One Out of Three

One Out of Three

IMMIGRANT NEW YORK IN THE TWENTY-FIRST CENTURY

Edited by Nancy Foner

COLUMBIA UNIVERSITY PRESS
NEW YORK, NEW YORK

Columbia University Press
Publishers Since 1893
New York Chichester, West Sussex
cup.columbia.edu

Library of Congress Cataloging-in-Publication Data
One out of three : immigrant New York in the twenty-first century /
edited by Nancy Foner.
pages cm
Includes bibliographical references and index.
ISBN 978-0-231-15936-4 (cloth : alk. paper)—ISBN 978-0-231-15937-1
(pbk. : alk. paper)—ISBN 978-0-231-53513-7 (ebook)
1. Minorities—New York (State)—New York. 2. Immigrants—New York (State)—New York.
3. New York (N.Y.)—Social conditions. 4. New York (N.Y.)—Emigration and immigration.
5. New York (N.Y.)—Economic conditions. I. Foner, Nancy, 1945- II. Title.
F128.9.A1N38 2013
305.086'9120747—dc23
2012046205

Columbia University Press books are printed on permanent and durable acid-free paper.
This book is printed on paper with recycled content.
Printed in the United States of America

CONTENTS

ACKNOWLEDGMENTS

Many people have helped to make this book possible. I am grateful, above all, to the authors of the chapters in this volume for their responsiveness and commitment to the book, from the very start when it began to take shape to the end of the publication process.

Once again, it has been a great pleasure to work with the editorial staff at Columbia University Press. I would like to thank Philip Leventhal, editor at the press, for his enthusiasm for the project, helpful advice, and for shepherding the book through the review and editorial process. I am also grateful to his editorial assistants, Alison Alexanian and Whitney Johnson, for their help along the way.

Thanks, as well, to my husband, Peter Swerdloff, for his unfailing support; my daughter, Alexis, a dyed-in-the-wool fourth-generation New Yorker; and my mother, Anne Foner, who has always been there as a sounding board and source of wise advice.

As some readers will note, this volume builds on two editions of an earlier volume, *New Immigrants in New York*, but it is a very different book and, fittingly, has a new title. The phrase "new immigrants," in any case, no longer rings true for many groups discussed in the pages that follow. Now, in the second decade of the twenty-first century, the "new" immigration is not so new anymore. Many groups featured in the chapters have been a significant presence in New York City for nearly half a century, and a large and growing second generation is coming of age. Together, immigrants and their U.S.-born children represent more than one out of two New Yorkers—immigrants alone, as the title indicates, are about one out of three or, to be precise, 37 percent. As for the book itself, it has many new authors (Arun Peter Lobo and Joseph Salvo, David Dyssegaard Kallick, Bernadette Ludwig, Silvio Torres-Saillant and Ramona Hernández, and Philip Kasinitz, John Mollenkopf, and Mary C. Waters). Those who had chapters in the 2001 edition of *New Immigrants in New York* (Pyong Gap Min, Annelise Orleck, Robert C. Smith, Milton Vickerman, and Min Zhou) have written very different ones—in some cases with a completely new focus. My own introductory chapter has been totally revamped to reflect changes in the book, changes in the nature and consequences of immigration in New York City, and developments in my own thinking about immigration after many years of studying and writing about it. A final word of thanks, then, to the many immigration scholars in the United States and Europe, too numerous to mention, who have been a source of insights, ideas, and inspiration.

One Out of Three

1. *Introduction*

IMMIGRANTS IN NEW YORK CITY IN THE NEW MILLENNIUM

Nancy Foner

New York is America's quintessential immigrant city. It has long been a gateway for the nation's new arrivals and is a major receiving center today. By the end of the first decade of the twenty-first century, after nearly fifty years of massive immigration, just over 3 million immigrants lived in New York City. They have come, in the main, from Latin America, the Caribbean, and Asia, although sometimes it seems as if every country in the world is represented. In 1970, 18 percent of New York City's population was foreign-born, the lowest percentage in the twentieth century. By 2010, about one out of three New Yorkers were immigrants, or 37 percent to be exact. If we add the second generation—the U.S.-born children of the foreign-born—the figure is even more remarkable, an estimated 55 percent. How have immigrants affected New York City? And, conversely, how has the move to New York influenced their lives?

This collection of original essays offers an in-depth look at immigrant New York at the beginning of the twenty-first century as older post-1965 groups are replenished by new arrivals, as brand-new immigrant groups come to settle in significant numbers, and as a large and growing second generation takes its place in the city. The book's approach is two-pronged: it combines micro and macro levels of analysis. Case studies explore the move to New York City from the immigrants' viewpoint, analyzing the way New York has influenced their social and cultural worlds and the emergence among them of new meanings and new social and economic patterns. The essays also demonstrate that the city itself has been deeply affected by the huge immigrant influx of recent decades. The presence of such large numbers of immigrants and their children has had a dramatic impact on the city's neighborhoods and economy and a host of social, economic, and cultural institutions. In fact, a dialectical relationship or interplay exists between the two kinds of changes. As immigrants change when they move to New York City, they affect the life of the city in particular ways. And as immigrants play a role in transforming New York City, this "new" New York in turn influences them.

The seven chapters on particular national origin groups deal with the experiences of a broad range of populations: Chinese, Dominicans, Jamaicans, Koreans, Liberians, Mexicans, and Jews from the former Soviet Union. These groups were chosen to give a sense of the diversity of New York City's immigrant population: with the exception of Liberians, they are among the most numerous immigrant groups in the city. All of the studies are based on in-depth research and long-term familiarity with the group in question.[1] In fact, many authors of the chapters are immigrants themselves.

Setting the stage for the case studies, chapter 2, by Arun Peter Lobo and Joseph J. Salvo, provides a detailed portrait of how immigration has been transforming New York City's population, as it has created a remarkable mélange of ethnic and racial groups and has fueled population growth. Chapter 3, by David Dyssegaard Kallick, examines the way that newcomers are fitting into and contributing to New York's economy. While the case studies of particular immigrant groups touch on the experiences of the second generation, chapter 11, by Philip Kasinitz, John Mollenkopf, and Mary Waters, focuses on the pathways and prospects of the children of immigrants as they have entered and begun to move through adulthood.

In this introductory chapter, I provide general background on the immigration of the last five decades and special features of New York as an immigrant city. As I sketch out the factors shaping the experiences of the newest New Yorkers—and the ways in which they are transforming the city—I point to common themes as well as differences among immigrant groups and raise some questions about patterns in the future.

WHY IMMIGRANTS HAVE COME

The huge immigration since the late 1960s is not the first large influx to New York City, but it stands out from earlier immigration waves in a number of ways. Compared to the great wave of immigration at the turn of the twentieth century, today's arrivals come from a much wider array of nations and cultures. Whereas immigrants in New York City a century ago were overwhelmingly

European—the vast majority Russian Jews and Italians—today they are mainly from Latin America, the Caribbean, and Asia. More men than women came in the immigration stream a hundred years ago; in recent decades, female immigrants have outnumbered males (see chapter 2, this volume). Many arrive now, as in the past, with little education and few skills, but a much higher proportion of contemporary newcomers have college degrees and professional backgrounds. And while the proportion of immigrants in the city's population is lower than it was early in the twentieth century, as table 1.1 shows, the actual numbers are at an all-time high (see Foner 2000 for a full comparison of immigration today and a century ago).

The reasons for the current influx are complex and multifaceted. A crucial factor was the 1965 immigration act that repealed the national origins quota system favoring northern and western Europeans and amendments to the act in subsequent years (chapter 2, this volume; Kraly and Miyares 2001; Reimers 1992; Zolberg 2006). The big winners were Asians, who had been severely restricted from immigration before 1965, and natives of the English-speaking Caribbean, who had been subject to small quotas for dependencies. Since 1965, U.S. immigration policy has emphasized family reunification and, to a lesser extent, skills within the context of annual immigration ceilings, which, after a series of

TABLE 1.1. FOREIGN-BORN POPULATION OF NEW YORK CITY, 1900–2010

Year	*Total Population (in Thousands)*	*Foreign-Born Population (in Thousands)*	*Percentage of Foreign-Born in New York City*	*Percentage of all U.S. Foreign-Born in New York City*
1900	3,437.2	1,270.1	37.0	12.2
1910	4,766.9	1,944.4	40.8	14.3
1920	5,620.0	2,028.2	36.1	14.5
1930	6,930.4	2,358.7	34.0	16.5
1940	7,455.0	2,138.7	28.7	18.3
1950	7,892.0	1,860.9	23.6	17.8
1960	7,783.3	1,558.7	20.0	16.0
1970	7,894.9	1,437.1	18.2	14.9
1980	7,071.6	1,670.2	23.6	11.9
1990	7,322.6	2,082.9	28.4	10.5
2000	8,008.3	2,871.0	35.9	9.2
2010	8,185.3	3,046.5	37.2	7.6

Source: Foner 2000:5; chapter 2, this volume.

legislative changes, stood at a "flexible" cap of 675,000 per year at the beginning of the twenty-first century. (Immediate relatives of U.S. citizens—spouses, parents of citizens ages 21 and older, and unmarried children under 21—are admitted without numerical limitation.) Further, the United States has allowed the large-scale admission of particular groups as refugees, Soviet Jews and Cubans being especially prominent in the New York area. Recent refugees to New York come from other places as well, including Liberians (see chapter 8). The diversity visa program, created by the 1990 U.S. immigration act to provide permanent resident visas for those from countries with relatively few immigrants in the United States, has also led to new flows to the city, including Bangladeshis as well as Nigerians and Ghanaians.

Economic factors have also underpinned the large-scale immigration to New York City in recent years. Neither the resource base nor the levels of economic development in many immigrants' home countries are adequate to meet the needs and aspirations of their populations. New York City has held out the promise of employment, higher wages, and improved living standards. In chapter 7, Vickerman notes how migration has long been a flight response among West Indians from the Anglophone Caribbean who come from small, resource-poor economies plagued by high levels of unemployment and underemployment and an unequal distribution of land, wealth, and income. West Indians are well aware of American affluence and standards of living owing to the impact of American media and tourism and because so many have relatives in the United States. Chapters 9 and 10 also describe persistent harsh economic realities—low incomes and low standards of living—fueling migration to New York.

Political factors in sending countries have also played a role. Unstable or oppressive conditions have driven some people out of their homelands, Liberians perhaps the most dramatic case in this book, who fled a country torn by bloody civil wars that were marked by torture and other gruesome atrocities (chapter 8, this volume). Changing exit policies in some sending countries have enabled large numbers to emigrate in recent years. In China, as Min Zhou explains (chapter 5), emigration was highly restricted between 1949 and 1976 (the end of the Great Cultural Revolution), a period when communication with overseas relatives was seen as antirevolutionary and subversive. In the late 1970s, when China opened its doors, it also relaxed emigration restrictions. Another group described in this book, Soviet Jews, were only allowed to emigrate in significant numbers after 1971, although in the early 1980s Soviet authorities again slammed shut the doors. By the late 1980s, in the context of political changes in the Soviet Union, the policy toward Jewish emigration was again liberalized, a situation that leads Annelise Orleck to speak of a Fourth Wave of émigrés in the post-1989 period although, as she also notes, after 2006 the influx of Jews from the former Soviet Union dropped off dramatically (see chapter 4, this volume).

Once begun, immigration tends to have a kind of snowball effect. Network connections lower the costs, raise the benefits, and reduce the risks of international migration. Every new migrant, as Douglas Massey has noted, "reduces the costs and risks of subsequent migration for a set of friends and relatives, and some of these people are thereby induced to migrate, thus further expanding the set of people with ties abroad and, in turn, reducing the costs for a new set of people, some of whom are now more likely to decide to migrate, and so on" (1999:43). By allocating most immigrant visas along family lines, U.S. immigration law reinforces and formalizes the operation of migrant networks.

"We opened the road," is how a Mexican migrant, Don Pedro, described the beginning of migration to New York City from the municipality of Ticuani in the early 1940s. Don Pedro and his two companions initiated a migration from the Mixteca region that now accounts for a significant portion of the city's Mexican population. By the start of the twenty-first century, new migration chains from other Mexican areas had taken hold so that more Mexican New Yorkers are from Mexico City as well as elsewhere (chapter 10, this volume; Smith 2001).

As in the past, New York City continues to be one of the major gateways for new immigrants in this country. (Los Angeles is the other major new immigrant destination, with large numbers also settling in Miami, San Francisco, Chicago, Houston, and Washington, DC.) New York City has a particular attraction for certain groups, the Caribbean connection being especially strong. In 2010, 43 percent of the Dominican immigrants, 37 percent of the Trinidadians, and 26 percent of the Jamaicans in the United States lived in the city. Alternatively, only about 2 percent of Mexican immigrants, by far the largest foreign-born group in the nation, lived in New York City.

Some groups, like West Indians, have a history of settlement in New York and initially gravitated there in the post-1965 years because of the presence of a long-established immigrant community (Foner 2001). In general, the presence of large numbers of friends and relatives continues to attract immigrants to the city and the surrounding region. Once an immigrant community develops, it tends to expand as compatriots are on hand to offer newcomers a sense of security and the prospect of assistance. "Moving to New York," as one Jamaican woman told me, "became the thing to do. Most of my friends were here" (Foner 1987:198). New York is also appealing because newcomers do not stand out; the city has a tradition of immigration, with many different immigrant and racial groups.

The city itself has an image that draws certain groups. With large numbers of Caribbean people in New York, the city has become, in the words of Bryce-Laporte, the special object of their "dream[s], curiosity, sense of achievement, and desire for adventure" (1979:216). The city is salient in Caribbean immigrants' mental map as a center of North American influence and power and as a logical entry point into the country. New York has become significant for other populations, too. Migration from Neza, the nickname for an area outside of Mexico City from which many recent migrants have come, has become so common these migrants often say that they live in "Neza York" (Smith 2001, 2006).

NEW YORK AS A SPECIAL IMMIGRANT CITY

"Our deity La Ciguapa, arrived in New York City," goes a poem by a New York–based Dominican. "The subway steps changed her nature" (quoted in Torres-Saillant 1999:44). The move to New York City has a profound effect on immigrants, and their lives change in innumerable ways when they move there. New York, as a major U.S. city, offers newcomers economic opportunities of an advanced industrial society and exposes them to values and institutions of American culture. But New York City is special in many respects. That immigrants have settled there rather than, say, Los Angeles or Miami influences them in particular ways.

A host of features make New York distinctive as an immigrant city. New York City served as the historic port of entry for southern and eastern European immigrants in the late nineteenth and early twentieth centuries so that by 1920, Jewish and Italian immigrants and their children made up over two-fifths of the population. In the newest wave of immigration, since the late 1960s, the city has continued to attract a significant share of the nation's new arrivals. From 1900 to 2000, around 10 percent or more of the nation's foreign-born population has lived in New York City—in 2010, it was slightly lower, at about 8 percent, but still a substantial share. For much of the twentieth century, a fifth or more of New York City's residents were foreign-born; the figure reached 41 percent in 1910 and by 2010 it was nearly as high, at 37 percent (see table 1.1).

The result of these inflows is that the vast majority of New Yorkers have a close immigrant connection. If they are not immigrants themselves, they have a parent, grandparent, or great-grandparent who is. Many of the roughly 1 million Jewish New Yorkers have grandparents or great-grandparents who arrived at the turn of the twentieth century from eastern Europe; hundreds of thousands of others have roots in Italy and Ireland. New York's white population is dominated by first-, second-, and third-generation Catholics (Irish and Italians) and Jews, and white Protestants are practically invisible, if still economically and socially powerful (Mollenkopf 1999:419). Although Puerto Ricans are not considered immigrants—those born on the island are U.S. citizens at birth—the more than 700,000 Puerto Rican New Yorkers have their roots outside the mainland United States. Most African Americans in New York have their origins in the internal migration from the South between World War I and the 1960s, but many are descended from immigrants who arrived in the early twentieth century from what was then the British Caribbean.

A striking feature of New York City's immigrant population is its extraordinary diversity. No one, two, three, or even four countries dominate, and the city has attracted sizable numbers of many European as well as Asian, West Indian, and Latin American nationalities. In 2010, the top three immigrant groups accounted for under a third of all immigrants in the city—the top ten groups, just over half (55 percent). As chapter 2 shows, this is different from many other major gateways, where Mexicans are the overwhelmingly dominant group—in Chicago and Houston, Mexicans are close to half of all immigrants, and in Los Angeles, Mexicans, Salvadorans, and Guatemalans are almost three-fifths of the foreign-born population (see also Foner and Waldinger 2013). In New York City, a substantial fraction (more than a quarter) of the non-Hispanic black and white populations are immigrants—something that distinguishes New York from most other major American gateway cities, where "immigrant" generally means Latino or Asian. To put it another way, in New York City, every major ethnoracial group—non-Hispanic blacks and whites as well as Asians and Hispanics—has a significant proportion of foreign-born (Foner 2007).[2]

Ethnic diversity is the expectation in New York—a fact of life, as it were. This is welcoming for many immigrants, although for some it can be confusing. Soviet Jewish teenagers whom Orleck studied in the 1980s were confounded when they entered high school, wanting to know where the Americans were. "It is . . . hard to know what we are supposed to be becoming. Everybody here is from someplace else" (Orleck 1987:295).

There is also a long list of "place-specific conditions" that mark off New York City as an immigrant destination. By U.S. standards, New York City's government provides a wide range of social, health, and educational services, including the City University of New York (CUNY), the largest urban public university system in the nation, with about 240,000 undergraduate students enrolled in 2011, the majority of them immigrants or children of immigrants. Owing to its immigrant history, the city is home to a wide array of institutions that owe their existence, or many features, to earlier European immigrants and their children—and that provide support and assistance to new arrivals. These include settlement houses, churches and synagogues, hospitals, and labor unions (Foner forthcoming). Immigrants in New York City profit from the fact that labor unions have been consistently strong and politically influential for many decades. Indeed, in 2010–11, 23 percent of all wage and salary workers in New York City were union members, higher than any other major U.S. city; among the foreign-born in New York City, the unionization rates of those who had become U.S. citizens and entered the United States before 1990 were comparable to or higher than those of U.S.-born workers (Milkman and Braslow 2011).

New York City's political culture bears the stamp of earlier European immigration and is used to accommodating newcomers from abroad. Ethnic politics is the lifeblood of New York City politics, and no group "finds challenge unexpected or outrageous" (Glazer and Moynihan 1963). In the 1930s, Fiorello LaGuardia—who some consider the city's greatest mayor—sprinkled his speeches with Italian and Yiddish, and in the postwar years aspiring leaders visited the three I's—Israel, Italy, and Ireland—the touchstones of so many Jewish and

Catholic voters (Wakin 2003). In the twenty-first century, Mayor Michael Bloomberg not only has made trips to Israel to woo the Jewish vote but, after two years in office in 2003, had already visited the Dominican Republic three times. In May 2005, he rolled out the first of his television campaign spots in Spanish.

Politics in the city "presents newcomers with a segmented political system, organized for mobilization along ethnic group lines, and a political culture that sanctions, indeed encourages, newcomers to engage in ethnic politics" (Waldinger 1996b:1084; see also Mollenkopf forthcoming). A large number of political prizes are up for grabs—including a fifty-one-member city council and more than seven dozen state assemblymen and senators. Despite the importance of party support in sustaining native white or minority incumbents in immigrant districts, New York City's primaries have proved to be an effective path for immigrant political mobility when one group becomes predominant in a district. As of the 2009 election, the city council had nine members with immigrant roots, including three West Indians, four Dominicans, and two Chinese. (Another seventeen were African American or Puerto Rican, giving minority representatives a bare majority of the total.) In that year, the city's second highest office, comptroller, was won by John Liu, born in Taiwan (Mollenkopf forthcoming; chapter 5, this volume).

Given New York's remarkable diversity and long history of absorbing immigrants, it is not surprising that the city's official commitment to cultural pluralism and cultural diversity stands out. Officials and social service agencies actively promote events to foster ethnic pride and glorify the city's multiethnic character and history. Even something as mundane as parking rules reflect a public recognition of ethnic diversity; alternate side parking regulations are suspended on thirty-four legal and religious holidays, including the Asian Lunar New Year, Purim and Passover, the Feast of the Assumption, the Muslim holiday of Idul-Fitr, and the Hindu celebration of Diwali.

In a city that prides itself on its immigrant history, New Yorkers—both old and new—generally feel comfortable with, or at least do not openly challenge the principle of, ethnic succession. If Italians "are yesterday's newcomers and today's establishment, then maybe Colombians are the new Italians and, potentially tomorrow's establishment. New Yorkers . . . are happy to tell themselves this story. It may not be completely true, but the fact that they tell it, and believe it, is significant and may help them make it come true" (Kasinitz et al. 2004:398).

FEATURES OF NEW IMMIGRANT GROUPS AND NEW PATTERNS IN NEW YORK CITY

Immigrants are inevitably influenced by New York's particular urban context, yet they do not become homogenized in a so-called melting pot in the city. The old and new blend in many ways in response to circumstances in the city—a kind of New Yorkization process (cf. Foner 1999). As Glazer and Moynihan wrote some fifty years ago, in New York immigrants become "something they had not been, but still something distinct and identifiable" (1963:14). The particular blend of meanings, perceptions, and patterns of behavior that emerges is shaped, to a large degree, by the culture, social practices, skills, and education that newcomers bring with them when they arrive—as well as by a variety of sociodemographic features of their particular immigrant group. Moreover, even as they settle in New York City, immigrants often continue to maintain ties with their homelands—and these transnational connections have consequences for their lives in the city.

PREMIGRATION CULTURAL AND SOCIAL PATTERNS

Immigrants come to New York City carrying with them a "memory of things past" that operates as a filter through which they view and experience life in the city. Some of their former beliefs and social institutions may persist intact, although usually they undergo change, if only subtly, in form and function in response to circumstances in New York. To put it another way, their premigration values, attitudes, and customs do not simply fade away; they shape, often in a complex fashion, how individuals in each group adjust to and develop new cultural patterns in New York.

Take something as basic as cooking and cuisine. Newcomers may add hamburgers, bagels, pizza, and fried chicken to their diets in New York City and concoct new dishes that use ingredients available there, but they still also eat such traditional foods as plantain and curried goat (Jamaicans), pickled herring and *shashlyk* (Jews from the former Soviet Union), and African peppers and cassava leaves (Liberians) (see, for example, Khandelwal 2002; Hauck-Lawson et al. 2008). Immigrant languages are alive and well in New York—indeed, lack of proficiency in English may limit patterns of association as well as the ability to obtain jobs in the mainstream economy.

Premigration family and religious patterns also have an impact. Of course, they may fill new needs and acquire new meanings in New York or be transformed in significant ways. South Asian families still often arrange their children's marriages or, in a modified "semiarranged" pattern, introduce suitable, prescreened young men and women who are then allowed a courtship period during which they decide whether they like each other well enough to marry (see Foner 1999; Khandelwal 2002; Kibria 2009; Lessinger 1995). In chapter 4, Orleck mentions that many Central Asian "Bukharan" Jews also continue to arrange their children's marriages in New York; when the children resist, serious conflicts, sometimes resulting in physical violence, may result. Child-rearing patterns may be modified too. Although West Indian parents continue to believe that sparing the rod is a recipe for disaster, and are outraged if they cannot use corporal punishment the way they did back home, some parents seek to adopt new techniques that are more in tune with mainstream American norms, something that Ludwig also notes of Liberians (chapter 8; see Waters and Sykes 2009).

Religious beliefs and practices from immigrants' homeland cultures are what draw many to places of worship in New York. Many have been founded and built in the city to cater to the growing number of new arrivals, from Pentecostal churches among West Indians to Hindu temples among Indians and Muslim mosques among West Africans, Pakistanis, Bangladeshis, and Middle Easterners; old-country beliefs also explain the continuation of customs like Haitian voodoo ceremonies (Abdullah 2010; Abusharaf 1998; Brown 1991; Guest 2003; Lessinger 1995; McAlister 1998).

TRANSNATIONAL CONNECTIONS

Home-country cultural patterns may be strengthened by ongoing ties with communities and people in the country of origin—what social scientists refer to as transnational ties. Immigrant New Yorkers often send money to relatives back home. Cheap phone calls, and the advent of cell phones, allow them to keep in touch with those they left behind, as does the Internet, through e-mail, instant messaging, and Skype. Frequent, fast, and relatively inexpensive flights, especially to nearby countries like the Dominican Republic, facilitate visits home and enable relatives and friends from the home country to visit New York, as well (see chapter 5, this volume). Given dual-citizenship provisions in a growing number of countries, many retain citizenship in their country of origin even after becoming U.S. citizens.

The consequences of involvement in home-country politics are complex—and sometimes contradictory. Although such involvement does not inevitably draw energies and interests away from political engagement in the United States, it can of course happen (see Jones-Correa 1998). Silvio Torres-Saillant and Ramona Hernández (chapter 9, this volume) note that while many Dominican New Yorkers see the U.S. political arena as the appropriate stage for their involvement—and younger local leaders are more committed to developing coalitions in New York than to homeland politics—others have their "hearts set on the affairs of one of the major political parties in the Dominican Republic." At the same time, concerns about the country of origin can provide a catalyst for engagement in U.S. politics, and involvement in homeland-based organizations can provide organizational skills and strengthen migrants' ability to mobilize a base of support for political issues and elections in New York (see Basch 1987; Guarnizo et al. 1999; Rogers 2006; Wong et al. 2011).

In general, an appreciation of the connections migrants maintain with the homeland should not blind us to—or detract attention from—efforts to build communities and develop a home in New York. Ties to the country of origin can go hand-in-hand with being deeply grounded in and attached to the United States. This is true for both the first and second generation. Second-generation Dominicans, for example, do not see loyalty to the United States as requiring cutting off links to the Dominican Republic, where they often maintain close affective ties to grandparents and other relatives (chapter 9, this volume).

For the vast majority of the U.S.-born second generation—who represent an ever-growing proportion of the Asian, Latin American, and Caribbean communities in New York City—the United States is truly home. Deep connections to the parents' country of origin and regular transnational practices are the exception, not the rule, Philip Kasinitz and his colleagues conclude from their large-scale study of the young adult children of immigrants in metropolitan New York. They found that few seriously considered living in their parents' homeland for a sustained length of time; indeed, visits there often made them feel more "American" than before (Kasinitz et al. 2008:262–64; chapter 11, this volume).

HUMAN CAPITAL AND ECONOMIC INCORPORATION

The concept of human capital refers to the knowledge or skills that individual migrants bring with them, but it can be applied to groups as well. Every group, of course, includes highly skilled people as well as those who are unlettered and have little training. Yet clearly some groups have human capital advantages that others do not share.

Asian and European groups in New York City have among the highest levels of education, many Latin American and Hispanic Caribbean groups among the lowest (Lobo and Salvo 2004). In 2010, about half of the adult Russian and Indian immigrants in New York City had a college degree—outpacing native-born New Yorkers—while this was true for only 5 percent of Mexican immigrants. Indeed, only about four out of ten Mexican immigrants in New York City were even high school graduates (chapter 2, this volume).

As one might expect, groups with high proportions of college graduates, like Russians and Asian Indians, do relatively well in New York's economy—though factors other than education and occupational skills also determine occupational success. Lack of U.S. job experience, credentials, and fluent English, for example, often prevents immigrants who held professional or highly regarded jobs in their home countries from getting work of comparable status here. Orleck speaks of an "intellectual holocaust" that has occurred as Jewish physicians, chemists, lawyers, and professors from the former Soviet Union have sometimes ended up driving cabs, doing filing, or working as home health care aides in New York City (chapter 4, this volume). Well-educated immigrants who cannot find jobs congruent with their occupational backgrounds frequently turn to entrepreneurial pursuits as a better alternative than low-level service or factory jobs—one reason for the proliferation of small businesses in the Korean community. Not surprisingly, very few of the Korean second generation have gone into small business; armed with American college and university degrees, many have obtained high-level jobs in the mainstream economy (Kim 2004).

As David Dyssegaard Kallick brings out (chapter 3), immigrants are a remarkable 45 percent of New York City's resident labor force. In 2009, about three-quarters of immigrant men and nearly three-fifths of immigrant women were in the city's labor force—which put the women on a par with, and men above, their native-born counterparts. Immigrants are well represented in occupations from the top to the bottom of the economic ladder, with nearly half working in white-collar jobs—a good number in managerial, technical, and professional occupations. To anyone familiar with the city, it would not be a shock to learn that three-quarters of New Yorkers who work as construction laborers and nursing aides are immigrants. It may come as a surprise, however, that immigrants are half of the accountants, a third of financial managers, and two-fifths of physicians living in New York City. Taken as a whole, immigrants have slightly lower poverty rates than the native-born, although for some groups the rates are higher—Mexicans and Dominicans are two prime examples (chapter 2, this volume).

Many immigrant groups are heavily concentrated in specific occupational niches. Kallick mentions Mexicans in food preparation services, Pakistani taxi cab drivers, and Haitian health care workers (chapter 3). Other chapters bring out different concentrations—Korean nail salon owners, Jamaican nursing aides and nannies, and Chinese restaurant workers, to mention a few. Immigrant occupational specialties take hold for a variety of reasons. They reflect a combination of the skills, cultural preferences, and human capital within a group as well as the opportunities available when they arrived. Sometimes members of a group come with previous experience in fields for which a demand exists—Filipino nurses, for example. English language ability plays a role in steering some groups into jobs where interpersonal communication is important. By the same token, lack of transferable skills and fluency in English limits immigrants' scope. Sheer happenstance can be involved, too, as a few pioneers from a group go into a particular line of work and pave the way for others. Once a group becomes concentrated in an industry or occupation, this facilitates the entry of additional coethnics through job referrals and training so that ethnic niches become, as Roger Waldinger (1996a) puts it, self-reproducing (on the making of ethnic niches in the city, see also Foner 2000; Model 1993).

Much depends on the kinds of niches a group establishes. Koreans have benefited from their concentration in small business—and their web of trade associations, ethnic media and organizations, and churches that have reinforced, supported, and encouraged entrepreneurial activity (Min 2001). Jamaican niches in health care and public employment have not provided anything like the opportunity to employ coethnics, accumulate capital, or establish credit that small business ownership does. In fact, educational credentials and bureaucratic requirements limit the scope of network hiring in white-collar and especially in public sector employment (Kasinitz 2001). On the positive side, concentration in health care and social assistance jobs largely accounts for high unionization rates among Jamaican as well as Guyanese, Haitian, and African immigrants; unionized jobs typically provide higher wages and more job security than nonunion jobs (Milkman and Braslow 2011).

The young adult children of immigrants, as chapter 11 shows, have largely exited from parental occupational niches owing to greater opportunity as well as distaste for "stereotypical ethnic jobs." The most common jobs among the second generation in their study were mainstream retail, white-collar manager, and clerical positions. "I don't do that factory thing," said one young man of Colombian origin, explaining why he would not follow in his father's footsteps. Or as the daughter of a Chinese immigrant jewelry store owner put it when asked if her father would like her to take over the business: "No, he doesn't hate me that much!" (chapter 11, this volume).

DEMOGRAPHIC FACTORS

The demographic composition of an immigrant group can have an impact on patterns that develop in New York City. The group's sheer size as well as spatial concentration influences, among other things, whether it can support a sizable number of ethnic businesses and provide enough votes to elect its own candidates. Dominicans' concentration in northern Manhattan as well as neighborhoods in other boroughs has been an asset at the ballot box in putting Dominicans into office; residential segregation among West Indians, while clearly disadvantageous in many respects, has helped them gain seats in the city council and New York State legislature. Conversely, as Smith (chapter 10, this volume) argues, Mexican immigrants' geographical dispersion contributes to making political mobilization among them problematic.

Gender and age ratios in each group affect marriage and family patterns. For example, a markedly unbalanced gender ratio will encourage marriage outside the group or consign many to singlehood or the search for spouses in the home country or elsewhere in the United States. A sizable proportion of old people in an immigrant group's population may, as among Russian Jews in Brighton Beach, ease the child care burden of working women (Orleck 1987). Korean families have often brought elderly relatives to New York City for this reason. Pyong Gap

Min has described how his own mother-in-law came to this country in 1981 "at the age of 58 as a temporary visitor to help with childcare and housework as my wife and I were struggling with three children, a small business, and my Ph.D. program. The next year my wife, a naturalized citizen, filed petitions for her parents' permanent residence" (1998:87). The presence of an elderly mother or mother-in-law in Korean immigrant households has other implications—it puts less pressure on husbands to help out and thus may end up reinforcing patriarchal practices.

RACE, RELIGION, AND LEGAL STATUS

Immigrants' race has crucial consequences for their experiences and reactions to New York life. Nativism, or opposition to groups because they are foreign, may not be strong in New York City, especially compared to other parts of the United States, but racial inequality is deeply entrenched (Waters forthcoming). Whereas whiteness is an asset for newcomers of European ancestry, dark skin brings disadvantages. People of color continue to experience prejudice and discrimination, and residential segregation between whites and blacks in New York City persists at remarkably high levels. In an analysis of black-white segregation in fifty American metropolitan areas with the largest black populations in 2010, New York was the third most segregated area, just behind Detroit and Milwaukee (Logan and Stults 2011; see also Beveridge et al. 2013).

Immigrants with African ancestry develop new attitudes and perceptions of themselves in New York City, where their racialization as blacks reflects different racial conceptions than those in their home societies. As chapter 7 shows, Jamaicans may identify as Jamaican or West Indian, but other New Yorkers often just see them as "black." Jamaican immigrants find it painful and difficult to cope with the degree of interpersonal racism they encounter in their daily lives (see Waters 1999). Apart from everyday slights and insults, racial discrimination places constraints on where they and other black immigrants can live and affects treatment by the police and opportunities on the job (see Foner 1987, 2000, 2001, 2005; Vickerman 1999; Waters 1999). Other immigrants of color confront racial discrimination too, but this tends to be less problematic than for immigrants of African ancestry who are defined as black. Indeed, research shows that dark-skinned Latino immigrants face barriers and discrimination that their light-skinned coethnics do not experience.

For the vast majority of immigrants, who are Christian or Jewish, religion is not a barrier, indeed tends to facilitate acceptance in New York (Foner and Alba 2008). However, Muslim newcomers from South Asia (Pakistan, Bangladesh, India) and the Middle East, whose numbers have grown in recent years, may face difficulties. In the backlash after the September 11 attacks on the World Trade

Center, some have been victims of discrimination, harassment, and occasionally even hate crimes owing to their religion or nationality. "Why you live here, go back to your country," a Palestinian woman in Brooklyn found written on her door, to give one example (Bakalian and Bozorgmehr 2009:144). The public controversy in 2010 over building a Muslim community center a few blocks from the World Trade Center—which was vocally supported by the Lower Manhattan Community Board and Mayor Bloomberg but attacked by many Republican politicians such as former mayor Rudolph Giuliani—also no doubt reflected and reinforced anti-Muslim prejudices among many New Yorkers.

Lack of legal status is a significant basis of inequality and exclusion for large numbers of Latino, Caribbean, and Asian immigrants. In 2010, an estimated 499,000 immigrants in New York City were undocumented (chapter 2, this volume), but because they often live in mixed-status families—for example, with U.S.-born citizen children—a much larger number are affected by legal status issues. As Robert Smith indicates (chapter 10), a remarkably high proportion of Mexican immigrants live in the legal shadows. The undocumented are particularly vulnerable in the labor market, commonly found in low-paid jobs with unpleasant, sometimes dangerous, working conditions (chapter 3, this volume). Without legal status, they are ineligible for most federally funded social welfare and health benefits (emergency Medicaid is one exception), and the record number of deportations in the United States in recent years—nearly 400,000 in fiscal year 2011—has heightened fears among them.

New York City is sometimes referred to as a sanctuary city, which follows practices to protect undocumented immigrants—in 2006, for example, the city distributed a letter in eleven languages assuring immigrants that no one would question their legal status when they sought care at the city's public hospitals, and undocumented immigrants in New York State are eligible for in-state tuition at public colleges. But New York City has little influence on federal policies which, as Smith notes (chapter 10), reign supreme when it comes to the all-important matter of legalization. As of this writing, federal laws have yet to provide a path to legalization and ultimately citizenship for the undocumented.

IMMIGRANTS' IMPACT ON NEW YORK CITY

The massive immigration of the last five decades has been remaking New York City in profound ways. At its most basic, immigration has brought about a dramatic demographic transformation; it is a major factor fueling population growth and has led to remarkable ethnoracial diversity, as chapter 2 describes in detail.

Many groups have been continually replenished by new members—Dominicans, Chinese, and Jamaicans, to mention three that have been in the top ten for several decades. New arrivals, fresh off the plane, often join compatriots who have been in New York for decades as well as the U.S.-born children—and grandchildren—of the earlier arrivals. Some belong to groups that are new to the city's immigrant scene, Liberians among them, who only began arriving in significant numbers in the last ten or fifteen years. The Mexican population, which was practically invisible before 1990, has grown by leaps and bounds, now ranking as the third largest immigrant group in New York City official statistics. Taken together, the millions of new New Yorkers and their children have been changing the sights, sounds, and tastes of the city as well as a wide range of institutions and communities.

NEIGHBORHOODS AND COMMUNITIES

The more than doubling of the city's immigrant population since 1970 has given rise to dense ethnic neighborhoods. With continuing immigration, new ethnic neighborhoods and ethnic conglomerations have cropped up in every borough.

Many neighborhoods of the city have taken on a distinct ethnic character. In Crown Heights, Flatbush, and East Flatbush in central Brooklyn—and many bordering neighborhoods like Canarsie—West Indian beauty parlors, restaurants, record stores, and bakeries dot the landscape, and Haitian Creole and West Indian accents fill the air. "[When I walk] along . . . Nostrand Avenue," the novelist Paule Marshall (1985) has noted, "I have to remind myself that I'm in Brooklyn, and not in the middle of a teeming outdoor market in St. George's, Grenada or Kingston, Jamaica." Several neighborhoods in the northeastern Bronx (Wakefield, Williamsbridge, and Baychester) and southeastern Queens (Laurelton, St. Albans, Springfield Gardens, Rosedale, and Cambria Heights) also now have a definite West Indian flavor. In chapter 8, Bernadette Ludwig describes a new immigrant neighborhood—Little Liberia—on the northern end of Staten Island, which now has an outdoor market where women sell African foods.

Several chapters show how the number of settlements in different groups has multiplied in response to growing immigration. Although Brooklyn's Brighton Beach, or "Little Odessa," remains an emotional and cultural home base for Russian Jews across the New York area, they have spread out to nearby Sheepshead Bay, Manhattan Beach, and Bensonhurst. A community of Central Asian Jews flourishes in Forest Hills and Rego Park in Queens, where 108th Street is now known as "Bukharan Broadway"; the neighborhood, according to Orleck (chapter 4), is affectionately known as "Queensistan." Manhattan's expanding Chinatown has spilled over into adjacent districts, including the City Hall area, Little Italy, and the Lower East Side, and two new satellite Chinatowns are thriving in Flushing and Sunset Park; visible Chinese clusters can also be found in places like Woodside and Elmhurst in Queens and Bay Ridge, Bensonhurst, and

Sheepshead Bay in Brooklyn. Dominicans have branched out from their ethnic enclave in upper Manhattan's Washington Heights to areas of the Bronx, Brooklyn, and Queens. By 2008, the Bronx, with heavy Dominican concentrations in neighborhoods in the southwest such as Morris Heights and Tremont, had surpassed Manhattan as the most popular borough for people of Dominican ancestry, with 39 percent of all Dominicans as compared to 29 percent in Manhattan (Caro-Lopez and Limonic 2010).

Immigrants have created not only large and dense ethnic settlements but also polyethnic neighborhoods that are amalgams of newcomers from all parts of the world. The number 7 train that connects Times Square in Manhattan with Flushing in Queens has been dubbed the International Express, as it weaves through multiethnic neighborhoods in Queens that have no parallel in previous waves of immigration. Queens is in fact the most ethnically and racially diverse county in the United States (chapter 2, this volume). Elmhurst, to mention one Queens neighborhood, is a true ethnic mélange, with large numbers of Chinese, Colombians, Koreans, Mexicans, Filipinos, Asian Indians, Dominicans, and Ecuadorians. Although Flushing (also in Queens) is often referred to as a new Chinatown, it is home to a growing number of Central and South American as well as Chinese, Indian, and Korean immigrants who join a native-born white population that, though declining, remains substantial. At the other end of Queens, Astoria, once a predominantly Italian and Greek neighborhood, has attracted large numbers of Bangladeshis, Brazilians, Ecuadorians, Mexicans, and Middle Easterners, among others, thereby becoming another ethnic stew.

As the chapters on the different groups in the volume demonstrate, clusters of recent immigrants have given rise to new ethnic businesses and have affected the composition of schools and places of worship all over the city. Neighborhood-based immigrant institutions and organizations like community centers, voluntary associations, and political groups have emerged and grown as have new churches, mosques, and temples.

Immigrants have played a central role in revitalizing many neighborhoods. When immigrants began arriving in Brighton Beach in the mid-1970s, the neighborhood was in decline: apartments stood empty as elderly Jewish residents died or moved to Florida, and the main commercial avenue was a dying strip of old stores. Soviet Jews filled apartments and turned the avenue into a thriving commercial center, with nightclubs, restaurants, state-of-the-art electronics stores, and clothing boutiques selling European designer clothing (chapter 4, this volume). Another Brooklyn neighborhood, Sunset Park, was in the "throes of a long twilight" that began in the 1950s when the area was devastated by, among other things, a drastic cutback in jobs on its waterfront and in industry and the exodus of tens of thousands of white residents to the suburbs. Louis Winnick argues that in Sunset Park, as in many other city neighborhoods "outside the yuppie strongholds of Manhattan and other favored areas of Brooklyn and Queens," immigrants have been the leading factor in neighborhood revitalization. "Owing to their high employment rates and multiple wage earners, the new foreigners have injected large doses of new purchasing power into the rehabilitation of an aging housing stock and the resurrection of inert retail stores" (Winnick 1990:62). The Chinese—who make up a growing proportion of Sunset Park's population—have opened numerous retail stores, service businesses, and garment factories where they and their coethnics work and shop, and they have bought, and fixed up, many of the two- and three-story houses in the neighborhood (chapter 5, this volume). The process has been repeated in the Queens neighborhood of Richmond Hill, where Indians and Indo-Caribbeans have established an array of new businesses—roti stands, sari stores, and groceries—that draw not only local customers but also immigrants from the suburbs looking for Indo-Caribbean and Sikh products. Throughout the five boroughs, immigrants have expanded the number of businesses, many of them catering to a growing ethnic market, one of the ways that new arrivals have contributed to economic growth in the city (chapter 3, this volume).

CUISINE AND POPULAR CULTURE

Immigrants have added to the city's cultural and culinary life. Restaurants and groceries run by newcomers have exposed New Yorkers, native and immigrant alike, to new cuisines and foods. Some thirty years ago, Bernard Wong (1982) wrote about Chinese immigrants broadening New Yorkers' tastes beyond Cantonese cooking to regional dishes from Shanghai, Hunan, and Szechuan. Since then, Indian, Thai, Vietnamese, Korean, and Jamaican restaurants—to name but a few—have become common on the city's restaurant scene. Korean food, relatively unknown to New Yorkers twenty years ago, has become more familiar with the proliferation of Korean restaurants in "K-Town" in mid-Manhattan. In the wake of the huge Mexican immigration, New York, one journalist quipped, finally shed its reputation as a city with terrible Mexican food (Asimov 2000). The city's ubiquitous street food vendors serve up a multicultural feast, from chalupas to souvlaki; the winner of New York City's sixth annual Vendy award—for the best street food vendor—was a Palestinian-born "falafel king" who normally parked his van in Astoria (Pearson and Schapiro 2010).

Musically, too, immigrants have had an influence, from Jamaican reggae and dance hall to Dominican merengue (Allen and Wilcken 2001; Austerlitz 1997; Flores 2000). Hip-hop was originally as much a creation of Afro-Caribbean and Latino youth in New York as it was an African American form, and many famous hip-hop artists have Caribbean origins, including Biggie Smalls (Brooklyn-born Christopher Wallace of Jamaican parents), rapper-producer Wyclef Jean, whose work celebrates his Haitian origins, and the Jamaican-born Kool Herc (born Clive Campbell) (Kasinitz forthcoming; chapter 7, this volume). Music and visual arts with immigrant roots have imported, built on, and altered cultural forms from the homeland in the New York context. "African American young people dance to Jamaican dance hall music and imitate Jamaican patois," Kasinitz (1999:29) has written; "Puerto Ricans dance to [Dominican] merengue."

New ethnic parades and festivals represent practically every immigrant group in the city. The largest is the West Indian American Day Parade, which attracts between 1 and 2 million people every Labor Day on Brooklyn's Eastern Parkway and has become a mandatory campaign stop for politicians seeking citywide office. The annual Dominican Day Parade, described by Torres-Saillant and Hernández, held every August in midtown Manhattan, also attracts politicians of all stripes and provides an opportunity for Dominicans to "flaunt their ethnicity, their flag, and their resolve to affirm their belonging in the city" (chapter 9, this volume). Since 2004, the city has sponsored an annual Immigrant Heritage Week honoring "the vibrant immigrant cultures, heritages, and communities found in every corner of the City" through film screenings, art exhibits, walking tours, and other programs. The ethnic media are flourishing. By one count in 2001, at least 198 magazines and newspapers were publishing in thirty-six languages, including seven New York daily newspapers in Chinese with a combined circulation of half a million (Scher 2001). There are also many radio and television stations with programs that draw listeners and viewers in different ethnic constituencies.

A spate of novels emerging out of the experiences of recent immigrants and their children has enriched the city's literary tradition, among them *Typical American* by Gish Jen (1992, Chinese); *Native Speaker* by Chang-Rae Lee (1995, Korean); *Breath, Eyes, Memory* by Edwidge Danticat (1995, Haitian), and *Russian Debutante's Handbook* by Gary Shteyngart (2003, Soviet Jews). The literary output in the Dominican community is a subject of chapter 9 as part of the analysis of the creation of a Dominican American culture, which considers, among others, the award-winning *The Brief Wondrous Life of Oscar Wao* by Junot Díaz (2007) and *How the Garcia Girls Lost Their Accents* by Julia Alvarez (1992).

RACE AND ETHNICITY

The massive immigration of recent years has changed the racial and ethnic dynamics of New York City. In street-level and popular discourse, New Yorkers think of a four-race framework: white, black, Hispanic, and Asian. The proportion of Asians and Hispanics has mushroomed; the proportion of whites has been steadily declining. Between 1980 and 2010, non-Hispanic whites went from 52 to 33 percent of New York City's population, Hispanics from 20 to 29 percent, Asians from 3 to 13 percent, and non-Hispanic blacks held fairly steady, 24 percent in 1980, 23 percent in 2010.

Gone are the days when Hispanic meant Puerto Rican; in 2010, Puerto Ricans accounted for just under a third of the city's Hispanic population, outnumbered by a combination of Dominicans, Mexicans, Ecuadorians, Colombians, and other Latin Americans. Asian no longer means Chinese but also Asian Indian, Korean, Filipino, and Bangladeshi (to name the largest non-Chinese groups). The black population increasingly has been Caribbeanized—and Africans are adding more diversity. By 2010, the Caribbean- and African-born populations were about a third of non-Hispanic blacks, up from less than 10 percent in 1970 (chapter 2, this volume).

This new racial and ethnic amalgam has been changing perceptions of race and ethnicity as well as creating new alliances, relationships, and divisions. All over the city, countless examples exist of amicable relations developing among immigrants from different countries, as well as between immigrants and the native-born, in workplaces, schools, and neighborhoods. Among the second generation, these patterns are especially pronounced, as young people mingle with each other and native minorities (less often with native whites) and become comfortable with those from different national backgrounds and take for granted the incredible ethnic mix in their classes, on the subway, in stores, and on the streets as a basic part of life in the city. As Kasinitz and his colleagues write, they may feel the sting of disadvantage and discrimination, but members of the second generation "move in a world where being from 'somewhere else' is the norm" and being ethnic is taken for granted as part of "being an American New Yorker" (2004:397, 286). Because established minority and second-generation young people in New York City under the age of eighteen dominate their age cohort, they have a great deal of contact with each other in their neighborhoods and a variety of institutions. Most respondents in the New York second-generation study had a diverse group of friends, describing social networks that included a "veritable United Nations of friends" (Kasinitz et al. 2008:339–40). Many defined themselves as "New Yorkers"—meaning people who "could come from immigrant groups, native minority groups, or be Italian, Irish, Jews, or the like" (Kasinitz et al. 2004:17).

Less happily, conflict is also part of the story. In this volume, Min Zhou writes of tensions between immigrant Chinese and longtime white residents in Flushing, as the remaining whites in what was once a virtually all-white area often feel locked out of what has become an Asian majority neighborhood (chapter 5). Black boycotts of Korean stores were visible in the city in the 1980s and 1990s (Min 2006), although they seem to be a thing of the past, according to Min (chapter 6), who argues that the reduction in the number of Korean businesses and growing racial and ethnic diversity in black neighborhoods help to explain the change.

In chapter 7, Milton Vickerman gives a nuanced picture of relations between Jamaicans and African Americans, which are characterized by both distancing and identification; Jamaicans seek to assert their ethnic identity and show they are different from African Americans at the same time as they feel a shared bond with African Americans as blacks and victims of racial discrimination (see also Foner 1987, 2001; Vickerman 1999; Waters 1999). Among the second generation, he argues, evidence suggests a gradual blurring of boundaries between African American and West Indian youth. Immigrants in other groups, too, engage in strategies to avoid being lumped with, and experiencing the same kind of discrimination as, African Americans and Puerto Ricans. Torres-Saillant and Hernández (chapter 9) report that members of the Dominican second generation may use Dominican-inflected Spanish to avoid being taken for African American, while also attempting to distance themselves from the anti-Haitian and antiblack prejudices prominent in the Dominican Republic (also see Itzigsohn 2009). According to Robert Smith (2006), Mexicans see themselves as "not black" and "not Puerto Rican" although, interestingly, some academically successful Mexican youths in New York City high schools identify and seek out their black counterparts as a way to become incorporated into the African American middle-class culture of mobility and facilitate their own upward path.

ETHNIC DIVISION OF LABOR

As immigrants have entered New York's economy and set up businesses, they have changed the ethnic division of labor—and perceptions of it. If you hail a taxi, your driver is likely to be South Asian; if you are a patient in a hospital, it is a good bet that the nursing aide taking your temperature will be West Indian; the vendor at the corner newsstand is Indian.

Nearly half of all small business owners living in New York City are immigrants, making up a whopping 90 percent of owners of dry cleaners and laundries, 84 percent of small grocery store owners, and 70 percent of beauty salon owners in the New York metropolitan area, to name a few (chapter 3). As particular groups concentrate in certain specialties, they often put their own stamp on them. Koreans reinvented the corner grocery, adding salad bars, deli counters, and bouquets of flowers, although Korean retail stores—grocery, produce, and fish stores—have recently declined in number owing in good part to the emergence of chain megastores. Koreans have also pioneered businesses, such as the now-ubiquitous nail salons, by taking what were once more exclusive products or services and making them cheaper (Lee 1999). Nail salons and dry cleaners are now the two major Korean businesses in the New York–New Jersey metropolitan area. By 2006, Koreans owned the vast majority of the nail salons in this area—about 4,000 in all, a nearly threefold increase since 1991 (chapter 6; for an ethnographic account of Korean nail salons in New York City see Kang 2010). The number of Korean-owned dry cleaners has also grown astronomically, up to about 3,000 in the New York–New Jersey metropolitan area in 2006 and constituting around half of all such establishments (Min 2008:37–38). West Indians have brought the concept of a privatized network of passenger vans to New York City, as their jitneys ply the streets of Queens and Brooklyn, offering lower prices and more frequent and convenient services than city buses (chapter 7). West African merchants have altered the city's street-vending business, bringing high-end items like "Rolex" watches and "Prada" bags to the street corner (Stoller 2001).

MAINSTREAM INSTITUTIONS

Immigrants are leaving their mark on a broad range of mainstream institutions in the city, from schools and hospitals to churches and museums.

The surge of immigration has led to major increases in public school enrollment, which is now over the 1 million mark, with the majority of students either immigrants or children of immigrants. With so many students and a limited budget, the public schools are squeezed for space. Although many immigrant students are doing remarkably well in the schools, there is no denying they bring with them a host of special needs. Many have to overcome poor educational preparation in their home countries or, at the least, unfamiliarity with subjects, teaching methods, and the discipline used. In addition to adjusting to new norms and customs in New York, many have a language problem to contend with. The diverse mix of immigrants in New York City means a dazzling array of languages. In one Queens elementary school, nearly 80 percent of the incoming students arrived speaking no English; among them the children in the school spoke thirty-six languages (Hedges 2000). In 2010–11, about 154,000 students in New York City's public schools were classified as English language learners (not proficient in English), with 168 home languages represented among them; Spanish was the home language for some two-thirds, and another quarter spoke Chinese (Mandarin, Cantonese, and other dialects), Bengali, Arabic, Haitian Creole, Russian, or Urdu (New York City Board of Education 2010–11). In response to the immigrant influx, the city has opened a number of schools specifically designed for recent immigrant children with limited English proficiency, the most well-known being the International High School in Long Island City. Higher up the educational ladder, new ethnic studies programs have emerged at universities and colleges, most notably CUNY, including one (the Dominican Studies Institute) headed by an author in this volume (Ramona Hernández). CUNY has recently instituted an outreach program, based on an agreement with the Mexican Consulate, to promote education in the city's Mexican community, including a Web site offering information about CUNY in English and Spanish (chapter 10, this volume).

The city's Roman Catholic schools have also experienced an influx of immigrant children. Although many newcomers have formed their own churches, temples, and mosques—witness the more than 500 Korean Protestant churches in the New York–New Jersey metropolitan area (chapter 6, this volume; Min 2010)—large numbers have been drawn to the Catholic church and established Protestant congregations. New York's Catholic church has a growing Latino presence, and an increasing number of Catholic churches conduct masses in Spanish as well as other languages, including Haitian Creole (McAlister 1998). Catholic churches in Washington Heights have emerged as Dominican congregations, holding mass in Spanish and inviting officials from the island to participate in church activities; elsewhere in the city, Mexican immigrants have been "Mexicanizing" many Catholic churches, including adding devotional practices dedicated to the Virgin of Guadalupe, the patron saint of Mexico (Galvez 2009; Semple 2011; Smith 2006; see Ricourt and Danta 2003 on the Latinization of the Catholic church in Queens).

The composition of the staff and patients of the city's hospitals has changed as well. The nurses, aides, and orderlies are often West Indian or Filipino; patients, especially at municipal hospitals run by New York City's Health and Hospitals Corporation, are frequently non-English-speaking immigrants who bring with them their own set of cultural values regarding health and medical treatment—which, in the New York context, means a bewildering assortment of patterns. New York City hospitals have established programs to address the need for better interpreter and translation services (language assistance is now mandated by law), and some have programs to serve the cultural and medical needs and health risks of particular groups. Lutheran Medical Center, for example, a nonprofit hospital close to Sunset Park, has special language, food, and cultural services available to the Chinese community (Zhou et al. 2013); Coney Island Hospital, a municipal hospital in southern Brooklyn, touts its treatment of the high incidence of thyroid cancers among Ukrainian and Russian survivors of the Chernobyl nuclear reactor accident and a healthy heart program geared to nearby Pakistani and Bangladeshi immigrants. In general, however, what is available in the health care system, in terms of language services and responsiveness to cross-cultural health care, is unfortunately still often inadequate

(Tung 2008; see Guo 2000 on the problems elderly Chinese immigrants face in New York in dealing with the health care system).

Immigration has also been reshaping mainstream cultural institutions. New York City's public library branches offer a growing number of books, DVDs, and CDs in many languages. In 2012, non-English titles made up 12 percent of items in the stacks of the Queens system, which had large collections in Spanish and Chinese as well as Korean, Russian, French, Hindi, Italian, and Bengali (Berger 2012). New museums have sprouted up to spotlight the history or arts of Asian and Latino groups. Two notable additions are the Museum of the Chinese in America in lower Manhattan, founded in 1980 and moved in 2009 to a building designed by the architect Maya Lin, and El Museo del Barrio in East Harlem, created in 1969 to focus on the Puerto Rican diaspora but since then changed to include all Latin Americans and Puerto Ricans in the United States. Older museums dedicated to Ellis Island–era immigrants are taking steps to include the post-1965 arrivals; the Tenement Museum has added "then and now" walking tours on the Lower East Side, and the Ellis Island Immigration Museum is slated to open a new section on the post–Ellis Island era in 2013.

CONCLUSION

Immigrants, it is clear, are not only influenced by social, economic, and political forces in New York City, but are also agents of change in their new environment. The newest New Yorkers have radically transformed the city—and more changes are in store. Predicting the future is a risky business, yet it is worth reflecting on some ways that the influx of newcomers will leave its stamp on the city and the lives of immigrants and their children in the years ahead.

The signs are that high levels of immigration will continue, at least in the near future. The United States is likely to remain an immigration country for many years to come, allowing hundreds of thousands per year to enter; New York City can expect to receive a substantial share, if only because of the networks that link newcomers to settlers. Immigrants from abroad will not be the only new arrivals, of course. As Lobo and Salvo show, New York City receives large numbers of domestic, often college-educated, migrants from other parts of the country, who will remain a part of the demographic picture (chapter 2). At the same time, immigration is bound to continue to play a critical role in the city's population vitality, especially in the context of a growing proportion of elderly and the exit of many native-born New Yorkers to greener pastures in the suburbs and elsewhere. If first- and second-generation immigrants are the majority in New York City today, we can expect this to be the case for some time to come.

Continued inflows will enrich and replenish the city's ethnic communities. With fresh memories and connections to the homeland, new arrivals will help to keep alive old-country traditions and orientations as well as actual transnational ties. A number of trends already evident in New York's racial-ethnic dynamics are also likely to continue—and indeed, may well accelerate. Puerto Ricans' share of the city's Latino population is bound to shrink; the proportion of Dominicans, Mexicans, Ecuadorians, and Colombians will rise. In addition to ongoing immigration, many Latino groups have high fertility rates, which will add to their numbers (chapter 2).

The Caribbeanization of the city's black population will no doubt persist—and its Africanization will become more prominent. Although the number of Africans is still relatively small, legal immigration from West African countries has grown substantially in the last two decades. Given the network-driven nature of immigration, the dominant role of family preferences in the allocation of immigrant visas, and push factors in West African sending countries, the African influx is sure to accelerate. The proportion of Asians in the city will also grow, owing to immigration as well as fertility. Here, too, new players will be increasingly important, among the most notable Bangladeshis, who have gone from a tiny population in 1990 to one of the top twenty immigrant groups in 2010.

The growing number of newcomers—and naturalized and birthright citizens—will make immigrants (and especially their children) more important in New York City's political arena. Dominicans and West Indians, with their large numbers and geographic concentration, are likely to build on their history in the past two decades of electing coethnics to city and state positions. The Chinese, another large population, have begun to elect their own to city offices, including Taiwanese-born John Liu, who won the race for comptroller in 2009 through significant African American as well as Asian support in addition to the endorsement of many of the city's ethnic newspapers and other media outlets (chapter 11). In 2012, Grace Meng, the Queens-born daughter of Taiwanese immigrants, became the first Asian American elected to Congress from New York City, representing a newly drawn Queens district. Mexicans, a large and fast-growing group, are poised to make gains, although as Smith (chapter 10) argues, they have been hampered by residential dispersion throughout the city, a high proportion of undocumented, and a crowded field of ethnic politics with longer-established Latino groups.

Of course, immigrants' political influence is limited by the fact that noncitizens cannot vote—and continued large influxes will swell this population. In the late 1990s, John Mollenkopf wrote that "the full [political] incorporation of the Caribbean, Dominican, and Chinese populations must await the political maturing of the second generation, just as the full impact of the turn-of-the-century immigration was not felt until their children voted for the New Deal"

(1999:419). At the beginning of the twenty-first century, we are fast approaching this time—in 2008, immigrants and their children accounted for nearly half of voting-age citizens in the city. Although they have yet to enter the city's political leadership proportionate to their numbers, immigrant-origin candidates have won seats in the city council, the state assembly and senate, and the U.S. Congress. Young people from immigrant backgrounds are also emerging as leaders of student groups and nonprofit organizations (chapter 11, this volume; Mollenkopf forthcoming). How their political influence will be felt, and how they will enter the precincts of power, in the years ahead are critical questions.

As chapter 11 suggests, first-generation immigrants along with their second-generation children—born and bred in New York City—will provide fresh, and no doubt surprising, twists and turns in the process of creating a new kind of multicultural city out of the mixture and interplay of their different cultural backgrounds. The New York second-generation study conducted by Kasinitz, Mollenkopf, and Waters provides many grounds for optimism about the prospects for the children of immigrants. Contrary to fears about second-generation decline, most of the young adult children of immigrants in the survey were moving into the economic mainstream. The young adults were generally comfortable with racial and ethnic diversity, having grown up in neighborhoods where almost everyone's family was from somewhere else. They were at ease with their American and ethnic identities, seeing themselves as Americans and New Yorkers, albeit ethnic ones.

Yet there are some clouds on the horizon. The second-generation study was done in good economic times, before the recent recession, and one question is whether New York City will provide sufficient economic opportunities to absorb the children of immigrants now coming of age. Another question posed in chapter 11 is whether the city's schools and higher educational system can meet the challenge of preparing newcomers and their children for managerial and professional jobs of the twenty-first century. In addition, will racial inequalities continue to create barriers for many immigrants and their children? Issues of legal status also loom large. As chapter 10 makes clear, the prospects of Mexican immigrants are of particular concern, in good part because so many are undocumented and thus lack basic rights and opportunities. The U.S.-born children of undocumented parents, despite birthright citizenship, often grow up with economic insecurity, the threat of parents' deportation, and limits on their access to an array of government programs (Yoshikawa 2011). In looking ahead, a crucial question is whether the federal government will enact legislation providing a pathway to legal status, and ultimately citizenship, for the many undocumented immigrants in the city, young and old alike.

These are just some of the questions about the shape of immigrant New York in the years to come. If the United States is a permanently unfinished country, as Nathan Glazer (1988:54) has written in another context, to an even greater degree the same can be said for New York City. In the second decade of the twenty-first century, fresh immigrant recruits keep entering New York City; newcomers who arrived in the 1980s and 1990s are by now old-timers; and a huge second generation is growing up and entering the labor market. The chapters that follow provide a view of immigrant New York after a half century of massive inflows. They offer insights and raise questions that will enrich our understanding of the newcomers in America's ever-changing and quintessential immigrant city and, in the end, also broaden our perspective on immigration generally.

NOTES

1. There is a growing number of full-length ethnographic accounts of contemporary immigrant groups in New York City (see, for example, Grasmuck and Pessar 1991, Pessar 1995, and Ricourt 2002 on Dominicans; Roth 2012 on Dominicans and Puerto Ricans; Margolis 1994, 1998 on Brazilians; Kang 2010, Park 1997, Min 1996, 1998 on Koreans; Khandelwal 2002 and Lessinger 1995 on Asian Indians; Chen 1992, Chin 2005, Guest 2003, Guo 2000, Lin 1998, Louie 2004, Wong 1982, and Zhou 1992 on Chinese; Bashi 2007, Kasinitz 1992, Vickerman 1999, and Waters 1999 on West Indians from the Anglophone Caribbean; Brown 1991, Pierre-Louis 2006, Laguerre 1984, and Glick-Schiller and Fouron 2001 on Haitians; Jones-Correa 1998, Ricourt and Danta 2003, Sanjek 1998 on Latinos in Queens; Markowitz 1993 on Russian Jews; Smith 2006, and Galvez 2009 on Mexicans; Stoller 2002, and Abdullah 2010 on West Africans).

2. According to the pooled 2005–10 American Community Survey, a little over a quarter of non-Hispanic whites and almost a third of non-Hispanic blacks were foreign-born, as compared to 72 percent of Asians and about half of Hispanics (Waters forthcoming).

REFERENCES

Abdullah, Zain. 2010. *Black Mecca: The African Muslims of Harlem*. New York: Oxford University Press.

Abusharaf, Rogaia. 1998. "Structural Adaptations in an Immigrant Muslim Congregation in New York." In R. Stephen Warner and Judith G. Witner, eds., *Gatherings in Diaspora*. Philadelphia: Temple University Press.

Allen, Ray, and Lois Wilcken, eds. 2001. *Island Sounds in the Global City: Caribbean Popular Music and Identity in New York*. Urbana: University of Illinois Press.

Alvarez, Julia. 1992. *How the Garcia Girls Lost Their Accents*. New York: Penguin.

Asimov, Eric. 2000. "Now in New York: True Mexican." *New York Times,* January 26.

Austerlitz, Eric. 1997. *Merengue: Dominican Music and Dominican Identity.* Philadelphia: Temple University Press.

Bakalian, Anny, and Mehdi Bozorgmehr. 2009. *Backlash 9/11: Middle Eastern and Muslim Americans Respond.* Berkeley: University of California Press.

Basch, Linda. 1987. "The Vincentians and Grenadians: The Role of Voluntary Associations in Immigrant Adaptation to New York City." In Nancy Foner, ed., *New Immigrants in New York.* New York: Columbia University Press.

Bashi, Vilna. 2007. *Survival of the Knitted: Immigrant Social Networks in a Stratified World.* Stanford: Stanford University Press.

Berger, Joseph. 2012. "Queens Libraries Speak the Mother Tongue." *New York Times,* January 2.

Beveridge, Andrew A., David Halle, Edward Telles, and Beth DuFault. 2013. "Residential Diversity and Division: Separation and Segregation among Whites, Blacks, Hispanics, Asians, Affluent, and Poor." In David Halle and Andrew Beveridge, eds., *New York and Los Angeles: The Uncertain Future.* New York: Oxford University Press.

Brown, Karen McCarthy. 1991. *Mama Lola: A Vodou Priestess in Brooklyn.* Berkeley: University of California Press.

Bryce-Laporte, Roy S. 1979. "New York City and the New Caribbean Immigrant: A Contextual Statement." *International Migration Review* 13: 214–34.

Caro-Lopez, Howard, and Laura Limonic. 2010. "Dominicans in New York City, 1990–2008." Report 31, Latino Data Project, Center for Latin American, Caribbean, and Latino Studies, Graduate Center, City University of New York.

Chen, Hsiang-Shui. 1992. *Chinatown No More: Taiwan Immigrants in Contemporary New York.* Ithaca, NY: Cornell University Press.

Chin, Margaret. 2005. *Sewing Women: Immigrants and the New York City Garment Industry.* New York: Columbia University Press.

Danticat, Edwidge. 1995. *Breath, Eyes, Memory.* New York: Vintage.

Díaz, Junot. 2007. *The Brief Wondrous Life of Oscar Wao.* New York: Riverhead.

Flores, Juan. 2000. *From Bomba to Hip Hop: Puerto Rican Culture and Latino Identity.* New York: Columbia University Press.

Foner, Nancy. 1987. "The Jamaicans: Race and Ethnicity among Migrants in New York City." In Nancy Foner, ed., *New Immigrants in New York.* New York: Columbia University Press.

——. 1999. "The Immigrant Family: Cultural Legacies and Cultural Changes." In Charles Hirschman, Philip Kasinitz, and Josh DeWind, eds., *The Handbook of International Migration.* New York: Russell Sage Foundation.

——. 2000. *From Ellis Island to JFK: New York's Two Great Waves of Immigration.* New Haven, CT: Yale University Press.

——. 2005. *In a New Land: A Comparative View of Immigration*. New York: New York University Press.

——. 2007. "How Exceptional Is New York? Migration and Multiculturalism in the Empire City." *Ethnic and Racial Studies* 30: 999–1023.

——. Forthcoming. "Immigrant History and the Remaking of New York." In Nancy Foner, Jan Rath, Jan Willem Duyvendak, and Rogier van Reekum, eds., *New York and Amsterdam: Immigration and the New Urban Landscape*. New York: New York University Press.

Foner, Nancy, ed. 2001. *Islands in the City: West Indian Migration to New York*. Berkeley: University of California Press.

Foner, Nancy, and Richard Alba. 2008. "Immigrant Religion in the U.S. and Western Europe: Bridge or Barrier to Inclusion?" *International Migration Review* 42: 360–92.

Foner, Nancy, and Roger Waldinger. 2013. "New York and Los Angeles as Immigrant Destinations: Contrasts and Convergence." In David Halle and Andrew Beveridge, eds., *New York and Los Angeles: The Uncertain Future*. New York: Oxford University Press.

Galvez, Alyshia. 2009. *Guadalupe in New York: Devotion and the Struggle for Citizenship Rights among Mexican Immigrants*. New York: New York University Press.

Glazer, Nathan. 1988. "The New New Yorkers." In Peter Salins, ed., *New York Unbound*. New York: Basil Blackwell.

Glazer, Nathan, and Daniel Patrick Moynihan. 1963. *Beyond the Melting Pot*. Cambridge, MA: MIT Press.

Glick-Schiller, Nina, and Georges Fouron. 2001. *Georges Woke Up Laughing: Long-Distance Nationalism and the Search for Home*. Durham, NC: Duke University Press.

Grasmuck, Sherri, and Patricia Pessar. 1991. *Between Two Islands*. Berkeley: University of California Press.

Guarnizo, Luis, Arturo Sanchez, and Elizabeth Roach. 1999. "Mistrust, Fragmented Solidarity and Transnational Migration: Colombians in New York and in Los Angeles." *Ethnic and Racial Studies* 22: 367–96.

Guest, Kenneth. 2003. *God in Chinatown: Religion and Survival in New York's Evolving Immigrant Community*. New York: New York University Press.

Guo, Zibin. 2000. *Ginseng and Aspirin: Health Care Alternatives for Aging Chinese in New York*. Ithaca, NY: Cornell University Press.

Hauck-Lawson, Annie and Jonathan Deutsch eds. 2008. *Gastropolis: Food and New York City*. New York: Columbia University Press.

Hedges, Chris. 2000. "Translating America for Parents and Family." *New York Times*, June 19.

Itzigsohn, Jose. 2009. *Encountering Faultlines: Race, Class, and the Dominican Experience in Providence*. New York: Russell Sage Foundation.

Jen, Gish. 1992. *Typical American*. New York: Penguin.

Jones-Correa, Michael. 1998. *Between Two Nations: The Political Predicament of Latinos in New York*. Ithaca, NY: Cornell University Press.

Kang, Miliann. 2010. *The Managed Hand: Race, Gender, and the Body in Beauty Service Work*. Berkeley: University of California Press.

Kasinitz, Philip. 1992. *Caribbean New York: Black Immigrants and the Politics of Race*. Ithaca, NY: Cornell University Press.

—. 1999. "A Third Way to America." *Culturefront* 8: 23–29.

—. 2001. "Invisible No More? West Indian Americans in the Social Scientific Imagination." In Nancy Foner, ed., *Islands in the City: West Indian Migration to New York City*. Berkeley: University of California Press.

—. Forthcoming. "Immigrants, the Arts, and the 'Second Generation Advantage' in New York." In Nancy Foner et al., eds., *New York and Amsterdam: Immigration and the New Urban Landscape: New York and Amsterdam*. New York: New York University Press.

Kasinitz, Philip, John Mollenkopf, and Mary Waters, eds. 2004. *Becoming New Yorkers: Ethnographies of the New Second Generation*. New York: Russell Sage Foundation.

Kasinitz, Philip, John Mollenkopf, Mary Waters, and Jennifer Holdaway. 2008. *Inheriting the City*. Cambridge, MA: Harvard University Press.

Khandelwal, Madhulika. 2002. *Becoming American, Being Indian: An Immigrant Community in New York City*. Ithaca, NY: Cornell University Press.

Kibria, Nazli. 2009. "Marry into a Good Family: Transnational Reproduction and Intergenerational Relations in Bangladeshi American Families." In Nancy Foner, ed., *Across Generations: Immigrant Families in America*. New York: New York University Press.

Kim, Dae Young. 2004. "Leaving the Ethnic Economy: The Rapid Integration of Second-Generation Korean Americans in New York." In Philip Kasinitz, John Mollenkopf, and Mary Waters, eds., *Becoming New Yorkers: Ethnographies of the New Second Generation*. New York: Russell Sage Foundation.

Kraly, Ellen, and Ines Miyares. 2001. "Immigration to New York: Policy, Population, and Patterns." In Nancy Foner, ed., *New Immigrants in New York*, rev. ed. New York: Columbia University Press.

Kwong, Peter. 1997. *Forbidden Workers: Illegal Chinese Immigrants and American Labor*. New York: New Press.

Laguerre, Michel. 1984. *American Odyssey: Haitians in New York City*. Ithaca, NY: Cornell University Press.

Lee, Chang-Rae. 1995. *Native Speaker*. New York: Riverhead.

Lee, Jennifer. 1999. "Retail Niche Domination among African American, Jewish, and Korean Entrepreneurs: Competition, Coethnic Advantage, and Disadvantage." *American Behavioral Scientist* 42: 1398–1416.

Lessinger, Johanna. 1995. *From the Ganges to the Hudson: Indian Immigrants in New York City*. Boston: Allyn and Bacon.

Lin, Jan. 1998. *Reconstructing Chinatown: Ethnic Enclave, Global Change*. Minneapolis: University of Minnesota Press.

Lobo, Arun Peter, and Joseph Salvo. 2004. *The New New Yorkers 2000*. New York: New York City Department of City Planning.

Logan, John, and Brian Stults. 2011. "The Persistence of Segregation in the Metropolis: New Findings from the 2010 Census." Census Brief prepared for Census 2010 Project. http://www.s4.brown.edu/us2010/Data/Report/report2.pdf.

Louie, Vivian. 2004. *Compelled to Excel: Immigration, Education, and Opportunity among Chinese Americans*. Stanford, CA: Stanford University Press.

Margolis, Maxine. 1994. *Little Brazil: An Ethnography of Brazilian Immigrants in New York*. Princeton, NJ: Princeton University Press.

——. 1998. *An Invisible Minority: Brazilians in New York City*. Boston: Allyn and Bacon.

Markowitz, Fran. 1993. *A Community in Spite of Itself: Soviet Jewish Emigres in New York*. Washington, DC: Smithsonian Institution Press.

Marshall, Paule. 1985. "Rising Islanders of Bed-Stuy." *New York Times Magazine* (November 3): 179–82.

Massey, Douglas. 1999. "Why Does Immigration Occur? A Theoretical Synthesis." In Charles Hirschman, Philip Kasinitz, and Josh DeWind, eds., *The Handbook of International Migration*. New York: Russell Sage Foundation.

McAlister, Elizabeth. 1998. "The Madonna of 115th Street Revisited: Vodou and Haitian Catholicism in the Age of Transnationalism." In R. Stephen Warner and Judith G. Witner, eds., *Gatherings in Diaspora*. Philadelphia: Temple University Press.

Milkman, Ruth, and Laura Braslow. 2011. "The State of the Unions 2011: A Profile of Organized Labor in New York City, New York State, and the United States." New York: Joseph Murphy Institute for Worker Education and Labor Studies, City University of New York.

Min, Pyong Gap. 1998. *Changes and Conflicts: Korean Immigrant Families in New York*. Boston: Allyn and Bacon.

——. 2001. "Koreans: An Institutionally Complete Community in New York." In Nancy Foner, ed., *New Immigrants in New York*, 2nd ed. New York: Columbia University Press.

——. 2006. *Caught in the Middle: Korean Communities in New York and Los Angeles*. Berkeley: University of California Press.

——. 2008. *Ethnic Solidarity for Economic Survival: Korean Greengrocers in New York City*. New York: Russell Sage Foundation.

——. 2010. *Preserving Ethnicity through Religion in America: Korean Protestants and Indian Hindus across Generations*. New York: New York University Press.

Model, Suzanne. 1993. "The Ethnic Niche and the Structure of Opportunity: Immigrants and Minorities in New York City." In Michael Katz, ed., *The "Underclass" Debate.* Princeton, NJ: Princeton University Press.

Mollenkopf, John. 1999. "Urban Political Conflicts and Alliances." In Charles Hirschman, Philip Kasinitz, and Josh DeWind, eds., *The Handbook of International Migration.* New York: Russell Sage Foundation.

——. Forthcoming. "The Rise of Immigrant Influence in New York City Politics." In Nancy Foner, Jan Rath, Jan Willem Duyvendak, and Rogier van Reekum, eds., *New York and Amsterdam: Immigration and the New Urban Landscape.* New York: New York University Press.

New York City Board of Education. 2010–11. "The 2010–11 Demographics of New York City's English Language Learners." Report of the New York City Board of Education, Office of English Language Learners.

Ng, Mei. 1998. *Eating Chinese Food Naked.* New York: Washington Square Press.

Orleck, Annelise. 1987. "The Soviet Jews: Life in Brighton Beach, Brooklyn." In Nancy Foner, ed., *New Immigrants in New York.* New York: Columbia University Press.

Park, Kyeyoung. 1997. *The Korean American Dream.* Ithaca, NY: Cornell University Press.

Pearson, Jake, and Rich Schapiro. 2010. "Falafel King Freddy Zeideia, Who Parks His Falafel Truck in Astoria, Wins Vendy Food Title." *New York Daily News,* September 26.

Pessar, Patricia. 1995. *A Visa for a Dream.* Boston: Allyn and Bacon.

Pessar, Patricia, and Pamela Graham. 2001. "Dominicans: Transnational Identities and Local Politics." In Nancy Foner, ed., *New Immigrants in New York,* rev. ed. New York: Columbia University Press.

Pierre-Louis, Francois. 2006. *Haitians in New York City: Transnationalism and Hometown Associations.* Gainesville: University Press of Florida.

Reimers, David. 1992. *Still the Golden Door,* 2nd ed. New York: Columbia University Press.

Ricourt, Milagros. 2002. *Dominicans in New York City: Power from the Margins.* New York: Routledge.

Ricourt, Milagros, and Ruby Danta. 2003. *Hispanas de Queens: Latino Panethnicity in a New York City Neighborhood.* Ithaca, NY: Cornell University Press.

Rogers, Reuel. 2006. *Afro-Caribbean Immigrants and the Politics of Incorporation: Ethnicity, Exception or Exit.* New York: Cambridge University Press.

Roth, Wendy. 2012. *Race Migrations: Latinos and the Cultural Transformation of Race.* Stanford, CA: Stanford University Press.

Sanjek, Roger. 1998. *The Future of Us All: Race and Neighborhood Politics in New York City.* Ithaca, NY: Cornell University Press.

Scher, Abby. 2001. "NYC's Ethnic Press." *Gotham Gazette.com* http://old.gothamgazette.com/commentary/80.scher.shtml.

Semple, Kirk. 2011. "Mexicans Fill Pews, Even as Church Is Slow to Adapt." *New York Times*, March 25.

Shteyngart, Gary. 2003. *Russian Debutante's Handbook*. New York: Riverhead.

Smith, Robert C. 2001. "Mexicans: Social, Educational, Economic, and Political Problems and Prospects in New York." In Nancy Foner, ed., *New Immigrants in New York*, rev. ed. New York: Columbia University Press.

——. 2006. *Mexican New York: Transnational Lives of New Immigrants*. Berkeley: University of California Press.

Stoller, Paul. 2001. "West Africans: Trading Places in New York." In Nancy Foner, ed., *New Immigrants in New York*, rev. ed. New York: Columbia University Press.

——. 2002. *Money Has No Smell: The Africanization of New York City*. Chicago: University of Chicago Press.

Torres-Saillant, Silvio. 1999. "Nothing to Celebrate." *Culturefront* 8: 41–48.

Tung, Larry. 2008. "Language Barrier Begins to Fall at City Hospitals." Gotham-Gazette, July. http://old.gothamgazette.com/article/immigrants/20080722/11/2589.

Vickerman, Milton. 1999. *Crosscurrents: West Indian Immigrants and Race*. New York: Oxford University Press.

Wakin, Daniel. 2003. "Religion and Mayoralty: In a City of Diverse Faiths, a Deft Touch Is Often Required." *New York Times*, August 31.

Waldinger, Roger. 1996a. *Still the Promised City? African-Americans and New Immigrants in Postindustrial New York*. Cambridge, MA: Harvard University Press.

——. 1996b. "From Ellis Island to LAX: Immigrant Prospects in the American City." *International Migration Review* 30: 1078–86.

Waters, Mary C. 1999. *Black Identities: West Indian Immigrant Dreams and American Realities*. Cambridge, MA: Harvard University Press.

——. Forthcoming. "Nativism, Racism, and Immigration in New York City." In Nancy Foner, Jan Rath, Jan Willem Duyvendak, and Rogier van Reekum, eds., *New York and Amsterdam: Immigration and the New Urban Landscape*. New York: New York University Press.

Waters, Mary C., and Jennifer Sykes. 2009. "Spare the Rod, Ruin the Child? First- and Second-Generation West Indian Child-Rearing Practices." In Nancy Foner, ed., *Across Generations: Immigrant Families in America*. New York: New York University Press.

Winnick, Louis. 1990. *New People in Old Neighborhoods*. New York: Russell Sage Foundation.

Wong, Bernard. 1982. *Chinatown: Economic Adaptation and Ethnic Identity of the Chinese*. New York: Holt, Rinehart and Winston.

Wong, Janelle, S. Karthick Ramakrishnan, Taeku Lee, and Jane Junn. 2011. *Asian American Political Participation*. New York: Russell Sage Foundation.

Yoshikawa, Hirokazu. 2011. *Immigrants Raising Citizens*. New York: Russell Sage Foundation.

Zhou, Min. 1992. *Chinatown: The Socioeconomic Potential of an Urban Enclave.* Philadelphia: Temple University Press.

Zhou, Min, Margaret M. Chin, and Rebecca Kim. 2013. "The Transformation of Chinese America: New York vs. Los Angeles." In David Halle and Andrew Beveridge, eds., *New York and Los Angeles: The Uncertain Future.* New York: Oxford University Press.

Zolberg, Aristide. 2006. *A Nation by Design: Immigration Policy in the Fashioning of America.* Cambridge, MA: Harvard University Press.

2. *A Portrait of New York's Immigrant Mélange*

Arun Peter Lobo and Joseph J. Salvo

The success of any great city lies in its capacity to reinvent itself over time. What aids New York in this enterprise is the vitality provided by the inflow of people from all over the globe who have made the city their home. The energy unleashed by a city continuously remaking itself demographically—and by the dreams of upward social mobility that immigrants embody—allows it to reinvent itself socially, culturally, and economically. Immigrants are an integral part of the changing social and economic fabric of New York City, which helps explain why the city has benefited from immigration throughout its history.

New York City has been an ethnic mélange since its earliest years under the Dutch and English. Later, in the 1830s and 1840s, famine and oppression in Europe drove large numbers of Irish and German settlers to the city, but by 1880 immigrant origins had shifted to southern and eastern Europe. New York grew even larger when it was incorporated as a city of five boroughs in 1898, with its population of more than 3 million living primarily in lower Manhattan and northwestern Brooklyn. It was a very densely settled place, with more than two-thirds of the population living on less than 10 percent of the city's land mass. Population densities in the tenements of the Lower East Side were above 500 persons per acre (by comparison, today's high-rise neighborhoods of the Upper East Side or Upper West Side rarely exceed 300 persons per acre).

Starting in 1904, the subways became the circulatory system for the creation of new neighborhoods in the boroughs outside of Manhattan. These new neighborhoods helped relieve population pressures in Manhattan, a result of the surging inflow of Italians and Jews from southern and eastern Europe. In the first two decades of the twentieth century, New York City absorbed large numbers of these immigrants, who went on to build the great infrastructure that was to become the backbone for a population that rose to 6.9 million by 1930. By the 1940s, the mélange now included hundreds of thousands of domestic African American migrants from the South and Puerto Ricans from the Caribbean island.

It was the 1965 Immigration Act that put an end to country quotas and opened up immigration to the world. The law allowed for multiple family and employment pathways to the United States that brought another great surge to New York, which would once again put the city on a course to reinvent itself. Largely unanticipated was a great wave of immigrants from the Caribbean, Latin America, and Asia—immigrants seeking opportunities in an increasingly service-based economy. While New York City lost 10 percent of its population in the 1970s, it avoided the collapse experienced by many older cities in the East and Midwest. Immigrants and their fertility buffered losses in the 1970s and then propelled the city to new heights in the 1980s and 1990s. By 2000, New York reached an official population of 8 million for the first time, formed on the heels of immigration flows that brought an unprecedented mix of ethnicities to the city.

New York's growth continued into the first decade of the twenty-first century, with its population reaching nearly 8.2 million in 2010. Its mix of population has become even more varied, with a further diversification by country of origin. Immigration is still part of the continuous cycling of population, as people who have lived in the city move on and are replaced by immigrants. This "demographic ballet" is a source of strength for the city because it provides a supply of talent upon which its institutions rest. This stands in contrast to cities that have been unable to attract people and face demographic and economic decline. New York offers a social and economic environment that continues to attract newcomers, making the city a major hub for those across the globe searching for opportunities.

GROWTH AND CHANGING ORIGINS OF THE FOREIGN-BORN, 1970–2010

The 1965 Immigration Act is the seminal piece of federal legislation that has shaped the demography of New York City for nearly half a century.[1] The law repealed immigration quotas of the 1920s that favored northern and western Europe and, for the first time, placed all countries on an equal footing. The

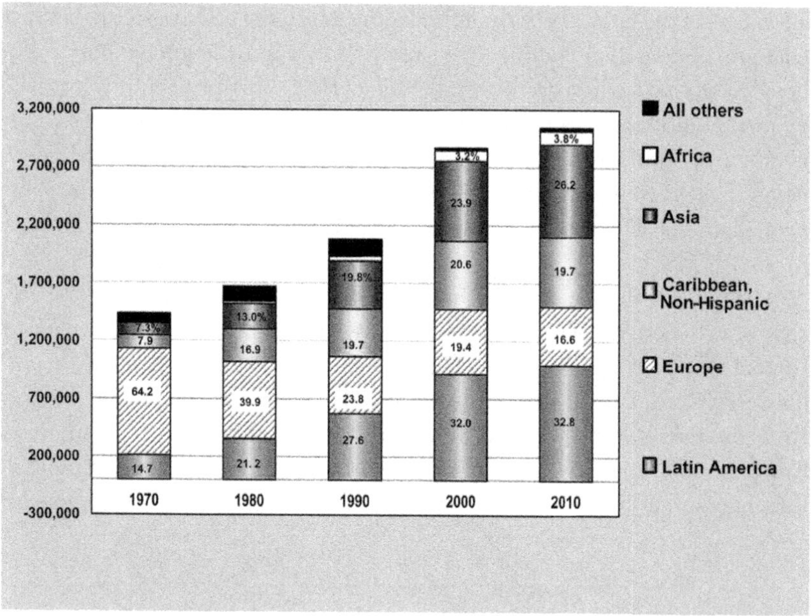

FIGURE 2.1. FOREIGN-BORN BY REGION, NEW YORK CITY, 1970–2010. *Source:* U.S. Census Bureau, 1970–2000 Census; 2010 American Community Survey, Public Use Microdata Sample; Population Division, New York City Department of City Planning.

1965 act made family reunification the main pathway of entry to the United States, but also created a path for those with needed occupational skills and for refugees and asylum seekers (Lobo and Salvo 1998). When the law was passed, New York's foreign-born population was aging and in decline, since immigration had not fully recovered after having dropped precipitously during the Great Depression and World War II. The foreign-born were enumerated at 1.4 million in the 1970 census (figure 2.1); they accounted for just 18 percent of the city's population—a twentieth-century low—of 7.9 million.

The new law and its subsequent amendments were crucial to the resurgence of immigration to the city. By 1980, New York City's foreign-born population had grown to 1.7 million, increasing to 2.1 million in 1990. Immigration law was revised with the Immigration Act of 1990, which provided immigrants expanded opportunities to enter the nation. These additional avenues included an increase in the number of employment visas and a new diversity visa program which, since 1995, has made 55,000 permanent resident visas available by lottery annually to those from countries that sent relatively few immigrants to the United States (Lobo 2001). Diversity visas provided an entry path for those with no close relatives in the United States and who were thus unable to take advantage of the family-based visas under the 1965 law. Partly as a result of these changes, immigration continued to surge and by 2000, the foreign-born numbered nearly 2.9 million. In the first decade of the twenty-first century, the pace of growth had slowed, with the city's foreign-born numbering just over 3 million in 2010—still an all-time high. However, the immigrant share of the population (37 percent) was below the peak attained in the preceding century—41 percent in 1910. The United States as a whole was nearly 13 percent foreign-born in 2010.

The last four decades have seen a surge in immigration, but also a dramatic change in the origins of the city's foreign-born. In 1970, Europe accounted for 64 percent of the city's foreign-born. The top five countries of origin of the foreign-born were Italy, Poland, the (then) USSR, Germany, and Ireland; the United Kingdom ranked eighth and Austria ranked ninth (figure 2.2). The only non-European countries in the top ten were Cuba (ranked sixth), the Dominican Republic (seventh), and Jamaica (tenth). By 2010, Russia was the only European

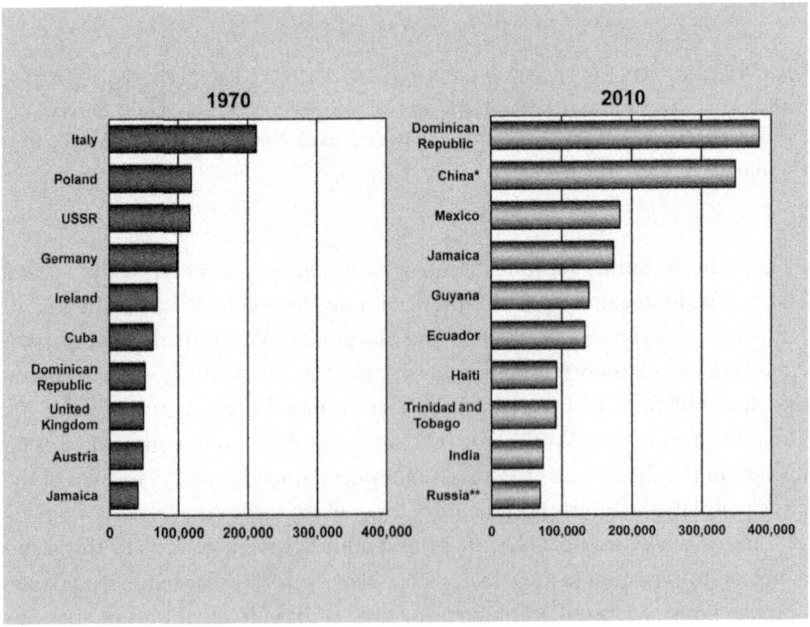

FIGURE 2.2. TOP SOURCES OF NEW YORK CITY'S FOREIGN-BORN, 1970 AND 2010.
*Includes Hong Kong and Taiwan.
**If the former Soviet Union existed, it would rank fifth.
Source: U.S. Census Bureau, 1970 Census; 2010 American Community Survey, Fact-Finder; Population Division, New York City Department of City Planning.

country to make the top ten list, coming in at number ten, with 69,000 immigrants. Due to continued large flows from Russia and Ukraine, the former USSR was the only European entity that actually saw its numbers increase significantly between 1970 and 2010; if the USSR still existed as a country, it would have ranked fifth in 2010, compared to third in 1970. The flow of Russians and Ukrainians has helped increase the number of European-born persons modestly, from 496,000 in 1990 to 504,000 in 2010. But since overall immigration has increased dramatically, the share of Europeans among the foreign-born has declined to just 17 percent in 2010.

In 2010, Latin America was the top area of origin, accounting for nearly one-third of the city's immigrants. Three Latin American countries were among the city's top ten sources of immigrants: the Dominican Republic, Mexico, and Ecuador. China, with 348,000 residents, was the second largest source country of immigrants; India was the only other Asian country that figured among the city's top ten foreign-born groups. However, an additional four Asian countries figured in the top twenty: Korea (eleventh), Philippines (thirteenth), Bangladesh (sixteenth), and Pakistan (eighteenth). Asians accounted for over one-quarter of the foreign-born in 2010.

Non-Hispanic Caribbean countries were disproportionately represented among the city's top immigrant groups. The top ten included fourth-ranked Jamaica (174,000 immigrants) and fifth-ranked Guyana (139,000), as well as Haiti (seventh) and Trinidad and Tobago (eighth). The diversity visa program helped Africans establish a foothold in New York. Africans were nearly 4 percent of the foreign-born population in the city, but no African country made the top twenty list of source countries.

New York's immigrant diversity is unique among large cities in the United States in that no one group dominates the immigrant population (figure 2.3). In New York, Dominicans, the largest immigrant group, comprise just 13 percent of the immigrant population, and it takes the top eight immigrant groups to account for half of the immigrant total. In comparison, in Los Angeles, Mexicans, the largest group, account for 38 percent of immigrants, and along with Salvadorans make up nearly half of immigrants in that city. In both Chicago and Houston, Mexicans account for 46 percent of all immigrants. In most other cities as well, one or two groups dominate the immigrant population, compared to the mosaic of groups in New York City, each with a substantial population. Among other things, this immigrant diversity leads to multiethnic constituencies that often coalesce around specific issues, since no one group commands a majority. The city's immigrant diversity is also likely to increase, thanks to the diversity visa program. These visas have helped countries such as Bangladesh and West African nations, particularly Ghana and Nigeria, to gain a firm foothold in New York. Given that these visas are aimed at those underrepresented

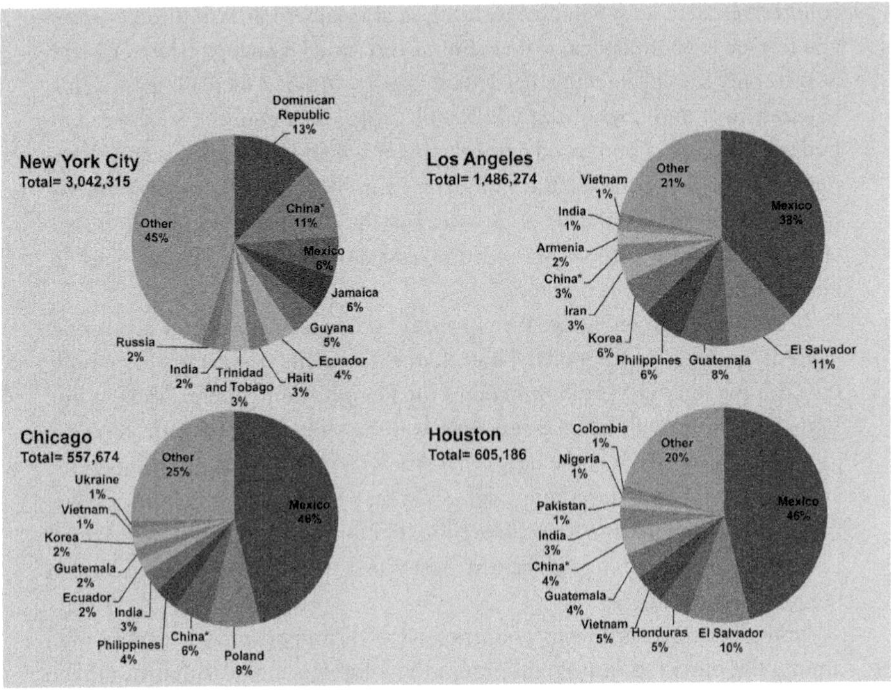

FIGURE 2.3. TOP SOURCES OF THE FOREIGN-BORN FOR MAJOR U.S. CITIES, 2010.

*Includes Hong Kong and Taiwan.

Source: U.S. Census Bureau; 2010 American Community Survey, FactFinder; Population Division, New York City Department of City Planning.

in the immigration stream, it is a built-in mechanism in immigration law to further diversify the sources of immigration.

BOROUGH AND NEIGHBORHOOD OF SETTLEMENT

New York City's five boroughs have unique patterns of immigrant settlement. There are distinct ethnic enclaves across the city, as neighborhoods that are home to one immigrant group tend to also attract more recent entrants (Winnick 1990). Figure 2.4 maps immigrant concentrations across the city's community districts and highlights the major immigrant neighborhoods within these districts,[2] while table 2.1 shows the top immigrant groups in each of the city's five boroughs in 2010. Some immigrant groups were concentrated in specific boroughs—and in specific

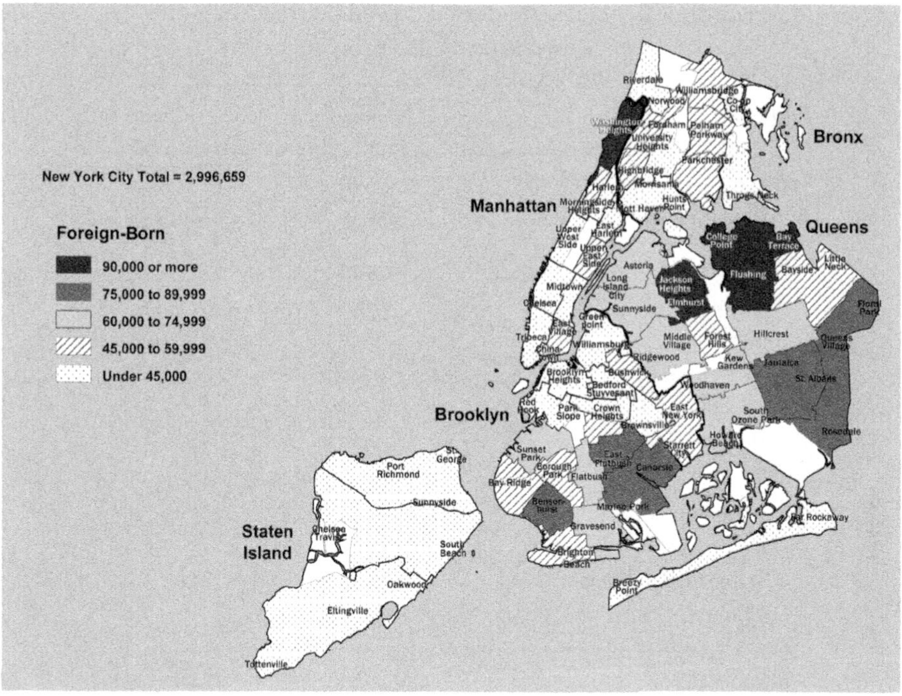

FIGURE 2.4. TOTAL NEW YORK CITY FOREIGN-BORN BY COMMUNITY DISTRICT, 2008–10.*

*Approximated by 55 Public Use Microdata Areas.

Source: U.S. Census Bureau; 2008–2010 American Community Survey, Public Use Microdata Sample; Population Division, New York City Department of City Planning.

community districts within boroughs—while other groups were found across the five boroughs. Two-thirds of immigrants made their home in just two boroughs—Queens and Brooklyn. Queens was home to over 1 million immigrants, and the top immigrant neighborhoods were Flushing, Jackson Heights, Elmhurst, and Jamaica. The Chinese were the largest immigrant group in Queens, with a significant presence in Flushing, one of the city's three Chinatowns. Queens was home to a diverse array of immigrant groups, with no one dominant group. The Chinese, for example, accounted for just 14 percent of all immigrants in the borough, and they were followed by immigrants from Guyana, Ecuador, the Dominican Republic, and Mexico. Together, these countries accounted for just 38 percent of the overall foreign-born population of Queens, indicative of the diverse nature of the foreign-born in the borough. As a result of its large and diverse immigrant population, Queens would qualify as the most racially and ethnically heterogeneous county in the United States.

TABLE 2.1. PLACE OF BIRTH OF THE FOREIGN-BORN BY BOROUGH, 2010

BRONX	*Number*	*Percent*
Total	**1,386,657**	**100.0**
Foreign-born	**475,734**	**34.3**
Foreign-born	**475,734**	**100.0**
Dominican Republic	161,957	34.0
Jamaica	49,053	10.3
Mexico	47,164	9.9
Ecuador	22,029	4.6
Honduras	18,372	3.9
Ghana	17,449	3.7
Guyana	10,085	2.1
Italy	6,584	1.4
Trinidad and Tobago	6,156	1.3
China*	5,626	1.2

BROOKLYN	*Number*	*Percent*
Total	**2,508,340**	**100.0**
Foreign-born	**948,052**	**37.8**
Foreign-born	**948,052**	**100.0**
China*	126,309	13.3
Jamaica	69,550	7.3
Dominican Republic	59,145	6.2
Trinidad and Tobago	57,590	6.1
Mexico	55,222	5.8
Haiti	54,248	5.7
Guyana	45,457	4.8
Ukraine	43,667	4.6
Russia	43,359	4.6
Ecuador	26,642	2.6

MANHATTAN	*Number*	*Percent*
Total	**1,586,698**	**100.0**
Foreign-born	**451,770**	**28.5**
Foreign-born	**451,770**	**100.0**
Dominican Republic	104,031	23.0

MANHATTAN	*Number*	*Percent*
China*	59,622	13.2
Mexico	21,389	4.7
Ecuador	13,001	2.9
United Kingdom	12,803	2.8
Canada	11,840	2.6
India	11,311	2.5
Korea	9,871	2.2
Japan	9,685	2.1
Philippines	9,145	2.0

QUEENS	*Number*	*Percent*
Total	**2,233,841**	**100.0**
Foreign-born	**1,066,262**	**47.7**
Foreign-born	**1,066,262**	**100.0**
China*	150,274	14.1
Guyana	77,628	7.3
Ecuador	71,895	6.7
Dominican Republic	55,697	5.2
Mexico	51,592	4.8
Jamaica	49,600	4.7
India	48,879	4.6
Korea	48,106	4.5
Colombia	46,399	4.4
Philippines	34,333	3.2

STATEN ISLAND	*Number*	*Percent*
Total	**466,676**	**100.0**
Foreign-born	**97,228**	**20.8**
Foreign-born	**97,228**	**100.0**
Mexico	8,345	8.6
China*	7,565	7.8
Italy	7,482	7.7
Ukraine	5,548	5.7
Russia	5,087	5.2
Philippines	4,561	4.7

(*continued*)

TABLE 2.1. *continued*

STATEN ISLAND	*Number*	*Percent*
India	3,649	3.8
Poland	3,371	3.5
Korea	2,755	2.8
Pakistan	2,563	2.6

*Includes Hong Kong and Taiwan.

Source: U.S. Census Bureau, 2010 American Community Survey, FactFinder. Staten Island only: U.S. Census Bureau, 2008–2010 American Community Survey, FactFinder. Population Division, New York City Department of City Planning

Brooklyn's 948,000 immigrants were concentrated in neighborhoods such as Bensonhurst, Canarsie, and Flatbush, as well as Sunset Park—Brooklyn's own Chinatown. As in Queens, the Chinese were the largest immigrant group in Brooklyn, followed by immigrants from Jamaica, the Dominican Republic, Trinidad and Tobago, and Mexico. These five groups made up just 39 percent of the immigrant population; Brooklyn now rivals Queens in terms of diversity of its immigrant population.

The Bronx was home to 476,000 immigrants, with large numbers concentrated in the borough's western and northern neighborhoods—Highbridge, University Heights, Wakefield, Williamsbridge, and Norwood. The Dominican Republic accounted for over one-third of all immigrants in the Bronx, followed by Jamaica and Mexico. These three sources together accounted for over half of the borough's foreign-born; every other group accounted for under 5 percent. Newly emerging immigrant groups in the city, such as Ghanaians, have a relatively large concentration in the Bronx, which places them among the borough's top ten groups.

Manhattan was home to 452,000 immigrants, and the largest concentrations were on either end of the borough: Washington Heights to the north and Chinatown to the south. Washington Heights was home to a great number of Dominicans, who were the largest immigrant group in Manhattan. The Chinese, the second largest group, were concentrated in the city's original Chinatown in lower Manhattan. The Dominicans and Chinese together accounted for over one-third of the borough's immigrant population. The third largest group, Mexicans, accounted for just 5 percent of the borough's immigrants, making their homes primarily in East Harlem. Every other immigrant group accounted for less than 3 percent of the immigrant population in the borough.

Staten Island's 97,000 immigrants were heavily present in the northern part of the borough. Though Staten Island's growing immigrant population is relatively small, its diversity rivals that of Queens and Brooklyn. The top five source countries in the borough were Mexico, China, Italy, Ukraine, and Russia, which together accounted for 35 percent of the borough's foreign-born; the top ten accounted for just over half.

In terms of immigrant concentrations, Queens ranked first: its 1.1 million immigrants comprised 48 percent of the borough's population. Brooklyn was next, with immigrants comprising 38 percent of its population, followed by the Bronx (34 percent), Manhattan (29 percent), and Staten Island (21 percent). Unlike the other boroughs, immigrant concentrations in Staten Island and the Bronx reflect major increases since 2000.

As we will discuss later, New York's population is characterized by huge immigrant inflows and an even larger outflow of city residents to other parts of the United States. In the 1950s, 1960s, and 1970s, when whites left a neighborhood (usually en masse, giving birth to the term "white flight"), they were succeeded primarily by native-born minority groups. This pattern of "invasion-succession" led to all-minority neighborhoods and high levels of segregation in the city—and in inner cities across the Northeast and Midwest. Today, departing native-born whites have been joined by native-born blacks, Hispanics, and Asians, and outflows from the city are now seen as part of a life cycle. Moreover, in the past three decades, as neighborhoods in the city have continued to absorb immigrants from Latin America and Asia, the wholesale racial turnover of neighborhoods is no longer as evident. Rather, many neighborhoods, especially in Queens, have become integrated (Lobo et al. 2002)—integration being defined as neighborhoods including both whites and racial minorities—and have stayed that way.

Figure 2.5 presents two kinds of integrated neighborhoods: melting pot integrated neighborhoods and two-group integrated neighborhoods. In melting pot integrated neighborhoods, whites and at least two other groups (from among blacks, Hispanics, and Asians) each comprised at least 10 percent of the neighborhood's population. In two-group integrated neighborhoods, whites and one minority group each comprised at least 10 percent of the population. In 2010, there were 690 melting pot integrated neighborhoods in the city and 413 two-group integrated neighborhoods, for a total of 1,103 integrated neighborhoods—up from 1,055 in 2000.[3] In both 2000 and 2010, integrated neighborhoods accounted for over half of all neighborhoods in the city. Thus, while many new immigrants move into enclaves—for example, Dominicans moving into Washington Heights or Chinese from across the diaspora moving to Chinatowns—in which they cluster with coethnics, the presence of immigrants across the city has also resulted in a relatively new pattern of stable, multiracial neighborhoods. This pattern has

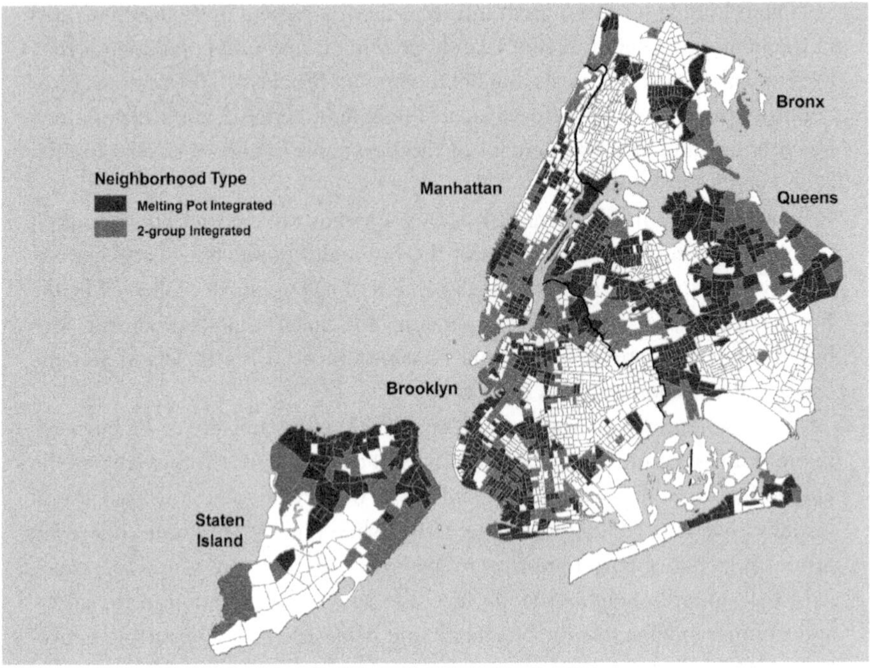

FIGURE 2.5. INTEGRATED NEIGHBORHOODS IN NEW YORK CITY, 2010.*

*Census tracts used as a proxy for neighborhoods. Excludes tracts with population less than 100.

Source: U.S. Census Bureau, 2010 Census Public Law 94–171 Files; Population Division, New York City Department of City Planning.

also been found across the larger New York region (Alba et al. 1995; Logan and Zhang 2010).

Stable, melting pot integrated neighborhoods in New York, however, are more likely to be composed of whites, Asians, and Hispanics, and are generally less inclusive of blacks (Flores and Lobo 2013). Non-Hispanic blacks in New York City—both native- and foreign-born—remain the group most segregated from whites.

SELECTED SOCIODEMOGRAPHIC CHARACTERISTICS OF IMMIGRANTS

The diverse patterns of immigration to New York are reflected in the disparate social, economic, and demographic characteristics of immigrants. Initial gender patterns of immigrants, for example, are reflected in the sex ratio, defined as the number of males per 100 females (table 2.2). This can be clearly seen among Mexican immigrants in New York City, who had among the highest sex ratios, 144 males for every 100 females. Mexicans are relatively recent, young entrants. Mexicans, as well as Ecuadorians, start out with very high sex ratios, with males first establishing themselves before being joined by their spouses and children, which will eventually lower the sex ratio. This pattern of immigration also holds true for the city's myriad South Asian groups.

In contrast, immigrants from the non-Hispanic Caribbean had the lowest sex ratios, with the Trinidadian and Tobagonian sex ratio at 66, and Jamaicans and Guyanese at 75 and 83, respectively. For these groups, females are in the vanguard of immigration and are later followed by males. Often an immigrant group disproportionately uses certain classes of immigration law that can benefit one gender, as with Filipinos, who have a sex ratio of just 52. Filipinos have made use of a special provision in U.S. law that allows for the entry of nurses into the United States, and these nurses are overwhelmingly female.

Given that most immigrants come from non-English-speaking countries, it is no surprise that many do not speak English well. In 2010, half of the foreign-born and 24 percent of city residents overall were limited English proficient (LEP), defined as those speaking English "less than very well."[4] The city's LEP population totaled 1.8 million (data not shown), with those speaking Spanish at home accounting for one-half of the total, followed by Chinese (17 percent), Russian (6 percent), and Haitian Creole and Korean (each with 3 percent). Thus these top five languages accounted for nearly 80 percent of the LEP population. Among the city's top ten immigrant groups, 83 percent of Mexicans, 78 percent of Chinese, and 77 percent of Ecuadorians were LEP. By comparison, immigrants from Trinidad and Tobago and Jamaica, where English is the lingua franca, had very low LEP levels.

Educational attainment among immigrants was significantly lower than the New York City average. Among adult immigrants, just 72 percent had completed high school and 26 percent had a college degree, compared to 79 percent and 33 percent, respectively, for the city overall. Mexicans, who had the highest proportion who were LEP, had the lowest educational attainment: just 42 percent had completed high school and just 5 percent had a college degree. Educational attainment was also below average for Dominican, Ecuadorian, and Chinese immigrants. Among the top ten immigrant groups, college attainment only for Indians (53 percent) and Russians (49 percent) was higher than that of the city overall, and even higher than that of the native-born (40 percent).

The labor force participation rate is defined as the percentage of people working or looking for work. Among males ages sixteen to sixty-four, the foreign-born had a labor force participation rate (83 percent) higher than that of their native-born counterparts (70 percent); for the city overall, the rate was 76 percent. The

TABLE 2.2. SELECTED SOCIOECONOMIC CHARACTERISTICS OF NEW YORK CITY'S TOP TEN FOREIGN-BORN GROUPS, 2010

				Educational Attainment[3]				Income and Poverty	
						Labor Force Participation Rate[4]			
	Total Population	Sex Ratio	Limited English Proficient (%)[2]	High School Graduate or Higher (%)	College Graduate or Higher (%)	Males	Females	Median Household Income	Poverty Rate
Total	8,185,314	90	23.7	79.3	33.3	75.9	66.7	$48,366	20.3
Native-born	5,138,863	93	6.5	86.2	39.7	70.3	67.1	$51,792	21.3
Foreign-born	3,046,451	87	50.0	71.7	26.3	83.2	66.1	$44,335	18.6
Dominican Republic	378,199	71	69.9	55.6	10.7	77.6	66.4	$30,229	25.9
China[1]	351,314	89	78.3	59.9	25.1	76.7	66.4	$40,506	21.5
Mexico	187,086	144	83.3	42.2	4.8	94.3	48.9	$37,282	28.5
Jamaica	169,863	75	0.7	77.9	19.3	78.8	82.9	$49,374	13.4
Guyana	138,549	83	2.3	77.2	19.0	81.7	76.5	$60,457	9.0
Ecuador	138,097	112	77.0	58.8	9.8	89.1	59.8	$43,731	17.2
Haiti	97,516	72	50.2	79.7	17.6	80.8	74.4	$44,940	16.2
Trinidad and Tobago	84,347	66	0.4	86.3	15.9	80.4	77.2	$42,320	14.3
India	72,803	112	37.9	81.9	52.8	81.9	56.5	$61,667	13.1
Russia	70,123	70	63.5	91.3	49.3	83.2	73.3	$42,320	14.8

[1]Includes Hong Kong and Taiwan.
[2]Persons 5 years and over.
[3]Persons 25 years and over.
[4]Persons 16–64 years old.
Source: U.S. Census Bureau, 2010 American Community Survey, Public Use Microdata Sample; Population Division, New York City Department of City Planning.

labor force participation rate for each of the city's top ten immigrant groups exceeded the city's overall rate. Among females, the overall labor force participation of the foreign-born (66 percent) was similar to the city average. However, women from the non-Hispanic Caribbean had higher-than-average labor force participation, particularly Jamaicans (83 percent) and Trinidadians (77 percent).

Given the socioeconomic characteristics of immigrants, it is not unexpected that they have a lower median household income ($44,000) than the city overall ($48,000). But three groups, Indians ($62,000), Guyanese ($60,000), and Jamaicans ($49,000) had household incomes at or above the city average, primarily as a result of the high labor force participation of household members. At the same time poverty was lower for immigrants. Immigrant poverty stood at 18.6 percent, compared to 20.3 percent for the city; at 21.3 percent, the native-born had the highest poverty rate. Income among the native-born was concentrated, while the income distribution was more equitable among immigrants, resulting in a lower poverty rate. Dominicans, Mexicans, and Chinese were the only groups in the top ten with a poverty rate higher than the city average.

Immigrant groups arrive in the United States with disparate skills, which partly accounts for differences in their socioeconomic attainment. Some groups are also comprised primarily of recent arrivals who have just entered the U.S. labor market (Lobo et al. 2012). Newly arrived immigrants often accept lower-level jobs than they may have held in their home countries. But after acquiring experience in the U.S. labor market and becoming more proficient in English, earnings tend to increase. Thus, groups such as Mexicans in New York City, who are overwhelmingly composed of recent entrants, tend to have among the lowest socioeconomic attainment.

IMMIGRANTS IN THE NEW YORK METROPOLITAN REGION

The entry of immigrants to New York City has had a major impact on the wider New York metropolitan region. In addition to the city's five boroughs, the metropolitan region encompasses twenty-six other counties, for a total of thirty-one counties spread over 12,600 miles across portions of New York State, New Jersey, and Connecticut (figure 2.6). While the initial impact of post-1965 immigration was felt primarily in New York City, over time many of these immigrants left the city to settle in the region's suburban towns, villages, and cities. They were joined by many entering immigrants who bypassed the city altogether and moved directly to the suburban counties of the New York metropolitan region. While New York City accounted for nearly 8.2 million, or 37 percent of the 22 million residents in the region, it remains the epicenter of immigrant settlement, being home to over half of the region's 5.9 million immigrants.

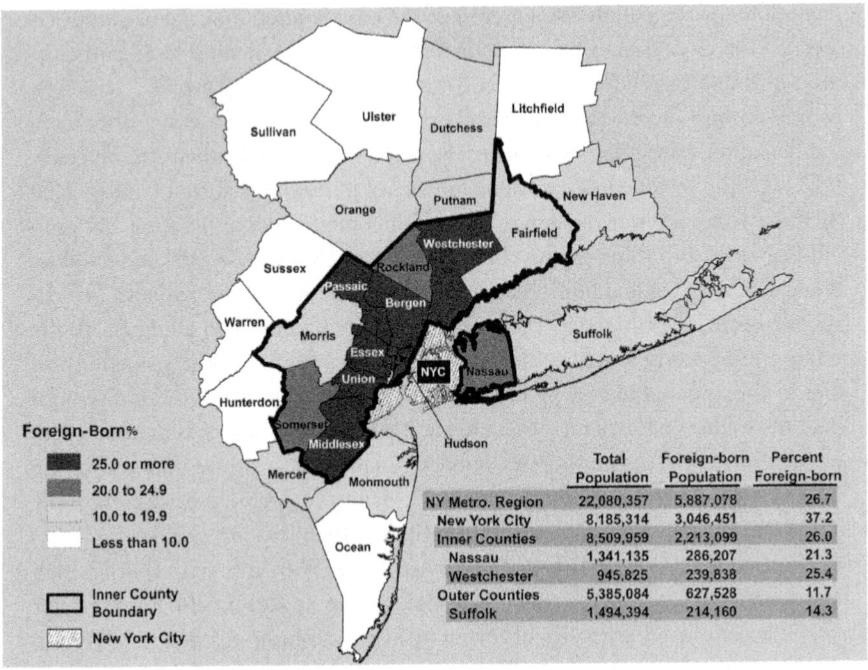

FIGURE 2.6. FOREIGN-BORN IN THE NEW YORK METROPOLITAN REGION BY COUNTY, 2010.
Source: U.S. Census Bureau; 2010 American Community Survey, Public Use Microdata Sample; Population Division, New York City Department of City Planning.

The subregion adjacent to New York City also had significant immigrant concentrations. This subregion, composed of the twelve counties closest to the city, labeled "inner counties," was one-quarter foreign-born. The percentage foreign-born in these counties ranged from a high of 42 percent for Hudson—second in the entire region only to Queens—to a low of 19 percent for Morris. The subregion comprising the fourteen counties farthest from the city, labeled "outer counties," was only 12 percent foreign-born, but this was up from 7 percent in 1990.

Neighborhoods in the region with high immigrant concentrations tend to have low income and a housing stock that includes older, multifamily, rental units, which produce high population densities. However, many immigrant neighborhoods—such as Edison, West Orange, Fair Lawn, Dix Hills, Morganville, and Princeton North—have socioeconomic characteristics superior to those of the subregion in which they were located (Lobo and Salvo 2004).

NEW YORK'S UNAUTHORIZED POPULATION

A major issue in the United States is policy concerning unauthorized immigrants. For New York City, a key question is the size of the unauthorized population and its pace of growth. In 1986, that segment of the unauthorized population which continuously resided in the United States since January 1, 1982, and those employed as seasonal agricultural workers became eligible for legalization under the Immigration Reform and Control Act (Salvo and Lobo 2005). In New York State, 174,000 unauthorized immigrants were legalized under this program, 125,000 of whom were in New York City. Just four years later, New York State's unauthorized immigrant population was estimated at 358,000 (figure 2.7), 261,000 or 73 percent of whom lived in New York City. Most unauthorized immigrants in New York City entered the country with a valid visa. But by overstaying their visas, that is, staying in the United States beyond the required departure dates, they become part of the unauthorized population. The growth in this

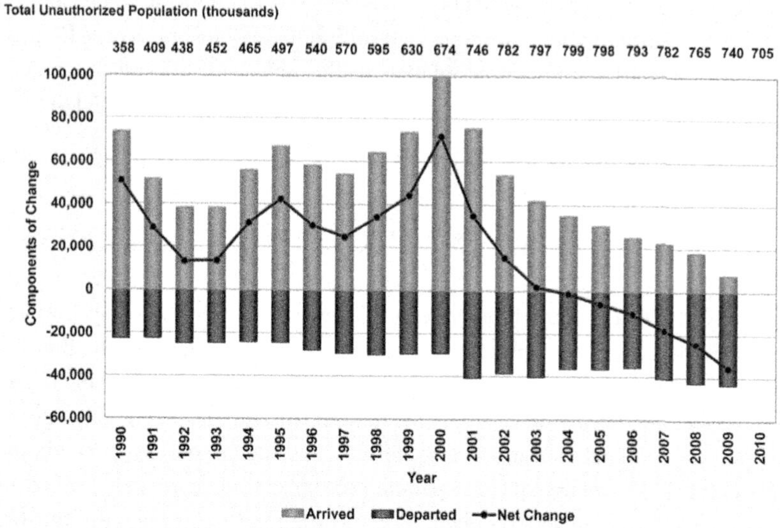

FIGURE 2.7. ANNUAL ESTIMATES OF THE UNAUTHORIZED POPULATION AND COMPONENTS OF CHANGE, NEW YORK STATE, 1990–2010.

Source: Robert Warren, Unpublished estimates; Population Division, New York City Department of City Planning.

population is the net effect of those entering and those leaving unauthorized status—the latter being an important, though often overlooked, component of change in the unauthorized immigrant population.

In the 1990s, the addition to New York State's unauthorized immigrant population averaged 57,000 each year. At the same time, an average of nearly 26,000 unauthorized immigrants exited each year—either returning home, moving to another state, or becoming legalized (through marriage to a U.S. citizen, for example). Thus, in the 1990s, the number of those entering the unauthorized population each year was, on average, more than twice as large as those leaving. The net effect was an increase in the unauthorized immigrant population by nearly 32,000 each year, resulting in the total unauthorized immigrant population increasing 88 percent over the decade, to 674,000 in 2000. Indeed, unauthorized immigrants were the fastest-growing component of the state's foreign-born population in the 1990s. This growth continued in the early years of the twenty-first century and, by 2004, New York State's unauthorized population reached a high of nearly 799,000, of whom 583,000 are estimated to have lived in New York City.

But patterns changed dramatically by the end of the first decade of the twenty-first century, with those leaving the unauthorized population exceeding those entering, resulting in a decline in unauthorized immigrants. By 2009, those entering the unauthorized population numbered only 8,000, while those leaving this population numbered over 43,000, resulting in a net loss of 35,000. By 2010, the unauthorized immigrant population in the state had dropped to 705,000, with 499,000 living in the city. The unauthorized population is estimated to comprise between 15 and 20 percent of the city's foreign-born population.

A CITY DEPENDENT ON IMMIGRATION

As is already clear, immigration is a central element in understanding how New York City has been able to grow and reinvent itself demographically. But it is interesting to place these inflows in the context of broader demographic trends in the city and in other cities across the nation. In 2000, New York City's population was enumerated at just over 8 million, and in the following decade the city added approximately 167,000 people (bottom tier of figure 2.8). Growth is often viewed as a small increment added to the existing population, but the underlying dynamic is more complicated. Between 2000 and 2010, New York City had a net loss of 1.4 million people through domestic migration, that is, the number of city residents who left for the rest of the country exceeded those who arrived from within the United States by 1.4 million. But the city gained back a big portion of that loss—926,000—through net international flows, which reflects the exchange of people with other countries. The net result was a loss through

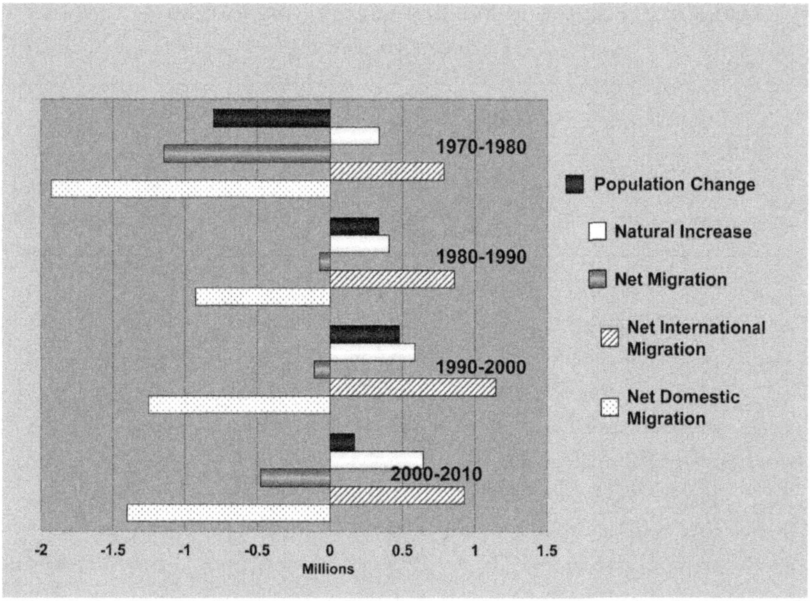

FIGURE 2.8. COMPONENTS OF POPULATION CHANGE FOR NEW YORK CITY BY DECADE, 1970–2010.
Source: Adjusted U.S. Decennial Census data 1970–2000; 2010 Decennial Census as revised by Population Division, New York City Department of City Planning.

migration of 474,000 people. Despite this loss, the city's population continued to grow, thanks to natural increase (the difference between births and deaths) of 641,000, resulting in a population increase of 167,000.

Thus, what may seem like a small population change can mask large movements of people into and out of the city. Each day, new people move into the city, while even more leave. Outflows from the city take place for a host of reasons, including the desire for a larger home, a new job, and retirement. The inflow—the constant injection of new energy into the city—is what makes New York City special. It may seem that there is something unusual about a city that had a net loss in a decade of 1.4 million people through domestic exchanges with the fifty states. But there is nothing inherently wrong with this dynamic. The fact that population losses are largely ameliorated through immigration inflows is a testament to New York City's demographic dynamism.

One way to illustrate this point is to examine the top ten cities in the United States in 1950 and then again in 2010 (table 2.3). New York was the largest U.S. city in 1950, followed by Chicago, Philadelphia, and Los Angeles. The fifth-ranked city was Detroit, followed by Baltimore, Cleveland, St. Louis, Washington, DC, and Boston, but by 2010, none of these cities were among the nation's ten largest.

TABLE 2.3. TOP U.S. CITIES IN 1950, AND GROWTH BETWEEN 1950 AND 2010

Rank			*Population*			
1950	2010	*City*	1950	2010	*Growth (%)*	2010 *Foreign-Born (%)*
1	1	New York City, NY	7,891,957	8,175,133	3.6	37.2
2	3	Chicago, IL	3,620,962	2,695,598	−25.6	20.7
3	5	Philadelphia, PA	2,071,605	1,526,006	−26.3	11.6
4	2	Los Angeles, CA	1,970,358	3,792,621	92.5	39.1
5	18	Detroit, MI	1,849,568	713,777	−61.4	4.8
6	22	Baltimore, MD	949,708	620,961	−34.6	7.1
7	43	Cleveland, OH	914,808	396,815	−56.6	4.5
8	50	St. Louis, MO	856,796	319,294	−62.7	7.2
9	25	Washington, DC	802,178	601,723	−25.0	13.5
10	23	Boston, MA	801,444	617,594	−22.9	26.9

Source: U.S. Census Bureau, 1950 Census; 2010 Decennial Census, Summary File 1; 2010 American Community Survey, FactFinder; Population Division, New York City Department of City Planning.

All had lost population, with St. Louis, Detroit, and Cleveland losing more than half their 1950 populations. These cities could not attract immigrants (as they once did) to replace those leaving; indeed, but for Boston and Washington, DC, the percentage of foreign-born in these cities was in the single digits in 2010.

In contrast to this one-sided population (out) flow, New York's population movements are dynamic, with immigrants replacing those who leave. The city remains a magnet for immigrants, who come to take advantage of the opportunities the city has to offer and are attracted by the large communities of coethnics who live there. As a result of immigrant inflows, New York remained the largest city in the nation in 2010, followed by Los Angeles, which saw a near doubling of its population, also due to a heavy inflow of immigrants. New York's population dynamic is not of recent vintage, as can be seen in figure 2.8. However, in the 1970s, a period of grave economic crises, immigration and natural increase could not mitigate the large outflows from New York City, resulting in a population decline of around 806,000. This decline was primarily due to a high level of out-migration; while natural increase added nearly 339,000 persons to the city's population, a net of 1.15 million persons left New York, resulting in a substantial population loss for the city. The decline would have been much greater were it not for the entry of 783,000 immigrants in that decade. In the 1980s and 1990s, however, outflows moderated, and thanks to higher immigration and to natural increase, the city enjoyed renewed population growth. As noted earlier, this trend has continued in the first decade of the twenty-first century.

In addition to the direct effect of immigration on population growth, immigrants have an indirect effect by way of their fertility. Immigrants are heavily concentrated in the younger childbearing ages, and immigrant fertility is higher than that of native-born residents. Table 2.4 shows that in 2010, 54 percent of the 115,000 births in the city of New York were to foreign-born women—62 percent of these newborns had a foreign-born mother or father. Women from five countries accounted for nearly one-quarter of all births in New York City: the Dominican Republic, Mexico, China, Jamaica, and Ecuador. Being younger, immigrants also have lower mortality; thus higher immigrant fertility and lower mortality disproportionately contribute to positive natural increase in New York. With respect to the overall population, immigrants and their U.S.-born offspring account for an estimated 55 percent of the city's population.

While inflows to New York continue to be smaller than outflows, the start of the twenty-first century has shown a change in the relative profiles of those

TABLE 2.4. BIRTHS IN NEW YORK CITY TO FOREIGN-BORN MOTHERS, 2010

	Number	*Percentage*
Total births	114,908	100.0
Foreign-born mothers	61,671	53.7
Dominican Republic	7,635	6.6
Mexico	7,378	6.4
China*	7,144	6.2
Jamaica	2,947	2.6
Ecuador	2,905	2.5
Guyana	1,921	1.7
Bangladesh	1,755	1.5
Haiti	1,522	1.3
Trinidad and Tobago	1,440	1.3
Pakistan	1,263	1.1
India	1,250	1.1

*Includes Hong Kong and Taiwan.
Source: Department of Health and Mental Hygiene, New York City, 2010; Population Division, New York City Department of City Planning.

entering and leaving the city (table 2.5). Historically, those coming to the city have had a lower socioeconomic profile, compared to those leaving. For example, during the 1985–90 period, in-migrants to the city had lower earnings compared to out-migrants ($45,100 vs. $54,900), lower household income ($50,900 vs. $56,000), and higher poverty (21.9 percent vs. 17.2 percent). The lower socioeconomic profile of in-migrants relative to out-migrants was also evident in flows between 1995 and 2000. However, there was a shift in the first decade of the twenty-first century, with socioeconomic characteristics of in-migrants in the 2008–10 period similar to those of out-migrants (in the case of mean earnings and median household income), though poverty remained significantly higher.

This shift is related to another major source of in-migrants—domestic migrants—who are also critical to the vitality of New York City. The higher socioeconomic profile of in-migrants at the beginning of the twenty-first century was partly due to a compositional change in inflows to the city (figure 2.9). In the 1995–2000 period, the inflow to New York City was almost equally divided between domestic migrants coming from the fifty states and immigrant flows

TABLE 2.5. ECONOMIC CHARACTERISTICS OF MIGRANTS TO AND FROM NEW YORK CITY: 1985–90, 1995–2000, 2008–10

	1985–90	1995–2000	2008–10
Mean earnings, 21 years and over			
In-migrants	$45,130*	$57,959*	$54,760
Out-migrants	$54,880	$61,857	$58,463
Median household income			
In-migrants	$50,933*	$54,304*	$54,761
Out-migrants	$56,026	$58,884	$51,564
Percentage below poverty			
In-migrants	21.9*	23.9*	24.5*
Out-migrants	17.2	15.7	20.8
Percentage college graduates, 25 years and over			
In-migrants	39.0*	46.0*	55.0*
Out-migrants	32.4	37.4	47.9

*Difference with out-migrants is statistically significant at the .10 level.
All dollar figures in 2010 constant dollars.
Source: U.S. Census Bureau, 1990–2000 censuses; 2008–2010 American Community Survey, Public Use Microdata Sample; Population Division, New York City Department of City Planning.

from outside the United States. Domestic migrants from the fifty states have traditionally had higher socioeconomic characteristics compared to those coming from abroad, which remains true even today. Domestic migrants entering between 1995 and 2000 had mean earnings of $65,000, compared to $41,000 for immigrants entering during this period, a differential that has narrowed—though is still present—in the years since 2000 (data not shown). The lower earnings of immigrants have historically pulled down the overall socioeconomic profile of those entering the city.

In 2008–10, however, the share of domestic migrants increased to 67 percent of all in-migrants, and there was a concomitant decline in the share of immigrants, to 33 percent (figure 2.9). Thus, while immigrants remain an important part of the flow, the city has become a more attractive destination for domestic migrants, who now comprise a larger share of the total inflow to the city. Many of them are college-educated young adults who move to New York—primarily to Manhattan, but increasingly to Brooklyn and Queens—for jobs in vibrant sectors of the economy, including financial services, the arts, and publishing. The higher socioeconomic attainment of domestic in-migrants, coupled with their increased share of the total inflow to the city, has resulted in a higher socioeconomic profile of all

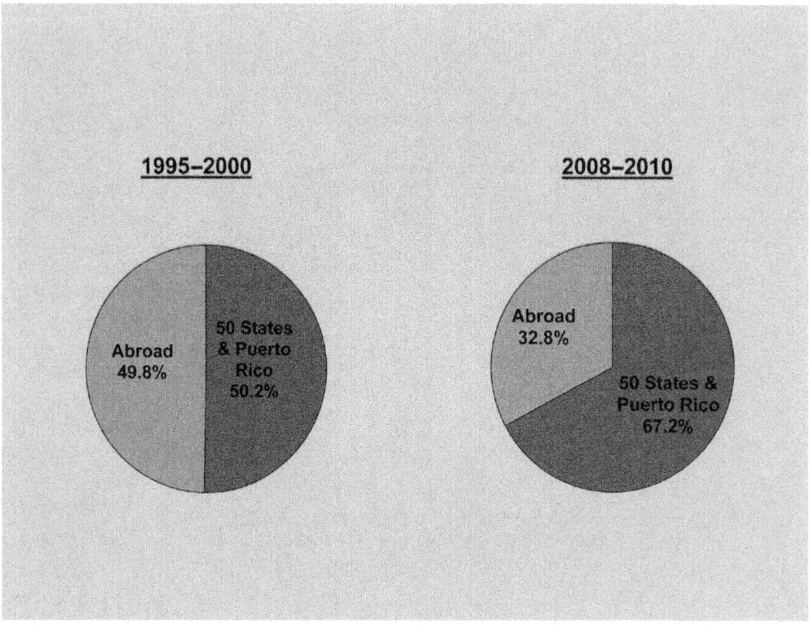

FIGURE 2.9. CHANGING ORIGINS OF IN-MIGRANTS TO NEW YORK CITY, 1995–2000 AND 2008–2010.
Source: U.S. Census Bureau, 2000 Census; 2008–2010 ACS Public Use Microdata Sample; Population Division, New York City Department of City Planning.

in-migrants to the city. It is too early to tell whether this pattern will continue, but these changes testify to the dynamic nature of migration flows to New York City, and the dramatic effect they can have on the city's overall well-being.

THE CHANGING FACE OF NEW YORK CITY

In the nearly five decades since the passage of the landmark 1965 Immigration Act, the large influx of immigrants from Latin America, Asia, and the Caribbean has transformed the racial and ethnic composition of New York City, from one that was largely white non-Hispanic to a diverse mix where no one group is in the majority. While white non-Hispanics were still the largest group in 2010, they comprised just 33 percent of the population (figure 2.10), down from 63 percent in 1970. Hispanics were the largest minority group in 2010, with a 29 percent share, followed by blacks (23 percent) and Asians (13 percent). (These figures include both the native- and foreign-born in each group.)

The role of immigration in the changing racial and ethnic distribution is even more apparent when we look at the borough level (figure 2.10). In the Bronx,

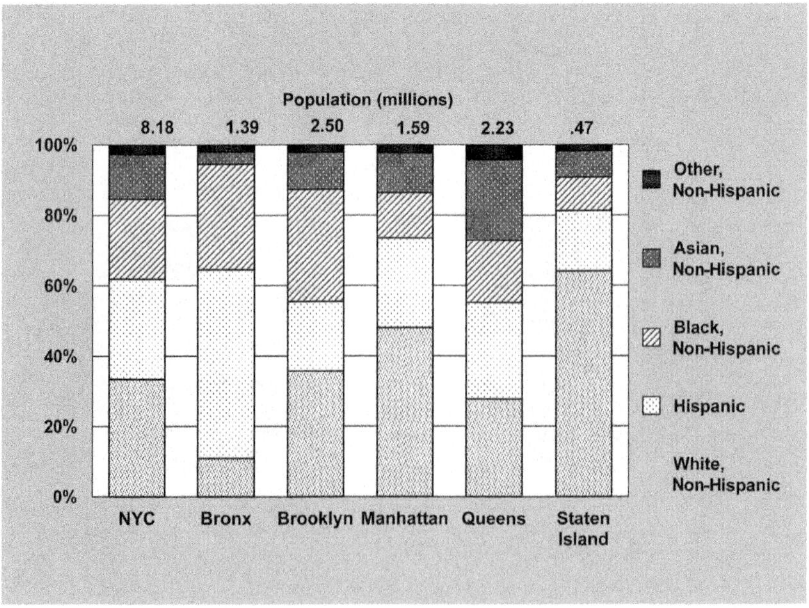

FIGURE 2.10. NEW YORK CITY'S RACE/HISPANIC GROUPS BY BOROUGH, 2010.
Source: U.S. Census Bureau, 2010 Census, Summary File 1; Population Division, New York City Department of City Planning.

where immigrants are primarily from Latin America and the non-Hispanic Caribbean, Hispanics, not surprisingly, were over half of the borough's population, while blacks were at 30 percent. In Brooklyn, where immigrants are mainly from the non-Hispanic Caribbean and Europe, whites and blacks each comprised approximately one-third of the population. In Manhattan, whites were just under half of the population, with immigrant enclaves in the northern and southern sections of the borough accounting for the strong presence of Hispanics and Asians. Immigration has made Queens the most diverse county in the country. Whites and Hispanics each comprised 28 percent, while Asians and blacks accounted for 23 percent and 17 percent, respectively. Staten Island is the only borough in the city where whites comprised a majority (64 percent)—in 1970, each of city's five boroughs was majority white.

There is also increasing ethnic diversity within each of the four major ethnoracial groups in the city. The Caribbean- and African-born populations, for example, made up approximately one-third of the black non-Hispanic population in 2010, up from less than 10 percent in 1970. In 2010, the Hispanic population, long synonymous with Puerto Ricans, had no single ethnic group with a majority. Puerto Ricans remained the largest group, but accounted for under one-third of Hispanics in 2010 (data not shown), and were followed by a host of other ethnic groups, including Dominicans (25 percent), Mexicans (14 percent), Ecuadorians (7 percent), and Colombians (4 percent). Among Asians, the Chinese were a near majority (49 percent) in 2010, but down from their 59 percent share in 1970. They were followed by Asian Indians (19 percent), Koreans (9 percent), Filipinos (7 percent), and Pakistanis and Bangladeshis, each with a 4 percent share of the Asian non-Hispanic population.

Immigration has had an especially profound effect in changing the ethnoracial composition of the youngest age cohorts, who represent the city's future. Indeed, one can peek at the demographic future of the city by examining its ethnic and racial population by age (figure 2.11). In 2010, among the city's population ages 65 years and over, close to half was white non-Hispanic, mirroring the city's demographic past. In contrast, children under 18, who represent what the city will look like, demographically, in the years ahead, were disproportionately nonwhite. Hispanics were the largest group (36 percent), followed by black and white non-Hispanics (each with 25 percent), Asian non-Hispanics (11 percent), and those of multiracial non-Hispanic backgrounds (4 percent).

New York City continues to grow, with an estimated population of nearly 8.25 million in 2011, but irrespective of its pace of growth, it will see further changes in its overall ethnoracial composition. In the coming decades, as older New Yorkers—who are disproportionately white non-Hispanic—pass on, the city will reflect the makeup of its extremely diverse younger age cohorts as they move into adulthood and old age.

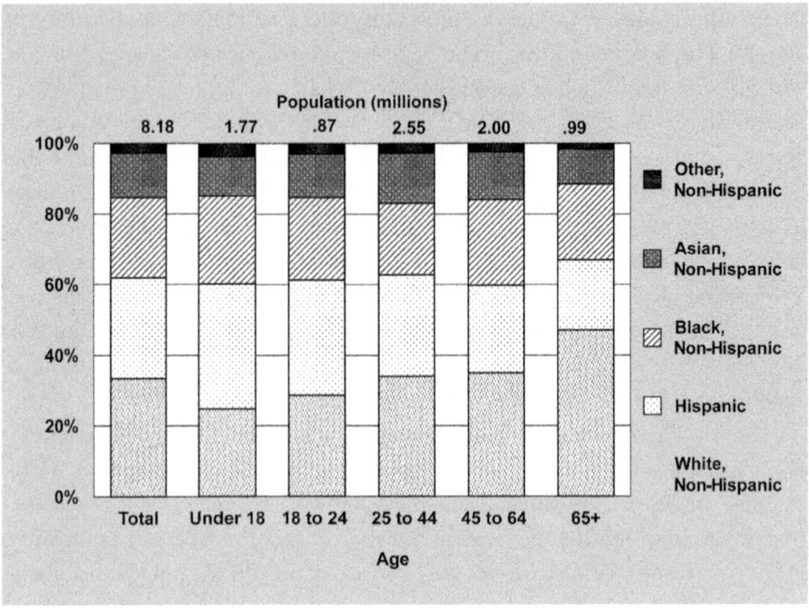

FIGURE 2.11. NEW YORK CITY'S RACE/HISPANIC GROUPS BY AGE, 2010.
Source: U.S. Census Bureau, 2010 Census, Summary File 1; Population Division, New York City Department of City Planning.

CONCLUSION

Recent statistics about the racial and ethnic diversity of New York City's population tell a remarkable story. The words of Major Samuel Shaw of Boston, referring to New York in 1776 as "a motley collection of all the nations under heaven" (Shaw and Quincy 1847) are even more appropriate today. New York City is arguably more multiracial and multiethnic than at any time in its history. No single chart or graph can adequately characterize this diversity. Indeed, categories that are available in the decennial census and the American Community Survey barely do the city justice on this subject. As we have seen, in just a few decades, New York City has shifted from a place consisting largely of the descendants of European immigrants to a city that now has no dominant racial, ethnic, or national origin group. And the latest data show that New York City is continuing in the direction of unprecedented diversity.

As we move forward, in this decade and into the next, two factors will come to dominate the demographic landscape. First, the descendants of earlier European immigrants will enter retirement age in very large numbers, owing to the size of the aging baby-boom cohorts—a process that has already begun. Second, the economy of New York City will continue to depend on the flow of young working age people—many of them from other parts of the world—in search of economic opportunities.

Given the aging of New York City's population, the reliance on immigrants is as important today as it was in past eras. In every city, there is a demographic balance between those who supply labor for the economy and the elderly who are dependent on it. In demographic parlance, this is expressed as the aged dependency ratio, which refers to the ratio of persons 65 and over to those 20 to 64 years of age. While an increasing ratio is an issue of national concern, it is also relevant at the city level. The fact is that some places do a better job than others at attracting workers who are the essence of a vital city. As populations age, as they are doing in a number of American cities, the capacity to provide services will depend on ensuring that dependency does not rise to unsustainable levels. New York City has been able to benefit from the strength of its immigrant flows to maintain a diverse and vibrant labor force, one that keeps its dependency ratio in check. Just as immigrants a century ago provided New York City with the labor necessary for creating its infrastructure, the city now relies on its immigrants to shore up its labor force and to provide services for its aging population. Looking ahead, there is every reason to expect that the incorporation of what is likely the most diverse mélange of immigrants it has ever seen will reaffirm New York City's status as a great, open, and welcoming city.

ACKNOWLEDGMENTS

The authors thank Vicky Virgin and Donnise Hurley for their research assistance. The views expressed in this chapter are those of the authors and do not necessarily reflect those of the Department of City Planning, where they are employed, or the City of New York.

NOTES

1. Data used in this chapter include decennial data from the 1950–2010 censuses, vital statistics data for the years 1970–2010 from the New York City Department of Health and Mental Hygiene, 2011 population estimates from the U.S. Census Bureau, and unpublished estimates of the undocumented population in New York State by Robert Warren, former head of the Statistics Division of what was the U.S. Immigration and Naturalization Service. Data on social and economic characteristics, such as place of birth and income, have historically come from the decennial census long form. The long form was discontinued with the 2010 census, and data on socioeconomic characteristics are now obtained from the American Community Survey (ACS). The

ACS utilizes a monthly sample of the nation's population, which is "rolled up" to create estimates of characteristics for places throughout the nation. These estimates can be for one, three, or five years, depending upon the size of the geographic area for which estimates are created. The one-year ACS data used in this analysis include summary files as well as the Public Use Microdata Samples from the 2010 releases. Thus, for the same year, the estimate of the foreign-born may differ, depending on which source of data is used. These differences, however, are within sampling limits. Due to sample size constraints with the one year ACS, three years of pooled data were used from the 2008–10 ACS to examine subcounty settlement patterns of the foreign-born and the socioeconomic characteristics of recent domestic and international migrants to New York. For more information on the ACS and the correct use of these data, please see Salvo et al. (2009) and Anderson et al. (2012).

2. There are fifty-nine community districts (CDs), which are part of New York City's government structure. Each CD has a community board whose members are charged with identifying local needs and articulating neighborhood concerns. To protect data confidentiality, the Census Bureau combines a few small CDs in the Bronx and in Manhattan and provides data for the resulting fifty-five Public Use Microdata Areas (PUMAs), which are largely coterminous with CDs. Figure 2.4 maps immigrant concentrations for these fifty-five areas. For more information on the use of ACS data for CDs or PUMAs, please see Salvo and Lobo (2010).

3. Data are presented at the census tract level, which is used as a proxy for neighborhoods. Data at two time points were made comparable by aggregating 2000 census block data into census tracts that matched 2010 tract boundaries. While there has been an increase in melting pot integrated neighborhoods, they are more likely to be composed of whites, Asians, and Hispanics, and are generally less inclusive of both native- and foreign-born blacks.

4. Those who were ages five and over and spoke a language other than English at home were asked whether they spoke English "very well," "well," "not well," or "not at all." According to the Census Bureau, data from other surveys suggest a major difference between the category "very well" and the remaining categories. Thus, those with LEP were defined as persons who spoke a language other than English at home and who spoke English less than very well; i.e., it included those who spoke English "well," "not well," or "not at all." The percent LEP was obtained by dividing the LEP population by the population ages five and over.

REFERENCES

Alba, R. D., N. A. Denton, S. J. Leung, and J. R. Logan. 1995. "Neighborhood Change under Conditions of Mass Immigration: The New York City Region, 1970–1990." *International Migration Review* 29: 625–56.

Anderson, Margo, Constance Citro, and Joseph Salvo, eds. 2012. *Encyclopedia of the U.S. Census: From the Constitution to the American Community Survey (ACS)*, 2nd ed. Washington, DC: Sage CQ Press.

Flores, Ronald O., and Arun Peter Lobo. 2013. "The Reassertion of a Black-Nonblack Color Line: The Rise in Integrated Neighborhoods without Blacks in New York City, 1970–2010." *Journal of Urban Affairs*, forthcoming.

Lobo, Arun Peter. 2001. "U.S. Diversity Visas Are Attracting Africa's Best and Brightest." *Population Today* 29 (5): 1–2.

Lobo, Arun Peter, Ronald Flores, and Joseph Salvo. 2002. "The Impact of Hispanic Growth on the Racial/Ethnic Composition of New York City Neighborhoods." *Urban Affairs Review* 37 (5): 703–727.

Lobo, Arun Peter, and Joseph J. Salvo. 1998. "Changing U.S. Immigration Law and the Occupational Selectivity of Asian Immigrants." *International Migration Review* 32 (3): 737–60.

Lobo, Arun Peter, and Joseph J. Salvo. 2004. *The Newest New Yorkers, 2000: Immigrant New York in the New Millennium*. New York: New York City Department of City Planning.

Lobo, Arun Peter, Joseph J. Salvo, and Donnise Hurley. 2012. "The Confluence of Immigrant Ethnicity and Race in New York: A Socioeconomic Perspective." *Journal of Immigrant and Refugee Services* 10 (1): 31–53.

Logan, J., and C. Zhang. 2010. "Global Neighborhoods: New Pathways to Diversity and Separation." *American Journal of Sociology* 115: 1069–1109.

Salvo, Joseph J., and Arun Peter Lobo. 2005. "Undocumented Immigration." In Peter Eisenstadt, ed., *The Encyclopedia of New York State*. Syracuse, NY: Syracuse University Press.

Salvo, Joseph J., and Arun Peter Lobo. 2010. "The Federal Statistical System: The Local Government Perspective." *Annals of the American Academy of Political and Social Science* 631 (1): 75–88.

Salvo, Joseph J., Arun Peter Lobo, and Joel Alvarez. 2009. *A Compass for Understanding and Using American Community Survey Data: What State and Local Governments Need to Know*. Washington, DC: U.S. Government Printing Office.

Shaw, Samuel, and Josiah Quincy. 1847. *The Journals of Samuel Shaw: The First American Consul at Canton. With a Life of the Author by Josiah Quincy*. Boston: William Crosby and HP Nichols.

Winnick, Louis. 1990. *New People in Old Neighborhoods: The Role of Immigrants in Rejuvenating New York's Communities*. New York: Russell Sage Foundation.

3. *Immigration and Economic Growth in New York City*

David Dyssegaard Kallick

Immigration has dramatically changed the face of New York in the past several decades, and with it the New York economy. The immigrant share of the city's population has rebounded from a twentieth-century low point of 18 percent in 1970 (and 27 percent of the resident labor force) to 36 percent (and 45 percent of the resident labor force) in 2009.[1]

The increase in the number and proportion of immigrants in the city has fueled economic growth, filled in neighborhoods that had become underpopulated during the 1970s, and helped make New York the extraordinarily diverse global city it is today, with immigrants working in a wide range of jobs from the top to the bottom of the economic ladder.

Immigration has brought some challenges as well. There are legitimate worries about the effect of immigration on some U.S.-born workers, as well as concerns about immigrants, especially undocumented immigrants, being caught in—and perhaps fueling—an unregulated labor market.

At the same time, there are serious problems in the New York economy that affect both U.S.-born and foreign-born workers. New York's economy has expanded over the past decades, but it has also grown increasingly polarized. In providing an analysis of immigrants' role in a changing New York economy, I show how immigrants make up a large and growing part of the city's labor force, and have been part of virtually every aspect of the city's economic picture over the past four decades.

IMMIGRANTS AS A KEY COMPONENT IN NEW YORK'S REBOUND FROM THE 1970s

POPULATION CHANGE

A substantial part of New York City's post–World War II history can be read from the simple trend line of the city's overall population change, which mirrors its economic trajectory. From 1950 to 1970 the population was fairly stable, followed by a steep drop in the course of the 1970s, and a strong rebound from 1980 to the present.

A closer look at that rebound, however, shows that the post-1980 population increase was driven by immigrants. As figure 3.1 shows, from 1980 to 2009, the U.S.-born population changed only slightly—and in a downward direction. The total population grew because of increases in the foreign-born population.

FISCAL CRISIS IN THE 1970S

New York City's population numbers reflect underlying economic trends. In the 1950s and 1960s, the economy was humming along at a good clip. True, white middle-class residents were leaving in significant numbers for the suburbs, attracted by the promise of green lawns, and lured by government policies—from federal mortgage agencies that graded white suburban areas as safer areas for banks to make loans than racially mixed urban areas, to road construction that literally paved the way for an outflow from the city (see, for example, Jackson 1987; Dreier et al. 2004). During the 1950s and 1960s, however, the decrease of the white population was offset by an increase in the number of blacks, who were moving to New York from the South, and by Puerto Ricans, who were moving to New York from the island, as figure 3.2 dramatically shows.

Then came the 1970s. In mid-decade, a serious national recession hit the city hard. The already established white population decline escalated to a more panicked "white flight" as race riots around the country and deteriorating city services made the suburbs feel like a necessary haven for many of the city's middle-class white residents. Modest increases in the city's black and Latino populations between 1970 and 1980 were not enough to offset the substantial decline in the city's white population.

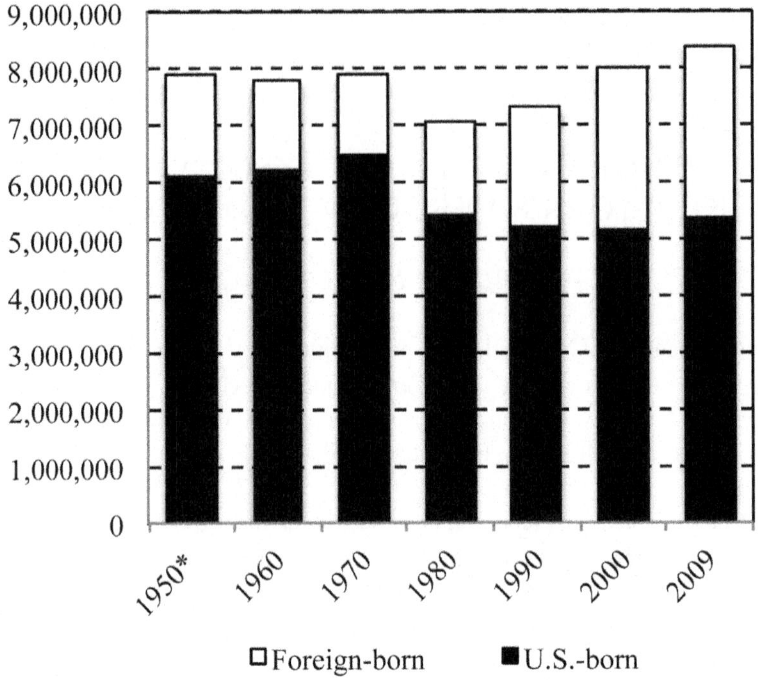

FIGURE 3.1. TOTAL NEW YORK CITY POPULATION BY NATIVITY.
*In the 1950 census, foreign-born included only foreign-born whites.
Source: New York City Department of City Planning, analysis of census data 1950–2000; Fiscal Policy Institute analysis of 2009 American Community Survey.

The cost of providing government services had been rising for some time, but in the 1960s the city was able to rely on greater federal and state aid to cover part of what it owed, and turned to short-term borrowing rather than tax increases to cover the rest. In the course of the 1970s, total city population fell by almost a million residents—which meant that substantially fewer people were paying city taxes. The recession pushed tax revenues down further and the cost of providing city services increased, while federal and state aid to the city decreased. The result was a severe fiscal crisis, a defining moment in New York City politics, when the city seemed at risk of defaulting on its bonds.

The story of how New York got into the fiscal crisis, and how it was finally addressed, has been extensively documented. Civic-minded leaders of finance and labor unions were crucial in what was often referred to as "saving New York." So was a financial control board designed to reign in as well as provide transparency to the city budget. Eventual aid from reluctant state and federal governments was a third crucial factor in solving the crisis (Shefter 1985; Freeman 2000).

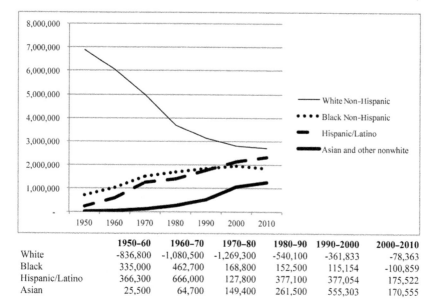

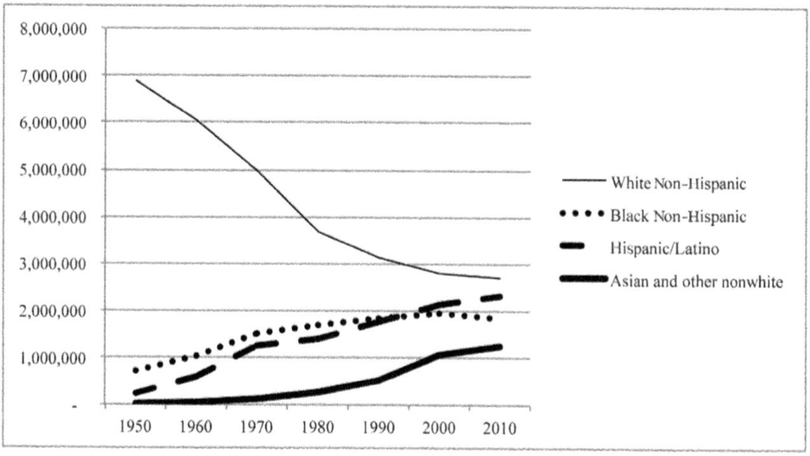

	1950–60	1960–70	1970–80	1980–90	1990–2000	2000–2010
White	-836,800	-1,080,500	-1,269,300	-540,100	-361,833	-78,363
Black	335,000	462,700	168,800	152,500	115,154	-100,859
Hispanic/Latino	366,300	666,000	127,800	377,100	377,054	175,522
Asian	25,500	64,700	149,400	261,500	555,303	170,555

FIGURE 3.2. GROWTH AND DECLINE IN WHITE, BLACK, LATINO, AND ASIAN POPULATIONS OF NEW YORK CITY, 1950–2010.
Source: Population Division, New York City Department of City Planning; Hispanic population for 1950 through 1970 imputed from characteristics such as Puerto Rican origin and language spoken.

Once the city's finances were put on a stable basis, however, reversing the declining population was a crucial factor in keeping the city fiscally solvent and economically vibrant. Some residents remained fiercely committed to the city through the years when "the Bronx was burning," memorialized in Spike Lee's movie *Summer of Sam*. (The phrase "the Bronx is burning" was famously used by sports announcer Howard Cosell to describe to a national audience the spectacle of buildings near Yankee Stadium being torched by absentee landlords to collect on insurance money; "Summer of Sam" refers to a series of murders committed in the same year, 1977, by a man who called himself the Son of Sam.)[2] In the 1970s, many people played a role just by remaining in the city and going about their lives as usual at a time when others were leaving. But many longtime New Yorkers also pushed hard to rebuild their neighborhoods, by forming civic groups and community organizations, cleaning up neighborhoods, and pushing city, state, and federal governments to reinvest in the city.

The 1980s and 1990s were crucial decades in the city's history—a time when urban planners shifted from 1970s discussions of "planned shrinkage" to more recent concerns about low- and moderate-income people being squeezed out by gentrification and scarcity of affordable housing. Yet, looking back on these

TABLE 3.1. DECLINE IN U.S.-BORN POPULATION BETWEEN 1980 AND 2009

Change in Population, 1980–2009						
U.S.-born	1980	1990	2000	2009	*Change 1980–2009*	
0–19	1,816,820	1,609,103	1,814,223	1,905,141	88,321	4.9%
20–34	1,361,760	1,307,347	1,132,224	1,249,095	−112,665	−8.3%
35–64	1,674,160	1,653,803	1,592,980	1,676,522	2,362	0.1%
65 and older	564,300	647,665	594,197	575,421	11,121	2.0%
All	5,417,040	5,217,918	5,133,624	5,406,179	10,861	−0.2%
Foreign-born	1980	1990	2000	2009	*Change 1980–2009*	
0–19	215,280	249,299	320,389	193,581	−21,699	−10.1%
20–34	426,200	619,298	798,001	734,146	307,946	72.3%
35–64	649,140	891,568	1,401,819	1,614,591	965,451	148.7%
65 and older	384,540	302,023	350,926	442,569	58,029	15.1%
All	1,675,160	2,062,188	2,871,135	2,984,887	1,309,727	78.2%

Source: Fiscal Policy Institute analysis of decennial census and American Community Survey 2009.

years, it is clear that immigration was also a crucial part of the story of reviving the city's underpopulated neighborhoods. Although there were many U.S.-born newcomers—the city population is constantly churning, with people coming and leaving—figure 3.1 shows that the result of this churning was a U.S.-born population that was a little smaller in 2009 than it was at the low point in 1980. All of the net population growth was due to immigration.

Even more striking is the 8 percent drop—after 1980—in the number of U.S.-born young adults (24–34 years old), a decline of 113,000 between 1980 and 2009. The number of U.S.-born 35–64-year-olds remained about flat over this period; the only increase among the U.S.-born over these four crucial decades is for those over 65 (the result of an aging population) and 19 and under (driven in part by U.S.-born children of immigrants) (see table 3.1).

IMMIGRANTS AND LABOR DEMAND

The 1965 change in federal immigration law made it possible for immigrants to come to the United States in much larger numbers than in the previous decades. But what was especially important in drawing immigrants to New York City (and not, for example, in substantial numbers to St. Louis or Pittsburgh) was increased labor market demand: the economy was expanding while the working-age U.S.-born population was declining.

As the city's economy began to revive and grow in the 1980s, it also significantly changed. New York in the mid-twentieth century was an important center for manufacturing. As the city found a more solid economic footing after the 1970s, it did so on a foundation of growth in high-end jobs in finance and business headquarters, as well as in low-end jobs in the service sector—with a substantial shift away from jobs in manufacturing (Mollenkopf 1992; Waldinger 1996; Wright and Ellis 2001). The low-end service sector jobs included restaurant workers, retail clerks, child care workers, home health care aides, dry cleaners, security guards, beauty salon workers, and a host of other jobs that provided inexpensive and convenient services to city residents.

As the city added low-wage jobs, it shed many of the middle-wage jobs that had been the underpinning of the city's middle class. Disappearing manufacturing—unionized and with solid wages by midcentury—on average paid considerably higher wages than newly created, generally nonunion service jobs. In addition, a large number of the manufacturing jobs that remained were in the by-then poorly paid apparel industry. At the same time, wages went up at the top, as management and finance industry executives received increasingly exorbitant salaries.

Immigrants were part of all aspects of the city's changing economy. Large numbers ended up working in the newly created service jobs—by 2009, 63 percent of service workers living in the city were foreign-born, compared to the 45 percent immigrant share of jobholders overall. Yet considerable numbers also wound up working in higher-wage jobs. In 2009, 30 percent of New York City immigrants worked in service jobs, 25 percent in managerial and professional specialties, 23 percent in technical, sales, and administrative support, and 22 percent in blue-collar jobs.

By 2007, the city's economy had become so highly polarized that the top 1 percent of taxpayers received 44 percent of all income in the city—far more than the already record high 23 percent share of income controlled by the top 1 percent nationally (Fiscal Policy Institute 2010). There were immigrants at the top, bottom, and middle of this economic ladder, with immigrants generally living in families that were clustered in the middle. In 2005, 55 percent of New Yorkers living in immigrant families (those with at least one foreign-born adult) had annual family incomes of $20,000 to $80,000, compared to 44 percent of those living in U.S.-born families. New Yorkers living in families with only U.S.-born adults were more likely to be at the top and bottom—that is, in families making less than $20,000 or over $80,000 a year (Fiscal Policy Institute 2007).

WHAT ABOUT U.S-BORN WORKERS?

One frequently raised question is how U.S.-born workers have been affected by immigration. Did the economy grow to accommodate the added workforce, or did immigrants displace U.S.-born workers?

While the new jobs in New York have not all been good jobs, immigration does not seem to have increased faster than the city's ability to absorb immigrants and U.S.-born workers into the workforce together. Yet, while this is the overall trend, there is a significant exception: black men and women who did not finish high school.

The unemployment rate is one clear measure of whether U.S.-born workers are able to find jobs. The unemployment rate varies greatly in the course of the business cycle—it is lower (better) for all groups during an economic expansion, and is higher (worse) for all groups in a recession. To consider whether different groups of U.S.-born residents have had an easier or harder time finding a job during a period when the number of immigrants in the city was increasing, table 3.2 shows the unemployment rate for different groups at the top of each of the past four business cycles, the peak years, when unemployment could be expected to be lowest for all groups.

In all race and ethnic categories, and at all education levels, the unemployment rate for U.S.-born workers declined from 1980 to 2007, with just two exceptions: U.S.-born black men and women with less than a high school degree. For these black men, the unemployment rate went from an already alarmingly high 14.2 percent at the peak of the 1980 expansion to a staggering 20.2 percent

TABLE 3.2. UNEMPLOYMENT RATES FOR NEW YORK CITY WORKERS AT THE TOP OF EACH OF THE LAST FOUR BUSINESS CYCLES

	1980 (%)	1990 (%)	2000 (%)	2005–07 (%)	*Percentage Point Change 1980–2007*
All (U.S.- and foreign-born)	7.0	5.8	4.6	4.2	−2.8
All U.S.-born	6.8	5.5	4.6	4.4	−2.4
U.S.-born men					
White, non-Hispanic	4.9	3.6	2.4	2.9	−2.0
Less than high school	7.6	8.0	7.5	6.2	−1.4
High school	5.1	4.7	4.0	3.4	−1.7
Some college	5.2	3.9	2.6	4.2	−0.9
College graduate and higher	3.5	2.4	1.5	2.3	−1.2
Black, non-Hispanic	11.5	10.3	8.9	8.1	−3.4
Less than high school	14.2	16.7	20.2	17.0	2.8
High school	10.8	11.4	9.9	9.7	−1.1
Some college	10.4	8.4	6.9	6.6	−3.9
College graduate and higher	6.8	3.3	3.1	3.8	−3.0
Hispanic/Latino	10.1	8.9	6.5	6.0	−4.1
Less than high school	11.3	11.7	11.9	10.9	−0.4
High school	8.9	9.1	6.7	6.2	−2.8
Some college	10.0	6.4	4.1	5.2	−4.8
College graduate and higher	4.9	3.5	2.2	2.6	−2.3
U.S.-born women					
White	5.3	3.4	2.3	2.8	−2.5
Less than high school	8.5	7.8	12.1	4.1	−4.4
High school	5.1	4.5	3.9	3.4	−1.7
Some college	5.5	3.7	3.0	4.1	−1.4
College graduate and higher	4.2	2.3	1.4	2.3	−1.9
Black	8.3	7.4	7.5	6.0	−2.3
Less than high school	12.6	16.3	19.9	15.6	3.1
High school	7.9	8.8	10.6	7.1	−0.9
Some college	5.9	5.5	5.4	5.6	−0.2
College graduate and higher	3.9	2.3	2.5	3.1	−0.8
Hispanic/Latino	11.5	8.2	7.5	6.0	−5.5
Less than high school	14.9	13.8	15.9	11.7	−3.2
High school	9.5	9.0	9.0	6.2	−3.3
Some college	9.7	5.0	5.5	6.0	−3.7
College graduate and higher	5.9	3.8	2.5	3.0	−2.9

Source: Fiscal Policy Institute analysis of decennial census and American Community Survey 2005–7. Unemployment rates adjusted using Local Area Unemployment Statistics. Asian and "other race" are not shown due to small sample size.

at the peak of the 2000 expansion, retreating only a little to 17.0 percent at the most recent economic peak year. As for U.S.-born black women without a high school degree, the rate increased from 12.6 percent in 1980 to a high of 19.9 percent in 2000, falling back to 15.6 percent in 2007. It is worth noting that these groups are shrinking as blacks gain in educational attainment: there are considerably fewer black men and women without a high school degree in 2007 than in 1980. Still, the fact that these already very high unemployment rates grew even higher over time is a matter of serious concern.

The unemployment rate for immigrants at each of the past four economic peaks has been within one percentage point of the rate for U.S.-born, and has also seen long-term improvements, suggesting that there is room in the New York City labor market, at least in economic peak years, for both immigrants and U.S.-born workers.

How much of the predicament of black men and women without a high school degree can be explained by immigration is unclear. Econometric studies that look at data at the national level have found that immigration has had only a very modest negative impact on U.S.-born black men with a high school diploma or less (and have generally not found a negative effect for black women), even while U.S. workers overall have benefited from immigration (Shierholz 2010). These national studies are consistent with in-depth research on New York City (Waldinger 1996; Wright and Ellis 2001). What is most troubling about these findings is not the magnitude of the negative impact for black men and women without a high school diploma, which is generally relatively modest, but that the negative impact affects a group already at such a stark disadvantage in the labor market. Racial discrimination is no doubt part of the story; employers may prefer employees other than black men or women with little formal education. In addition, black men without a high school degree are far more likely than other groups to be affected by increasing incarceration rates. Not surprisingly, it is extremely difficult to find employment after serving in prison.

In considering the impact of immigrants on U.S.-born workers, it is important to bear in mind that in addition to taking available jobs, immigrants also create jobs in New York City—not just for other immigrants but for U.S.-born workers as well. It is sometimes assumed that new workers add to the labor force and do not otherwise change an economy, leading to the erroneous conclusion that they reduce the number of jobs available for the existing labor force. However, adding workers to an economy also adds people who buy goods and services, which in turn creates more consumer demand, and can create a positive feedback loop of job creation. Indeed, the large immigrant inflow to New York in recent decades has expanded the number of people shopping in stores, eating in restaurants, frequenting beauty salons, using the services of lawyers, sending children to schools and colleges, and purchasing all manner of goods and services—and thus boosting job growth throughout the economy in the process.

IMMIGRANT BUSINESSES

Immigrants also have been among the entrepreneurs who found ways to meet new consumer demands. Between 1994 and 2004, the number of businesses in the city overall increased by 10 percent, while the number of businesses in neighborhoods with particularly high concentrations of immigrants grew far faster: Flushing had 55 percent more businesses at the end of that ten-year period than at the beginning; Sunset Park had 48 percent more; Sheepshead Bay–Brighton Beach had 34 percent more; and so on down the list (Bowles and Colton 2007).

Speaking about one heavily immigrant community—Richmond Hill, Queens—a community leader named Raymond Ally told a team of researchers, "Back in 1979–80, the area was depressed. There was nothing here and there were very few businesses." As the area attracted immigrants from Guyana and Trinidad and Sikhs from India, there was a gradual sprouting of roti stands, sari stores, jewelers, and groceries to serve those communities. Muslim mosques and a Sikh *mandir* helped root the communities, and as the area became more established as an immigrant center, it began to draw shoppers from the suburbs looking for Indo-Caribbean or Sikh products. Before long, Richmond Hill was buzzing with activity on the streets and in the stores. "Now, it's thriving," said Ally. "The number of businesses has quadrupled compared to what it was before." Rents have risen dramatically—reflecting increased demand—and the only vacancies researchers found were due to landlords holding out for even higher return on their investment (Bowles and Colton 2007:14).

CRIME

Immigrants not only have set up many businesses but also appear to have affected crime rates—another issue related to New York City's comeback from the 1970s low point. In the 1970s, '80s, and early '90s high crime rates were a frequently cited cause of concern for both businesses and residents. It is commonly agreed that the turnaround in crime in the 1990s was an important factor in the improved business climate in the city. Safer neighborhoods drew more residents, shoppers, and business owners.

Changes in policing policy were certainly important in reducing crime. Policies put in place by Mayor Rudy Giuliani such as "broken-windows" policing and the Compstat system of tracking crime were undeniably critical to this improvement. Important, too, though less commonly acknowledged was Mayor

David Dinkins's Safe Streets, Safe Cities program that raised taxes to put more police on the street.

Immigration—sometimes associated in the public view with increasing crime—has been an underappreciated factor in reducing crime in New York City. In the 1980s and 1990s, many New Yorkers, both U.S.- and foreign-born, took part in projects to clean up parks, reinvent community institutions, and reclaim neighborhoods. This helped create a climate in which people moved into previously abandoned apartments and started to repopulate neighborhoods. As the neighborhoods became more densely populated, the streets became safer (as any New Yorker knows, a busy street is safer than an empty one). In neighborhood after neighborhood, population growth was driven by immigrants. Community policing may have prevented windows from being broken, but damaged windows were also more quickly fixed in areas where every apartment was occupied than in those where many buildings stood empty. Indeed, as safety improved and the popularity of many neighborhoods increased, the people who helped rebuild them frequently ended up being victims of their own success. In many cases, the problems of underinvestment gave way to the problems of gentrification, making neighborhoods increasingly difficult to afford for low- and moderate-income families, immigrant and U.S.-born alike.

In addition to helping crime prevention by adding eyes on the street, there is considerable evidence that, contrary to popularly held views, immigrants are less likely than their U.S.-born counterparts to commit crimes. An analysis of 2000 national census data shows that the incarceration rate of the foreign-born was four times lower than for the U.S.-born—though the longer immigrants have lived in the United States the more immigrant crime rates begin to look like those of U.S.-born residents (Rumbaut et al. 2006).

CHOOSING THE CITY

Also of significance in the post-1970s era has been immigrants' very willingness to live in central cities in general, and New York City in particular. There is a strong pull for city residents in the United States to move outward to the suburbs, especially when they have children approaching school age. Even in metropolitan areas with little overall growth, there is still a tendency for residents to move from the city to the suburb—a phenomenon Rolf Pendall (2003) terms "Sprawl without Growth." Although immigrants are also increasingly moving to the suburbs (Singer et al. 2008), they are nevertheless considerably more likely than their U.S.-born counterparts to live in central cities.

"Smart growth"—an alternative to sprawl that concentrates on town and city hubs, public transportation, walkable streets, and mixed commercial and residential neighborhoods—has numerous advantages for effective utilization of resources. This is particularly clear where cities have already developed infrastructure that is underutilized—as was the case in New York in the 1970s and '80s (and is still the case today in cities like Detroit and Buffalo). When public transportation, school buildings, sewers, and other major infrastructure investments are used at less than the capacity for which they were built, the money spent on them goes at least partially to waste. Worse, if the same population moves to sprawling suburbs, much of the same infrastructure has to be built anew there, at additional expense. As "Planning for Smart Growth," a report by the American Planning Association, summed it up, "Planning reforms and smart growth provide long-term savings by eliminating inefficiencies caused by inconsistent and uncoordinated planning. . . . There is a growing awareness, too, that poorly planned development is a hidden tax on citizens and communities alike" (2002:8).

The hundreds of thousands of immigrants, together with the U.S.-born residents who made a commitment to live in New York City in the 1970s and '80s, were critical to putting the city on a path toward fiscal sustainability. Among other things, they made efficient use of the city's already existing infrastructure, allowing their taxes to support other government services.

IMMIGRANTS' CENTRAL ROLE IN TODAY'S NEW YORK CITY ECONOMY

Having contributed to the city's rebound from the 1970s, immigrants are most certainly pulling their weight in the city's economy today.

In 2006 immigrants made up 21 percent of New York State's population and accounted for 22 percent of the state's $1 trillion gross domestic product (GDP) (Fiscal Policy Institute 2007). Zeroing in on New York City—where three-quarters of the state's immigrants live—figure 3.3 shows that immigrants in 2009 made up 36 percent of the city's population, and accounted for 35 percent of economic output, the broad equivalent of GDP for the city.[3]

The finding that immigrants contribute to the economy in almost exact proportion to their share of the population may seem surprising, since immigrants earn on average less than U.S.-born workers. Three main factors explain this apparent puzzle. First and simplest, immigrants make up a bigger share of the labor force than their share of the population. In New York City, immigrants are 36 percent of the population, but 45 percent of the resident labor force. Having proportionately more people working offsets immigrants' lower wages, resulting in the immigrant share of total earnings being the same as the immigrant share of population (see figure 3.3).

To some small extent, immigrants make up a disproportionate share of the labor force because they have slightly higher labor force participation rates than U.S.-born New Yorkers—66 percent of immigrants over age 16 are in the labor force, compared to 62 percent of U.S.-born New Yorkers. (What accounts for this difference is the higher labor force participation rate for immigrant men.

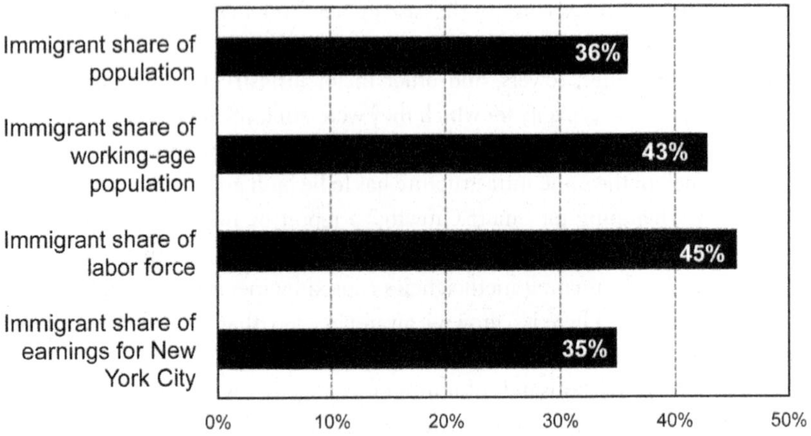

FIGURE 3.3. IMMIGRANT SHARE OF POPULATION, WORKING-AGE POPULATION, LABOR FORCE, AND ECONOMIC OUTPUT, NEW YORK CITY, 2009.

Source: Fiscal Policy Institute analysis of 2009 American Community Survey. Working age is 16–64 years old. Immigrant share of earnings is a proxy for immigrant share of economic output.

U.S.-born and immigrant women in New York City have the same level of labor force participation; see figure 3.4.) A much bigger factor in the overrepresentation of immigrants in the labor force is that they are considerably more likely than U.S.-born New Yorkers to be in the prime working ages (16–64 years old). To put it another way, immigrant economic output is boosted by the fact there are proportionately more working-age immigrants than immigrant children or retirees. Immigrants generally come to the United States as young adults, and it is important to bear in mind that the U.S.-born children of immigrants are counted in the U.S.-born population.

The second factor that helps explain why immigrants' economic output is proportionate to their population share is that they are spread over a broad array of occupations; immigrants are not nearly as concentrated in low-wage occupations as one might imagine from reading the popular press. Immigrants who live in New York City work in a wide range of jobs across the economic spectrum, making up 28 percent of management analysts, for instance, half of accountants, a third of receptionists, and half of building cleaners. Indeed, immigrants make up between 25 and 80 percent of virtually all occupations, from the bottom to the top of the economic ladder.

Much of the media coverage, and even a good deal of scholarly literature, focuses on low-wage immigrants and those with less than a high school education, but it is a mistake to equate this narrow focus with the broader experience of immigrants in the city. Consider a few of the figures. In finance, immigrants represent a quarter of securities, commodities, and financial service sales

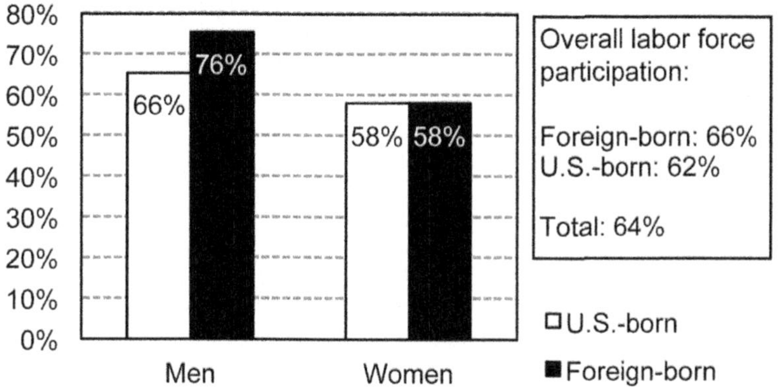

FIGURE 3.4 IMMIGRANT AND U.S.-BORN LABOR FORCE PARTICIPATION RATES, NEW YORK CITY, 2009.
Source: Fiscal Policy Institute analysis of 2009 American Community Survey.

agents, and a third of financial managers who live in New York City. In real estate, immigrants make up four out of ten brokers, four out of ten property managers, three out of ten architects, and three-quarters of construction laborers. In health care, four out of ten doctors, more than half of all registered nurses, and three-quarters of all nursing aides are foreign-born.

There are hundreds of occupations at this level of detail, so the above numbers are just a sampling. Grouping all these detailed occupations into twenty-one occupational categories gives a more comprehensive view of where immigrants are clustered, and the extent to which they work in occupations across the entire spectrum. As table 3.3 shows, immigrants make up 45 percent of the New York City resident labor force. Their share of generally well-paid executive, administrative, and managerial jobs is 33 percent, and in professional specialties such as doctors and engineers, 31 percent. Immigrants are overrepresented at 49 percent of registered nurses, pharmacists, and health therapists. They are most starkly overrepresented in blue-collar jobs such as machine operators, fabricators, construction trades, drivers, and construction laborers and other material handlers. Immigrants are also starkly overrepresented in low-wage service jobs such as dental, health, and nursing aides and food preparation services, and among workers in private households and personal service. Yet only among firefighters, police, and supervisors of protective services are immigrants less than 25 percent of the workers, and in no instance do immigrants make up more than 75 percent of one of the twenty-one occupational categories.

These figures, as noted, are for New York City residents, but many of the people contributing to New York City's economic output live in the suburbs and commute to the city. Yet even among the commuters, immigrants play an important part. Nearly a third of the 868,000 commuters to New York City are immigrants, with immigrant commuters—like U.S.-born commuters—concentrated in

TABLE 3.3. NEW YORK CITY OCCUPATIONS OF IMMIGRANTS

	Foreign-Born in Occupation (%)
White-collar jobs	
Executive, administrative, managerial	33
Professional specialty (incl. doctors, engineers, lawyers)	31
Registered nurses, pharmacists, and health therapists	49
Teachers, professors, librarians, social scientists, social workers, and artists	28
Technicians (incl. health, engineering, and science)	40
Sales (supervisors, real estate, finance, and insurance)	36
Sales (clerks and cashiers)	43
Administrative support (incl. clerical)	35
Service jobs	
Private household and personal service	67
Firefighters, police, and supervisors of protective services	21
Guards, cleaning, and building services	54
Food preparation services	69
Dental, health, and nursing aides	73
Blue-collar jobs	
Mechanics and repairers	55
Construction trades	63
Precision production	64
Machine operators	74
Fabricators	67
Drivers (incl. heavy equipment operators)	66
Construction laborers and other material handlers	67
Gardening	
Farming, forestry, and agriculture (incl. gardeners)	46
Total	**45**

Source: Fiscal Policy Institute analysis of 2009 American Community Survey, New York City resident labor force. For detail on occupational categories, see *Immigrants and the Economy* (Fiscal Policy Institute 2009).

higher-wage jobs that contribute substantially to total economic output. (The calculation for immigrant share of New York State GDP includes commuters; the calculation for New York City is for the resident labor force, and so does not include commuters.)

Finally, the third factor in accounting for the unexpectedly high immigrant share of economic output is that many immigrants are business owners. Immigrants make up 48 percent of incorporated self-employed people living in New York City—a good indicator of small business ownership. Of the thirteen broad industrial sectors, immigrant small business ownership is highest in transportation and warehousing (81 percent, with Colombians and Dominicans playing the biggest role) and lowest in information and communications (19 percent), with levels between these two extremes in industries such as finance, insurance, and real estate (35 percent); educational, health, and social services (47 percent); and retail trade (64 percent). The overall immigrant share of these small business owners is well above the immigrant share of the population, and is slightly above the overall immigrant share of the labor force (see table 3.4).

Immigrants are making a particularly significant contribution in small businesses that shape the character of neighborhoods, including those that provide

TABLE 3.4. BROAD SECTORS OF IMMIGRANT SMALL BUSINESS OWNERS IN NEW YORK CITY

Sector	*Foreign-Born Business Owners*	*All Small Business Owners (U.S.- and Foreign-Born)*	*Small Business Owners Who Are Foreign-Born (%)*
Construction	8,089	13,059	62
Manufacturing	3,284	6,178	53
Wholesale trade	4,733	8,732	54
Retail trade	12,145	18,877	64
Transportation and warehousing	5,802	7,190	81
Information and communications	1,040	5,555	19
Finance, insurance, real estate	4,867	13,969	35
Professional and business services	9,497	31,891	30
Educational, health, and social services	6,564	13,971	47
Leisure and hospitality	7,582	16,421	46
Other services	5,685	8,677	66
Total	69,411	144,674	48

Fiscal Policy Institute analysis of American Community Survey 2005–09. "Small business owners" are people who live in New York City who own an incorporated business in the New York metro area and whose main job is to run that business. Small numbers of mining and agriculture, and forestry, fishing, and hunting businesses that are below the threshold of statistical significance are included in the total.

TABLE 3.5. DETAILED TYPES OF SMALL BUSINESSES OWNED BY IMMIGRANTS IN NEW YORK CITY

Type of Business (Ranked by Immigrant Concentration in Industry)	*Foreign-Born Business Owners*	*All Small Business Owners (U.S.- and Foreign-Born)*	*Small Business Owners Who Are Foreign-Born (%)*
Dry cleaning and laundry services	1,381	1,536	90
Taxi and limousine service	3,777	4,214	90
Grocery stores	1,544	1,831	84
Child day care services	2,162	2,876	75
Beauty salons	1,475	2,097	70
Restaurants	5,574	8,032	69
Truck transportation	1,076	1,659	65
Clothing stores	1,370	2,162	63
Construction	8,089	13,059	62
Computer systems design	1,533	3,790	40
Architectural, engineering, and related services	1,046	2,635	40
Real estate	2,970	7,700	39
Offices of physicians	1,202	3,428	35
Specialized design services	1,375	4,209	33
Securities, commodities, funds, trusts, and other financial investments	1,105	3,975	28
Management, scientific, and technical consulting services	1,375	5,615	24
Independent artists, performing arts, and spectator sports	1,310	6,363	21
All other	31,047	69,493	45
Total	69,411	144,674	48

Source: Fiscal Policy Institute analysis of American Community Survey 2005–9. Sectors with fewer than 1,000 small business owners are excluded from the analysis due to small sample size.

services that make life convenient for middle- and upper-class New Yorkers—though many immigrant businesses rely on long hours by family members or the low-wage labor of other immigrants. Table 3.5 shows that immigrants who live in New York City virtually monopolize certain small business fields in the New York metropolitan area: grocery stores (where immigrants represent 84 percent of local store owners), dry cleaning and laundry services (90 percent), and taxi and limousine services (90 percent). Immigrants make up a substantial share of small business owners in a range of other fields, from restaurants (69 percent) to construction (62 percent) to computer design services (40 percent).

Beyond small business ownership, immigrants also play an integral role in leading many of the city's larger businesses. There are 9,500 immigrant chief executive officers living in New York—comprising 30 percent of all CEOs living in the city. Both famous and notorious, former Citicorp CEO Vikram Pandit, media mogul Rupert Murdoch, and financier George Soros are all immigrants, as are well-known names in the fashion industry from Oscar de la Renta to Diane von Furstenberg.

OVERALL ECONOMIC STRENGTH, BUT GENUINE PROBLEMS

While immigrants are working in jobs across the economic spectrum, the popular image of immigrants working in low-wage jobs is not wholly unfounded. Pakistani cab drivers, Chinese apparel workers, Mexicans working in the back of the house in restaurants—these are very real experiences of daily life in New York City. And the census data bear out these images: in 2009, 82 percent of taxi drivers living in New York City were foreign-born, as were 90 percent of sewing machine operators and 67 percent of food preparation workers.

One reason for the disparity between popular images and reality is that it is a very different matter to speak of immigrants on average than to focus on particular groups of immigrants. On average, for example, as figure 3.5 shows, about half of all immigrants living in New York City work in white-collar jobs (as do 75 percent of U.S.-born New Yorkers). But this composite is made up of a wide range of immigrant experiences. Among immigrants born in India, Hong Kong, or Russia, for example, about three-quarters of workers are in white-collar jobs, matching the share for U.S.-born workers. Yet less than a quarter of Mexican or Ecuadorian workers are in white-collar jobs. And there is a wide range in the middle, with, for example, about half of Jamaican and Guyanese workers in white-collar jobs.

Looking in greater detail, it is clear that, while some immigrant groups are well spread across a range of occupations, others are strongly clustered in particular occupations, as the sociological literature has documented (Waldinger

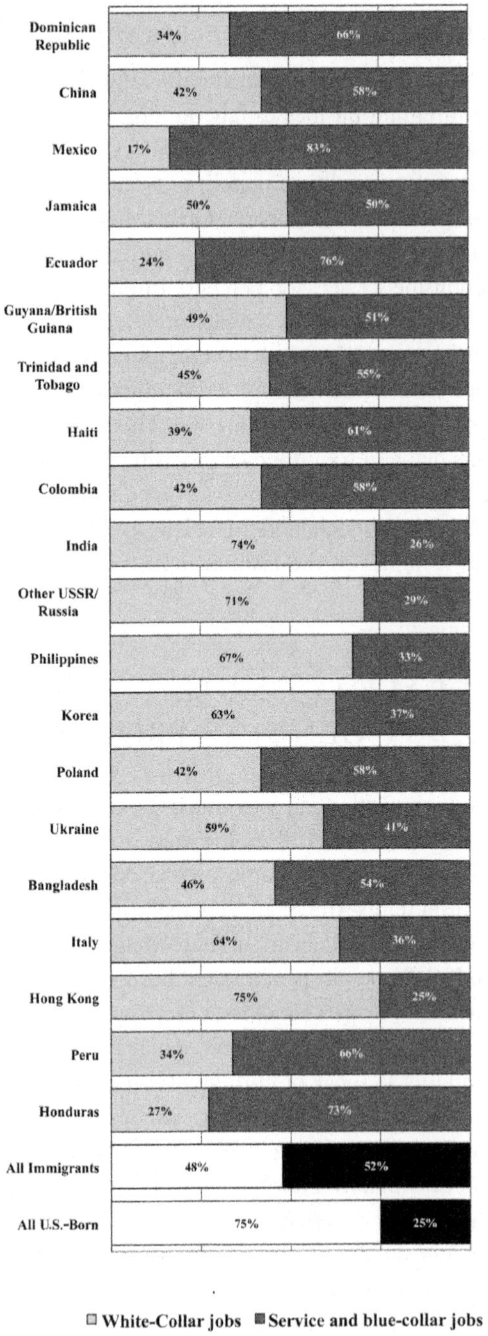

FIGURE 3.5. PROPORTION OF NEW YORK CITY IMMIGRANTS IN WHITE-COLLAR AND ALL OTHER JOBS, BY COUNTRY OF ORIGIN. *Source*: Fiscal Policy Institute analysis of 2009 American Community Survey, based on broad occupations as defined in *Immigrants and the Economy*, Fiscal Policy Institute, 2009. Universe is New York City residents 16 years and older, employed in the civilian labor force. The service and blue-collar category also includes a very small number of farm, fishing, and forestry jobs.

1996; Foner 2000; Logan and Alba 1999). In many cases, the clusters are in jobs at the lower end of the occupational ladder. Consider the most intensively concentrated immigrant groups. In 2009, fully 30 percent of all Mexican and 21 percent of Chinese immigrants living in New York City worked in food preparation services. Nearly a quarter of New York City workers born in Haiti were dental assistants, health aides, or nursing aides. Some immigrant clusters are at the higher end of the occupational ladder: a quarter of those born in Hong Kong were in executive, administrative, managerial, and management-related jobs; 21 percent of Filipino immigrants worked as registered nurses, pharmacists, and health therapists. Not all immigrant groups are so strongly concentrated at either the high or low end: Jamaicans, Guyanese, and Colombians, for example, are fairly evenly spread across the occupational spectrum.

Labor market outcomes in New York City are strongly shaped by the race and ethnicity of workers, whether they are U.S.- or foreign-born. Table 3.6 shows the earnings for full-time, year-round workers in different racial and ethnic groups compared to those of U.S.-born whites. At each level of educational attainment, white U.S.-born workers have the highest wage (this is thus shown as 100 percent). Even after accounting for differences in education levels, there are considerable disparities between the earnings of white, black, Latino, and Asian immigrants. U.S.-born whites earn more than all other groups, U.S.- or foreign-born, at every level of educational attainment. Using U.S.-born whites as a benchmark, we see that even at the same level of educational attainment, foreign-born workers consistently earn less than U.S.-born whites, generally between 50 and 80 percent of the amount of U.S.-born whites, and in one instance (Latinos with an advanced degree) as little as 40 percent of the level of U.S.-born whites. White immigrants also do uniformly better than immigrants of color, while Latino immigrants are at or near the bottom of earnings for each level of educational attainment.

American racial and ethnic categories (white, Black, Latino, Asian), of course, affect not only immigrants but also U.S.-born workers. Among the U.S.-born, whites have a decided advantage. The only instance in which a nonwhite U.S.-born group approaches the wages of the white group is Asians with an advanced degree, who typically earn 94 percent of the level of whites with an advanced degree. U.S.-born blacks and Latinos generally earn 70 to 80 percent the level of whites at the same level of educational attainment.

Nativity, in other words, is hardly the only dividing line in the New York economy. Race and ethnicity are significant predictors of how both U.S.- and foreign-born workers will fare in the economy. Indeed, it could be argued that race and ethnicity are more important than nativity in predicting earnings. White immigrants, for example, have higher earnings than U.S.-born blacks and Latinos at every level of educational attainment. Black immigrants at each

TABLE 3.6. MEDIAN ANNUAL WAGES BY RACE OR ETHNICITY AND NATIVITY, INDEXED TO WAGES FOR U.S.-BORN WHITES

	Earnings Compared to U.S.-Born White Earnings (%)	
	Foreign-Born	*U.S.-Born*
Less than high school		
White	80	100
Black	75	70
Latino/Hispanic	52	75
Asian	55	50
High school		
White	82	100
Black	69	78
Latino/Hispanic	64	82
Asian	62	87
Some college		
White	82	100
Black	73	73
Latino/Hispanic	58	75
Asian	65	89
College completion		
White	88	100
Black	71	69
Latino/Hispanic	58	71
Asian	74	83
Advanced degree		
White	94	100
Black	66	72
Latino/Hispanic	58	76
Asian	79	94
All		
White	74	100
Black	54	60
Latino/Hispanic	40	57
Asian	57	83

Source: Fiscal Policy Institute analysis of American Community Survey 2009. Annual wages for full-time workers (at least fifty weeks per year and thirty-five hours per week), 25 years and older, in the civilian labor force.

educational level have earnings that are closer to those of U.S.-born blacks than they are to any other foreign-born group.

Then there is legal status, which also makes a difference in how immigrants fare, and in their role in the New York City economy. There were about a half million undocumented immigrants in New York City in 2010 (chapter 2, this volume). Using somewhat earlier data, combining the years 2000 to 2006, the Pew Hispanic Center showed the countries of birth of undocumented immigrants in New York City. About equal numbers came from Mexico and Central America (27 percent), South and East Asia (23 percent), and the Caribbean (23 percent), and the balance—about a quarter—were from other parts of the world (Pew Hispanic Center estimate using 2000–2006 Current Population Survey data, in Fiscal Policy Institute 2007).

Undocumented immigrants are highly concentrated at the bottom of the occupational and wage spectrum, enough to make up a very substantial portion of workers in some jobs. The Pew study estimated that 11,000 undocumented immigrants worked as dishwashers in New York City, making up more than half of all dishwashers. About a third of the city's sewing machine operators, painters, cooks, construction laborers, and food preparation workers were estimated to be undocumented, as were between a quarter and a third of waiters and waitresses, maids and housekeeping cleaners, automotive service technicians and mechanics, and carpenters.

Immigrants in low-wage jobs, and undocumented immigrants in particular, are vulnerable to being mistreated by employers—to receiving reduced wages and enduring severely trying, sometimes dangerous, working conditions in the low-wage labor market. Immigrants, and especially undocumented immigrants, are frequently caught in jobs where there is little enforcement of basic labor rights. Yet the plight of undocumented workers should not blind us to the fact that a remarkable number of workers in general have their basic labor rights violated on a daily basis. The prevalence of workers at the low end of the job ladder who are paid below minimum wage, do not receive overtime, or are simply not paid by employers upon completion of a job has led some researchers to talk about a "gloves-off economy" (Bernhardt et al. 2009).

A recent study of labor law violations in New York City found that labor violations are widespread in low-wage jobs. Although undocumented immigrants were the most likely to be victimized, other groups were clearly at high risk as well. Looking at minimum wage violations, for example, the survey found that among men, 17 percent of low-wage workers experienced violations—for U.S.-born workers, the figure was 10 percent; for legal immigrants, 15 percent; and for undocumented immigrants, 29 percent. Among women, 24 percent of all low-wage workers experienced minimum wage violations—13 percent for U.S.-born women, 24 percent for legal immigrants, and an astonishing 40 percent for undocumented immigrants (Bernhardt et al. 2010). Part of what keeps this unregulated labor market viable is that unscrupulous employers have not been prevented from taking advantage of workers in a precarious position in the labor market. Certain groups are especially vulnerable: undocumented immigrants, former welfare recipients, and ex-offenders, for example. But the problem is widespread enough that even removing the most vulnerable from this picture would not change its basic contours.

In addition to the external challenges facing undocumented immigrants, there is some evidence that they may also be less likely than legal immigrants to invest in education, job training, or English language skills that would help them advance—for the logical reason that they are uncertain of their future status in this country. A national study, done after the 1986 law providing amnesty to undocumented immigrants went into effect, found that an unexpected positive economic effect of the amnesty law was that once workers gained legal status they became more likely to invest in their own education, enabling them to advance in their careers, earn higher wages, and benefit the economy through higher productivity (Kossoudji and Cobb-Clark 2000).

CONCLUSION

Immigration has been centrally important to the economy of New York City in recent decades. Immigrants—driving overall population growth—have often been an important part of neighborhood revitalization and have helped the city as a whole rebound from the days of underinvestment, abandoned buildings, and fiscal crisis of the 1970s.

The city's growth over the past four decades has been highly polarized. Gains have been concentrated in high-wage finance and business headquarters and in low-wage service industries, while losses included many middle-wage unionized manufacturing jobs, and the top 1 percent of taxpayers have taken the lion's share of economic gains. Immigrants have been part of New York City's growth at all levels; they are particularly concentrated in low-wage jobs, but are also substantially represented in middle- and high-wage positions in the city. Although wages have been under pressure, there seems to be room in the labor market for both U.S.- and foreign-born workers. Over the past four business cycles, peak-to-peak unemployment rates for both foreign and U.S.-born workers have been declining. One notable exception is U.S.-born black men and women with less than a high school education, a shrinking group, but one that experienced higher unemployment rates as the immigrant share of the labor force grew.

Immigrants are playing a central role in the city economy today, contributing to the city's overall economic output in nearly exact correlation to their share of the population. Immigrants' economic role is so large because they are particularly likely to be of prime working age, because they play a big role as owners of small businesses and managers of businesses large as well as small, and because—contrary to common misperception—immigrants are significantly represented in jobs all across the occupational spectrum. Immigrants are a diverse group. It is easy to get the impression that immigrants as a whole are highly concentrated at the bottom of the economic ladder, but while this is true for some groups, it is not true overall—indeed, race and ethnicity may well be more important than nativity in predicting success in New York City's labor market.

Finally, although economic output is driven in large measure by wages earned, low-wage immigrants—and other low-wage workers—also play very significant roles in the New York economy. Low-wage workers—in particular immigrants, and most especially undocumented immigrants—often work under harsh conditions, and are frequently paid less than the law requires. But they also provide low-cost amenities of city life such as free delivery, keep bodegas open twenty-four-hours a day, add value to products in garment factories, wash dishes in New York's dynamic restaurant industry, provide child care to a large number of New York City families, and in numerous other ways contribute to the economy in the city. There is no reason these jobs have to pay low wages, and there have been numerous campaigns to change that (Ness 2005). Even when they are drastically underpaid, however, low-wage immigrants are greatly improving the quality of life of New Yorkers, and there is no denying that, as a whole, New Yorkers benefit.

NOTES

1. "Immigrant" is defined as a person born in another country and residing in the United States. Immigrants include both documented and undocumented persons, except where specified. U.S.-born includes people born in the United States, including U.S. territories such as Puerto Rico and the U.S. Virgin Islands, as well as children born abroad to U.S. citizen parents. "Immigrant" and "foreign-born" are used interchangeably. All data in this report come from the Fiscal Policy Institute analysis of the 2009 American Community Survey, except where otherwise noted. The author would like to thank Jonathan DeBusk for his meticulous work in preparing the data, James Parrott and Frank Mauro for their input on the content, and Nancy Foner for her sharp editorial eye.

2. Jonathan Mahler took the phrase "the Bronx is burning" as part of the title of his 2005 book, *Ladies and Gentlemen, the Bronx Is Burning: 1977, Baseball, Politics, and the Battle for the Soul of a City*; Spike Lee's film *The Summer of Sam* came out in 1999.

3. Total economic output of an area can be estimated by looking at the total earnings of residents—wage and salary earnings, as well as proprietors' earnings, data that are available from the American Community Survey. This is the way the Bureau of Economic Analysis makes official estimates for GDP by metro area. Here we use the

same general method to estimate immigrant share of economic output. The New York State–level estimates were further refined by taking into consideration commuters and industries where immigrants are concentrated.

REFERENCES

American Planning Association. 2002. "Planning for Smart Growth: 2002 State of the States." Washington, DC: American Planning Association.

Bernhardt, Annette, Heather Boushey, Laura Dresser, and Chris Tilly. 2009. *Confronting the Gloves-Off Economy: Workplace Standards at the Bottom of America's Labor Market*. Ithaca, NY: Cornell University Press.

Bernhardt, Annette, Diana Polson, and James DeFilippis. 2010. *Working without Laws: A Survey of Employment and Labor Law Violations in New York City*. New York: National Employment Law Project.

Bowles, Jonathan, and Tara Colton. 2007. *A World of Opportunity*. New York: Center for an Urban Future.

Dreier, Peter, John Mollenkopf, and Todd Swanstrom. 2004. *Place Matters: Metropolitics for the Twenty-First Century*, 2nd rev. ed. Lawrence: University Press of Kansas.

Fiscal Policy Institute. 2007. *Working for a Better Life: A Profile of Immigrants in the New York State Economy*. New York: Fiscal Policy Institute.

——. 2009. *Immigrants and the Economy*. New York: Fiscal Policy Institute.

——. 2010. "Grow Together or Pull Further Apart? Income Concentration Trends in New York." New York: Fiscal Policy Institute.

Foner, Nancy. 2000. *From Ellis Island to JFK: New York's Two Great Waves of Immigration*. New Haven, CT: Yale University Press.

Freeman, Joshua B. 2000. *Working Class New York*. New York: New Press.

Jackson, Kenneth. 1987. *Crabgrass Frontier*. New York: Oxford University Press.

Kossoudji, Sherrie A., and Deborah A. Cobb-Clark. 2000. "IRCA's Impact on the Occupational Concentration and Mobility of Newly-Legalized Mexican Men." *Journal of Population Economics* 13: 81–98.

Logan, John R., and Richard D. Alba. 1999. "Minority Niches and Immigrant Enclaves in New York and Los Angeles: Trends and Impacts." In Frank D. Bean and Stephanie Bell Rose, eds., *Immigration and Opportunity: Race, Ethnicity, and Employment in the United States*. New York: Russell Sage Foundation.

Mollenkopf, John. 1992. *A Phoenix in the Ashes*. Princeton, NJ: Princeton University Press.

Ness, Immanuel. 2005. *Immigrants, Unions, and the New U.S. Labor Market*. Philadelphia: Temple University Press.

Pendall, Rolf. 2003. "Sprawl without Growth: The Upstate Paradox." Washington, DC: Brookings Institution.

Rumbaut, Rubén, Roberto G. Gonzales, Golnaz Komaie, and Charlie Morgan. 2006. "Debunking the Myth of Immigrant Criminality: Imprisonment among First- and Second-Generation Young Men." Washington, DC: Migration Policy Institute.

Shefter, Martin. 1985. *Political Crisis/Fiscal Crisis.* New York: Columbia University Press.

Shierholz, Heidi. 2010. "Immigration and Wages: Methodological Advancements Confirm Modest Gains for Native Workers." Washington, DC: Economic Policy Institute.

Singer, Audrey, Susan Hardwick, and Caroline Brettell, eds. 2008. *21st Century Gateways: Immigrant Incorporation in Suburban America.* Washington, DC: Brookings Institution Press.

Waldinger, Roger. 1996. *Still the Promised City? African Americans and New Immigrants in Post-Industrial New York.* Cambridge, MA: Harvard University Press.

Wright, Richard, and Mark Ellis. 2001. "Immigrants, the Native-Born, and the Changing Division of Labor in New York City." In Nancy Foner, ed., *New Immigrants in New York,* rev. ed. New York: Columbia University Press.

4. *Soviet Jews*

THE CONTINUING RUSSIFICATION OF JEWISH NEW YORK

Annelise Orleck

From computers to finance, partying to politics, Soviet and post-Soviet émigrés have made their mark on New York City over the past four decades.[1] This immigrant group has appeared in the headlines in sensational ways. The criminal and the infamous—mobsters and money launderers—along with the admired and celebrated—from Pulitzer Prize–winning poet Joseph Brodsky and novelist Gary Shteyngart to pianist Bella Davidovich and pop singer Regina Spektor—are part of the story of acculturation, accommodation, and economic mobility among Soviet Jewish émigrés in New York. But, as with any immigrant group, these spotlit moments show only glints on the surface of the sea. The larger history of these now-not-so-new New Yorkers is deep, substantive, complicated, and emotionally gripping. And it requires some history to understand.[2]

SOVIET JEWS AND THE TRANSFORMATION OF NEW YORK JEWISH LIFE

Soviet Jewish émigrés began to arrive in the United States during the early 1970s. From that time through the early twenty-first century—when the immigration largely dried up—between 40 percent and 50 percent of each year's new arrivals have stayed in the New York area, putting down deep roots. Energetic entrepreneurs created bustling commercial strips in South Brooklyn and Forest Hills, Queens. Computer wizards and commercial artists flooded the city's financial and design worlds. Émigré painters, sculptors, playwrights, and dancers made New York one of the world's centers of Russian Jewish culture. And the mass of immigrants from Russia, Belarus, Ukraine, and Uzbekistan both revitalized and forever transformed the tenor and flavor of New York Jewish life.

Most Soviet émigrés to New York got their first taste of America in communities that had been Jewish ethnic enclaves long before they arrived, settling in crowded Brooklyn or Queens neighborhoods among elderly East European Jews who were themselves once immigrants to the United States. In Brighton Beach, Sheepshead Bay, and Bensonhurst, Brooklyn; Forest Hills and Rego Park, Queens; and a patchwork of other neighborhoods throughout the New York area, these new immigrants breathed fresh life into withering communities. Under elevated subway tracks in three-story walk-ups that had formerly housed kosher delicatessens and dairy restaurants, tailor shops and glaziers, they opened black-and-silver-accented nightclubs, Georgian restaurants and sushi bars, and groceries selling sausage and smoked fish, European chocolate and jam.

Russian émigrés created new cultural institutions to replace those that were disappearing as earlier Jewish immigrants died or moved to Florida or to nursing homes nearer their now-suburban children. But at the same time, "the Russians" changed these neighborhoods in ways that were hard for many older Jewish New Yorkers to accept. During the long years of Communist rule, some Soviet Jews had carved out a sense of Jewish identity defined by their disproportionate representation in Russian theater, music, and literature. In New York many tried to sustain that identity by opening schools of music, art, dance, and gymnastics. These schools marked both the change and the continuity in longtime Jewish communities as immigrant academies appeared in the mildewing shells of synagogues, yeshivas, and Yiddish cultural centers.

Older East European Jewish immigrants who came to New York decades earlier were grateful to the Russians in the 1970s and '80s for revitalizing their neighborhoods, but tensions arose over Soviet émigrés' expressions of Jewish identity or lack thereof. The earlier immigrants had been raised speaking Yiddish and reading Hebrew religious texts. The post-1975 immigrants were raised under the virulently antireligious Stalin, Khruschev, and Brezhnev regimes, a time when publications in Yiddish or Hebrew were largely banned or at least very tightly controlled. The heritage that these new immigrants sought to pass on to their children seemed to many older Jewish New Yorkers more Russian than Jewish.

During the massive outpouring of the early 1990s that brought 1.6 million Jews from the former Soviet Union (FSU) to Israel, the United States, and Germany, New York City lost some of its allure. The best-educated among the émigrés often chose to settle elsewhere. And Brighton Beach, epicenter of the immigration, became an ambivalent symbol of the immigration's early years, a place to shop, to gather for family parties, to visit one's elderly parents, maybe to indulge in a bit of nostalgia. By 1999, fewer than 40 percent of Soviet Jewish immigrants to the United States chose New York City—preferring Los Angeles, Miami, and Chicago (Liff 1999). Still, large numbers continued to arrive in the city—at least 114,000 during the 1990s alone. (That does not include an estimated 40,000 more—many of them non-Jews—who came on tourist visas and never left.) Of the city's Soviet émigrés, 75 percent initially settled in Brooklyn, and most have stayed until today (Miller and Ukeles 2004).

Half of all Russian-speaking Jews in the United States live in New York City and, according to a 2011 survey, about 60 percent of those live in Brooklyn. They are most geographically concentrated in the Brighton Beach, Manhattan Beach, Sheepshead Bay, Bensonhurst, and Gravesend sections of Brooklyn, which are home to about a third of Russian-speaking Jews in the city (Cohen et al. 2012). About a quarter of Soviet Jewish émigrés in the city live in Queens—including approximately 50,000 Bukharan Jews from Uzbekistan and other Central Asian countries—most heavily concentrated in Forest Hills and Rego Park. The region's remaining Soviet émigrés are scattered through the Bronx, Staten Island, Manhattan, Westchester, New Jersey, and Long Island—creating a vast patchwork of Russian-speaking Jewish communities. More than a third are from the Ukrainian port city of Odessa, but many are also from Moscow, St. Petersburg, Minsk, Kiev, Tashkent, and Samarkand (U.S. Census Bureau 2009, New York City Department of City Planning 2004; Miller and Ukeles 2004). Different sources offer different numbers, but the best estimate is that between 200,000 and 300,000 Jews from the former Soviet Union currently live in the wider New York area.

Some more affluent émigrés and children of immigrants have carved out greener niches—"ethnoburbs"—in Long Island, Connecticut, and New Jersey. More often, they have simply moved to more upscale Brooklyn or Queens neighborhoods—Dyker Heights, Mill Basin, Manhattan Beach—where midcentury faux Tudor, brick, and faux Spanish–style homes are fast being replaced by massive, modern, flashy showcases for Soviet émigré wealth. The vast majority have remained in the regions of the city where they first settled, with a substantial number in the twenty-first century still concentrated in the southern tier of Brooklyn—rarely, as they put it, "going out to America."

Many young people, who came as children or were born in the United States, have done well for themselves economically, especially in the fields of high technology and finance. Most of New York's Soviet émigrés are not economically thriving, however. Despite high levels of education, 69 percent of Russian-speaking Jewish households in the eight-county New York City area in 2011 earned less than $50,000 a year, a very modest income in an area as expensive as New York (Cohen et al. 2012). One reason for their low income is that about a third of Russian-speaking Jews were elderly. In Russian Jewish households with seniors over 65 in the eight-county area, the poverty rate was as high as 73 percent. Russian Jews have been consistently among the largest immigrant consumers of public assistance in the city, with a rate comparable to that of native-born African Americans and Puerto Ricans. At the turn of the twenty-first century over a third of Soviet Jewish New Yorkers were receiving food stamps, Social Security, and/or Medicare. One 2008 study found that children of Soviet immigrants in metropolitan New York were more likely than children of Chinese, Dominican, West Indian, or South American immigrants to have grown up with someone in their household receiving public assistance (Lakhman and Goldiner 1999; Treiman 2003; Miller and Ukeles 2004; Kasinitz 2008).

Because so many Soviet Jews came as refugees, many had access to government benefits right away—and Jewish social service agencies were on hand in New York to make them aware of and to help them apply for these benefits (Kasinitz 2008). In 1995–1996, when over 40,000 Soviet Jewish émigrés came to New York City, 85 percent came with full refugee status, which meant that they received federal subsidies to ease housing, job training, and education costs and were able to apply right away for various kinds of public assistance.

As of 2010, though there were still anywhere from 330,000 to nearly a million Jews in the former Soviet states (depending on how the Jewish population is defined), immigration to the United States has largely stopped. After the late 1990s, of those who left the FSU, most headed for Israel or Germany, which now has a population of Soviet Jews almost half that of the United States. The dropoff was so dramatic that the primary agency for Soviet refugee resettlement in the city, the New York Association for New Americans (NYANA), closed its doors in 2008. Large numbers of Jewish and non-Jewish Russians continue to express a desire to emigrate. A 2011 poll of urban Russians found that more than 50 percent of entrepreneurs and students and more than 30 percent of professionals (including sizable numbers of Moscow's remaining Jews) would like to leave Russia in the near future ("The Mood of Russia" 2011). Still, it is possible that large-scale immigration of Soviet Jews to New York has come to an end. Whether it has or has not remains to be seen, but the impact of Soviet Jews on New York City is a current and ongoing story.

BACKGROUND OF THE IMMIGRATION

Soviet Jews began to agitate for the right to emigrate from the USSR during the early 1960s, part of a larger movement by Eastern bloc intellectuals for human rights. Israel's military success in the Six-Day War of 1967 had a strong emotional impact on Soviet Jews. Across the USSR, they held unprecedented demonstrations demanding the right to emigrate. The government of Leonid Brezhnev responded with a flood of anti-Semitic pronouncements and publications, equating Israel with the Third Reich and the Israeli army with Hitler's SS (Low 1990; Levin 1988).

This campaign encouraged longtime anti-Semites to be open about their feelings, creating an increasingly ugly atmosphere for Jews in many parts of the USSR. Émigrés now living in New York recall those painful days. Physician Khaya Reznikov's husband, whose dark hair and dark eyes distinguished him from his Russian neighbors, was pushed and chastised on trains and buses. "They would say, 'Your place is in Israel. We don't need you here.'" Computer programmer Sophia Shkolnikov remembers children being asked at the beginning of each school year to stand and identify themselves by nationality. Those who said they were Jewish were soon subjected to taunts and verbal abuse by other children, and sometimes by teachers as well.

Popular hostility against Jews was intensified by government reports about "overrepresentation" of Jews in universities and in the performing arts. Energetic government enforcement of ethnic quotas in Moscow, Leningrad, Minsk, Odessa, and Kiev forced even successful and assimilated Soviet Jews to question what would become of their children if they remained in the Soviet Union (Altshuler 1987:143–44). Jewish actors, directors, musicians, and athletes felt the sting of discrimination. Alexander Sirotin recalls being denied roles on Moscow television because he "did not have a Russian face." Pianist Edith Shvartsmann, who opened a dance, music, and gymnastics school on Ocean Parkway in Brooklyn, was working as an accompanist for the Russian gymnastics team in the 1970s. "It was the Olympic Games in Montreal. I think it was 1976. And everybody knew, anyone who was Jewish, they would never go. It didn't matter how much work you had put in or how much talent you had. This was true for coaches, athletes, everyone." Shvartsmann remembers deciding to emigrate. "I had a small son," she says. "I just began to wonder what he could look forward to."

Few exit visas were granted before 1971. Most who tried to emigrate in those years were dedicated Zionists who understood the dangers involved in applying. Applicants lost their jobs and those who were refused permission faced unemployment and prosecution under a Soviet law prohibiting "parasitism." Applicants for visas to Israel were sometimes jailed on charges of Zionism, which Soviet prosecutors defined as treasonous allegiance to an enemy state. Those denied permission to emigrate came to be known as refuseniks. Each year there were more of them.

Suddenly, during the spring of 1971, the Soviet government did an abrupt about-face and began to grant exit visas to tens of thousands (Lewis 1978:356). There was a fear that protests might continue to escalate and spread to other ethnic minorities. Appeals by Soviet Jews had also generated political pressure from the United States, Western Europe, and the western communist parties (Gilbert 1984:74–76; Birman 1979).

Before 1976, the Hebrew Immigrant Aid Society (HIAS) had bowed to pressure from the Israeli government and had given Soviet émigrés no choice but to go to Israel. American Jews began to exert their own preferences. That year, HIAS began offering departing Soviet Jews freedom to choose where they wished to resettle (Sawyer 1979:207–12; Weinstein 1988:610). During the second half of the 1970s, according to the U.S. government, more than 110,000 Soviet Jews emigrated to the United States. Émigré organizations in New York put the number at nearly twice that (Miller and Ukeles 2004).

The 1970s emigration was made up primarily of assimilated, successful urban professionals from the largest cities of Russia and Ukraine seeking to escape the limitations that Soviet anti-Semitism placed on their careers and on the prospects of their children. Without a keen Zionist commitment, few wished to trade the hardships of Soviet life for the dangers and difficulties of life in Israel. They saw a brighter future for their children in America.

The early 1980s saw Soviet authorities again shut the doors. A handful of Jews were granted exit visas, but after a high of 51,320 in 1979, emigration slowed to a trickle; just 522 were permitted to leave in 1984. These cuts in Jewish emigration were accompanied by renewed government campaigns against the study and promotion of Jewish culture, and by official condemnations of Zionism. Arrests and show trials began again. Some Jewish activists were sentenced to long terms of hard labor in gulags. While not as lethal as those of Stalin's day, these prison camps still bore a shocking resemblance to the conditions described in the writings of Aleksandr Solzhenitsyn.

Soviet Jews living in the United States and Israel feared for the safety of relatives left behind. Nearly 400,000 Jews still living in the USSR had asked for and received the invitations from relatives in Israel that were the first step in the process of applying for exit visas. Though not technically refuseniks, this huge pool of people experienced many of the same economic, personal, and legal difficulties that had made the lives of 1970s refuseniks so trying and uncertain. Then, political winds began to shift (Gilbert 1984; Wiesel 1987; Friedgut 1989).

Mikhail Gorbachev became general secretary of the Soviet Communist Party in 1985. At first, the government of this lifelong party apparatchik (functionary) held little promise for change. Within a year, though, he began releasing Jewish political prisoners—and took steps to make emigration easier. In May 1987, 871 Jews were permitted to leave, nearly as many in one month as had been allowed out the year before. Then a negative effect of Gorbachev's new policy of glasnost (greater government openness and candor) sparked a dramatic increase in applications to emigrate.

Though the democratization of speech and the press in the Soviet Union certainly had its benefits for Jews, who could now openly practice their religion, mount Jewish plays and exhibitions, and safely protest the imprisonment of Jewish activists, it also created space for deeply-rooted anti-Semitism among Russians and ethnic groups in the outlying republics to resurface. No longer sponsored by the government, anti-Semitic organizations nevertheless proliferated at the grass roots. The most influential of these was Pamyat, which mounted mass protests in Moscow against alleged Jewish meat hoarding and alcohol dealing.

In 1989, on the 1,000-year anniversary of the Russian Orthodox Church, Jews across Moscow found violently hostile leaflets in their mailboxes, threatening pogroms. Crosses were painted on Jewish apartment doors. One Jewish journalist described the poisonous climate, even among educated professionals: "At the editorial office of a progressive newspaper, two sweet women of my age approached me, hissing into my face: 'Leave amicably before they slaughter the lot of you'" ("I'm Not Fleeing" 1991:18). Rebecca Pyatkevich recalls that even small children were chased from playgrounds by older neighbors, who shouted, "'Go back to your part of town. Go away.' It was not a pleasant thing to grow up with."

A panic emigration ensued. Even as the Soviet Union continued to liberalize, even after the Berlin Wall fell, hundreds of thousands of Jews applied for exit visas. Between 1989 and 1991, 106,677 Soviet Jews emigrated to the United States. By 1996, another 156,901 had come, well over a quarter million people in six and a half years. These numbers count only legal immigrants. There were numerous illegals as well. In this same period more than 700,000 Soviet Jews went to Israel and to Western Europe, most of the latter to Germany. Between 1997 and 2005, half a million Soviet Jews emigrated to Israel; Germany received 156,000, while approximately 45,000 came to the United States (Tolts 2008). Since 2006, emigration from the FSU has slowed to a trickle.

Three factors were significant in driving the majority of immigrants to leave in the 1997–2005 period: a desire for family reunification, resurgent anti-Semitism, and the aftermath of the 1986 Chernobyl nuclear reactor explosion, which created skyrocketing rates of thyroid cancer and myriad other diseases across Byelorussia and parts of Russia and Ukraine. Other factors were food and housing shortages, spiraling inflation, ethnic violence, and violence against women, the same forces that caused a flood of non-Jewish citizens from former Soviet republics to head to Western Europe.

To highlight the differences between those who left the Soviet Union during the 1970s and early 1980s and those who left after 1989, I refer to them here as Third and Fourth Wave émigrés, respectively. This places them in the context of earlier Jewish out-migrations from Eastern Europe, the First Wave beginning in the 1880s and lasting through the 1910s, and the Second Wave coming after World War II. As one Brighton shopkeeper explained to me in 1980: "From this side of the Atlantic it may look like three different kinds of immigrants. From the other side I saw it this way. My grandfather left before the First World War. My uncle, who was in the Red Army, escaped after the Second. And I came thirty years after him."

SETTLING AN EXODUS

Counting American-born children, Soviet Jewish immigrants in the New York metropolitan area may well number over half a million. Since World War II most Soviet Jews had been big-city dwellers. They were accustomed to subways and buses, high-rise dwellings, and the speed of city life. And they came with skills to offer. A survey of late 1980s arrivals in nine U.S. metropolitan areas found that they described themselves as academics, scientists, professionals, or technical workers (Tress 1996:263–79). In the New York eight-county area in 2011, 52 percent of Russian-speaking Jewish men and 55 percent of women had either a bachelor's or postgraduate degree (Cohen et al. 2012).

Almost all Soviet Jews arriving in New York before 2004 received help from NYANA, founded after World War II to offer counseling, job placement, and housing assistance for Jewish Holocaust survivors. NYANA caseworkers settled as many Soviet Jewish immigrants as they could in historically Jewish neighborhoods where, they assumed, the local populations would be most welcoming and where a social service system was already in place to care for the Jewish elderly who had long been living there. Affordability was a pressing concern since immigrants were not allowed to bring cash with them from the USSR. So NYANA looked for apartments in aging inner-city Jewish communities with good housing stock and high vacancy rates (Fisher 1975:267–69; Jacobson 1975:190–94).

Once new immigrants found permanent housing, NYANA assigned vocational counselors to each working-age adult, tested them for English proficiency, and enrolled them in English courses. The NYANA method of teaching enabled many new arrivals to grasp basic conversational English in just a few weeks. The agency then offered vocational training in business and accounting, industrial trades, carpentry, building maintenance, and food service. It also provided retraining and licensing courses for engineers, computer scientists, and health care professionals (NYANA 1996). Unfortunately, only a small percentage of these immigrants were able to enroll in these programs. NYANA did not have the resources to reach most of the immigrants, especially during the periods of heaviest immigration. The vast majority had to fend for themselves or make use of networks established by friends and family members who had been in New York longer. How successful immigrants were at making the transition to the American work world depended a great deal on their gender, age, and class.

GENDER AND GENERATION

Perhaps one of the most striking features of the Soviet Jewish community in New York City is the experience of downward occupational mobility that has been so widespread among them. Arriving without English and with professional credentials that did not easily translate in the American context, middle-aged professionals have had a hard time picking up their careers where they left off in the old country. Those who applied for competitive high-level positions comparable to those they had held in the USSR were rarely hired—and many, perhaps most, realized it was futile to even try. Some émigrés have described what happened to them in the United States as an "intellectual holocaust" that has forced physicians, chemists, lawyers, engineers, and professors to drive cabs, work in garment factories, file, deliver pizza, and become home health care aides. *Science* magazine estimated that, between 1987 and 1990, 15 percent of all Soviet Jewish immigrants to the United States possessed PhDs or equivalent degrees in science and engineering. (That does not count those with MDs or advanced degrees in arts and humanities.) The very top Soviet mathematicians, scientists, and recent PhDs were snapped up by U.S. universities and corporations, particularly in the high-tech sector. But most were not. Frustratingly, many were turned down even for low-level technical positions because they were "overqualified." One out-of-work engineer commented bitterly: "In Russia, we had to hide that we are Jews. Here, to get a job, we have to hide that we have a PhD." Facing intense ageism, many tried to pretend they were younger than they were. Greying émigré scientists reported dyeing their hair, eyebrows, and beards (Rubin 1975; Holden 1990).

If the job market has been dismal for male professionals over 40, it has been even harder for women. For the large number of middle-aged Soviet women immigrants who had worked as pediatricians in their home country, the loss of professional status and the fall down the economic ladder was devastating. Of all the émigré physicians to enter the United States since the 1960s, these women had the least success in rebuilding their careers (Office of Refugee Resettlement 1995, cited in Tress 1996).

After thirty-two years of pediatric practice near Minsk, Bertha Klimkovitch, who came to Brooklyn in 1979, could find no better job than sewing machine operator in a Williamsburg garment shop. "I cried so much. But I know that for the children it will be better here." She found happiness "because the children are working and the grandchildren go to college." But she sometimes mourned for the premature end of her career. Sonya, fifty-one when she moved to Brighton Beach from Leningrad, had also practiced medicine for decades. After several unsuccessful attempts to pass the language exams required for relicensing, she was forced to take a minimum-wage job as a companion and chore worker for an elderly woman in Brooklyn. She too comforted herself with the thought that her son, an electronics engineer who was in his twenties when he arrived and found well-paid work in Houston, has done far better for himself in the United States than he could have in Russia. "As for myself," she sighed, "I could be more fulfilled."

Almost all women in the Soviet Union worked outside the home. Nearly two-thirds worked in high-skilled jobs prior to emigration. Once in the United States they have been less likely than their male counterparts, even over time, to be able to continue their careers. Fewer than a third managed to work in the same fields they had left in the FSU. More than 55 percent had to take jobs in service or clerical fields (Office of Refugee Resettlement 1994, cited in Tress 1996). It is possible that some of these women—like their male counterparts—have managed to receive additional training and improve their lot. A significant number of Soviet émigré women professionals have retrained to become social workers in New York, some of them specializing in the problems of the émigré community. A much smaller number have been able to pass U.S. licensing requirements and become physicians—also primarily serving their own community. More frequently, former physicians have become biomedical researchers, health technicians, secondary school teachers, or nursery school assistants (Orleck 2001; Reminnick 2005). It is the exception, not the norm, for a woman professional among Soviet émigrés to be able to find work in her own field in the United States. A good number say they prefer to focus on the achievements of their children.

Still, for many émigré women, initial adjustments to a severe decline in occupational status were very difficult. After the first months of elation following their arrival in New York, a period when mothers were incredibly busy taking care of the needs of family members, many adult women among the Soviet émigrés sank into profound depression over the loss of respect, professional identity, and the years of work they had put into building careers. Like Bertha Klimkovitch, women who were professionals in the FSU describe months and even years when they cried every day on their way to jobs that offered little pay and less in the way of professional satisfaction (Halberstadt and Nikolsky 1996; Reminnick 2007).

Such dramatic loss of professional status, coupled with frustration over inability to speak English and feelings of incompetence at basic tasks—shopping, filling out applications for schools, driver's licenses, and so on, not to mention disappointment in job hunting—caused serious emotional and psychological problems for many older working-age immigrants. Adele Nikolsky, coordinator of Russian immigrant services for a Brooklyn community health center, noted in 1996 that area mental health clinics were seeing "overwhelming numbers of middle-aged immigrants" with debilitating symptoms of depression and anxiety (Halberstadt and Nikolsky 1996). Many complained of poor health and stress caused by emigration.

Two groups that came in the 1990s and early twenty-first century were particularly plagued. Upwards of 30,000 victims of Nazi war crimes came as part of the post-Soviet influx in the 1990s. They are the poorest group of Jews in New York City, according to the 2002 Jewish Community Survey, and 85 percent claimed to be in poor or only fair health (Miller and Ukeles 2004). Second, exposure to fallout from the 1986 Chernobyl nuclear reactor accident created anxiety among émigrés from western Ukraine, Russia, and Belarus as well as real illnesses, especially elevated rates of thyroid cancer. Tellingly, 77 percent of Soviet émigrés in New York over the age of 57 in a 2004 study cited serious health issues.

Community health centers in Brooklyn and Queens struggle to serve thousands of Soviet elderly, as do Jewish social service agencies. This is especially true in the most crowded enclaves like Brighton Beach (Halberstadt and Nikolsky 1996; Weinberg et al. 1995; Miller and Ukeles 2004:92–93).

Despite a remarkably high educational profile, Soviet Jewish émigrés have among the lowest annual incomes and one of the highest rates of poverty in New York City. According to a report on poverty in the New York City Jewish community, about half of all Russian-speaking Jewish households were poor (150 percent of the federal poverty line) (Rapfogel et al. 2007; Miller and Ukeles 2004; New York City Department of City Planning 2004; Gamboa 2001; Popper 2004).

On the bright side, the children of immigrants are doing well. Nearly three-quarters of Russian Jews in a large-scale survey of second-generation young adults (18–32 years old) in the New York City metropolitan area were either attending or had graduated from a four-year college (Kasinitz et al. 2008). This is not surprising given their parents' educational background—more than two-thirds have at least college degrees—and a strong parental push to regain the family's lost professional status (Kasinitz 2008). Still, they have been less focused on attending elite private universities and colleges than have some other recent immigrant groups. Many Soviet émigré youth have chosen to attend colleges and universities in New York, and a good number continue to live at home into their mid-twenties. There is no stigma attached to that choice—quite the opposite.

They are consumers of American popular culture. Though almost all speak Russian, a majority in the second-generation survey said they preferred speaking English and read, watched, or listened to the city's Russian-language media only rarely (Zeltzer-Zubida and Kasinitz 2005). And they have fared well in the New York job market, the most common employment sectors for young Russian Jews in New York being computers and finance. Still, they have not developed much of a sense of community with American-born Jewish young people. Part of this is because so many remain concentrated in the South Brooklyn ethnic enclaves where their parents first settled.

"LITTLE ODESSA": MOURNING, MEMORY, COMMUNITY, AND A LITTLE FRAUD

The first Soviet Jews to arrive in New York City settled in Brighton Beach in the early 1970s. The neighborhood quickly became a mecca for Russian and Ukrainian immigrants. The housing stock on the ocean side of Brighton Beach Avenue—mostly 1920s Art Deco apartment buildings—was inexpensive and in excellent condition. Commercial space was plentiful. And there were well-established services for the elderly, as Brighton already had the second-highest concentration of senior citizens in the nation (Markowitz 1993).

Brighton was also emotionally appealing. Its residents back then were almost all Eastern European Jews, many of whom spoke Yiddish as their first language. This meant that Soviet elderly could begin to communicate with their neighbors immediately. Unlike many other Jewish neighborhoods in Brooklyn, Brighton was culturally Jewish but not overwhelmingly religious. Finally, it was located on a narrow strip of land facing the sea, perfect for walking and meeting neighbors, for breathing the fresh salt air. By the 1980s it had come to be known as Little Odessa, a reflection of the Ukrainian origins of nearly three-quarters of the new arrivals.

Thousands of Odessans and other Ukrainians, pining for the Black Sea, found in Brighton Beach a little of the feel of home—and something more. Fanya emigrated from Odessa in 1978 with her daughter and two young granddaughters. "The first time I heard Yiddish spoken on the street here, I couldn't believe my ears," she recalled in an emotional whisper. "Then I saw little boys wearing yarmulkes, walking down the street unafraid and I cried." Although Fanya's daughter, who opened a small grocery store on Brighton's main commercial strip, spoke no Yiddish, her granddaughters learned it as students in a Brooklyn yeshiva (religious school). Fanya reminisced in the mid-1980s: "In the First World War I lost my father, in the Second World War my husband. Since then I have had a bad heart. I could not cry at all. Here for the first time I cried. Here, when my little ones speak to me in Yiddish, my heart feels better."

With its fruit stands and street peddlers, barrels of pickles and swimming carp, haggling shoppers, and bantering merchants, Brighton evoked the lost Jewish world of an earlier era: the crowded small-town marketplace, the courtyards and ghetto streets of early twentieth-century urban Eastern Europe. Brighton has that feel in part because most of its buildings were constructed in that era. It became popular among First Wave Jewish émigrés as a summer resort in the late 1910s. By the 1930s the neighborhood was home to a thriving and diverse community of Jews from Russia, Poland, Czechoslovakia, and Romania, most of whom were active in the city's two major garment unions.

A hotbed of radical protest, Brighton supported not only a dozen synagogues and myriad charitable and cultural organizations, but also branches of the Jewish Labor Bund, the Socialist Arbeiter Ring (Workmen's Circle), the Zionist Farband, and active branches of the Socialist and Communist Parties. The Jewish immigrant culture of the area was enriched and transformed after World War II by the arrival of Holocaust survivors from across Central and Eastern Europe, then again in the late 1960s when the Amalgamated Clothing Workers' Union opened the Warbasse houses. These were soon filled with thousands of union retirees, who intensified Brighton's immigrant feel, its radical politics, and the density of its large population of seniors. By the late 1970s Brighton had begun to wither as its elderly residents died or moved to Florida. This opened up an abundance of commercial and residential space. For that and other reasons, it became the first and best choice of NYANA caseworkers looking to settle hundreds of Soviet émigrés arriving daily in New York.

Given the East European Jewish character of the neighborhood, it seemed likely that the mixing of newcomers with older residents would be smoother and easier than in areas where residents were of entirely different cultural, linguistic, and religious backgrounds. Instead, tempers soon flared. Each group developed quick and strong impressions of the other as they interacted on Brighton streets, in the hallways of apartment buildings, and in senior centers, shops, and synagogues. The neighbors fell into a strained sort of intimacy like estranged cousins bound by bloodlines from a distant past, related but completely unlike each other in habit and style. Each side had high expectations of the other, nurtured during the long struggle to "free Soviet Jewry." These gave way, perhaps inevitably, to disappointments, turf wars, and misunderstandings.

The issue of Jewish identity was perhaps the greatest bone of contention during the early days of the immigration and, to some extent, continues to be. Observant New York Jews reached out to the newcomers, hoping to school them in the fundamentals of a religious practice that Soviet Jews had been prevented from observing for half a century. Brooklyn synagogues and yeshivas launched outreach programs to attract and teach new immigrants. They leafleted apartment buildings with invitations to attend special Russian-language holiday services. Of the eleven synagogues in Brighton, only five were able to attract Russian speakers to join. And these were almost all people over sixty. Outreach efforts have continued to the present day—using all sorts of lures to draw in Soviet émigrés. In the summer of 2009, young émigrés and children of Soviet immigrants were bused to a weekend in the Hamptons where they were immersed in Jewish culture and history seminars (Goelman 2008; Berger 2010).

Years of lukewarm responses to such efforts evoked anger in some non-Russian New York Jews. So did differences in style. Many felt that the Soviets were pushy and unfriendly, unwilling to return greetings or wait their place in line. Others railed against generous subsidies that the immigrants received from Jewish charitable agencies, perhaps forgetting that earlier waves of émigrés also received help. You could hear the comments on the boardwalk, in stores, and on the streets. "Why did we fight to bring them here? Why did they want to come here? They're not even Jews. They don't want to be Jews."

Some of the most Jewish-identified immigrants tried to mediate. Alexander Sirotin, a playwright and director from Moscow and one of the earliest immigrants to arrive in Brighton, formed the Jewish Union of Russian Immigrants to sponsor activities with a Jewish theme. During the 1980s and '90s he hosted *Gorizont* (Horizon), a Russian-language radio show on the Lubavitch Hasidic radio network. He urged Russian-speaking listeners to deepen their Jewish knowledge. He suggested that New York Jews back off and let émigrés nourish their Jewish identities in their own ways.

"American Jews try to teach the Russian immigrant about Jewishness using a strange language," Sirotin wrote, "and then wonder why he does not understand." Sirotin compared the émigrés to concentration camp survivors when it came to their knowledge and comfort with Yiddishkayt (Jewishness). "We are not starving technically but we are starving for Jewishness. You can't shove food down a starving man's throat. It is the same with these Jews. They must be fed Yiddishkayt with a teaspoon" (Sirotin 1981).

And yet surveys show that most Soviet Jewish émigrés feel very Jewish—especially the elderly. They recall being forced to carry internal passports stamped with the letter J to prevent them from passing as Christian. Jewish looks or last names and school or work documents revealing a Jewish ancestor subjected them to both petty and serious harassment. Every Jewish family from Russia, Belarus, and Ukraine has paid a price in blood for the crime of being Jewish—exacted by the Nazis, the Soviets, or both. Those old enough to remember "the black years of Soviet Jewry" from 1939 to 1954 express bitter resentment toward anyone who dares tell them they are not really Jews, especially American Jews who spent those years comfortable and safe on this side of the Atlantic.

In fact, Soviet émigrés have expressed their Jewishness in myriad ways and their increasing comfort doing so has been an important part of their acculturation process. Émigré theater troupes have performed Soviet Yiddish plays. Community Passover seders have incorporated tales of the exodus from Odessa. Then there have been the public gatherings in commemoration of the 1941 massacre at Babi Yar (the forest near Kiev where the Nazis shot more than 100,000 Jews); Dyen Pyobyedi (the holiday honoring World War II Red Army veterans); and the 1943 Warsaw Ghetto Uprising. In New York, Los Angeles, Chicago, Tel Aviv, and Berlin Soviet survivors have stood up in public for the first time since World War II to tell horrific stories of the Nazi invasion and harrowing tales of survival—feigning death, surrounded by the bodies of friends and family until the Nazi execution squads left and they could crawl away under cover of darkness.

As for religious observance, Soviet émigrés have, like American Jews, embraced a wide range of Jewish identities. Some are quite religious, others less so. Some began attending synagogue and studying Hebrew before emigrating in the 1960s, '70s, and '80s as an act of resistance against the antireligious Soviet regime. Others have always seen religion as a throwback, a superstition. Surveys show that a large majority of Soviet émigrés strongly identify as Jewish, even more strongly than most American-born Jews. More than one-third enroll their children in Jewish day schools or Sunday schools. And most celebrate popular Jewish holidays like Passover and Hanukkah with family gatherings and ritual meals at home (Miller and Ukeles 2004; Goelman 2008). A staggering number of adult men had themselves circumcised after their arrival in the United States, more than 10,000 in New York City alone (Sugarman 1992). And Soviet storekeepers throughout Brooklyn, who at first stayed open on the Jewish High Holy Days, soon began to close on Rosh Hashanah and Yom Kippur.

Some émigré children have pushed their families to observe Jewish rites at home. Since these observances sometimes caused tension with irreligious parents, they have turned to grandparents to help them. Sparking memories in these elderly immigrants can be disturbing, however. They lived through Stalin's purges; the Nazi occupation, during which one in two Soviet Jews was murdered; and the years after World War II, when so many Jewish artists, intellectuals, and physicians were executed or sentenced to years of hard labor in the gulag. Almost all have lost loved ones to violent death and feel crippling guilt over having survived and leaving family graves behind. The symptoms of post-traumatic stress disorder are common in Soviet émigré communities.

Traumatic memories sometimes make it difficult for elderly émigrés to meet their needs in a new and alien place. Sophie Spector, who for many years taught English to elderly émigrés at the Shorefront Y and Senior Center, found that simply calling for an ambulance could evoke memories of the era in Soviet history when political dissidents were whisked off to hospitals and never heard from again. In Brooklyn, if a police car arrived before the ambulance, says Spector, some elderly immigrants would panic. An uncomprehending medic, arriving moments later, would then try to push the terrified old man or woman into the vehicle. On more than one occasion, Spector recalled, this escalated into near-brawls between police, medics, and a gathering crowd of immigrants.

Many émigrés have found New York health care facilities to be cold and impersonal compared to small neighborhood clinics in the USSR. Some grow angry and frustrated at not being able to find physicians near their homes who will accept Medicare or Medicaid and, when they do, at waits up to four hours (Caroll 1995). Though only a small percentage of those who came to this country with medical degrees were able to get licenses to practice in the United States, increasing numbers of children of immigrants are working their way through medical school and setting up offices in Russian communities.

Some émigrés have turned to alternative medicine. Pharmacies in émigré neighborhoods carry a bewildering array of dried herbs in hand-labeled bags. Street-corner vendors sell everything from garlic-skin pastes to powdered reindeer horn, assuring prospective customers that these "alternative antibiotics" can cure ills that bedevil physicians. The emergency room staff at Coney Island Hospital, South Brooklyn's major public medical facility, began keeping a Russian-language herbal remedy book on hand so that they could find out from patients what they had already ingested (Garrett 1997).

Confusions notwithstanding, most elderly Soviet émigrés have come to think of South Brooklyn as home and are quite content there. It has been a place where they have been able to heal and put down roots—conduct public ceremonies of communal mourning, watch their grandchildren play on the beach, and meet friends on the boardwalk and in local parks. In recognition of their presence in Brighton, the city renamed a tiny vest pocket park off Brighton's back streets Babi Yar Triangle. The green New York City parks sign is the kind of public marker one could not find in Kiev. It represents a freedom to mourn, to finally name the dead aloud without fear of reprisal.

But late in 2010, this bit of tarred ground, with its perpetually filled benches and inlaid stone chess tables where old men in berets bent in concentration, was abuzz with a new Holocaust story that was making front pages from New York to Jerusalem. On a crisp day in November, federal agents swarmed an Art Deco apartment building on Brighton Twelfth Street as elderly émigrés watched intently from folding chairs on the street.

The targets of this raid were building residents Tatiana and Abram Grinman. They, along with fifteen other Soviet émigrés, were charged with massive fraud—filing 5,600 false claims for Holocaust restitution monies totaling $42 million. Other émigré fraud schemes have made the headlines. There have been dramatic and not infrequent instances of bilking Medicare and Medicaid, fraudulent claims on funds set up to assist victims of the Chernobyl meltdown, ATM fraud, and mortgage fraud. One doctor's office near Coney Island was reputed to have a "kickback room" where émigrés received their share of fraudulent claims. The room sported a World War II–era Soviet poster warning people to keep quiet (Fisher and Mangan 2010; Italiano and Messing 2005).

These activities may be related to long-imprinted patterns carried over from Soviet days (Fishman 2010). Sociologist Lydia Rosner identified a significant group of Soviet émigrés she calls "survivors" who engaged in "extralegal" activities to support their families in the USSR and who continued such activities once in New York. Émigré writer Boris Fishman describes a lingering "poison" inside some of these survivors of the Soviet regime. Still, it is important to remember that the vast majority of émigrés live upstanding lives and that crime by Soviet émigrés tends to hurt their fellow immigrants most (Rosner 1986). Not only are immigrants victims of many of the crimes, but the reputation of Soviet Jewish immigrants, especially in Brighton, has suffered as a result of adverse publicity generated by the criminals.

VOROVSKOY MIR (THIEVES' WORLD)

The 2010 Holocaust restitution fraud is just the most recent manifestation of wide-ranging and sophisticated criminal activities perpetrated by Soviet immigrants in New York City. Some of that crime has been open, organized, and violent. Back in the late 1970s, a small group of Ukrainian Jewish gangsters known as the "Odessa Mob" first made Brighton Beach infamous as a hub of immigrant crime. Gang members had learned their craft back in Odessa, trading on the black market, diamond and heroin smuggling, and gun running. Over the past thirty years members of many other crime gangs have found their way to New York. The first came when Soviet authorities emptied their prisons in the 1970s and '80s, allowing criminals to slip in among honest citizens leaving for Israel and the United States. Nominally Jewish gangsters recast themselves as refugees fleeing Soviet anti-Semitism. Non-Jewish gangsters used the identification papers and visas of deceased Odessan Jews. And for a long time, public law enforcement failed to question their stories. Not until the mid-1980s did the FBI or New York City police begin to take this criminal immigration seriously.

Brighton was a good spot for Russian mobsters for a variety of reasons. It was a short drive from JFK International Airport, an excellent port for smuggling. Its teeming streets gave perfect cover; it was easy to blend in among thousands of Soviet immigrants. A few corrupt police were willing to provide protection. And in the 1970s there were plenty of vacant apartments, some of which were bought up in blocks by crime bosses. One immigrant who moved to Brighton the early 1980s recalled that entire buildings in one part of the neighborhood—huge Art Deco edifices with turrets, mosaics, and long, dark hallways—were occupied by members of immigrant crime syndicates who were brought over directly from Russia and installed there (Rosner 1986).

Evsei Agron was the most powerful of the early gangster immigrants. A short Joseph Stalin lookalike, he listed his occupation as jeweler when he first arrived at Kennedy Airport in 1975, neglecting to mention the seven years he had served in a Soviet prison camp for murder or the gambling and prostitution rings he had just been running in West Germany. He quickly transferred his skills to Brighton Beach where, like most immigrant criminals, he began by preying on his own (Friedman 1994, 2000).

By 1980, Agron was averaging $50,000 per week, extorting funds from Soviet émigré business owners with plausible threats of violence, illustrated by the electric cattle prod he liked to carry. His loan sharks lent money at astronomical rates. Soviet émigrés' suspicion of official paperwork made them particularly vulnerable to this sort of attack. Car theft rings soon prowled the streets of New York, Chicago, Los Angeles, and San Francisco, recruiting underage boys—who could not be sentenced to long prison terms—to do the actual stealing. The most famous victim of these carjackers was Ennis Cosby, son of the famed comedian Bill Cosby, who was murdered in California in 1997 by an 18-year-old Ukrainian car thief. Still, most of the victims of Soviet émigré crime were other Soviet immigrants, at least in the beginning (Sterngold 1998).

Several ambitious young émigré thugs made attempts on Agron's life, one in a brazen daylight shooting on the Brighton Beach boardwalk. He walked away more than once but, in 1985, was shot at close range waiting for the elevator in his apartment building. The Byelorussian émigré Marat Balagula, his closest aide, and the man most likely responsible for his murder, then became the city's top ex-Soviet gangster.

Learning from Agron's mistakes, Balagula followed the time-honored practice of other immigrant crime bosses, creating a protective buffer around himself by taking care of struggling fellow émigrés. One recalled:

> Marat was the king of Brighton Beach. . . . People would come over from Russia and he'd give them jobs. He liked professional men. Guys came over and couldn't practice medicine or use their engineering degrees. He sought them out. He was fascinated with intellectuals. He co-opted them. He put them into the gasoline business, he put them into car washes or taxi companies. He'd reinvest his own money in their business if they were having trouble. He had a heart. (Friedman 2000:42)

Echoing a tradition among mobsters in the former Soviet Union, Balagula became the judge and jury of his own Brighton "people's court," convened in an upstairs room at his nightclub, the Odessa. Some say that sentences were also carried out there. Attempts to kill him were swiftly punished. Protected by the Lucchese crime family, Balagula became one of the longest survivors in the Soviet émigré criminal underworld.

The arrival of Soviet crime families in Brighton brought a level of violence to the neighborhood that it had never seen before. The 1980s and 1990s were a frighteningly bloody time. A Soviet hit man who had made an attempt on Balagula's life was shot to death in front of the Odessa restaurant. A well-known former journalist was gunned down in a jewelry store. One Yom Kippur (Day of Atonement) a man was shot to death at close range on the boardwalk in front of elderly First and Second Wave Jewish immigrants gathered for the High Holidays. One angry voice could be heard above the crowd: "There is something very sick happening in this neighborhood. They shoot each other on the holiest day of the year. These cannot be Jews."

Since the collapse of the Soviet Union in 1991, an increasing percentage of émigrés are in fact not Jewish—upwards of 30 percent by some accounts. There are enough of them now living in South Brooklyn that there have been reports of street fights between Jewish and non-Jewish émigrés over anti-Semitic slurs uttered in Russian. Non-Jewish Soviet émigrés have also included some well-connected criminals, most famously Vyacheslav Ivankov, who moved to Brighton in 1992 with false papers identifying him as Jewish. Dispatched to New York by Moscow crime bosses to lay foundations for criminal networks that stretched throughout the world, Ivankov was jailed in 1995 for kidnapping two crooked Soviet émigré investment bankers from the bar of the New York Hilton at gunpoint. Extradited to Russia to face murder charges there, he was assassinated by a sniper in 2009 (Friedman 2000:136; Mustain and Capeci 1997; Finkenauer and Waring 1998:chap. 9).

Still, a good many of the most infamous Soviet émigré criminals have been Jews, including the man who claims to be the most prolific hit man of all time—Monya Elson, who has been tied to upwards of 100 murders. A self-styled tough guy from Kishinev, Elson had established crime enterprises in Brighton Beach, Eastern Europe, and Israel by the 1980s. In the early 1990s, operating out of the Brighton Beach nightclub Rasputin, he launched a bloody reign of terror that stretched from Brooklyn to Los Angeles as he and his rivals fought for dominance.

By the twenty-first century, Russian émigré crime networks with bases in Brooklyn, Tel Aviv, and Europe had been caught running drugs through Miami, diamonds through Sierra Leone, and weapons through Russia. They have laundered billions through banks, including an estimated $7 billion through the Bank of New York alone, have run the largest Medicare and Medicaid frauds in U.S. history, and, according to one Brooklyn detective, "they have invaded Wall St. from boiler room operations to brokerage houses." Most shocking of all to American sports fans has been the alleged Soviet émigré mob involvement, through Russian players, in the National Hockey League. Acculturation takes many forms (Friedman 2000:286; "Mafia Power Play" 1999).

EATING, DRINKING, AND ACCULTURATING

Beneath these sensational headlines are the quieter stories of honest immigrants who run an array of small businesses in Brighton and other neighborhoods. From the beginning of the immigration, entrepreneurship has generated income for new arrivals—both those who had bought and sold goods to supplement their meager wages in the FSU and former professionals who were unable to find work in their fields once in the United States. One early study of Soviet immigrants in New York indicated that three-quarters hoped or planned to open their own businesses (Simon 1985).

Partly this was an idealized vision of American capitalism. To own a business was to have no boss, no restrictions on where one could settle, and no limitations on what one could earn. It was also a recognition that, with limited English, it might be difficult to find work outside the immigrant enclaves where Russian was the language of commerce. Many new arrivals believed that they could create thriving businesses catering to the Russian immigrant community without becoming fluent in English. Brighton Beach Avenue and other Brooklyn commercial strips filled with Russian-speaking merchants and shoppers are testament to the success of that vision.

The first Soviet immigrant-owned stores to appear in the late 1970s were groceries. Clean and brightly lit, they stood in stark contrast to the old-fashioned corner stores run by an earlier generation of immigrants. For the past three decades, these stores have occupied an important place in the lives of newly arrived immigrants—concrete reminders of the differences between years of rationing and substandard food back in the USSR and the miracle of abundance that is shopping in America. In Soviet-era Russia and Ukraine, keeping a family fed meant standing in one line after another for hours each day just to purchase the essentials. It meant bribing truckers, farmers, and grocery workers, and scouring the city for the latest black market shipments. In Brooklyn, immigrants can choose between dozens of groceries offering Polish, Hungarian, German, Russian, Turkish, Greek, Italian, and American meats, cheeses, juices and chocolates. Bakeries, butcher shops, fish stores, and fruit stands compete with each other, lining street fronts and packing windows with eye-catching displays. These stores quickly became informal community centers where shoppers lingered to talk, exchange news, or offer congratulations or condolences. For some Soviet émigrés who have moved to greener pastures, these stores and immigrant enclaves are places they come to remind them of their roots—the smells, the packaging, the Russian banter all evocative of childhood neighborhoods.

Brighton's Russian restaurants and nightclubs—known as much for their glitz and excess as for their food—have been perhaps even more important in defining both the internal life of the community and the image of it held by outsiders. They are public gathering spaces where a sense of group identity has been forged, reinforced, and continually reinvented. They reflect the geographic and cultural diversity of this immigration—serving up food, music, and dance from the Caucasus, Central Asia, Moscow, and Odessa. Ukrainian food is the most commonly served cuisine, along with some traditional Ashkenazi (Northern European Jewish) specialties and an odd fusion cuisine known as Odessan continental that reflects Odessa's heritage as a seaport visited by sailors from throughout the world. Georgian restaurants are also popular, as are restaurants serving Uzbek and other Central Asian cuisines. Meat, cheese, and potato-filled dumplings are found most everywhere but called different names—*pirogi* in Ukrainian, *pyelmeni* in Central Asian restaurants, and *vareniki* in Russian. *Shashlyk* is also ubiquitous (shish kebab, made with lamb, chicken, or sturgeon and served on a swordlike skewer), as is chicken Kiev (fried and stuffed with butter and mushrooms).

Whatever the restaurateurs' region of origin, groaning banquet tables are the norm, covered with *zakuski* (appetizers), flowers, and elaborate place settings. Plates of smoked fish, pickled vegetables, and cold vegetable salads greet arriving guests. Bottles of vodka, water, wine, and soda rise like islands in the sea of food.

To what extent have these stores and restaurants been touched by organized crime? That is difficult to assess. The two studies of Soviet émigré crime in the United States came to starkly different conclusions. One argues that every Soviet émigré family in Brighton has been either victimized by or involved in organized crime (Friedman 2000). The other study is based on a large number of interviews with émigrés who said that they have had no contact with Soviet organized crime except through the media (Finckenauer and Waring 1998). The truth, almost certainly, lies somewhere in between.

Brighton's restaurants and nightclubs vary dramatically in size and levels of grandeur, undoubtedly depending on the cash flow of their owners, but all share an extravagant taste in interior design that make even the smallest feel more like a stage set than a dining room. Red walls, colored lights, stained glass sailing ships, marble bathrooms, crystal chandeliers, chrome and black enamel banquettes, live bands, and strobe-lit dance floors infuse these restaurants with a sense of the fantastic. So do the blonde Russian torch singers in skintight, low-cut Spandex, Stevie Wonder impersonators with Russian accents, and big bands with congas and horns. The food, the music, the decor, and the free-flowing vodka work together to create moments of shared release and a sense of belonging.

The mystery and secrecy surrounding Brighton's Russian restaurants stem from several sources. First, they are products of mistrust and persecution, arising out of the harsh realities of life in the USSR, where from the 1930s to the early 1990s it was not only difficult but dangerous for Jews to gather in groups. With undercover agents infiltrating synagogues, and house parties subject to police raids, restaurants were among the only places where Soviet Jews could gather in a relaxed atmosphere. "The spirit of Soviet Jewry really came to life in restaurants," émigré author and actor Alexander Sirotin (1981:10) has written. "There ordinary workers, by day forced to comply with Soviet officials, to submit to constant harassment, could finally become people of character, of unique identity. This was the only place where they could remove all masks to reveal openly a Jewish face. In the absence of other possibilities, the restaurant became the center of life for many Jews in Soviet cities. That custom was carried here." In the USSR, these spaces were hidden from prying eyes, with few signs marking entrances and no windows open to the street. That custom, too, was carried to New York.

For many years, Russian restaurants in Brighton hid their fabulous interiors behind blank fronts, heavy curtains, and blackened street-facing windows. This camouflage reflected both a lingering distrust of strangers and a desire to discourage casual entry by outsiders. Owners of the lavishly decorated National removed a large plate-glass window from what used to be a furniture store and replaced it with a metal, windowless, street-facing facade. At Sadko, a two-floor black-and-silver discotheque, they were even more intent on hiding. Its street front for years was an abandoned pizzeria, as it was on the day it closed, with white formica counter and pizza ovens. Over a faded sign for Mama Mia Pizzeria, a tiny sign said Sadko. There was no indication that a nightclub lay within. Yet each weekend, dark cars and limousines pulled up at a side entrance around the corner, where a signless wooden door admitted those in the know. Sometime during the mid-1980s, the owners erected a more inviting nautical facade, but the porthole windows were placed so high they were impossible to peek into.

These masked facades were not simply legacies of Soviet repression, however. For the National, Sadko, the Odessa, Rasputin, and several other local restaurants were more than just places for hard-working Soviet émigré families to celebrate reunions, birthdays, weddings, and bar mitzvahs. Some of these restaurants were owned by and served as watering holes for members of émigré crime families. And when wars broke out between these violent rivals, they were sometimes fought out against surreal strobe-lit, music-pulsing backdrops. During Brighton's most violent years—from the mid-1980s through 1995—Sadko, the National, the Odessa, Cafe Arbat, and the Winter Garden on the boardwalk were all sites of mob killings. Most of these crimes went unsolved for years (Tri-State Joint Soviet-Émigré Organized Crime Project 1995).

By the late 1990s, the violence had largely disappeared, and long-silent witnesses began to come out of the woodwork. Some cases have been reopened, if the perpetrators are still alive. Since that time, Brighton's restaurants and clubs have become more normalized and integrated into the complex culinary life of the city. Newspapers and Web sites review them, and outsiders are more welcome.

Extravagance, however, is still the rule in Brighton's Russian nightclub parties. This seems particularly true of bar and bat mitzvahs—the Jewish coming-of-age rituals for 12- and 13-year-olds. Like earlier generations of Jewish immigrants in New York, many Soviet émigrés use these occasions to demonstrate how well they have done in America. More about affirming a communal Jewish identity than about embracing religion, Soviet émigré bar and bat mitzvahs (like so many now held by American Jews) are often an irreverent mix of traditional religious rites and cheerfully irreligious food and music. Shrimp (strictly forbidden under Jewish dietary laws) is piled high on the tables, served alongside gefilte fish (a traditional Jewish dish of ground carp, whiting, and onions). Hebrew blessings are accompanied by electric guitar. Synthesizers approximate the violin and clarinet sounds of East European klezmer music, interwoven with the heavy beats of electronic house music. Over the decades, the Jewish content of these events has faded. At one party, the band insisted that they didn't know any horas (celebratory Jewish circle dances), though the same restaurant's band had played them just months earlier.

Brighton's nightclubs have become objects of fascination well beyond South Brooklyn. Small numbers of hip and arty New Yorkers venture down for a taste of South Brooklyn "exotic." Online gamers anywhere in the world can now role-play as Soviet émigré gangsters in the Big Store (criminal slang for the U.S.)—a game set on the streets of Brighton and in its clubs. And in 2011 television viewers could watch Brighton's Russians show off on reality TV in Lifetime's *Russian Dolls*, which first aired in the summer of that year.

Vlad Iorsh, a fervent nightclub patron until he joined the military and saw combat in Afghanistan before returning to Brooklyn in 2003, had this to say about the new media interest in Brighton's Soviet émigrés: "Television is making them really look bad. They will do a better job—maybe not so much in ratings—if they show the hard-working side of the Russian community, instead of just the mafioso side or the women who are gold-diggers. Not to say that's not true but they only show one side."

QUEENSISTAN

New York's other large Soviet-émigré neighborhood, Forest Hills, Queens, also broke into the headlines in recent years in a splashy and violent way that shone a distorting light on a community long closed to outsiders, sparking a local debate that continues to simmer. Since the 1970s, some 50,000 Central Asian Jews from Uzbekistan, Tajikistan, and Kazakhstan have settled there, opening synagogues, restaurants, barber shops, doctors' offices, a museum, a religious school, live theater, and food markets. Forest Hills' 108th Street has come to be known as Bukharan Broadway and the neighborhood is affectionately called Queensistan.

Culturally, linguistically, and religiously distinct from their western Soviet counterparts, Bukharan émigrés believe themselves to be descended from Persian Jews of the ancient world. They trace their Uzbek roots back to the fifth century, and have never spoken Yiddish but instead use a dialect of Persian known as Bukhori, which is written in Hebrew characters. Just as Jews from the western republics see themselves as Russians, Bukharan Jews share the cultural identity of Tajiks and Iranians. They have more in common with Muslim Middle Easterners than they do with Christian Europeans, and some from the western areas of the FSU do not consider them real Russians (Carr 1997).

Central Asian Jews have a long history of entrepreneurship even in the Soviet Union, where they were given economic freedoms others did not enjoy. Excellent businesspeople, their economic adjustment to New York life has been rapid and successful. Family businesses, which rely on the combined labor of children, parents, and grandparents, can be found flourishing both in Queens and in Manhattan. Bukharan émigrés run furniture stores in Manhattan on Lower Broadway and jewelry stores on 47th Street where Hasidic diamond cutters practice their craft.

Their cultural transition has been more difficult, especially for older Bukharans who hold onto ancient traditions of prayer, food, and relationships between men and women. For some it has been a difficult leap from the ancient domed and pinnacled cities of Bukhara, Tashkent, and Samarkand to the twenty-story apartment buildings and sprawling grid of streets and highways that dominate Rego Park, Queens. Unlike their counterparts from the west, Bukharan Jews were deeply religious before emigration, and most have remained so in New York. Though some have joined the Lubavitch Hasidic sect, most have continued to observe in the traditionally Persian style: the language and melody of their prayers, the holiday foods and customs, and their religious clothing are quite different from those of western Jews.

If Ukrainian immigrants in Brighton have bristled at charges that they are not "real Jews," Bukharans in Queens are angered by immigrants from the western republics who insist that the Central Asians are not "real Russians." Queens courtroom translator Alla Lupyan Grafman, an émigré from Minsk, admitted that many émigrés from Belarus, Ukraine, and Russia believe Bukharans to be primitive, savage, dirty, and prone to violence (Malcolm 2010). Such sentiments have created tensions in some Queens public schools, says Susan Sokirko, who runs a program for Russian-speaking students at Forest Hills High School. David, a 13-year-old Ukrainian Jew, opines, "We get offended when you call them Russians." Bukharan children in public schools where they are in the minority can end up "outcasts because of their accents and backgrounds," Sokirko says. And this has contributed to a disproportionately high dropout rate (Gorin 1995).

Adolescents and young adults sometimes face problems at home as well, fighting against parents who try to arrange marriages or to restrict children's choices of schooling or occupation. *Toys* (weddings) remain one of the central rituals of life in the community, and when girls try to carve out their own way, or when wives resist control by husbands, it has too often resulted in physical violence. Anna Halberstadt for many years ran a NYANA support program for battered women from the Soviet émigré community. Though Bukharans represent only about 15 percent of Soviet Jews in New York, they were more than 50 percent of participants in NYANA's domestic violence programs. Victoria Neznansky, a program counselor, says that these adult Bukharan women seek treatment and support but few are willing to leave their marriages for fear of being cut off from community or losing custody of their children.

Younger Bukharan girls have proven bolder. After years of watching her father beat her mother, one 17-year-old Bukharan girl began flouting his authority openly—wearing short skirts and red lipstick to school. She warned him that she would never marry a Bukharan man because they abuse their wives. When the father began beating her as well, she ran away from home. Fifteen-year-old Nellie called New York City Child Welfare services and asked to be placed in foster care because she could no longer bear to watch her father beat her mother (Halberstadt and Nikolsky 1996).

Some young Bukharan girls have tried to bring social workers (often Soviet immigrants themselves) into the closed community in hope that it will bring an end to the abuse of Bukharan women. They feel that they need outside eyes because the community's most traditional male leaders view charges of domestic violence skeptically. "If a father taps a child on the back of the head that doesn't mean he beat him," said Boris Kandov, president of the Bukharian Jewish Congress of the United States and Canada. "But if it's recorded by the police—that's it. He's a criminal." Kandov also argues that restraining orders break up marriages, "preventing husbands from apologizing" (Barnard 2009).

Concern about violence and about intrusion by outsiders has moved some religious leaders to develop their own programs to improve marital relationships and to create stronger bridges between parents and children.

These concerns were heightened in 2009–10 by a now-infamous case that brought the inner world of Bukharan marriage, or at least one particularly troubled Bukharan marriage, into the local and national media spotlight. A 35-year-old physician from Samarkand in Uzbekistan was accused of hiring a cousin to kill her husband who, among other things, she claimed sexually abused her child and beat her; the two were convicted and sentenced to life in prison, a verdict that held despite appeals (Malcolm 2010).

As the case made headlines, the subjects of domestic violence and gender relations were hotly debated in Queensistan. Rafael Nektalov, editor of the Russian-language newspaper the *Bukharian Times*, argued that, since immigration, Bukharan women have started leveling charges of violence and sex abuse to get the better of their husbands in court. "A woman understands that, to take everything, all she has to do is say 'I have been abused.' It has become like feminine blackmail." But for Margarita Nektalova, a physical therapist who won custody of her children after immigrating to New York, it is a comfort that women and children "are more protected here." Mediation involving community elders is fine, she said, but it does little to protect women and children if an abusive husband "has no conscience."

CONCLUSION

As we enter the second decade of the twenty-first century, Soviet Jewish New Yorkers remain a remarkably diverse group. The elderly, those less educated, and those who speak English less well remain deeply embedded in the ethnic enclaves of South Brooklyn and Forest Hills, Queens. The younger generation and U.S.-born children of the immigrants are, by contrast, integrated into many aspects of the city's life. "Some of our friends are Russian," says Vlad Iorsh, "but we have friends of all kinds. I think mine now are mostly American." Still, though Iorsh has lived in Virginia and traveled the world with the military, like many children of the immigrant generation he has returned to the neighborhood of his parents and grandparents. "I felt myself tugged back to Brighton Beach because of my parents. Having them literally two blocks away is a blessing. Family. That's what is important."

With out-migration from the former Soviet Union reduced to a trickle, the story of Soviet Jewish émigrés in New York has become for now a tale of the city and the changes they continue to bring to it. In the last few years, their increasing involvement in New York politics has shifted the city's Jewish political profile, with some districts that were reliably Democratic now in flux. Though Russian émigrés in the city are mostly registered Democrats, they remain swing voters. Since 2000 they have driven both Democratic and Republican victories. Assemblyman Alec Brook-Krasny, a Democrat who won election in 2006, was the country's first Soviet émigré state official. Running against a Republican who was also a Soviet émigré, Brook-Krasny won by tapping the alliances he had painstakingly built with the city's largely Democratic Jewish political establishment (see Soehl 2011). However, in fall 2011, New York's Ninth Congressional district sent a Republican to Washington for the first time since the 1920s. This dramatic upset was in large part determined by a heavy Republican vote among Soviet émigrés in Brooklyn and Queens who cited concern over Israel as the primary factor guiding their vote. Around 80 percent of Soviet émigrés in New York have primary or secondary relatives living in Israel, and their devotion to it is fierce (Gordon 2011; Kliger 2004; Fishman 2006).

How Jewish émigrés from the FSU will vote in future New York elections remains uncertain, but their willingness to break with the politics of a heavily Democratic New York Jewish electorate reflects deep fissures and tensions that continue to separate Soviet Jewish Americans from the larger American Jewish community—even in the most Jewish city in the United States. Though Soviet Jewish émigrés and their children are building bonds with other Jewish New Yorkers through political, cultural, and religious organizations, their poverty, their politics, and their strongly Russified expressions of Jewishness continue to distinguish and separate them from earlier generations of Jewish immigrants to New York. That shows no sign of changing any time soon.

NOTES

1. Although the Soviet Union has been gone for more than twenty years, its politics, bureaucracy, economics, and anti-Semitism have continued to leave a profound

imprint on the hundreds of thousands of Russian-speaking Jewish immigrants and their children who live in New York City and surrounding areas. For that reason, this chapter refers to them as Soviet Jews.

2. This essay was greatly enriched by the research and analysis of Alyssa Penick. It also draws on my own field research in Brighton Beach in the 1980s and 1990s, which is the source of much of the uncited information in this chapter and a number of the quotations.

REFERENCES

Altshuler, Mordecai. 1987. *Soviet Jewry since the Second World War: Populations and Social Structure.* Westport, CT: Greenwood.

Barnard, Anna. 2009. "As One of Their Own Is Tried for Murder, Bukharans Debate Loss of Old Ways." *New York Times,* February 8.

Berger, Paul. 2010. "For Russian Speaking Holocaust Survivors, A Passover to Remember," *The Forward,* April 9.

Birman, Igor. 1979. "Jewish Emigration from the USSR: Some Observations." *Soviet Jewish Affairs* 9 (September): 46–63.

Caroll, Linda. 1993. "Seeking Care in a Strange Land: Medical Culture Shock." *Newsday,* October 10.

Carr, Donna. 1997. "The Jews of Bukhara." Unpublished paper.

Cohen, Steven, Jacob Ukeles, and Ron Miller. 2012. *Jewish Community Study of New York.* New York: UJA Federation of New York.

Finkenauer, James O., and Elin J. Waring. 1998. *Russian Mafia in America: Immigration, Culture and Crime.* Boston: Northeastern University Press.

Fisher, Janon, and Dan Mangan. 2010. "Hushin' Russian in Brooklyn Med 'Fraud'." *New York Post,* July 17.

Fisher, Leon D. 1975. "Initial Experiences in the Resettlement of Soviet Jews in the United States." *Journal of Jewish Communal Service* (March): 275–79.

Fishman, Boris. 2006. "Politborough." *New Republic,* October 6.

——. 2010. "Old Ways." *The Tablet,* November 18.

Friedgut, Theodore. 1989. "Passing Eclipse: The Exodus Movement in the 1980s." In Robert Friedman, ed. *Soviet Jewry in the 1980s: The Politics of Anti-Semitism and Emigration and the Dynamics of Resettlement.* Durham: Duke University Press.

Friedman, Robert I. 1994. "The Organizatsya." *New York Magazine,* November 7.

——. 2000. *Red Mafiya: How the Russian Mob Has Invaded America.* New York: Little, Brown.

Gamboa, Suzanne. 2001. "The Slowing Progress of Immigrants." *Associated Press,* March 28, http://www.cis.org/articles/2001/back401coverage.html.

Garrett, Laurie. 1997. "Crumbled Empire, Shattered Health." *Newsday,* October 28.

Gilbert, Martin. 1984. *The Jews of Hope.* New York: Viking.

Goelman, Zachary. 2008. "Brighton Beach Revisited," *The Jerusalem Report*, March 3.

Gordon, Jerry. 2011. "There's More Than a Palestinian State at Stake for Obama: It's Jewish Votes in 2012." *New English Review*, September 18.

Gorin, Julia. 1995. "Along the Bukharan Broadway." *Newsday*, July 23.

Halberstadt, Anna. 1996. "A Model Assessment of an Émigré Family from the Former Soviet Union." *Journal of Jewish Communal Service* (Summer): 244–55.

Halberstadt, Anna, and Adele Nikolsky. 1996. "Bukharan Jews and Their Adaptation to the United States." *Journal of Jewish Communal Service* (Summer): 298–309.

Holden, Constance. 1990. "No American Dream for Soviet Refugees." *Science*, June 1.

"I'm Not Fleeing. I'm Being Evicted." 1991. *Harper's*, June.

Italiano, Laura, and Phillip Messing. 2005. "Fake Ache Scam." *New York Post*, March 23.

Jacobson, Gaynor. 1975. "Spotlight on Soviet Jewry: Absorption in the USA." *Journal of Jewish Communal Service* (December): 190–94.

Kasinitz, Philip. 2008. "Becoming American, Becoming Minority, Getting Ahead: The Role of Racial and Ethnic Status in the Upward Mobility of the Children of Immigrants." *Annals of the American Academy of Political and Social Science* 620: 253–69.

Kasinitz, Philip, John Mollenkopf, Mary Waters, and Jennifer Holdaway. 2008. *Inheriting the City*. Cambridge, MA: Harvard University Press.

Kliger, Sam. 2004. "Russian Jews in America: Status, Identity and Integration." Paper presented at the conference Russian-Speaking Jewry in Global Perspective: Assimilation, Integration and Community-Building, June 14–16, Bar Ilan University, Israel.

Lakhman, Marina, and David Goldiner. 1999. "Beacon of Liberty for New Russians Filled with Ambition: Immigrants Find Success in the City." *Daily News*, January 31.

Levin, Nora. 1988. *The Jews in the Soviet Union Since 1917*. 2 volumes. New York: New York University Press.

Lewis, Philippa. 1978. "The Jewish Question in the Open, 1968–71." In Lionel Kochan, ed. *The Jews in Soviet Russia Since 1917*. London: Oxford University Press.

Liff, Bob. 1999. "Breaking with Brighton Beach." *Daily News*, March 18.

Low, Albert D. 1990. *Soviet Jewry and Soviet Policy*. New York: Columbia University Press.

"Mafia Power Play: An Investigation into Links between Russian NHL Players and Russian Organized Crime." 1999. *Frontline*, PBS, www.pbs.org/wgbh/pages/frontline/shows/hockey/etc/script.html.

Malcolm, Janet. 2010. "Iphigenia in Forest Hills." *New Yorker*, May 3.

Markowitz, Fran. 1993. *A Community in Spite of Itself: Soviet Jewish Émigrés in New York*. Washington, DC: Smithsonian Institution Press.

Miller, Ron, and Jacob Ukeles. 2004. *Jewish Community Study of New York: 2002*. New York: UJA Federation of New York.

"The Mood of Russia: Time to Shove Off." 2011. *The Economist*, September 10.

Mustain, Gene, and Jerry Capeci. 1997. "Infamous from Moscow to N.Y." *Daily News*, April 21.

New York City Department of City Planning. 2004. *The Newest New Yorkers 2000: Immigrant New York in the New Millennium*. New York: NYC Department of Planning, Population Division.

NYANA. 1996. *Starting Over: The NYANA Resettlement Process*. New York: New York Association for New Americans.

Office of Refugee Resettlement. 1994. *Report to Congress FY 1993, Refugee Resettlement Program*. Washington, DC: U.S. Department of Health and Human Services.

——. 1995. *Report to Congress FY 1994, Refugee Resettlement Program*. Washington, DC: U.S. Department of Health and Human Services.

Orleck, Annelise. 2001. *Soviet Jewish Americans*. Hanover, NH: University Press of New England.

Popper, Nathaniel. 2004. "Jewish Poverty Deepens in New York." *The Forward*, February 6.

Rapfogel, W., I. S. Marcus, and E. Larson. 2007. "Understanding the Jewish Near Poor: An Analysis of the Population and How the Jewish Community Can Serve Them." *Journal of Jewish Communal Service* 82 (1/2): 97–104.

Reminnick, Larissa. 2005. "Being a Woman Is Different Here: Changing Attitudes toward Femininity, Sexuality and Gender Roles among Former Soviet Immigrant Women in the U.S." Working Paper Series No. 13. Boston: Hadassah-Brandeis Institute.

——. 2007. *Russian Jews on Three Continents: Identity, Integration and Conflict*. New Brunswick, NJ: Transaction.

Rosner, Lydia S. 1986. *The Soviet Way of Crime: Beating the System in the Soviet Union and the U.S.A*. South Hadley, MA: Bergin and Garvey.

Rubin, Burton. 1975. "The Soviet Refugees." *Journal of Jewish Communal Service* (December): 195–201.

Sawyer, Thomas E. 1979. *The Jewish Minority in the Soviet Union*. Boulder, CO: Westview.

Simon, Rita J. 1985. *New Lives: The Adjustment of Soviet Jewish Emigres in the United States and Israel*. Lexington, MA: Lexington Books.

Sirotin, Alexander. 1981. "The Wandering Jew." Trans. Annelise Orleck. Unpublished manuscript.

Soehl, Thomas. 2011. "The Ambiguities of Political Opportunity: Political Claims Making of Russian Jewish Immigrants in New York City." Program on International Migration, UCLA, http://escholarship.org/uc/item/9gr107hp, posted July 1.

Sterngold, James. 1998. "Man Convicted in Cosby Death." *New York Times*, July 8.

Sugarman, Rafael. 1992. "The Kindest Cut of All." *Urban Gazette*, December 10.

Tolts, Marc. 2008. "Migration since World War I," in G.D. Hundert, ed., *The YIVO Encyclopedia of Jews in Eastern Europe*. New Haven, CT: Yale University Press.

Tri-State Joint Soviet-Émigré Organized Crime Project. 1995. "The Nature of Russian Émigré Crime in the Tri-State Area." http://www.state.nj.us/sci/pdf/russian.pdf.

Treiman, Daniel. 2003. "Survey Finds Poverty Rate among Jews Soars in N.Y." *The Forward,* June 20.

Tress, Madeline. 1996. "Refugees as Immigrants: Revelations of Labor Market Performance." *Journal of Jewish Communal Service* 72 (4): 326–34.

U.S. Census Bureau. 2009. "American Community Survey, Fact Sheet 2005–2009."

Weinberg, Armin, Sunil Kripilani, Philip L. McCarthy, and Jack Schuli. 1995. "Caring for Survivors of the Chernobyl Disaster: What the Clinician Should Know." *Journal of the American Medical Association* 274: 408–12.

Weinstein, Lewis. 1988. "Soviet Jewry and the American Jewish Community." *American Jewish History* 77: 600–13.

Wiesel, Elie. 1987. *The Jews of Silence: A Personal Report on Soviet Jewry,* expanded edition. New York: Schocken.

Zeltzer-Zubida, Aviva, and Philip Kasinitz. 2005. "The Next Generation: Russian Young Adults in Contemporary New York." *Contemporary Jewry* 25: 193–225.

5. *Chinese*

DIVERSE ORIGINS AND DESTINIES

Min Zhou

> New York offers many fortunes but unequal opportunities to newcomers. Not everyone can make it here. It [New York] is like a happy melting pot for some, a pressure cooker for many others, and still a Dumpster for the unfortunate.
>
> —A *Chinese immigrant*[1]

New York has long been an immigrant gateway city, but until 1970 the majority of immigrants were European. Time has washed off the "colors" of the old-timers from Russia, Italy, and Ireland, "melting" them into an indistinguishable "white" racial group. Since the 1970s, however, a new ethnic mosaic has been in the making as a result of the arrival of hundreds of thousands of newcomers from Asia and the Americas.

This change is evident in any rush-hour subway ride in the morning or evening. An Anglo New Yorker commuting on the number 7 subway train through Queens remarked, "I feel I am riding a train through the globe. There are so many different faces, so many strange languages, and so many unfamiliar mannerisms that I suddenly become an alien. Once the train gets past Shea Stadium and goes underground, I feel I am on the Orient Express."[2] A visitor getting off the train in Flushing encounters a Little Asia. Flushing is often referred to as the Chinatown of Queens, while also known as Koreatown or Little India. A traveler who takes the N train to Brooklyn and gets off at Eighth Avenue comes out of the subway station to find what seems to be a street in China. That is Sunset Park, the Chinatown of Brooklyn.

At the end of the first decade of the twenty-first century, the Chinese were the second largest immigrant group in New York City. Between 1982 and 1989, 72,000 Chinese immigrants (including 10,000 from Hong Kong and 9,000 from Taiwan) entered the city of New York legally (NYCDCP 1992, 1999). Since 1990, hundreds of thousands more have arrived. Post-1990 arrivals have hailed from mainland China, Taiwan, Hong Kong, and other parts of the Chinese diaspora. In all, foreign-born Chinese numbered 351,314 in 2010 (chapter 2, this volume). Together with their native-born coethnics, the number of ethnic Chinese in New York City grew nearly fourteen times in just four decades, from 33,000 in 1960 to 487,532 in 2010.[3]

How are these newest New Yorkers adapting to their new homeland? This chapter explores the processes of transformation and adaptation among new Chinese immigrants in the past forty years and the divergent destinies that these immigrants experience. I use a combination of quantitative and qualitative data, including U.S. census data, immigration statistics from the U.S. Department of Homeland Security, data compiled by the New York City Department of City Planning (NYCDCP), and my own field observations and interviews. Specifically I discuss the changing trends of Chinese immigration, distinct characteristics of the newcomers, new patterns of settlement, and the impacts of immigration on the lives of new immigrants.

CHANGING TRENDS IN CHINESE IMMIGRATION TO NEW YORK CITY

THE EXCLUSION ERA

New York's Chinatown made its initial appearance in the 1870s in the four-block neighborhood across Canal Street from Little Italy in lower east Manhattan (Sung 1987). The city's Chinese population was relatively small but experienced steady growth, from 7,170 to 13,731 between 1900 and 1940, most of them coming to New York from the West Coast. By the 1940s, New York's Chinatown had become a ten-block enclave, accommodating the majority of the Chinese immigrants in the city. This increase in population occurred during the Chinese exclusion era, which began in 1882 when the U.S. Congress passed the Chinese Exclusion Act banning the immigration of Chinese laborers (the act was renewed in 1892 and later extended to exclude all Asian immigrants until World War II). In the exclusion years, Chinese immigrants in New York shared many common characteristics with their coethnics elsewhere in the country. First, most were from villages in the Sze Yap area, speaking Taishanese (a local dialect incomprehensible even to some Cantonese), and from other villages in Sam Yap and the greater Pearl River delta region of Guangdong Province.[4] Second, most left their families behind in China and came to America as sojourners with the aim of making a "gold" fortune and returning home. Third, most were poor and uneducated and had to work at odd jobs that few Americans wanted. Laundrymen, cooks, waiters, and household servants characterized most of the workers in Chinatown. Fourth, they spoke very little English. Not only did they seem unassimilated in the eyes of Americans, they were not allowed to assimilate as the law rendered them "aliens ineligible for citizenship."

POST–WORLD WAR II TRENDS

Chinese exclusion effectively reinforced the bachelors' society. In 1890, there were 495 men per 100 women in New York's Chinese population; by 1940, the sex ratio in New York had become even more skewed with 603 men per 100 women. After the repeal of the Chinese Exclusion Act in 1943 and the passage of the War Bride Act in 1945, Chinese women were allowed into the United States to join their husbands and families, and they comprised more than half of the postwar arrivals from China. As a result, the bachelors' society began to dissolve. However, the number of Chinese immigrants entering the United States each year was still very small because the annual quota was set at 105 (Sung 1987). Legal admissions of Chinese immigrants averaged only 965 annually in the 1950s, a drop from 1,670 in the 1940s when many war brides came.

The surge of Chinese immigration began in the late 1960s, due to the passage of amendments to the Immigration and Nationality Act, also referred to as the Hart-Celler Act of 1965. This act abolished the national origins quota system, lifted the ban on immigration from Asia, and established seven preference categories favoring family reunification and the importation of skilled labor. Since the Hart-Celler Act went into effect in 1968, immigration from China, Hong Kong, and Taiwan has grown at unprecedented rates (see figure 5.1). Altogether from 1970 to 2009, nearly 2 million Chinese immigrants were legally admitted to the United States as permanent residents (U.S. Department of Homeland Security 2009). Driven by international migration, the ethnic Chinese population in the United States grew exponentially, from 237,000 in 1960 to 3.8 million in 2010, when the foreign-born made up about two-thirds of the total. In New York City, Chinese immigrants arrived at an average annual rate of 12,000 in the 1980s and 1990s, accounting for almost 20 percent of all Chinese immigrants legally admitted to the United States (AAFNYCIC 2004; NYCDCP 1992, 1999, 2000). In 2010, New York City had the largest Chinese population of any city outside of Asia (NYCDCP 2011).

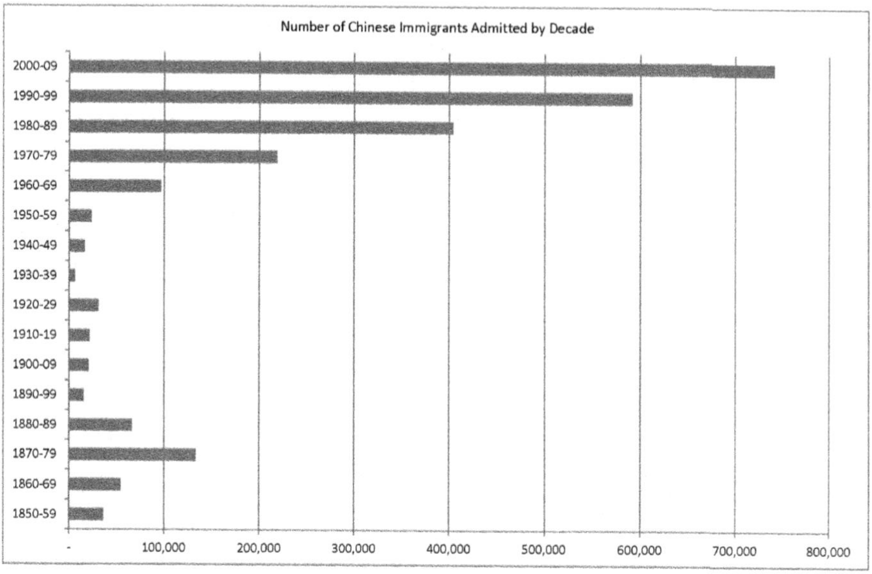

FIGURE 5.1. CHINESE IMMIGRANTS ADMITTED TO THE UNITED STATES, 1850–2009.
Source: U.S. Department of Homeland Security, *Yearbook of Immigration Statistics, 2009*, table 2. See http://www.dhs.gov/xlibrary/assets/statistics/yearbook/2009/ois_yb_2009.pdf.

DRIVING FORCES OF CONTEMPORARY CHINESE IMMIGRATION

Without question, the passage of the Hart-Celler Act of 1965 was critical in accelerating Chinese immigration. However, broader geopolitical factors, independent of or interacting with the act, also account for the surge in contemporary Chinese immigration. Between 1949 and the end of the Chinese Great Cultural Revolution (1966–76), China was sanctioned by the West and isolated from the rest of the world. Emigration from China was highly restricted and communications with overseas relatives were regarded as antirevolutionary and subversive. For many years the government banned the movement of Chinese people across borders and severely punished those who attempted border crossing illegally. Since the 1970s, several historical events have been particularly relevant for Chinese emigration: China gained admission to the United Nations at the expense of Taiwan in 1971; President Nixon visited China in 1972, marking the first official Sino-U.S. contact since the founding of the People's Republic of China; the Great Cultural Revolution ended in 1976 upon the death of Communist Party Chairman Mao Zedong and Premier Zhou Enlai; China and the United States established normal diplomatic relations in 1979; the Chinese government began to aggressively pursue an open-door policy in 1978 and implemented nationwide economic reforms in 1984; also in 1984, China and Britain signed an agreement on the 1997 return of Hong Kong to China; and last but not least, the Chinese military put down a pro-democracy student movement in Beijing's Tiananmen Square in 1989.

In China, liberalized emigration policy, economic reform, and the new opportunity to study abroad were among the most significant factors contributing to emigration. As China opened its door in the late 1970s, it relaxed emigration restrictions. The normalization of Sino-U.S. relations made it possible for relatives of U.S. citizens or longtime U.S. resident aliens to apply for U.S. immigrant visas in China. Initially, most of the U.S.-bound emigrants were from the historically important sending regions in Guangdong Province. Later on, newly established migration networks facilitated emigration from other parts of China.

China's open-door policy also unintentionally created pressure for emigration. Since 1978, China has aggressively pursued its modernization goal through scholarly and technological exchanges. Over the past forty years, China has sent hundreds of thousands of undergraduate and graduate students and visiting scholars to the United States, as well as to other Western countries, for postgraduate education and advanced professional training. During the 2009–10 academic year alone, nearly 128,000 international students (both graduate and undergraduate students) from China were studying in American universities and colleges, making China the number one source of international students in the U.S. higher education system (IIE 2010). A significant proportion of the students who come to the United States, estimated at two-thirds or more, decide to stay rather than return to China (Orleans 1988). Many foreign students find permanent employment in the United States after completing their studies or practical training. In fact, most employer-sponsored immigrants from China have had their nonimmigrant student visas adjusted to permanent residency status in the United States. Moreover, the 1989 crackdown on the student pro-democracy movement in Beijing's Tiananmen Square led to special U.S. legislation, the Chinese Student Protection Act of 1992, granting permanent residency to more than 48,000 Chinese nationals (mostly students and visiting scholars) and their families between 1993 and 1994 (USINS 1995, 1996:19).[5]

Since the 1980s, many tens of thousands of Chinese from the Fuzhou area of Fujian Province have come to the United States, a significant fraction of them undocumented and who have paid enormous fees to smugglers—more than $70,000 a person in 2010—to make the journey to New York. As the anthropologist Kenneth Guest notes, rural Fuzhounese continue to leave their homes in large numbers on an expensive and often dangerous trip despite the prospect of difficult work in restaurants, garment shops, and construction trades in the

United States to make more money than they could imagine earning at home, where the annual income in a farming or fishing village ranges from $500 to $750 and in export processing factories about $1,500 in 2010. "Outmigration has become part of the local culture of the towns and villages outside Fuzhou. . . . For a down payment of 10 to 20 percent, a villager can begin his journey arranged by any of the local snakeheads—the Chinese term for smugglers. . . . Snakeheads paint their cell phone numbers and post advertisements on the walls of stores, temples, and town halls" (Guest 2011:32–33).

As for immigration from Taiwan and Hong Kong, it was political uncertainty and anxiety about the future that spurred emigration in the late twentieth century. The ousting of Taiwan from the United Nations and the normalization of China-U.S. diplomatic relations in the 1970s caused a huge volume of capital outflow, as well as an exodus of middle-class Chinese to the United States from Taiwan (Li 2009). The return of Hong Kong to the sovereignty of China in 1997 also triggered the exodus of thousands of capitalists and members of the middle and upper-middle classes who sought safe havens in the West. The flight of middle-class professionals and businessmen coincided with the increasing globalization of the U.S. economy, which has attracted transnational capital investment and favored the importation of highly skilled foreign labor (Liu and Cheng 1994; Skeldon 1994). Starting in the early 1980s, capitalists from rapidly growing Asian economies saw the United States as a modern gold mine for investment. Many overseas Chinese from Hong Kong and Taiwan invested in Manhattan's Chinatown and new suburban Chinese communities (Li 2009; Lin 1998; Wong 1998).

Last but not least, the end of the Vietnam War in 1975 and subsequent political repression in Vietnam pushed thousands of refugees out of their homeland. The United States resettled over 600,000 of them, including some 200,000 ethnic Chinese, whose admission was not subject to the per-country limit. Many Sino-Vietnamese went to live in Chinatowns or in neighborhoods settled by other Chinese immigrants.

CHINESE NEWCOMERS TO NEW YORK

DIVERSE ORIGINS

During the past four decades, nearly one in four Chinese immigrants arriving in the United States has moved to New York City. Unlike old-timers, most of the new Chinese immigrants flew to New York directly from Asia, rather than remigrating after spending time in America's West. The majority came to join their families, while others were sponsored by their U.S. employers (Sung 1987; Wong

1987; Zhou 1992). For example, in 2009, about two-thirds of all Chinese immigrants receiving lawful permanent residence in the United States were admitted as family-based immigrants while 18 percent were employment-based immigrants (Terrazas and Batalova 2010). There were also those who were smuggled in without proper documents (Chin 1997; Kwong 1997; Liang 2001).

Diversity in origin is a distinct characteristic of contemporary Chinese immigration. Chinese immigrants now come from a much wider range of places than the few rural villages in the Sze Yap area of Guangdong Province that sent Chinese to New York in the exclusion era. In 2000, 75 percent of Chinese New Yorkers were foreign-born; 74 percent of the foreign-born were from China, 11 percent from Hong Kong, 8 percent from Taiwan, and 7 percent from other parts of the world (AAFNYCIC 2004). Since the 1990s, Chinese immigrants from Southeast Asia and the Americas have become increasingly visible in New York City. Those from Guangdong Province are from large cities as well as rural areas. Immigrants from outside Guangdong Province are from many places that historically sent few emigrants to the United States, including the capital cities of Beijing, Shanghai, and Tianjin, coastal cities in Fujian, Zhejiang, and Shangdong provinces, and inland cities in Sichuan and Hunan. Few Chinese immigrants today understand Cantonese or Toishanese, the dialect of the old-timers from South China. Among the more recent arrivals, those who speak Mandarin are more numerous than those who speak Cantonese. In Manhattan's Chinatown, Cantonese is still widely spoken, but Mandarin is increasingly common given the influx of immigrants from the Fuzhou area of Fujian Province who speak Mandarin and the Fuzhou dialect, as well as the Minnan dialect; the Fuzhounese now constitute a significant subenclave that has greatly expanded over the last two decades (Guest 2011; Kwong 1997).

DIVERSE SOCIOECONOMIC BACKGROUNDS

Contemporary Chinese immigrants also have diverse socioeconomic backgrounds. Some arrived with little money, minimum education, and few job skills, forcing them to take low-wage jobs and settle in deteriorating urban neighborhoods. Others have come with family savings, education, and skills. According to the 2010 American Community Survey, 60 percent of foreign-born Chinese adults in New York City had completed high school and 25 percent had a college degree (chapter 2, this volume). Most remarkable are foreign-born Taiwanese; seven out of ten Taiwanese-born adults in the United States in 2008 had a bachelor's degree or higher (S. Lin 2010). Not surprisingly, a higher proportion of foreign-born Taiwanese hold professional occupations than other Chinese foreign-born, no doubt an indication of employer-sponsored or investment migration among the Taiwanese that started before the mass emigration from China.

Compared to Chinese immigrants in the entire country, those in New York City have a lower proportion of college graduates, lower median family and per capita income, and a higher poverty rate (AAFNYCIC 2004). Although New York City receives a disproportionate number of low-skilled Chinese immigrants, not all are confined to low-paying jobs at the very bottom of the labor market. Highly skilled immigrants, especially those who received their graduate education in the United States, are able to enter the mainstream labor market as professionals in such occupations as finance, science and engineering, insurance, real estate, education, and even various levels of the government. Still others are self-employed. Immigrants with high levels of human capital (education and skills) as well as those with limited human capital but experience in a trade tend to be attracted to entrepreneurship, especially in business specialties where the Chinese are concentrated and which offer opportunities and resources for business creation. In sum, Chinese immigrants in New York have a wide variety of jobs, ranging from cooks, waiters, seamstresses, and housekeepers to research and development scientists, computer engineers, laboratory technicians, Wall Street stock brokers, midtown bankers, and "astronaut" (transnational) businessmen.

NEW PATTERNS OF SETTLEMENT

Historically, the majority of Chinese immigrants who came to New York clustered in Manhattan's Chinatown,[6] but by 2000 less than 15 percent had settled there. In fact, many immigrants have bypassed the century-old enclave to settle in the outer boroughs, where they have formed new Chinatowns while others have moved to upscale neighborhoods in affluent suburbs. Within New York City, as chapter 2 shows, the borough of Queens had the largest Chinese immigrant population in 2010 (150,274), followed by Brooklyn (126,309) and Manhattan (59,622). Figure 5.2 shows that ethnic Chinese were clustered in particular neighborhoods: in Manhattan's expanded Chinatown, in the western and southern parts of Brooklyn (Sunset Park, Bay Ridge, Bensonhurst, and Sheepshead Bay), and northeastern and north-central parts of Queens (Flushing, Elmhurst, and Woodside). In suburban communities, many Chinese have moved to areas associated with universities or high-technology corporations such as Stony Brook on Long Island and Princeton Junction, Plainsboro, and the Route 1 high-tech corridor in New Jersey.

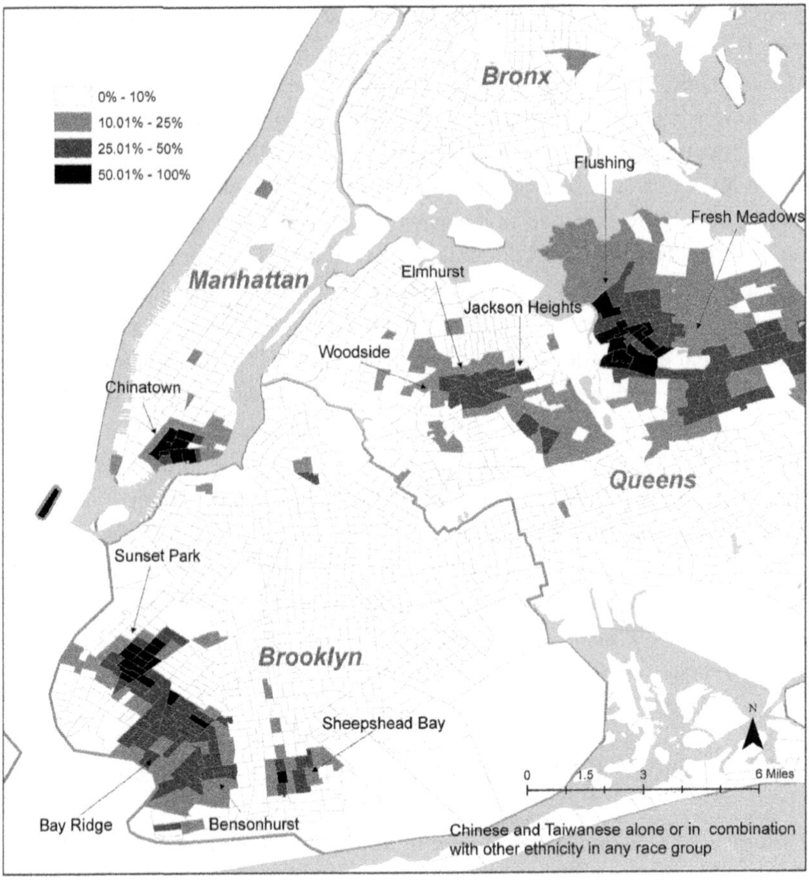

FIGURE 5.2. RESIDENTIAL DISTRIBUTION OF CHINESE AMERICANS IN NEW YORK CITY, 2010.
Source: U.S. Census of Population, 2010.

MANHATTAN'S CHINATOWN

Manhattan's Chinatown is a long-standing immigrant community. Only 120 Chinese lived in New York City according to the 1860 census, less than 1 percent of the total Chinese population (63,109) in the United States at the time (Zhou 1992). Legend has it that when a Chinese merchant, Wo Kee, opened a general store at 8 Mott Street in 1870, coethnic immigrants began to gravitate toward the area (Lee 1960; Sung 1987). The first eastbound group settled in a three-street area (Mott, Pell, and Doyer) on the Lower East Side of Manhattan (Jackson 1983; Wong 1987). Until the 1970s, most Chinese immigrants entering New York made Chinatown their home. Although decentralization of the Chinese population began as early as the 1950s, substantial out-migration and outer-borough settlement were not common until much later. According to census counts in 2000, 56 percent of Manhattan's Chinatown's residents were Chinese, up from 32 percent in 1970; out of fourteen census tracts in Chinatown's core, seven had a Chinese majority and another three contained 25 percent or more Chinese (Zhou 1992; Zhou et al. 2013). Census counts are no doubt too low and miss many undocumented immigrants who are too frightened to cooperate with census staff. Probably at least twice as many Chinese live in Manhattan's Chinatown and the surrounding area as census figures indicate.

Many Chinatown residents are still Cantonese from the traditional sending regions in South China. In recent years, a noticeable group of Sino-Vietnamese has settled in Chinatown; most are fluent in Cantonese and share many cultural characteristics with the Cantonese, as they originally immigrated to Vietnam from Guangdong and Guangxi provinces. The Fuzhounese are now a very significant group and, according to some sources, may even constitute a majority in lower Manhattan's Chinese community (Guest 2011). Because of cultural differences and coethnic stereotyping, Fuzhounese, who have generally arrived as undocumented immigrants, do not mingle with the Cantonese and have built their own subenclave in the area around East Broadway under the Manhattan Bridge and into neighborhoods of the Lower East Side (Guest 2011; Kwong 1997; Zhao 2008). Wherever they come from, many of Chinatown's residents are recent arrivals, have low levels of education, speak little or no English, hold low-wage jobs, and live in poverty.

In Chinatown, walk-up tenement and loft buildings line the streets. Overcrowding characterizes Chinatown living. Over 90 percent of residents live in rental housing and many housing units are in poor and deteriorating condition. New immigrants arriving in Chinatown are often shocked by the squalid living that provides a striking contrast to the glamorous skyscrapers in the background. One middle-aged woman who arrived to join her daughter's family in Chinatown recalled:

> I'd never imagined my daughter's family living in this condition. My daughter, who was about to give birth to her first child, lived with her husband in a one-room apartment. When I arrived in New York, my daughter had to squeeze me into their apartment. They had only one queen-size bunk bed that almost filled the room. I slept, and later with the baby, at the bottom, and my daughter and her husband on top. In China, I had a spacious three-bedroom apartment. It was just like hell living there.[7]

This woman's family eventually bought a house in Brooklyn. Like her, many immigrants came from relatively affluent middle-class backgrounds but lacked the money when they got here to afford adequate housing. Others who came from the working class seemed more optimistic when they first got to New York. One Chinatown man remarked, "Sharing a two-bedroom apartment with another family in Chinatown wasn't that bad. In China, I lived just like that and there were many people who lived in worse conditions. Here, you are pretty sure that this would change in a few years. But in China, you were not so sure."[8] Many Chinese immigrants reluctantly tolerate dank and filthy cubicle dwellings in the hope that someday they will move out of Chinatown. Indeed, many have been able to do so. In Chinatown, most residents are either recent arrivals or the elderly; there are very few second-generation young people who are raising their families there.

For many Chinese immigrants, Chinatown's inferior living is offset by the easy access to jobs and services. With the continuous arrival of new immigrants and the tremendous influx of foreign capital, the physical boundaries of Chinatown have expanded so that it now covers a huge area in lower Manhattan, including parts of the City Hall area, Little Italy, and the Lower East Side. The ethnic enclave economy has also been transformed. During the 1930s and 1940s, Chinatown's ethnic economy was highly concentrated in restaurant and laundry businesses. By the 1970s, the laundry business had shrunk substantially and the garment industry had become one of Chinatown's backbone industries. In the 1980s, Chinatown's garment industry had grown to more than 500 factories, run by Chinese entrepreneurs and employing more than 20,000 immigrant Chinese, mostly women. By the end of the twentieth century, many garment shops had moved out of Manhattan's Chinatown, and the garment industry there had shrunk to 240 factories employing 14,000 (Chin 2005). Since then, there have been further contractions. While this industry was still important in 2010 for low-skilled Chinese immigrant women in New York City, only an estimated 70 to 100 garment factories remained in Chinatown (Zhou et al. 2013).

The restaurant business, another backbone industry in Chinatown, has continued to prosper. Listed restaurants run by Chinese grew from 304 in 1958 to 781 in 1988, employing at least 15,000 immigrant Chinese workers (Kwong 1987; Zhou 1992). Since the 1990s, the restaurant trade has grown to include upscale places catering to suburban middle-class coethnics and non-Chinese tourists.

Another development among Fuzhounese immigrants is that East Broadway has become the staging platform for their circulation beyond New York to jobs as cooks, waiters, delivery men, busboys, and receptionists in the "ethnic economy of all-you-can-eat buffets and take-out restaurants" across the United States (Guest 2011:34). Buses owned by Fuzhounese entrepreneurs carry workers, as well as restaurant supplies, to states in the Midwest and South; workers return regularly to lower Manhattan "for rest and recuperation between strenuous jobs" before seeking out jobs again, posted by area code, type of work, and salary, in East Broadway employment agencies (Guest 2011:35–36). Fuzhounese entrepreneurs have also established passenger vans that link Manhattan's Chinatown to Flushing and Sunset Park, charging less than the New York subway and bus fare and delivering passengers door to door (Guest 2011:37).

In addition, various other businesses have experienced growth, ranging from grocery stores, import-export companies, barber shops, and beauty salons to such professional services as banks, law firms, financial, insurance, and real estate agencies, and doctors' and herbalists' clinics. Chinatown's economic development is described by the sociologist Jan Lin (1998) as a two-circuit phenomenon embedded in a postindustrial global city: sweatshops and tenements are the lower circuit, characterized by low-wage jobs, unskilled labor, sidewalk peddlers, and crowding or slum living; finance and redevelopment are the upper circuit, characterized by high-skilled and professional service jobs, capital-intensive redevelopment, transnational businesses, and modern tourism. In recent years, Chinatown has been built up and much of the Chinese investment goes to ethnoburbs or other emerging Chinese communities, but the Chinese two-circuit development in New York and other major metropolises still prevails (Li 2009; J. Lin 2010).

Chinatown has also witnessed a growth of civic and religious institutions. In Manhattan's Chinatown, family or clan associations, hometown associations, and merchants' associations and tongs ("brotherhoods" based on professions) were traditional ethnic organizations that were oriented toward cultural preservation and protecting Chinese immigrants against racial discrimination. They provided a refuge for sojourning laborers, meeting their basic needs, such as housing, employment, and various social services, as well as organizing economic activities (Kuo 1977; Zhou and Kim 2001). Some of these traditional organizations grew into underground societies that profited from illicit activities such as partitioning territories, extortion for business protection, exploitation of immigrant labor, gambling, prostitution, and drugs (Dillon 1962; Kuo 1977; Sung 1987). Perhaps the most important social organization was the Chinese Consolidated Benevolent Association (CCBA), which was established as an apex group representing some sixty Chinatown organizations, including different family and district associations, the guilds, the tongs, the Chamber of Commerce, and the Nationalist Party. Controlled by a few powerful tongs, the CCBA cooperated with all ethnic associations and operated as an unofficial government in Chinatown (Kuo 1977; Sung 1987; Zhou 2009).

In recent years, the rapid change in the nature of Chinese immigration has created pressing demands for services associated with resettlement and adjustment problems that have overwhelmed the existing traditional organizations in Chinatown. To accommodate these changes, traditional organizations have been pressured to redefine their role, and various new organizations have been established. A glance at the Chinese Consumer Yellow Pages New York City listing in 2011 reveals forty-four traditional Chinese associations, over fifty voluntary civic associations, thirty nonprofit community-based organizations, thirty-one ethnic employment agencies, fifty career training schools, thirty-five Chinese- and English language schools, nineteen educational consulting services, forty-seven after-school tutoring programs, thirteen dancing, music, and martial arts studios, twenty-one elderly or day care centers, and fifty-five churches and temples.[9] Except for traditional ethnic organizations, some of which have been around for more than a hundred years, most of these establishments have emerged since the 1980s and are located in Manhattan's Chinatown or in new satellite Chinatowns in Flushing, Queens, and Sunset Park, Brooklyn.

Traditional ethnic institutions have changed their orientation from sojourning to settlement and assimilation. To appeal to the settlement demands of new immigrants and their families, the CCBA established a Chinese language school, an adult English evening school, and a career training center, and instituted a variety of social service programs, including employment referral and job training services. The CCBA-operated New York Chinese School is perhaps the largest children- and youth-oriented organization in Chinatown. The school annually (not including summer) enrolls about several thousand Chinese children, from preschool to twelfth grade, in their Chinese language and specialty classes (e.g., band, choir, piano, cello, violin, tai chi, ikebana, dancing, and Chinese painting). The Chinese language classes run from 3:00 to 6:30 P.M. daily after regular school hours. Students usually spend one hour on regular school homework and two hours on Chinese language or other selected specialties. The school also has English classes for immigrant youths and adult immigrant workers.

The Chinese-American Planning Council (CPC), established in the late 1960s in Chinatown, is a rival organization to the CCBA, representing an assimilationist and mainstream agenda. Led by educated Chinese Americans in the U.S.-born second and 1.5 generation (who came to the United States as young children), the CPC has challenged the traditional patriarchal structure and conservative stance of the CCBA through grassroots class mobilization and obtaining support from the federal and local government and private foundations. Aiming to provide "access to services, skills and resources toward the goal of economic self sufficiency and integration into the American mainstream" (CPC 1993), the CPC offers a number of programs targeted at high-risk youth, such as drug use prevention and counseling, and also provides recreational activities for young people by renting places where they can play pool or video games and have parties and by organizing free field trips, shows, and museum visits (Kuo 1977). Most of these programs have continued, expanded, and diversified in recent years.

Many smaller civic and voluntary ethnic organizations have also been established to address concerns and demands of new immigrants and their children. The Chinatown History Museum, now the Museum of Chinese in the Americas, was established in 1980 primarily as a history project for reclaiming, preserving, and sharing Chinese American history and culture with a broad audience. The member-supported museum, now expanded and located in a new building designed by the architect Maya Lin, provides an array of educational and cultural programs for Chinese Americans as well as the general public. Ethnic religious institutions have also played an important role in helping immigrants adjust to life in the United States. Although Chinese immigrants were often not religious in China, in New York many initially affiliated with religious institutions, including Christian churches and Buddhist and Taoist temples, for practical support and later were converted through intense participation (Guest 2003; Yang and Tamney 2006).

Overall, the growth of the ethnic economy, ethnic organizations, and nonprofit community-based organizations in the last several decades has strengthened and expanded existing community social structures. The ethnic community, in turn, has furnished a protective social environment, helping immigrants cope with racism, unemployment, family disruption, school dropouts, drug abuse, and crime and providing access to resources that help them and their children adjust to and, in some cases, move ahead in mainstream American society (Zhou 1992, 2009). A counterargument is that Chinatown's enclave economy reinforces the traditional patriarchal social structure, privileging the elite, while exacerbating intraethnic conflicts and trapping working-class immigrants in permanent subordination (Kwong 1987, 1997). Another important question is how Manhattan's Chinatown will change and adapt in the face of gentrifying pressures—and rising rents for residents and businesses. Already, boutique hotels, high-rent office spaces, and luxury condominium apartments occupy many spaces that formerly housed warehouses and garment factories that provided jobs, clients, and customers for the local garment and restaurant economies. Whether and how gentrification will intensify—and how extensive its impact will be on Chinese immigrant residents and community institutions—are uncertain issues that have significant implications for the future of Chinatown as a viable immigrant gateway and venue for immigrant entrepreneurship (Guest 2011:42).

FLUSHING: THE SECOND CHINATOWN

Before the surge in contemporary immigration, the Flushing neighborhood in north-central Queens was mainly a white middle-income area, whose residents were of Jewish, Irish, Italian, and German ancestry. In 1960, 97 percent of the population was non-Hispanic white. The downtown area, especially the blocks within walking distance of the subway and the Long Island Railroad station, was a mixture of multifamily apartment buildings and low-density units; single and two-family houses, originally built for middle-income families, increased in number with distance from downtown.

Prior to the 1970s, nonwhites were not welcome in Flushing. A longtime Chinese resident arrived from China in 1946 to join her white American husband in Jamaica, Queens. When they decided to move to Flushing she sent her husband to look for housing, she explained, "because they [whites] didn't want to see Chinese here. At that time, there were few Chinese in the community. I was not the only one, but there weren't many." According to this resident, in the early 1960s, the Flushing business district had only one Chinese restaurant and one Chinese laundry.[10] In more affluent parts of Flushing in the 1950s, there were incidents of neighborhood action attempting to prevent Chinese families from moving into the area.

By the turn of the twenty-first century Flushing had a different face. It is often referred to as the second Chinatown, as well as Little Taipei. However, Flushing does not match Manhattan's Chinatown in ethnic density. Also, the ethnic label is highly contested as Flushing is not dominated by a single ethnic group. The core of Flushing, the area surrounding downtown (defined by eleven census tracts), is heavily Asian, with large numbers of Chinese, Koreans, and Indians.[11] By 2010, Asians were 68 percent of the neighborhood's population and whites had declined to only 8 percent; all but one of the eleven census tracts had an Asian majority (ranging from 57 to 85 percent Asian).

Flushing's Chinese are predominantly foreign-born and come from Taiwan, mainland China, and Hong Kong. Although most Taiwanese prefer Los Angeles—less than a fifth of the Taiwanese immigrants in the United States live in New York City—Taiwanese are very visible in Flushing. Among Chinese immigrants, those from Taiwan are significantly better educated and more concentrated in professional occupations. Many Taiwanese immigrants first came to Flushing because they did not identify with Manhattan's Chinatown, which was dominated by Cantonese culture and working-class immigrants. Moreover, Taiwanese had the educational backgrounds and economic resources to build their own enclave away from the existing center of Chinese settlement (Zhou and Logan 1991). Once the Taiwanese movement to Flushing began, other Chinese followed, and after a while a new type of immigrant enclave emerged that includes many from the mainland as well.

With the injection of massive amounts of capital and the influx of affluent, entrepreneurial, and highly skilled immigrants from Taiwan, Flushing's Chinese enclave economy began to develop in the 1980s. Property values in Flushing increased 50 to 100 percent during the 1980s, and commercial vacancy rates plummeted (Parvin 1991:22). Since 1975, new retail and office development has rejuvenated the downtown area. At present, the business center has expanded in all directions from the core. Modern office complexes house banks and service-oriented firms owned by Taiwanese immigrants and transnational Taiwanese, as well as subsidiary firms from the Asian Pacific. In the heart of the downtown commercial and transportation hub, the multilingual signs of several mainstream bank branches and Asian-owned banks stand at the busiest intersection. In what was until recently an aging neighborhood falling into decay is a vibrant scene of ethnic businesses, ranging from mom-and-pop stores to large supermarkets and office buildings. Stretching up and down Main Street and onto the side streets, Chinese restaurants and shops, interspersed with green groceries, drug stores, and fast-food restaurants, give the area an unmistakable look of Chinatown.

But it is not quite a new Chinatown. Flushing's commercial core is also filled with Korean, Indian, Pakistani, and Bangladeshi restaurants and stores, packed into shop fronts along the main streets. Korean, Indian, Pakistani, and Bangladeshi immigrants think of Flushing as their own community, just as the Chinese do. Suburban Chinese come to the neighborhood for multiple purposes, for example, to bring their children to Flushing's Chinese Cultural Center for Saturday afternoon language classes and recreational activities. While children are at the center, their parents usually shop at the local grocery and specialty stores. Others come to Flushing to study or browse in the crowded municipal public library that owns books, magazines, and newspapers in different Asian languages, staying afterward to shop and perhaps eat at one of the many ethnic restaurants.

The business expansion of the Chinese community is particularly noteworthy. Chinese businesses are booming as the rate of immigrant entrepreneurship remains high. There are as many Chinese realtors today as restaurants, and a substantial number of doctor and dentist offices and pharmacies. The development of Flushing as a comprehensive business center means that suburban Chinese residents no longer have to go to Manhattan's Chinatown to visit a restaurant or shop, or for Chinese cultural activities. Although Flushing is quite far from Manhattan's Chinatown, the subway makes the commute relatively easy. Many Chinese immigrants living in Flushing still commute to Chinatown to work or shop.

In recent years, the immigrant Chinese in Flushing have become more actively involved in local politics, mostly through direct political participation (Lin 1998; Lien 2006). They have formed various civic organizations, the most prominent being the Chinese American Voters Association, that work closely with ethnic businesses and other non-Chinese community-based organizations. Common economic concerns have encouraged different immigrant groups to work together to improve the neighborhood's image and to mediate interethnic misunderstanding and conflicts. New ethnic associations have organized street cleaning campaigns and voter registration drives, and have lobbied the city on a wide range of issues. In the early 1990s, eight of Community Board 7's forty-eight members were Asian; as of 2011, fourteen of the fifty-member board were Asian. The Chinese played an important role in the Downtown Flushing Development Corporation and other community organizations, such as the Friend's Reconciliation Project, which served to resolve neighbor disputes (Chen 1992).

The Chinese in Flushing have gained political influence as well in recent years. The election of John Chun Liu to represent a district including Flushing on the city council in 2001 was an important milestone: he was the first Asian American elected to the city council. Liu was born in Taiwan, migrated to the United States with his family at age 5, and after receiving his bachelor's degree in mathematical physics worked as a manager at a major management consulting firm. In 2009, when Liu won the race for New York City comptroller—becoming the first Asian American elected to a citywide office in New York City—he was succeeded on the city council by the Hong Kong–born businessman Peter Koo, who owns a chain of drugstores in Flushing. Koo, who started his American life working at Kentucky Fried Chicken, was an active member of Community Board 7, which represents Flushing and a few other neighborhoods. He has been called the mayor of Flushing because of his active involvement in civic organizations, his accessibility to the public, his philanthropic endeavors, and his leadership role in the business community, serving as the president of the Flushing Chinese Business Association.[12] Two other Chinese American "firsts" in New York City politics should also be noted. In 2009, Hong Kong–born Margaret S. Chin became the first Chinese American elected to the city council representing District 1, which includes Manhattan's Chinatown, where she grew up. More recently, in 2012, Queens-born Grace Meng, the daughter of Taiwanese immigrants, became New York City's first Asian American elected to Congress, representing a newly drawn Queens district that includes Flushing.

Flushing's Chinese community started as a mainly middle-class ethnic enclave but has become more diverse in terms of class over time. The ethnic economy has attracted growing numbers of low-skilled working-class immigrants. For example, many mainland Chinese, mostly of urban working-class background, have settled in Flushing because of the conveniences offered and job opportunities. Also, middle-class neighborhood pioneers have sent for their relatives—many of whom are less skilled and have fewer resources than their predecessors. The shift in class status has become increasingly visible since the mid-1990s. Nowadays, Chinese immigrants often refer to Flushing as the second Chinatown rather than Little Taipei, implying the increased visibility of immigrants from the mainland. The class diversity among Flushing's Chinese has important implications. For Chinese immigrants, class segmentation means greater social service burdens and higher risk of bearing a dual stigma—foreign and poor. More Chinese immigrants see Flushing as a temporary home on the route to suburbia. Since the mid-1990s, many of the more affluent Chinese immigrants have moved from Flushing to bedroom communities in Long Island, New Jersey, and Connecticut.

SUNSET PARK

Sunset Park is a working-class neighborhood in Brooklyn originally settled by European immigrants living in two- or three-story houses and brownstones that line surrounding streets. It is conveniently located along the B, N, and R subway lines and just about thirty minutes by subway from Manhattan's Chinatown. As in Flushing, earlier European immigrants and their children started gradually moving to the suburbs in the late 1960s, leaving many absentee-owned houses and many storefronts vacant. As white residents slowly abandoned the neighborhood, ethnic minorities and new immigrants, first Dominicans, then Puerto Ricans, then Asians and Arabs, began to move in (Winnick 1990). Like Manhattan's Chinatown, Sunset Park is dominated by renter-occupied housing. Most of the housing was built prior to 1950 but, unlike Manhattan's Chinatown, there has been little new real estate development in the neighborhood. In the neighborhood's core (defined by nine census tracts),[13] non-Hispanic whites went from 51 percent of the population in 1980 to 22 percent in 2000, while the Chinese increased from four percent to nearly a quarter.

Sunset Park's Chinese community, anchored by Eighth Avenue, houses recent Chinese immigrant arrivals as well as former Chinatown residents, who are mostly of working-class background. Some of the former Chinatown residents were families resettling in Sunset Park as they attained a measure of economic mobility; others were pushed out of Chinatown because of overcrowding and the fear that their teenage children might be pressured into joining gangs.

Sunset Park has offered affordable housing and easy access to Chinatown. The more upwardly mobile immigrant Chinese were unlikely to move to Sunset Park because of the neighborhood's working-class characteristics, but some have purchased houses there as rental property. Less upwardly mobile, hard-working immigrants often have been able to buy a house in Sunset Park on the condition that they rent out part of it to coethnic immigrant families to help meet the hefty monthly mortgage payments. Mr. Fu of Brooklyn's Community Planning Board explained that with continued high immigration from China and Hong Kong, "more and more Chinese will be coming to New York. There is no more room in Manhattan, and Queens is too expensive for newcomers. Brooklyn, being affordable and easily accessible, is the logical place to be" (Zhou 1992:191–92). With the revitalization of Sunset Park owing to the Chinese influx and growing gentrification of parts of the community, rents are now rising there, so that significant numbers of Chinese are moving further afield in Brooklyn, settling along the subway lines in Bensonhurst and Avenue U (Guest 2011; Hum 2004).

In revitalizing Sunset Park through home ownership, the arrival of immigrant Chinese families has attracted more immigrants from Manhattan's Chinatown and from abroad. Many of Sunset Park's Chinese immigrants are Cantonese from the mainland and Hong Kong, but a large number, perhaps by now a majority, are Fuzhounese, who have also moved into the neighborhood, often living in basement or subdivided units rented from coethnic homeowners (Guest 2011; Kwong 1997).

As increasing numbers of Chinese immigrant families moved into Sunset Park, so did ethnic businesses. The ethnic economy that has developed along Eighth Avenue between 39th and 65th streets can trace its origin to the opening of Fung Wong Supermarket, owned by a Hong Kong immigrant, Tsang Sun (Sunny) Mui in 1986 (Aloff 1997; Mustain 1997). In recent years, the number of garment factories has grown along with ethnic service-oriented businesses, such as restaurants, grocery stores, beauty salons, herbal medicine stores, health clinics, and accounting and legal offices. Immigrant Chinese often call Sunset Park *Bat Dai Do* (in Cantonese) or *Ba Da Dao* (in Mandarin), a translation of Eighth Avenue, which symbolically means the road to good fortune or prosperity. Like Manhattan's and Flushing's Chinatowns, Sunset Park has risen as an important community center serving to accommodate the pressing needs of new immigrants for jobs, housing, and a hospitable neighborhood in which to raise their children.

CAUSES AND CONSEQUENCES OF ETHNIC CLUSTERING

Even as New York City's Chinese immigrants have moved to new neighborhoods in Queens and Brooklyn, there has been a trend to continue to cluster together. This pattern of residential dispersion and concentration has to do with a number of factors.

The dispersion to new areas in the city is related to Chinese immigrants' diverse socioeconomic backgrounds. Highly skilled and economically resourceful Chinese immigrants have often bypassed Manhattan's Chinatown to buy homes in outer-borough middle-class neighborhoods without ever setting foot in Chinatown; they have been able to do so because they have stable incomes secured by well-paying professional jobs in the mainstream economy. Many of these affluent individuals have bought homes in Queens, where they can enjoy a semi-suburban life while also living close to their jobs in Manhattan. Low-skilled immigrants without well-paying jobs in the mainstream economy may also be able to buy homes in Queens or Brooklyn but must do so differently; they pool resources from extended families to purchase multifamily housing units, so that they can share the cost among several subfamilies or rent out part of the homes to other immigrants to help with mortgage payments. For many Chinese, purchasing a home, rather than improving English or advancing to a more desirable occupation, is considered a major achievement and a symbol of success in life.

Ethnic networks and ethnic preferences are important in ethnic clustering. Where one lives depends on whom one knows. Because of limited English proficiency, many Chinese immigrants depend on family or friendship networks to find work and housing. Family members and friends spread the word or obtain information about housing availability through informal social contacts. Chinese homeowners prefer Chinese renters who share the same language and culture and they put advertisements in Chinese-language newspapers to find renters.

The reliance on family members and friends has a direct effect on the concentration of immigrant Chinese from the same dialect group. Immigrant Chinese from different places of origin do not necessarily speak the same language, and a language barrier often separates Cantonese speakers from traditional sending regions in Guangdong and Mandarin speakers from Taiwan and elsewhere in the mainland. As a result, few Taiwanese are interested in living in Manhattan's Chinatown. Although Sunset Park was initially settled by Cantonese-speaking immigrants from Guangdong and Hong Kong, in recent years it has drawn large numbers from Fujian Province who speak Mandarin as well as the Fuzhou and Minnan dialects. If language and family networks help explain settlement patterns, ethnic realtors play an important role, too. For newcomers, coethnic realtors are indispensable in the housing business. Realtors not only help immigrants purchase housing but also steer them into particular neighborhoods (Zhou 1992, 2009).

Another factor explaining residential patterns is immigrants' dependency on the ethnic enclave economy. Regardless of where they live, most immigrant Chinese are tied to the opportunities offered by Manhattan's Chinatown (Zhou and Logan 1991). One of the most important considerations in residential location for Chinese immigrants is convenient access to Chinatown, and ethnic businesses, via public transportation. The neighborhood where they live must be within easy walking distance of bus and subway lines that can get them to work quickly. Those with disadvantages associated with immigrant status, such as lack of English language ability and lack of information about jobs and ties to individuals in the mainstream economy, can find work in the ethnic economy. Also, ethnic banks and credit institutions in the enclave facilitate home financing for coethnic immigrants. In terms of time and distance, Flushing, Sunset Park, and most of the other neighborhoods with sizeable Chinese populations are reasonably close to Manhattan's Chinatown and other job centers and significant Chinese ethnic communities in the city.

Because ethnic networking is a primary way that immigrants from diverse socioeconomic backgrounds are channeled into middle-class neighborhoods throughout the city, it has contributed to class segmentation within new ethnic enclaves. For example, Flushing started out as a new type of ethnic enclave: Mandarin-speaking and rich in financial and human capital. Most of the earlier Chinese immigrants in Flushing were from Taiwan. Investors from Hong Kong and mainland China, as well as non-Cantonese-speaking professional migrants from China (e.g., foreign exchange students who obtained permanent residency status through employment) gravitated to Flushing. These professional migrants or investors used their economic and human-capital resources to build up the area into the status of an enclave. The neighborhood pioneers invested heavily in real estate and business development, which helped to provide the financial capital, housing, and employment opportunities for subsequent immigrants who in turn paved the way for later arrivals. After a while, the middle-class neighborhood pioneers began to send for their families, many of whom were not as resourceful as their sponsors and experienced downward occupational mobility. Also, the ethnic economy drew in low-skilled working-class immigrants from Manhattan's Chinatown and Sunset Park. The class segmentation has reinforced the negative stereotypes of Chinese immigrants as foreign and poor and has added to social service burdens in Flushing.

The development of new ethnic enclaves has also affected interethnic relations. With the growing presence of Chinese immigrants, a certain amount of interethnic conflict has surfaced in community life. Longtime native-born residents often feel that they are being locked out of their own neighborhoods. Some complain bitterly about non-English signs on the local shops. In Flushing, blacks and Hispanics have often reported that they are automatically considered to be criminals by certain Chinese and Korean shopkeepers, many of whom keep their stores locked and use a buzzer system to allow entry only to customers they perceive (visually) to be desirable. Chinese immigrants also often complain that blacks and Hispanics are hostile. It is important to note that ethnic frictions manifest themselves differently in different neighborhoods. There may be tensions in Flushing and Sunset Park—both multiethnic neighborhoods in the truest sense of the word—but they have not led to any urban riots. Still, we would do well to remember that ethnic hostility is unpredictable and can sometimes flare up without much notice. In this sense, the existence of any level of interethnic tension is a cause for concern (Zhou et al. 2013).

DISCUSSION AND CONCLUSION

In the past, Chinatown was a bachelors' society sheltering immigrants from racism and discrimination. Even at the beginning of the twenty-first century, many immigrants continue to cluster in Chinatown, work in the ethnic enclave economy, and socialize among coethnics. Since the ethnic enclave provides jobs, housing, services, and a familiar cultural environment, many immigrants can conduct their daily life without learning English and communicating with the outside world. However, the present-day Chinese immigrant community is not quite as isolated and immigrants are not quite as unassimilable as many think. There are several significant ways that the ethnic community shapes the lives of Chinese immigrants as they strive to make America home.

Participation in the ethnic enclave economy has facilitated upward social mobility for some Chinese immigrants while also keeping others at arm's length from the mainstream society. The experiences of the sewing women in Manhattan's Chinatown's garment factories provide a prime example. In New York City, immigrant Chinese women comprise over half of the work force in the garment industry in the Chinese enclave economy. Most of the garment workers lack English proficiency, have few job skills, and are married to other immigrants similarly handicapped. Since their husbands alone cannot provide for the family, these women must work to bring in money. They often find working in Chinatown a better option than working in low-wage jobs in the larger secondary economy, because enclave employment enables them to fulfill their multiple roles more effectively as wage earners, wives, and mothers. In Chinatown, working hours are flexible, employers are tolerant of children's presence, and private child care within walking distance from work is accessible and affordable. Chinatown also offers convenient grocery shopping and various takeout foods. These amenities enable women to juggle work outside the home and household responsibilities. Moreover, women socialize at work with other coethnic women, who come from similar cultural backgrounds and share similar goals and concerns about family, child rearing, and mobility. By the sewing machine, they can gossip, brag about children, complain about insensitive husbands or nagging relatives back in the homeland, share coping strategies, and comfort each other over hardships. These ties serve as a source of emotional support and psychological comfort (Zhou 1992, 2009).

The enclave economy is a double-edge sword, however. While it facilitates upward mobility for many immigrant families, enabling some to buy homes and set up their own businesses, and provides various resources, such as after-school programs that help children get ahead, working in the enclave economy does not help with English proficiency or learning American ways. And many will be stuck in low-wage jobs there. A good many who arrive with little knowledge of English and few transferable job skills and those arriving as undocumented will end up "trapped" in Chinatown for life and find themselves toiling in dead-end jobs under poor working conditions and seeing little hope of ever making it in America.

Involvement in the ethnic economy has another impact: it heightens the salience of ethnicity. For one thing, jobs created, as well as goods and service produced, in Chinatown, Flushing, and Sunset Park tie immigrant Chinese from diverse socioeconomic backgrounds together despite spatial dispersion. Put another way, the ethnic enclave has directly or indirectly increased the degree of ethnic cohesion that cuts across class lines, thereby sustaining a sense of ethnic solidarity. At the same time, living and working in the ethnic enclave reinforces common values and norms and creates new mechanisms for sanctioning nonconformity among Chinese immigrant workers from diverse class backgrounds.[14] As one immigrant worker said when asked why Chinatown workers seemed reluctant to stand up for their rights, "I don't think you people get it. In Chinatown, if you fight, you lose your job. Nobody will ever hire you. When factories close down, other workers will blame you and your family will blame you."[15]

In a sense, the survival and success of many ethnic businesses depend on cheap immigrant labor as well as unpaid family labor. In Chinese ethnic enclaves, economic behavior is embedded in an ongoing structure of social relations. Ethnic entrepreneurs depend on a motivated, reliable, and exploitable coethnic labor force. In return, they create job opportunities to serve the short-term goals of coethnic workers who must choose between low wages and joblessness (Zhou 1992). However, ethnic cohesion is not inevitable and does not inhere in the moral convictions of individuals or the value orientations in which they were socialized in the country of origin. Rather, ethnic cohesion is contingent upon structural disadvantages that immigrants confront in the host society. Immigrant Chinese from various dialect groups, especially those from rival groups, did not display much solidarity in the homeland, nor did they need to stress the consciousness of being Chinese (Zhou et al. 2013). Upon arrival in the United States, however, ethnic cooperation becomes a strategy for survival and social mobility.

Another way the ethnic community affects Chinese immigrants is through ethnic organizations. The development of ethnic organizations has broadened the connections between the ethnic community and the larger society while also intensifying intraethnic competition over who governs the community. To many New Yorkers, Chinese immigrants seem to be socially isolated in their own ethnic circles with little interest and knowledge about metropolitan affairs. This is no longer true. Chinese immigrants are increasingly connected to New York City and American life through Chinese-language newspapers, such as the *World Journal*, and Chinese-language television and radio stations that feature news and stories about America and international affairs (Zhou et al. 2006). Chinese immigrants and, even more, their children have been increasingly engaged in political affairs in the city, especially in elections of their own to office, including, as we have seen, the successful campaigns of city council members from Queens and Manhattan.

Thanks to well-educated, well-informed, and dedicated members of the first and second generation who work with coethnic immigrants in various community-based organizations, there is no shortage of information about the larger society particularly relevant to Chinese immigrant life. Unlike the old ethnic associations, new civil organizations do not require membership based on family, kinship, or place of origin; they serve the entire Chinese community. Their leaders are not interested in translating power into economic self-interest, but in power to integrate the ethnic community into the larger society and to affect public policy. Nonetheless, new leaders and their civic organizations, with good intentions, often find themselves struggling with little money and the problems of generating grassroots support. The new leaders are sometimes criticized as being naive, insensitive to culturally specific needs, and ignorant of the power of family, kin, and friendship bonds; they also have been accused of using white middle-class formulas to solve Chinese immigrants' social problems (Zhou and Kim 2001). Indeed, one reason they have had so much trouble building their organizations is their dependency on outside funding. Often residing outside of the Chinese residential enclaves, new leaders lack a shared identity with new immigrants based on a common struggle for survival (Kuo 1977).

In sum, recent Chinese immigration to New York City has led to dramatic changes in the metropolitan Chinese community, and these changes, in turn, have had far-reaching effects on the way the immigrants come to see themselves in New York and how they relate to coethnics and other New Yorkers. Many Chinese New Yorkers revere the Statue of Liberty with high hopes for a better life—sharing the same dream as those who came before from Europe or other parts of the world. However, establishing a new life in New York involves divergent destinies. Many newcomers have continued to head to Manhattan's Chinatown as their first stop on the journey to attain the American Dream, but others have bypassed the traditional staging place, moving directly into outer-borough neighborhoods. In creating ethnic clusters outside of Manhattan's Chinatown, Chinese immigrant New Yorkers challenge the conventional wisdom about immigrant assimilation, which has it that residential mobility out of central city areas is associated with acculturation. Chinese immigrant residential patterns also suggest that the newcomers are not birds of passage. Like most early European immigrants, they too want to become American, although at the same time maintaining their ethnic identity and many home-country customs. However, their sheer numbers, economic resources, and achievements have not automatically translated into social acceptance. Indeed, Chinese immigrants' desire to assimilate, no less than ethnic succession, may be perceived as a threat to native-born Americans in middle-class neighborhoods. Resistance from established residents, intertwined with the Chinese way of making it in America, reinforces ethnicity and complicates the direction and meaning of assimilation.

ACKNOWLEDGMENTS

This chapter is an updated version of "Chinese: Divergent Destinies in Immigrant New York," which appeared in Nancy Foner (ed.), *New Immigrants in New York* (New York: Columbia University Press, 2001). It has benefited from insightful discussions with prominent scholars, civic and business leaders, community organizers, and residents in the Chinese immigrant community in New York City. I wish to thank Nancy Foner, who offered helpful comments and suggestions, Andrew Beveridge for his help in preparing the map in figure 5.2, and Rennie Lee and Ada Lingjun Peng for their research assistance. The research is supported by funding from the Walter and Shirley Wang Endowed Chair at UCLA.

NOTES

1. Personal interview, August 1999.

2. Personal interview, January 1995.

3. U.S. Census Bureau, American Fact Finder, viewed on July 15, 2011.

4. Sze Yap includes four counties—Taishan, Kaiping, Enping, and Xinhui—and the people share a similar local dialect. Sam Yap includes three counties—Nanhai, Panyu, and Xunde—in the Pearl River delta region of Guangdong Province.

5. For details, see U.S. Office of Personnel Management, "Employment of Non-Citizens," www.opm.gov/employ/html/chinaref.htm, viewed on July 15, 2011; also see Executive Order 12711, April 11, 1990, http://www.state.gov/documents/organization/28450.pdf.

6. Old Chinatown in 1980 and 1990 included fourteen tracts: core area, 6, 8, 16, 18, 27, 29, and 41; and extended area, 2.01, 2.02, 14.02, 22.01, 43, 15.01, and 25 (Zhou 1992). The total population in these tracts was 92,873 in 1990 and 88,485 in 2011, over half of the residents Chinese.

7. Personal interview, November 1989; reinterview, May 1993.

8. Personal interview, May 1993.

9. Chinese Consumer Yellow Pages, New York: http://www.ccyp.com/NYYP/, viewed on July 15, 2011. The actual number of community organizations in Chinatown was approximately twice as many as this list shows because many were not listed in this particular directory.

10. Personal interview, May 1993.

11. Flushing in this chapter refers to the core area in downtown Flushing, which is officially defined by the Queen's Community Board 7 as an area including eleven contiguous census tracts in both 1980 and 1990 censuses: 797, 845, 851, 853, 855, 857, 859, 865, 867, 871, and 875.

12. Council member representing District 20, see http://council.nyc.gov/d20/html/members/home.shtml, viewed on July 15, 2011.

13. Sunset Park in this chapter refers to the core area defined by nine contiguous census tracts in both 1980 and 2000 censuses: 20, 58, 70, 74, 98, 102, 118, 120, and 122.

14. The development of the enclave economy of course involves cutthroat competition and intense internal conflicts, making the sanctioning of nonconformity one of the key functions of ethnic economic institutions. Whether this function is effective or not, however, is a topic for another essay.

15. Personal interview, November 1994.

REFERENCES

AAFNYCIC. 2004. "Census Profile: New York City's Chinese American Population." Asian American Federation of New York Census Information Center. http://www.aafny.org/cic/briefs/newyorkbrief.pdf.

Aloff, Mindy. 1997. "Where China and Brooklyn Overlap." *New York Times*, February 7, C1.

Chen, Hsiang-Shui. 1992. *Chinatown No More: Taiwan Immigrants in Contemporary New York*. Ithaca, NY: Cornell University Press.

Chin, Ko-lin. 1997. "Safe House or Hell House? Experiences of Newly Arrived Undocumented Chinese." In Paul J. Smith, ed., *Human Smuggling: Chinese Migrant Trafficking and the Challenge to America's Immigration Tradition*, 169–95. Washington, DC: Center for Strategic and International Studies.

Chin, Margaret. 2005. *Sewing Women: Immigrants and the New York City Garment Industry*. New York: Columbia University Press.

CPC. 1993. *Chinese-American Planning Council: Program List*. New York: Chinese-American Planning Council.

Dillon, R. H. 1962. *The Hatchetmen: Tong Wars in San Francisco*. New York: Coward McCann.

Guest, Kenneth. 2003. *God in Chinatown: Religion and Survival in New York's Evolving Immigrant Community*. New York: New York University Press.

——. 2011. "From Mott Street to East Broadway: Fuzhounese Immigrants and the Revitalization of New York's Chinatown." *Journal of Chinese Overseas* 7: 24–44.

Hum, Tarry. 2004. "Immigrant Global Neighborhoods in New York City." In Jerome Krase and Ray Hutchison, eds., *Race and Ethnicity in New York City*. New York: Elsevier.

IIE. 2010. "International Student Enrollments Rose Modestly in 2009/10, Led by Strong Increase in Students from China." Press release, Institute of International Education, November 15. http://www.iie.org/Who-We-Are/News-and-Events/Press-Center/Press-Releases/2010/2010–11–15-Open-Doors-International-Students-In-The-US.aspx.

Jackson, Peter. 1983. "Ethnic Turf: Competition on the Canal Street Divide." *New York Affairs* 7 (4): 149–58.

Kuo, Chia-Ling. 1977. *Social and Political Change in New York's Chinatown: The Role of Voluntary Associations*. New York: Praeger.

Kwong, Peter. 1987. *The New Chinatown*. New York: Hill and Wang.

——. 1997. *Forbidden Workers: Illegal Chinese Immigrants and American Labor*. New York: New Press.

Lee, Rose Hum. 1960. *The Chinese in the United States of America*. Hong Kong: Hong Kong University Press.

Li, Wei. 2009. *Ethnoburb: The New Ethnic Community in Urban America*. Honolulu: University of Hawaii Press.

Liang, Zai. 2001. "The Rules of the Game and the Game of the Rules: The Political Dimension of Recent Chinese Immigration to New York." In Hector R. Cordero-Guzman, Robert Smith, and Ramon Grosfoguel, eds., *Migration, Transnationalization, and Race in a Changing New York*, 131–45. Philadelphia: Temple University Press.

Lien, Pei-te. 2006. "Transnational Homeland Concerns and Participation in US Politics: A Comparison among Immigrants from China, Taiwan, and Hong Kong." *Journal of Chinese Overseas* 2: 56–78.

Lin, Jan. 1998. *Reconstructing Chinatown: Ethnic Enclave, Global Change.* Minneapolis: University of Minnesota Press.

——. 2010. *The Power of Urban Ethnic Places: Cultural Heritage and Community Life.* New York: Routledge.

Lin, Serena Yi-Ling. 2010. "Taiwanese Immigrants in the United States." *Migration Information Source*, Washington, DC: Migration Policy Institute.

Liu, John M., and Lucie Cheng. 1994. "Pacific Rim Development and the Duality of Post-1965 Asian Immigration to the United States." In Paul M. Ong, Edna Bonacich, and Lucie Cheng, eds., *The New Asian Immigration in Los Angeles and Global Restructuring*, 74–99. Philadelphia: Temple University Press.

Mustain, Gene. 1997. "Chinatown Grows in Brooklyn, Too." *Daily News*, October 27, 34.

NYCDCP. 1992. *The Newest New Yorkers: A Statistical Portrait.* New York: New York City Department of City Planning.

——. 1999. *The Newest New Yorkers: 1995–1996, An Update of Immigration to NYC in the Mid '90s.* New York: New York City Department of City Planning.

——. 2000. *The Newest New Yorkers 2000.* New York: New York City Department of City Planning. http://www.nyc.gov/html/dcp/html/census/nny_overview.shtml.

——. 2011. "Population Facts." New York City Department of City Planning. http://www.nyc.gov/html/dcp/html/census/pop_facts.shtml.

Orleans, Leo A. 1988. *Chinese Students in America: Policies, Issues and Numbers.* Washington, DC: National Academy Press.

Parvin, Jean. 1991. "Immigrants Migrate to International City." *Crain's New York Business* 7 (27, July 8).

Skeldon, Ronald. 1994. "Hong Kong in an International Migration System." In Ronald Skeldon, ed., *Reluctant Exiles? Migration from Hong Kong and the New Overseas Chinese*, 21–51. Armonk, NY: M. E. Sharpe.

Sung, Betty Lee. 1987. *The Adjustment Experience of Chinese Immigrant Children in New York City.* New York: Center for Migration Studies.

Terrazas, Aaron, and Jeanne Batalova. 2010. "Chinese Immigrants in the United States." *Migration Information Source*, Washington, DC: Migration Policy Institute.

U.S. Department of Homeland Security. 2009. *Yearbook of Immigration Statistics.* Washington, DC: U.S. Government Printing Office.

USINS. 1995. *1994 Statistical Yearbook of the Immigration and Naturalization Service.* Washington, DC: U.S. Government Printing Office.

——. 1996. *1995 Statistical Yearbook of the Immigration and Naturalization Service.* Washington, DC: U.S. Government Printing Office.

Winnick, Louis. 1990. *New People in Old Neighborhoods: The Role of New Immigrants in Rejuvenating New York's Communities.* New York: Russell Sage Foundation.

Wong, Bernard. 1987. "The Chinese: New Immigrants in New York's Chinatown." In Nancy Foner, ed., *New Immigrants in New York*, 243–71. New York: Columbia University Press.

——. 1998. *Ethnicity and Entrepreneurship: The New Chinese Immigrants in the San Francisco Bay Area*. Boston: Allyn and Bacon.

Yang, Fenggang, and Joseph Tamney, eds. 2006. "Conversion to Christianity among the Chinese." Special issue, *Sociology of Religion: A Quarterly Review* 67.

Zhao, Xiaojian. 2008. "The Spirit of Change: Constructing a Chinese Regional Identity in New York." In Sucheng Chan and Madeline Hsu, eds., *Chinese Americans and the Politics of Race and Culture*, 219–45. Philadelphia: Temple University Press.

Zhou, Min. 1992. *Chinatown: The Socioeconomic Potential of an Urban Enclave*. Philadelphia: Temple University Press.

——. 1997. "Social Capital in Chinatown: The Role of Community-Based Organizations and Families in the Adaptation of the Younger Generation." In Lois Weis and Maxine S. Seller, eds., *Beyond Black and White: New Faces and Voices in U.S. Schools*, 181–206. Albany: State University of New York Press.

——. 2009. *Contemporary Chinese America: Immigration, Ethnicity, and Community Transformation*. Philadelphia: Temple University Press.

Zhou, Min, Wenhong Chen, and Guoxuan Cai. 2006. "Chinese Language Media and Immigrant Life in the United States and Canada." In Wanning Sun, ed., *Media and the Chinese Diaspora: Community, Communications and Commerce*, 42–74. London: Routledge.

Zhou, Min, Margaret M. Chin, and Rebecca Kim. 2013. "The Transformation of Chinese America: New York vs. Los Angeles." In David Halle and Andrew Beveridge, eds., *New York and Los Angeles: The Uncertain Future*. New York: Oxford University Press.

Zhou, Min, and Rebecca Kim. 2001. "Formation, Consolidation, and Diversification of the Ethnic Elite: The Case of the Chinese Immigrant Community in the United States." *Journal of International Migration and Integration* 2 (2): 227–47.

Zhou, Min, and John Logan. 1991. "In and Out of Chinatown: Residential Mobility and Segregation of New York City's Chinese." *Social Forces* 70 (2): 387–407.

6. *Koreans*

CHANGES IN NEW YORK IN THE TWENTY-FIRST CENTURY

Pyong Gap Min

At the beginning of the second decade of the twenty-first century, there have been major changes in New York's Korean community. Not surprisingly, the number of Koreans has grown, but much else is new as well. One new set of developments has been a change in the immigration process itself. There has been a gradual shift from a Korean family-based pattern to immigration based on high-status occupations as well as a dramatic increase in the proportion of Koreans who have arrived on temporary visas and adjusted their status to permanent residents. Other changes relate to Koreans' involvement in business. Koreans are still heavily involved in business, but the self-employment rate among Korean immigrants in the New York area has decreased; among those who own businesses, there has been a significant rise in the number of personal service businesses and a decline in retail businesses. A third major transformation is the disappearance of the business-related intergroup conflicts involving Korean immigrants that were so severe in the 1980s and the early 1990s. Finally, Korean ethnic organizations have changed as well, not only in number but also, among other things, in their roles and the characteristics of their members.

The chapter is organized so that I begin with background on the factors behind Korean migration to the United States and New York, the growth of the New York area's Korean population in the last half century, and new settlement patterns in the metropolitan area and New York City. I then turn to exploring changes in Koreans' involvement in business, business-related conflicts, and ethnic organizational life, and conclude with some comments on the trend for Koreans to become more integrated into American mainstream society while also maintaining stronger attachments to the ethnic community and their South Korean homeland.

KOREAN MIGRATION TO THE UNITED STATES AND NEW YORK

The mass migration of Koreans to New York is a fairly recent phenomenon. Indeed, the overwhelming majority of today's Korean Americans are post-1965 immigrants and their children. The Korean population in the United States was negligible before 1970. The 1970 census counted about 69,000 Koreans in the United States. As table 6.1 shows, in the wake of the liberalized 1965 Immigration Act, the annual number of Korean immigrants legally admitted to the United States gradually increased in the late 1960s and early 1970s. By 1976, 30,000 Koreans annually immigrated to the United States, and throughout the 1980s

TABLE 6.1. KOREAN IMMIGRANTS ADMITTED TO THE UNITED STATES BY FIVE-YEAR PERIOD, 1965–2009

		Proportion of Korean Immigrants Who Settled in New York State and New Jersey (%)	
Five-Year Period	*Number*	*New York*	*New Jersey*
1965–69	17,869	—	—
1970–74	92,745	12	4
1975–79	148,645	9	3
1980–84	162,178	10	4
1985–89	175,803	11	4
1990–94	112,215	14	6
1995–99	75,579	12	8
2000–4	89,871	9	7
2005–9	125,878	10	8

Sources: Immigration and Naturalization Service, *Annual Report*, 1965–78; *Statistical Yearbook*, 1979–2001; Office of Immigration Statistics, *Yearbook of Immigration Statistics*, 2002–9.

there was an annual flow of over 30,000. In that decade, South Korea was the second largest source country of Asian immigrants to the United States, right below the Philippines. It is important to note that in the 1970s and 1980s, U.S. military involvement in South Korea brought an annual average of 3,000 Korean women to the United States as wives of U.S. servicemen (Min 2006a:45).

In addition to the close political and military ties between South Korea and the United States, another set of factors contributed to the mass migration to this country between 1965 and 1990. The low standard of living in Korea, closely linked to the lack of job opportunities, was the major factor pushing Koreans to seek to move to the United States during that period. Political insecurity and repression of freedom by the military dictatorship between 1960 and 1987 was another push factor in those years. In addition, military and political tensions between South Korea and North Korea and fear of another war in the Korean peninsula led many higher-class Koreans to take refuge in the United States. Finally, extreme difficulties in giving their children a college education in Korea due to excessive competition for admission and high tuition played—and still plays—an important role in the exodus of many Koreans to the United States.

Statistics in table 6.1 indicate that the Korean immigration flow reached its peak in the late 1980s and began to decline in the early 1990s. Between 1992 and 2000, the annual number of Korean immigrants remained below 20,000. Economic conditions in South Korea greatly improved in the early 1990s, with its per capita income rising from about $1,400 in 1980 to about $6,000 in 1990 and to approximately $10,000 in 2000 (Min 2006b). South Korea's political conditions improved through a popular election in 1987, ending the twenty-six-year military dictatorship. With better economic conditions in Korea, fewer sought to leave. Additionally, media reports in South Korea on Korean immigrants' difficulties in adjusting to life in the United States discouraged many Koreans from seeking to move to this country.

By 1999, the annual number of Korean immigrants had dropped to 12,840, the lowest number since 1971. Immigration began to increase, however, beginning in 2000, and the annual number hovered around 25,000 in the latter half of the 2000s, with the exception of the 2003 anomaly (when only 12,512 Koreans immigrated to the U.S.). Two major factors contributed to the increase. One is the difficulty facing college-educated people in finding meaningful occupations in Korea, which has pushed many to leave for temporary work in the United States (H1B visas) or graduate school education. Another and perhaps more important factor behind the recent increase is the significant growth in the number of Koreans who initially arrived as temporary residents. In recent years, large numbers of Koreans have visited the United States for various purposes—to study, to obtain training and internships, to see family members and relatives, for temporary work, for sightseeing, and so forth. Many have changed their status to permanent residents. In particular, an exceptionally large number of Korean young people have come to the United States for further study. Korean international students in 2009–2010 numbered more than 72,000, the third largest group next to Chinese and Indian students (Institute of International Education 2010). These figures do not include Korean "early study students" enrolled in elementary and secondary schools. The total number of Korean international students, including early study students, may be close to 100,000. A large proportion of these Korean students eventually change their status to permanent residents each year after finding professional and managerial occupations upon completing their education.

The increase in the Korean American population in the United States (including those of Korean birth as well as ancestry) since 1970 has been dramatic, from about 70,000 in 1970 to over 350,000 in 1990, to over 1 million in 2000, and then over 1.7 million in 2010. Native-born Koreans comprised only 27 percent of single-race Koreans in 2008; the majority are second-generation Korean Americans, children of post-1965 immigrants. Korean Americans have become the fifth largest Asian group in the United States, right below Chinese, Indian, Filipino, and Vietnamese Americans.

THE GROWTH OF THE KOREAN POPULATION IN NEW YORK

Pre-1965 Korean immigrants concentrated heavily in California, Hawaii, and other West Coast states, but post-1965 Korean immigrants have dispersed much more widely throughout the United States. In particular, a large proportion has settled in the New York–New Jersey metropolitan area. As shown in table 6.1, 9–12 percent of Korean immigrants legally admitted to the United States between 1970 and 1989 chose to reside in New York State. Another 3–4 percent chose New Jersey. By 2005–2009, 8 percent chose New Jersey (an increase from 6 percent in 1990–94) while 10 percent selected New York (a decline from 14 percent in 1990–94). These statistics reflect the increasing popularity of New Jersey's Bergen County to Korean immigrants and their tendency to avoid New York City. According to figures from the 2010 U.S. Census, 221,705 people of Korean ancestry lived in the New York–New Jersey Consolidated Metropolitan Statistical (CMSA) Area (table 6.2). The New York–New Jersey area is the second largest Korean population center in the United States, just after the Los Angeles–Long Beach–Riverside area.

In the late 1960s and early 1970s, immigrants admitted on the basis of occupation (and their spouses and children) constituted the vast majority of Korean immigrants in the New York–New Jersey area, as there were few Korean naturalized citizens who could sponsor their relatives through family reunification preferences. Two factors made possible the creation of a new migration chain in

TABLE 6.2. GROWTH OF THE KOREAN POPULATION IN THE NEW YORK–NEW JERSEY CMSA, 1990–2010*

NY-NJ Area	1990 N	2000 N	Change 1990–2000 (%)	2010 N	Change 2000–2010 (%)
Total	118,096	170,509	44.4	221,705	30.0
New York City	69,718	90,208	29.4	102,820	14.0
Suburban areas	48,378	80,301	66.0	118,885	48.0

*In 2000 and 2010 the U.S. Census Bureau included both single-race Koreans (who chose only the Korean racial category) and multiracial Koreans (who chose the Korean and one or more other racial categories). I have included both single-race and multiracial Koreans in the table.

Source: U.S. Census Bureau, 1990 Census and 2000 Census; and 2009 American Community Survey.

New York in the 1970s. First, an expanding medical industry and demand for health care professionals in the New York–New Jersey area attracted many Korean medical professionals (Kim 1981:153–56; Liu et al. 1991). Korean and other Asian medical professionals filled vacancies in the peripheral specialties, such as family practice and radiology, and also in low-income minority neighborhoods that were not attractive to native-born whites (Kim 1981:155–56; Rosenthal 1995). More than one-third of the 6,200 Korean medical professionals admitted to the United States between 1965 and 1975 settled in the tri-state area (New York, New Jersey, and Connecticut) (Kim 1981:148–57).

Second, many Korean international students who had studied at major East Coast universities moved to the New York area in the 1960s and early 1970s to find professional or managerial jobs or to start small businesses. They changed their legal status to permanent residents in those years by marrying Korean nurses or through other mechanisms. In fact, most successful business owners in New York today typically arrived three or four decades ago as international students to pursue their graduate education in the United States. Many started their businesses because their masters' degrees in social sciences or humanities did not help them find prestigious and well-paying jobs.

The economic recession in the early 1970s and lobbying by U.S. professional organizations led the U.S. government to revise the 1965 Immigration Act in such a way that it made the entry of occupational immigrants, especially professionals, more difficult. The revisions included a requirement that prospective professional immigrants obtain job offers from U.S. employers before entry (Harper 1979:3–4).

The Health Professional Educational Act of 1976 also required foreign physicians and surgeons to pass the National Board of Medical Examiners' examination or its equivalent and a foreign language test to gain admission to the United States (Harper 1979:5; Ong and Liu 1994:60–61). As a result, the immigration of Korean medical professionals dropped significantly after 1976.

By the late 1970s and 1980s, as Korean occupational immigrants and their spouses admitted in the late 1960s and early 1970s became naturalized citizens, they were able to sponsor their parents and siblings, who could enter as permanent residents. Thus, the earlier influx of Korean occupational and international student immigrants created an immigration chain that has perpetuated the family-based migration of Koreans to the New York area. The Korean immigrants in New York admitted on the basis of family reunification, including siblings of Korean women married to U.S. servicemen, represent a more diverse cross-section of classes and occupations than the earlier professional and student immigrants.

Still further changes in Korean immigrant patterns occurred as a result of the U.S. Immigration Act of 1990. The new immigration law raised the number of immigrants admitted on the basis of employment preferences, especially the number in specialty occupations (professional and managerial occupations). It made it easier for international students with graduate school education in the United States to change their status to permanent residents. In this way, the 1990 law has helped to raise the class and occupational status of Korean immigrants, reversing the trend of the 1976–89 period. Korean international students with college or graduate school education in the United States have filled much of the immigration quota assigned to Koreans; those with specialty occupations have comprised an increasingly large proportion of annual Korean immigrants in recent years. For example, Koreans with professional, technical, managerial, and administrative occupations and their family members comprised 60–76 percent of all new Korean immigrants admitted between 2005 and 2009 (Min 2011:31).

The changed characteristics of immigrants, as well as the growth of the Korean community in the New York area, also owe much to the rising number of Koreans on temporary visas who have become permanent residents. The Office of Immigration Statistics provides tabulations for two separate groups of immigrants legally admitted to the United States each year: new arrivals (those admitted as immigrants directly from foreign countries) and status adjusters (aliens who previously entered the United States with nonimmigrant status and who have changed their legal status to permanent residents). The proportion of Korean status adjusters gradually increased after the late 1980s, accounting for over 50 percent of all new legal residents in 2000 and 81 percent in 2009 (Min 2011:17). Many Korean temporary residents, such as international students, employees of branches of Korean firms, temporary workers, trainees and interns, and long-term visitors in the United States have become legal residents, a process especially marked in the New York area. The Korean community in the New York–New Jersey area includes a larger proportion of temporary residents than smaller Korean communities in other states and metropolitan areas.

KOREANS' SETTLEMENT PATTERNS IN NEW YORK

The most conspicuous changes in Korean Americans' settlement patterns between 2000 and 2010 were the movement from Korean enclaves in Queens to suburban counties and the expansion of Korean business districts in Korean enclaves in Queens and Manhattan as well as Bergen County.

SUBURBANIZATION

Although the population of Korean ancestry in New York City is large—close to 103,000 in 2010—it increased by only 14 percent between 2000 and 2010, in contrast to a 48 percent increase in suburban areas (see table 6.2). In particular, Bergen County in New Jersey witnessed a 61 percent growth in its Korean population, from about 36,000 in 2000 to more than 58,000 in 2010, following a whopping 130 percent increase (from 16,000 to 37,000) between 1990 and 2000. If the current preference for Bergen County over Queens continues, Bergen County may have a larger Korean population than the borough of Queens by 2020.

Why has the Korean population in Bergen County increased so dramatically? Many Korean old-timers who originally settled in New York City pioneered the move to suburban Korean enclaves in Bergen County, such as Fort Lee, Palisades Park, and Leonia, in the search for better public schools and housing (Oh 2007). Once Korean residential enclaves (as well as Korean business districts) were established there in the mid-1990s, the communities attracted more Koreans from enclaves in Queens, who also found the areas attractive because of their suburban amenities as well as the availability of many Korean restaurants and other Korean culturally based businesses.

Mr. Cho, who had lived in Jackson Heights (Queens), moved to Palisades Park in 1991. When I asked why he had moved to Bergen County, his response echoed the sentiments of many other Korean immigrants who had followed a similar path:

> There are several reasons why I moved to Palisades Park in the early 1990s. Jackson Heights is too crowded with new immigrants and has a high crime rate. By contrast, Palisades Park or Fort Lee in Bergen County is more like a suburban neighborhood, with no crime and no fast-food stores, like

McDonald's. My friend told me when your car stops on the street in Palisades Park, you can leave it for one day without locking it. But in Jackson Heights, many people lost their cars, even if they locked them. Also, public schools are much better in Bergen County than in Queens. While we enjoy all these advantages in Palisades Park, we can still go to Korean restaurants and bakeries within five to ten minutes. When I tried to move to Palisades Park at that time, many Korean stores had been already established.

At the same time, overcrowding and escalating commercial rents led many Manhattan-based branches of Korean firms and wholesale stores to move to Bergen County in the 1990s and after. In a natural progression, Korean employees and business owners who now found themselves working in New Jersey moved there from Queens to be near their workplaces. Also, many Korean temporary residents with children attending school—for example, visiting scholars, trainees, and employees of Korean government agencies—have tended to prefer living in Bergen County rather than in Queens or Manhattan. Many have told me that New York City is "too wild" and "somewhat dangerous" for family life.

In addition to New Jersey's Bergen County, several other suburban counties saw high rates of growth in their Korean population between 2000 and 2010. Of New York State's suburban counties, Nassau County on Long Island now has the largest Korean population, with nearly 11,000 in 2010, representing a growth rate of 64 percent since 2000 (Min and Kim 2012). Suffolk and Westchester Counties experienced a 38 percent and 27 percent growth rate, respectively. Nassau and other suburban counties are attractive to Korean immigrants mainly because of their many good school districts with highly ranked public schools. The neighborhoods where Korean immigrants are concentrated on Long Island, such as New Hyde Park, Great Neck, Port Washington, Syosset, and Jericho, have many first-class high schools.

KOREAN ENCLAVES IN NEW YORK CITY

Within New York City itself, 64 percent of Koreans were concentrated in the borough of Queens in 2010 (Min and Kim 2012). Even so, the Korean population in Queens grew by only 3 percent between 2000 and 2010, in good part because many Korean immigrants who originally settled there have remigrated to suburban areas.

Flushing, Bayside, Little Neck, and Woodside in Queens are home to large clusters of Koreans. Queens Community District 7, which includes Flushing, College Point, Whitestone, and a few other nearby neighborhoods in the northeastern part of the borough, was home to approximately 26,000 people of Korean ancestry as of 2007 (New York City Department of City Planning 2009). They constituted a little more than a fifth of the Koreans in New York City. Within Community District 7 itself, Koreans are heavily concentrated in Flushing, which Korean immigrants consider the symbolic capital of the Korean community in the New York–New Jersey area. It is not only a Korean residential area but also a business, social, and cultural center. Residentially, though, Flushing is a multiethnic neighborhood in which several Asian and Latino immigrant groups and white Americans live together (see chapter 5, this volume). As of 2007, the Chinese (61,720) outnumbered Koreans (25,927) by more than two to one in Community District 7. Altogether, Asian Americans made up 44 percent of Community District 7's population, with white Americans the second largest racial group, constituting 36 percent of the population.

Another area in which Koreans are highly concentrated is Queens Community District 11, which encompasses Bayside, Oakland Gardens, Little Neck, and Douglaston; neighborhoods in this district have more suburban amenities (including many single-family homes with backyards) than those in Community District 7, and the best school district (District 26) in New York City. Approximately 14,000 Korean Americans lived in Community District 11 in 2007, along with about 20,000 Chinese Americans; altogether, Asian Americans comprised a third of the district's population, whereas white Americans made up the majority (52 percent) of the population.

Korean immigrants began to establish Korean businesses on Main Street in downtown Flushing beginning in the late 1970s. According to the Korean Directory published in 1984 by the Korean Merchants Association in Flushing, there were then about 125 Korean-owned stores in the Flushing area, with about sixty located on Main Street. These included clothing and produce stores, Korean restaurants, Korean grocery stores, furniture stores, accounting firms, and medical offices. In the late 1980s, when Taiwanese and Hong Kong immigrants were actively developing their businesses on Main Street with the benefit of overseas capital, Korean immigrants gradually moved away from Main Street and began to develop businesses on Union Street, one block east of Main Street. By the early 1990s, Korean immigrants had developed Haninsanga (the Korean business district) on Union Street extending about five blocks between Forty-First Street and Northern Boulevard.

Since the early 1990s, the Korean business district has been extended along Union Street northward up to Thirty-Second Avenue as well as about 2.5 miles along Northern Boulevard up to 220th Street in Bayside. Korean restaurants, groceries, and other stores selling mainly Korean cultural products and services with Korean-language commercial signs are scattered on Northern Boulevard for eighty-five blocks and dotted on Union Street for ten blocks. Since the Korean business district connects Flushing and Bayside along Northern Boulevard, I call it the "Flushing-Bayside Korean Business District" (Min 2008:40–41).

Manhattan has the second largest Korean population in New York City, with more than 22,000 Koreans in 2010, representing an 85 percent increase since 2000 (the highest rate of increase in the 2000s of any borough). A growing number of Korean young adults in the U.S.-born second or 1.5 generation (who moved to the United States at the age of twelve or before) now have professional and managerial occupations in finance companies in midtown and downtown Manhattan and choose—and can afford—to live in that borough. So do many others with high salaries as well as some of the increasing number of Korean international students who attend various colleges and universities in Manhattan, particularly those from affluent families in Korea.

Although Manhattan has no neighborhood where Koreans are residentially clustered, there is an area where many Koreans are visible day and night, and where many Korean stores with Korean language signs are located. It is the area that I referred to as the "Broadway Korean Business District" in my book *Caught in the Middle* (Min 1996:39) and that young people now commonly call K-Town. The Korean Business District is a rectangle area covering Twenty-Seventh Street through Thirty-Fifth Street on Broadway, Sixth, and Fifth Avenues. The heart of the district is the intersection between Broadway and Thirty-Second Street. In October 1995, the New York City government named the district Koreatown and posted an official sign, "Korean Way," at the intersection.

In the early 1990s, the Broadway Korean Business District had about 400 Korean-owned import and wholesale businesses as well as many Korean restaurants and other Korean culturally based businesses. As early as the late 1960s, Korean import and wholesale companies in the area sold wigs, leather bags, hats, clothing, jewelry, and toys. Korean immigrants initially imported these manufactured goods mainly from South Korea, taking advantage of their home country's export-oriented economy. However, as wholesale prices gradually went up in South Korea, they increasingly turned to China, India, and even South America for supplies. The import and wholesale companies distributed Korean- and Asian-imported manufactured goods to Korean retailers not only in New York, but also in other parts of the Northeast, as well as to Latino retailers. As many Korean import and wholesale companies became established in the business district, Korean restaurants, bakeries, travel agencies, accounting firms, and law firms, mainly serving Korean wholesalers, mushroomed.

In recent decades, the number of Korean-owned import and wholesale companies located in the Broadway business district has shrunk, from about 400 in 1992 to 250 in 2005 and then down to 150 as of 2011. Intense competition with Chinese- and Indian-owned wholesale stores, and rent hikes caused by urban renovations, forced many Korean wholesale stores in the area to close and others to move to New Jersey. Chinese- and Indian-owned import and wholesale companies now outnumber Korean-owned companies in the district by a large margin. Thus the dwindling presence of Korean-owned import and wholesale businesses no longer justifies calling the area the Broadway Korean Business District.

While the number of Korean import and wholesale businesses has been drastically reduced in the area, the number of Korean restaurants and other Korean culturally based businesses has increased exponentially over the past ten years or so. Many businesses with Korean-language signs are heavily concentrated in a one and a half block section of Thirty-Second Street between Broadway and Madison Avenue. As shown in table 6.3, as of March 2011, there were 106 Korean-owned businesses on this section of Thirty-Second Street. The Korean-owned businesses located there include twenty-eight Korean restaurants, five other Asian restaurants, thirteen drinking or karaoke establishments, and five Korean bakeries.

Many Koreans visit K-Town in Manhattan to meet their friends and relatives. Especially during evenings, huge numbers of young Koreans—younger generations who often work in Manhattan and international students who may or may not live in Manhattan—visit K-Town for social gatherings in Korean restaurants and other entertainment places. Many young Korean students attending colleges

TABLE 6.3. TYPES OF KOREAN BUSINESSES LOCATED ON THIRTY-SECOND STREET BETWEEN BROADWAY AND MADISON AVENUE, 2011

Type of Business	N
Korean restaurants	28
Other Asian restaurants (Japanese, Chinese, and Vietnamese)	5
Korean franchise restaurants	3
Korean bakeries	5
Drinking places and karaoke	13
Saunas	5
Beauty salons	5
Retail stores	10
Department stores	2
Medical and law firms	8
Travel agencies	3
Korean banks	2
Korean daily newspaper branches	2
Other	15
Total	106

Source: Fieldwork by the author and Sou Hyun Jang.

and universities on the East Coast outside of New York City visit K-Town at least a few times during their college years. For young Koreans, K-town has become the symbolic capital of the Korean community in the New York–New Jersey area and the East Coast.

K-Town is also popular with many young Chinese, Japanese, Indians, whites, and members of other minority groups. They come to K-Town at night to enjoy Korean restaurants, bars, bakeries, and Korean franchise stores (Kyochon, Pinkberry, and Red Mango). Some of them visit K-Town with their Korean and non-Korean friends or dating partners, as this second-generation Korean said: "Even though I live and work in Brooklyn, I go to K-Town once or twice a month. I usually go there to meet up with my non-Korean friends, mostly Hispanics and whites, to eat Korean barbecue and tofu stew. My non-Korean friends like Korean food a lot. After dinner we usually go to a yogurt place for dessert or a Korean bar to drink beer." Many other non-Koreans visit K-Town at night because they too like Korean food and also the youth and nightlife culture there.

Most Korean restaurants on Thirty-Second Street are full between 7 and 8:30 P.M. every night, mostly with non-Korean young people—professionals and managers working in corporations in Manhattan, undergraduate and graduate students, and tourists. As night progresses, the proportion of young customers continues to increase. By around 10 P.M., about 90 percent of the customers in Korean bakeries, drinking places, and yogurt bars in K-Town are young people, and approximately two-thirds are non-Korean. K-Town on Thirty-Second Street in Manhattan is significant not only for reinforcing or enhancing younger-generation Koreans' ethnicity, but also for publicizing Korean culture to New Yorkers. Until about twenty years ago, Korean food was relatively unknown to New Yorkers. But many young residents in Manhattan today are familiar with Korean cuisine through their visits to Korean restaurants in K-Town.

CHANGES IN KOREANS' BUSINESS PATTERNS AND THE DISAPPEARANCE OF INTERGROUP CONFLICTS

In the 1980s and 1990s, Korean immigrants in New York as well as other major metropolitan areas were highly concentrated in labor-intensive small businesses and were involved in numerous business-related intergroup conflicts. In earlier publications, I focused on New York Korean immigrants' business-related intergroup conflicts and their effects on ethnic solidarity (Min 1996, 2008). However, there have been significant changes in Korean immigrant entrepreneurship. First of all, while the self-employment rate among Korean immigrants in the New York area is still high, it declined between 1990 and 2006 (see table 6.4).

TABLE 6.4. CHANGING SELF-EMPLOYMENT RATES AMONG KOREAN IMMIGRANT FULL-TIME WORKERS* IN THE NY-NJ-CT METROPOLITAN AREA (%)

	Total	*Men*	*Women*
1980	28.5	35.6	16.2
1990	33.5	36.4	28.7
2000	25.3	29.3	20.3
2005–7	27.2	29.8	23.6

*Korean immigrants 25–64 years old who worked thirty-five or more weeks and thirty-five or more hours per week in the previous year.

Source: Author's compilation from 5 percent Integrated Public Use Microdata Sample (IPUMS) of the 1980, 1990, and 2000 U.S. Census and a 3 percent (aggregated from 1 percent sample for each year) IPUMS of the 2005–7 American Community Surveys.

More Korean immigrants now participate in the general economy than they did fifteen years ago. Second, there have been major changes in the types of Korean immigrant businesses; the proportion of Korean retail businesses has fallen, with a concomitant rise in service-related businesses. Third and most important, Korean immigrants' business-related intergroup conflicts in New York and elsewhere have nearly disappeared since the mid-1990s.

DECREASE IN KOREAN IMMIGRANTS' SELF-EMPLOYMENT RATE

Most Korean immigrants in the 1970s and 1980s were well educated, but faced a severe language barrier. Mainly because they did not speak English well (or at all), they could not find white-collar and professional occupations in the United States commensurate with their educational levels (Min 1984). Many new immigrants at that time had to accept low-paying, menial blue-collar jobs, such as work in factories, janitorial services, and cashiers in retail stores. As an alternative to these low-status, low-paying occupations, they started labor-intensive small businesses that were not attractive to native-born whites. The self-employment rate of Korean immigrants (25–64-year-old full-time workers) in the New York area was 29 percent in 1980, rising to 34 percent in 1990 (see table 6.4). Koreans had the second highest self-employment rate among all immigrant groups in the New York–New Jersey metropolitan area, just below Greek immigrants (Min 2008:29). Census data underestimate Korean and other immigrant groups' self-employment rates (Min 2008:31). Results of a survey I conducted in 1988 revealed that 49 percent of Korean married working women and 61 percent of their husbands in New York City were self-employed (Min 1996:48).

The census-reported self-employment rate of Korean immigrants in the New York area dropped to 25 percent in 2000, slightly increasing to 27 percent in 2006. This decline from 1990 might seem surprising given that more recent Korean immigrants had far more advantages in starting their own businesses in 2000 than those in 1990 because of access to stronger family and ethnic networks from which they could get business information and training. Also, they had greater class resources, particularly business capital, to start their own businesses.

Yet it is the very characteristics of the most recent immigrants that actually help to explain the fall-off in business involvement. As I noted, international students, early study students, and other temporary residents have comprised a much larger proportion of Korean residents in New York City since 2000. These temporary residents are less likely to open their own businesses than permanent residents with green cards. Moreover, the many Koreans who entered as international students, completed their higher education, and then received permanent resident status are more qualified to find high-level and well-paying jobs in the mainstream economy than the earlier Korean immigrants. Even newly arrived Korean immigrants now have less of a language barrier than earlier immigrants because they had more opportunities to speak English in Korea.

CHANGES IN KOREAN IMMIGRANTS' BUSINESS TYPES

The three types of businesses Korean immigrants in New York first developed in the 1960s and 1970s were wholesale businesses selling manufactured goods, retail businesses selling some of the manufactured goods supplied by the wholesalers, and subcontracted garment manufacturing (Kim 1981). In the late 1970s, Korean immigrants began establishing produce and grocery retail stores and dry cleaning services. In the early 1980s, they ventured into nail salons and retail fish stores. By the early 1990s, Korean immigrants had a virtual monopoly on seven (excluding garment subcontracting) of these eight business lines, establishing several hundred or, in some cases, more than a thousand stores in each line in the New York–New Jersey metropolitan area (Min 1996:54).

Retail trade dominated Korean-owned businesses in the early years of the post-1965 immigration, with retail stores comprising a remarkable 59 percent of Korean-owned businesses in 1980 and 44 percent in 1990 (Min 2008:38). Korean-owned businesses involving personal services increased from 7 percent in 1980 to 19 percent in 1990, which reflected the growing number of Korean-owned dry cleaners and nail salons in the New York–New Jersey area. In all, in 1990, Korean retail stores outnumbered Korean service businesses 2.5 times. In the

1980s and early 1990s, Korean-owned retail stores in New York City were heavily concentrated in black and Latino neighborhoods, such as Harlem (Manhattan), Flatbush (Brooklyn), and Jamaica (Queens). Many Korean immigrants purchased retail stores from retiring Jewish, Italian, and other white shopkeepers (Kim 1981:110–11). Many others established new shops in low-income minority neighborhoods where neither white corporations nor white independent store owners were willing to invest. Black residents in black neighborhoods owned service businesses, such as barber shops, beauty salons, and funeral homes, while Koreans and other immigrants monopolized retail stores.

Structural factors associated with racial inequality and racial segregation encouraged Korean immigrants to enter retail businesses in minority neighborhoods beginning in the late 1970s. As middleman minority theory emphasizes, immigrant merchants plug a "status gap" by assuming a role neither the elite wishes nor lower-class minorities are able to fill (Bonacich 1973; Rinder 1958–59). As Rinder suggested for early twentieth-century Jews in the United States, in "the urban Negro ghettoes, Jews [were] . . . prominent in venturing into this gap to service the commercial needs, even as they did for the medieval peasant" (257). Later, Loewen (1971) tried to explain the concentration of Chinese immigrants in the Mississippi delta in the black-oriented grocery business based on the white-black status gap. He argued that few whites were willing to operate grocery stores in black neighborhoods, providing Chinese immigrants with an opportunity to establish the grocery business in the black community. In previous writings (Min 1996, 2008), I considered the 1980s and 1990s Korean retail business owner as playing a typical middleman minority role in New York, replacing Jews and other white business owners in black neighborhoods.

By 2000, retail businesses had declined to less than a third of Korean businesses (4,772 businesses) in the New York–New Jersey area, down from 59 percent (5,504 businesses) ten years earlier (Min 2008:38). This decline was part of a general trend across the American economy, caused by the emergence of megastores. White-owned retail businesses in New York also showed a steady decline in the same years, but Korean-owned retail stores in New York were hit harder by the emergence of megastores because Korean immigrants were far more concentrated in retail trade than whites. Results of research I conducted in Harlem and two other low-income black neighborhoods in 1991 and 2006 show how the movement of megastores negatively influenced Korean retail stores (Min 2008:89–90). According to my interview with the president of the Korean Merchants Association in Harlem in 1991, there were then fifty-five Korean-owned stores in the heart of Harlem. In 2006, I counted only fourteen in the same area. Ten of the fourteen were beauty supply, clothing, and shoe stores. In 1991, ten of the fifty-five stores were middleman retail businesses, which included three grocery, four produce, and three seafood stores. By 2006, only one produce store and one seafood store survived. The three blocks between St. Nicholas Avenue and Lenox Avenue on

125th Street were filled with more than thirty chain megastores, among them, Modell's Sporting Goods, Old Navy, Duane Reade, Foot Locker, and Pathmark. The new presence of Pathmark, a chain supermarket, killed most Korean grocery, greengrocery, and seafood retail stores in the area. The movement of megastores into Harlem and other minority neighborhoods was made possible by changes in zoning laws in the late 1990s.

The spectacular increase in the number of Korean nail salons and dry cleaners in the New York–New Jersey metropolitan area largely explains the dramatic rise in the proportion of Korean personal-service businesses between 1980 and 2000 (7 percent of Korean businesses involved personal services in 1980, 32 percent in 2000, and 25 percent in 2006). Based on interviews with Korean business association leaders in 1991, I estimated that there were 1,400 nail salons and 1,500 dry cleaning shops in the New York–New Jersey area (Min 1996:54). According to my 2006 interviews with presidents of the nail salon and dry cleaning associations, the number of nail salons and dry cleaning shops in New York and New Jersey had increased to approximately 4,000 and 3,000, respectively. Even if the leaders in both years exaggerated the numbers, there was still a large increase between 1990 and 2006. Since the early 1990s, Korean immigrants in the New York–New Jersey area have monopolized nail and dry cleaning businesses, controlling more than 60 percent of all the shops in each line.

The astounding growth in nail salons and dry cleaning businesses reflects the greater demand for personal-service businesses, in the United States in general and the New York area in particular. In the early 1990s, dry cleaners primarily catered to middle-class Americans. Korean-owned dry cleaning shops in the 1980s and early 1990s were thus heavily concentrated in white and multiracial middle-class neighborhoods in the New York area. The gradual change in American consumer culture toward a greater dependency on commercial dry cleaning has led many working-class people to use it as well. Now, many Korean dry cleaning shops are located in lower-income black and Latino neighborhoods. About two-fifths of Korean-owned dry cleaners are family businesses run by husband-wife teams. These cleaners are usually drop shops, which means that items are sent out for cleaning because there are no dry-cleaning machines on the premises. Most shops have their own dry cleaning machines and four to six employees, mostly Latinos.

The 4,000 Korean-owned nail salons in the New York–New Jersey area in 2006 marked a nearly threefold increase from about 1,400 in 1991. The figures reflect the importance of the nail business in the Korean community. The average Korean nail salon has more paid workers (usually five to six) than other types of Korean businesses, predominantly Korean women. This means that a large proportion of Korean women in New York work in nail salons either as business owners or as employees. A former president of the Korean Nail Salon Association of New York told me, in 2006, that women alone owned about 30 percent of Korean nail salons, husband-wife teams about 60 percent, and male owners with women managers the remaining 10 percent. Employees of Korean nail salons include former retail business owners, wives of Korean international students, temporary visitors from Korea, and Korean women from China. By making what was once a more exclusive service provided in beauty salons much cheaper and more accessible, Koreans have established nail salons as a fixture of New York life, catering to lower-class as well as middle- and upper-middle-class women.

Many Korean women who now work in Korean nail salons as employees used to run retail businesses in minority neighborhoods in the 1980s and 1990s. Mrs. Kim's job history reflects this transition. She immigrated to New York with her husband in 1987, helped by her husband's sister, who had become a U.S. citizen. She and her husband received business training by working in the sister's gift shop and opened their own store in the same year in a black neighborhood in the Bronx. Their gift shop, which sold wigs, handbags, toys, and related items, was successful enough to allow them to save money to establish a bigger gift shop in a Bronx Hispanic neighborhood in 1994. However, in 1999, they could not continue their business because of competition from a megastore (99 Cents Only Store) and two Chinese-owned gift shops that had moved onto the same block. After training for six months or so, Mrs. Kim found a job in a Korean-owned nail salon in 2000 while her husband started a real estate business. When asked how she liked her current job as a manicurist compared to working in her own retail business, she commented:

> If you want to make money, a business is much better. But running a small store in a minority neighborhood involves a lot of stress every day, day and night. As an employee, I cannot make as much money as I made as a business owner. But a good part of my current job is that once I finish my work in the nail salon, I am free from stress and enjoy leisure time at home and I work only five days a week. Now, my daughter makes good money at a finance company, and she helps us financially. So we don't need a lot of money.

FROM THE PREVALENCE TO THE DISAPPEARANCE OF BLACK BOYCOTTS

According to middleman minority theory (Bonacich 1973; Loewen 1971), middleman merchants are usually subjected to boycotts, arson, riots, and other forms of rejection from minority customers. As I and other researchers have documented (Gold 2010:134–37; Joyce 2003; Min 1996, 2008), Korean merchants in New York City were targets of fifteen black boycotts in the 1980s and early 1990s, six of which were long-term boycotts with a duration of four weeks or longer

(Min 2008:76). Two Korean produce stores in Flatbush, Brooklyn, were boycotted for seventeen months starting in January 1990. All major boycotts started with a personal dispute between one or more customers and an employee or manager of a Korean-owned store. Black nationalist leaders usually organized and led long-term boycotts. While a personal dispute was the immediate trigger, its more fundamental causes were black residents' severe underrepresentation in retail businesses in their neighborhoods and their and black nationalists' perceptions of Korean merchants as exploiting blacks economically (Min 1996:109–18, 2008:82–83).

The boycott of two Korean stores in Flatbush between January 1990 and May 1991 was the last long-term black boycott of Korean stores in New York City. Five more black boycotts of Korean stores occurred in the early 1990s, but they were all brief, lasting twelve days or less (Min 2008:76). Korean merchants in New York City have not encountered any black boycotts since 1996. According to the Korean media, Korean merchants in Los Angeles, Chicago, and other cities also do not seem to have encountered any serious open conflict with black residents since the mid-1990s. Thus, Korean-black conflicts that attracted a great deal of scholarly attention between the late 1990s and early 2000s are no longer an important research issue. However, what is now important to explain is why serious Korean-black business-related conflicts, which were once so prevalent, have disappeared since the mid-1990s.

My research in black neighborhoods in New York City indicates that two major factors contributed to the disappearance of black boycotts of Korean stores. One is the drastic reduction in Korean-owned stores in the city's black neighborhoods. Korean retail stores have been mostly concentrated in minority neighborhoods while Korean service businesses (dry cleaners and nail salons) are concentrated in middle-class white or multiethnic neighborhoods. The major shift in types of Korean businesses from retail to service businesses means that the number of Korean-owned stores in black neighborhoods has been greatly reduced. As I have indicated, the movement of many megastores into black neighborhoods and severe rent hikes following urban renovations made it difficult for small Korean retail shopkeepers to survive.

In addition to the emergence of megastores, the movement of many other non-Korean immigrants into New York City's black neighborhoods made it difficult for Korean merchants to compete. Since the mid-1990s, Chinese, South Asian, Middle Eastern, and African immigrants have established commercial activities in central Harlem (Min 2008:91). Now that the racial and ethnic backgrounds of immigrant business owners in black neighborhoods have become so diverse, black residents no longer target Korean or any other specific immigrant group for boycotts. For example, Mr. Kim, who had run two Korean produce stores in Flatbush, explained in 2006 how the diversity of business owners' racial backgrounds had nearly eliminated the major source of Korean-black conflict:

"Earlier, some black residents came to my produce store and said, 'Why do you Koreans control businesses in my territory?' They can no longer ask that question. Should they ask that question, I can say, 'What about the Dominicans, Indians, and Arabs who have their shops here?'" (Min 2008:93).

The other factor helping to explain the disappearance of black boycotts is the change in the racial composition of residents in New York City's black neighborhoods, which seems to have seriously weakened African Americans' sense that they own or control the neighborhoods. From the black nationalist perspective, black residents should control the economy in their neighborhood, and the presence of many nonblack business owners is seen as an invasion. However, in recent years, the "ownership" of neighborhoods has come into question with changes in residential demographics. Central Harlem, for example, went from being 94 percent non-Hispanic black in 1980 to 77 percent in 2000, a period in which the Hispanic population grew from 4 to 17 percent. In addition, by 2000, almost a tenth of black residents in Harlem were Caribbean and African immigrants. African Americans, who earlier may have considered central Harlem their territory, made up around two-thirds of the neighborhood in 2000. Moreover, in the last decade or so, under the impact of gentrification, many middle-class white and black Americans have moved to Harlem, further contributing to its racial and class diversity. Similar changes in racial composition have occurred in Flatbush and Jamaica. The diversification of both the residents and the business owners in minority neighborhoods has resulted in the elimination of boycotts of Korean-owned or any other immigrant-owned businesses.

OCCUPATIONAL ASSIMILATION OF KOREAN AMERICANS

As I have noted, proportionally more Korean immigrants now work in the mainstream economy than in the 1990s. Moreover, a significant majority of 1.5- and second-generation young adults who graduated from college in the United States also work in the mainstream economy; their self-employment rates in the New York–New Jersey metropolitan area are less than 10 percent (Min 2008:95). The proportion of younger-generation Koreans in the total Korean American population has increased significantly since the early 1990s.

In short, Korean Americans in New York, as well as in other cities, have now achieved a much higher level of occupational assimilation than was true fifteen or twenty years ago. Koreans in the mainstream economy need to speak English at work, and they have more opportunities to have non-Korean friends and dating partners than Koreans in the ethnic economy (Min 1991). Thus Koreans' higher level of occupational assimilation is likely to have led to higher levels of cultural and social assimilation.

The increase in the proportion of Korean-owned service businesses and the concomitant decrease in retail businesses have also contributed to the cultural and social assimilation of Korean immigrants. This is especially so for Korean women involved in service businesses—which involve considerable communication with non-Korean clients. Korean female manicurists, for example, need to communicate with their clients—mostly native-born white American women—in English far more frequently than Korean female cashiers in retail stores. To establish and secure regular clients, Korean nail salon owners and employees often ask white clients about their jobs, hobbies, and family backgrounds. Some even become friends with their clients thanks to the nature of their services.

CHANGES IN SOCIAL SERVICE AND OTHER ETHNIC ORGANIZATIONS

At the end of the 1990s, there were already about 1,100 Korean ethnic organizations, including 550 Korean Protestant churches, in the New York–New Jersey metropolitan area (Min 2001). By 2011, the total number of Korean ethnic organizations had slightly increased to approximately 1,300, but there have been several more important changes in the twenty-first century. Korean social service and empowerment organizations now take a more active role in providing services for Koreans who need them; Korean business associations have become somewhat less influential; 1.5- and second-generation Koreans increasingly participate as board and staff members or donors in ethnic organizations; and many Korean cultural organizations now focus on Korean children's "roots education" emphasizing various aspects of Korean history and culture.

MORE ACTIVE ROLE OF SOCIAL SERVICE AND EMPOWERMENT ORGANIZATIONS

At the end of the 1990s, I located approximately forty Korean social service organizations in the New York–New Jersey area. The number had grown to approximately ninety in 2011. About twenty Korean Protestant social service organizations, which combine evangelical efforts with service provision, are mostly recently established organizations. Several social service organizations that focus on helping Korean elderly people and regional Korean elderly self-help associations also have been established recently, reflecting a greater demand in the Korean community for services to elderly Koreans, whose number has radically increased in recent years.

The establishment of two foundations that provide mini-grants for various social service agencies indicates the maturity of the Korean community in the

New York–New Jersey area. The Beautiful Foundation USA, founded in 2006, is the northeastern U.S. chapter of the Beautiful Foundation in Korea and has been led by Korean immigrant leaders. It gets donations mainly from individual Koreans and successful Korean businesses, and distributes funds to Korean social service organizations in the form of program grants. The Korean American Community Foundation, founded in 2002 by 1.5- and second-generation Korean leaders, also distributes funds to Korean social service organizations through grant competitions mainly to help Korean immigrant families in difficulty. This second-generation organization receives donations mostly from 1.5- and second-generation Koreans and American corporations. About 1,000 people attended its annual donation gala held in October 2010 at Chelsea Piers in Manhattan at a cost of $400 a ticket. I learned that the majority of Korean participants were 1.5-generation and U.S.-born Koreans, with non-Korean participants comprising a significant proportion. Second-generation leaders were able to use personal contacts to bring many representatives of American corporations to the gala.

Korean social service organizations have expanded not only in number but also in their revenues and programs. About ten Korean social service agencies, including the two foundations just mentioned, have annual budgets (as of 2011) of $300,000 or more. Korean Community Services is the largest Korean social service organization in the New York–New Jersey area with an annual budget of approximately $3 million. It has several different programs established in offices located in Queens, Brooklyn, and Manhattan. Minkwon Center for Community Action has grown into a powerful civil rights organization in New York City, involved in efforts to protect the rights of Korean and other documented and undocumented immigrants, and combining the provision of social services with advocacy and social action. It has organized several multiracial demonstrations in Washington, DC, to put pressure on Congress to enact laws to legalize undocumented immigrants. The Korean Young Women's Christian Association runs a number of elderly, youth, and other social service programs in Flushing, including a nursery school, classes for the elderly, a women's choir, and a children's choir. Founded primarily to provide services for the Korean community, the association has expanded its services to Chinese, Latino, and other immigrants and their children in recent years. It is one of the few Korean Christian social service organizations that focus on providing social services without mixing these efforts with missionary activities.

WEAKENING OF BUSINESS ASSOCIATIONS' INFLUENCE AND POWER

As I have pointed out elsewhere, Korean business associations increased their power and influence in the Korean community in the course of trying to resolve business-related intergroup conflicts (Min 1996:202–9). Data collected in 1991 showed that major Korean business associations had much larger annual budgets than Korean professional associations such as the Korean American Lawyers Association of Greater New York and the Korean Dental Association of Eastern U.S.A. The major Korean business associations had office spaces and one or more paid employees while professional associations usually had neither offices nor paid employees. To resolve long-term black boycotts, conflicts with white suppliers, and tough government regulations of commercial activities, Korean business associations mobilized community forces for ethnic collective action. This process enhanced their influence in the Korean community.

The disappearance of business-related intergroup conflicts has weakened the unity of Korean merchants and reduced the power of major business associations. The Korean Produce Association (KPA) received only a few cases of complaints monthly from members in 2006, as Korean greengrocers had little conflict with black customers or white suppliers (Min 2008:133). As the demand for services by its members declined, the KPA's membership and budget also declined. As a result, the KPA has less manpower and fewer resources to provide services for the Korean community. Other major Korean business associations have gone through similar changes in their budgets and services to members and the Korean community in general. Korean business associations, it must be emphasized, still provide more services to members than Korean professional associations—but the business associations have seen their power wane in recent years as major Korean social service and empowerment organizations have seen their influence grow.

PARTICIPATION OF THE YOUNGER GENERATION IN THE KOREAN COMMUNITY

Second-generation Koreans were not very visible in the Korean community in the New York–New Jersey area in the 1990s; they were then active only in several English-language religious congregations, mostly established within Korean immigrant churches. However, by the beginning of the twenty-first century, younger-generation Koreans had gradually begun to participate in Korean ethnic organizations. As of 2011, at least three major Korean social service and empowerment organizations were run by younger-generation leaders (executive directors and board members). Many other Korean social service, empowerment, and professional organizations, although headed by immigrant leaders, have several younger-generation staff members.

The three organizations run by 1.5- and second-generation Koreans include two already described—the Korean American Community Foundation and Minkwon Center for Community Action. The third, the Korean American Family Service Center (KAFSC), was created by an immigrant woman in the early 1980s to provide services to victims of family violence, but second-generation women assumed leadership in the late 1990s. About 700 people came to the 2011 banquet organized by KAFSC and held at the Grand Hyatt Hotel in Manhattan, with a $275 ticket price. The majority attending were 1.5- and second-generation young adults working in the mainstream economy, but many non-Koreans, mostly representing various nonprofit organizations and companies, were also there. It is interesting to note that the Korean American Community Foundation and KAFSC have drawn more people to their galas than any Korean social service agency headed by immigrant leaders.

EXPANSION OF ROOTS EDUCATION

Korean immigrants, originating from a country of great cultural homogeneity, have made notable efforts to preserve their language and culture in New York. As early as 1967, the Korean Church of New York, the first Korean church in the city, located near Columbia University, set up a Korean language school, providing a one-hour Korean language class on Sundays. In 1973, an independent Korean school was established inside Kennedy High School in the Bronx, offering classes in the Korean language, Korean music, calligraphy, and tae kwon do on Saturday mornings. The number of church-based Korean schools increased exponentially, especially in the 1980s and 1990s, as the number of Korean immigrants and Korean churches mushroomed. According to the director of the Korean Education Center at the Korean Consulate, as of 2011 there were about 170 Korean schools in the New York–New Jersey area, with about 140 (82 percent) of them established within Korean Protestant churches.

No doubt, the Korean community has an advantage in teaching children its ethnic language because of the presence of so many Protestant churches (about 520 in the New York–New Jersey area in 2011). But Korean schools in Korean Protestant churches are usually smaller than those established in other Korean religious institutions or independently. Moreover, Korean schools in Protestant churches, with some exceptions, were created partly or mainly for evangelical purposes and thus put less emphasis on teaching children Korean history and culture than other Korean schools. Korean schools established within Buddhist temples, Catholic churches, and independently focus on teaching Korean cultural traditions and national history.

The number of Korean schools in 2011 has not changed much since the late 1990s, but there has been a significant improvement in their quality. For one thing, the presence of many Korean temporary residents, including international students, has supplied well-qualified Korean-language teachers for Korean schools. Also, the local chapter of the National Association of Korean Schools has trained Korean-language teachers and published effective textbooks for the schools. It has also organized several community-wide Korean-language competitions, such as a Korean speech contest, a Korean writing contest, and a Bible translation contest, in close coordination with the Korean Education Center.

Korean culture is also kept alive and reinforced by five major Korean ethnic festivals in the New York–New Jersey area, including the Korean Children's Folk Festival, which involve Korean traditional and contemporary folk dances, music, and games in which many children participate every year. In addition, the Korean community has developed active ethnic media outlets. Television dramas and other programs produced in Korea, including popular shows like *K-pop*, are watched by many 1.5- and second-generation Korean children and adolescents.

A dozen homeland tour programs for 1.5- and second-generation young people's ethnic education have also been established. Almost all of these programs, which involve two- or three-week tours of Korea, require participants to pay their own airfare, although the New York–based organizers have arranged for government agencies and private organizations in Korea to cover expenses for hotel accommodations and local tours. Many universities in Korea have also created summer language and cultural programs for overseas Korean children and young adults. They actively recruit participants in New York and other Korean communities in the United States. In addition, many Korean college students and college graduates have visited Korea to teach English in elementary or high schools or private English-language institutes. Although English-language institutes in Korea prefer white native English speakers, some have hired 1.5- and second-generation Koreans. They usually stay in Korea for six months to three years, and some have ended up meeting—and marrying—Koreans and bringing them to the United States. The Korean government through the Ministry of Science, Technology and Education has also established the TALK (Teach and Learn in Korea) program, in which Korean Americans with two or more years of college education are eligible to teach English in elementary schools in Korean small towns. The TALK program was created both to meet the need for English teachers in Korean small towns and to provide cultural education for 1.5- and second-generation Koreans in the United States and other English-speaking countries. Native speakers who teach English in remote schools in the TALK program are paid less than teachers in urban Korean schools, but they benefit from free well-organized cultural education and tours and exposure to Korean cultural traditions in small towns. The Korean government has actively recruited Korean American students for the program through the Korean consulates in Los Angeles and New York.

CONCLUSION

In an earlier publication, writing about the late 1990s, I indicated that Korean immigrants in the New York area were highly segregated from mainstream society—culturally, socially, and linguistically—and that the participation of the majority of Korean immigrants in the Korean ethnic economy was a major factor accounting for this social segregation (Min 2001). Some fifteen years later, in 2011, Korean immigrants were still highly socially segregated from other New Yorkers compared to other Asian immigrant groups, such as Filipinos and Indians. However, in 2011, Korean immigrants seemed to be more culturally and socially incorporated into mainstream society by virtue of their lower level of participation in the ethnic economy and greater concentration in personal-service businesses involving social interactions with clients. The participation of the overwhelming majority of the 1.5 and second generation in the general labor market has further incorporated Korean Americans into mainstream society. In addition, Korean social service organizations obtain more grants from local and federal governments and American corporations to serve Koreans in need than they did in the 1990s.

In the 1980s and early 1990s, the Korean community in New York City was plagued by many business-related conflicts, which attracted local, national, and even international media attention. During that period, Korean merchants in black neighborhoods were targets of more than a dozen boycotts, while the Korean Produce Association organized several demonstrations and boycotts against produce suppliers at Hunts Point Market (Min 2008). Since the mid-1990s, as I have shown, Korean immigrants' business-related intergroup conflicts have almost disappeared in New York City. The disappearance of black boycotts represents a significant change in the Korean community and, as I have argued, has a lot to do with the reduced number of Korean retail shops in black neighborhoods. In a nutshell, Korean immigrants no longer play a prominent middleman minority role in New York City's black neighborhoods, which is yet another indicator of Koreans' incorporation into mainstream society.

That Korean immigrants and Korean Americans are more integrated into the mainstream has not necessarily reduced their cultural and social attachments to the ethnic community and their homeland. One indication is that more 1.5- and second-generation young adults participate in the operation of Korean social service and empowerment organizations than in the past. In general, Korean immigrants and their children maintain stronger attachments to both the New York ethnic community and South Korea than they did fifteen years ago. Nonimmigrant temporary residents, such as Korean international students, visiting scholars, trainees, employees of branches of Korean firms, and other visitors are present in larger numbers—and they maintain more extensive and intense cultural and social ties to family members and friends in Korea than Korean immigrants and naturalized citizens who have lived in the United States much longer. Indeed, temporary residents' close social ties to family members and friends in Korea have helped Korean old-timers establish new social networks with people in Korea. Temporary residents' active practice of Korean cultural traditions in New York has helped old-timers and their children preserve these traditions as well.

Technological advances have also facilitated Korean immigrants' and their children's transnational ties to their homeland. It is now easier (and less expensive) for Koreans to talk on the phone with their relatives and friends in Korea and to visit them than it was fifteen years ago. These days, they can also use Skype and instant messaging via the Internet to communicate with those in Korea. Moreover, the influence of Korean media is much stronger and more accessible now than it was fifteen years ago. For news and information about Korea, the vast majority of Korean immigrants primarily depend on Korean ethnic daily newspapers and TV or radio programs (all of which are now easily accessible via Internet) that largely reproduce media materials written and produced in Korea (Min and Kim 2009). Korean immigrants' transnational activities are not unidirectional, from New York and other American cities to cities in Korea. Rather, they are bidirectional; relatives and friends in Korea frequently visit Korean immigrants. Many political leaders, singers and other entertainers, and business executives from Korea participate in major Korean festivals organized in New York.

In sum, the Korean community in the New York–New Jersey metropolitan area has experienced dramatic changes in the last couple of decades, among them, as I have discussed, new characteristics of many of the latest arrivals, altered economic underpinnings of the community, and new aspects of ethnic organizational life. Paradoxically, at the same time as Koreans have become increasingly incorporated into American society, they have also displayed stronger attachments to the ethnic community and their home society. These more or less paradoxical dual changes—more incorporation into American society and at the same time more attachments to the Korean community and Korea—mean that Korean immigrants and their children are more bicultural and binational than before.

I can see the benefits of Korean immigrants' bicultural and binational orientations most clearly from my own personal life. I enjoy both Korean and American cuisines in New York and practice positive elements of both Korean and American customs and values. Coming to the United States in 1972 as an international student, I made my first visit to Korea in 1985 only when my father passed away. But I have visited Korea once or twice a year since 2000. That I would now be leading this kind of bicultural and binational life, after living in the United States for about forty years, is something I never would have imagined twenty years ago.

ACKNOWLEDGMENT

I would like to thank Nancy Foner for her editorial assistance, which has helped make this a better chapter.

REFERENCES

Bonacich, Edna. 1973. "A Theory of Middleman Minorities." *American Sociological Review* 35: 583–94.

Gold, Steven. 2010. *The Store in the Hood: A Century of Ethnic Business and Conflict*. Lanham, MD: Rowman and Littlefield.

Harper, E. J. 1979. *Immigration Laws of the United States, 1978 Supplement*. Indianapolis: Bobbs-Merrill.

Institute of International Education. 2010. *Open Doors 2009: The Annual Report on International Education*. New York: Institute of International Education.

Joyce, Patrick D. 2003. *No Fire Next Time: Black-Korean Conflicts and the Future of America's Cities*. Ithaca, NY: Cornell University Press.

Kim, Illsoo. 1981. *New Urban Immigrants: The Korean Community in New York*. Princeton, NJ: Princeton University Press.

Liu, John, Paul Ong, and Carolyn Rosenstein. 1991. "Dual Chain Migration: Post-1965 Filipino Migration." *International Migration Review* 25: 487–513.

Loewen, James. 1971. *The Mississippi Chinese: Between Black and White*. Cambridge, MA: Harvard University Press.

Min, Pyong Gap. 1984. "From White-Collar Occupations to Small Business: Korean Immigrants' Occupational Adjustment." *Sociological Quarterly* 25: 1370–94.

——. 1991. "Cultural and Economic Boundaries of Korean Ethnicity: A Comparative Analysis." *Ethnic and Racial Studies* 14: 255–41.

——. 1996. *Caught in the Middle: Korean Communities in New York and Los Angeles*. Berkeley: University of California Press.

——. 2001. "Koreans in New York: An Institutionally Complete Community." In Nancy Foner, ed., *New Immigrants in New York*, 2nd ed., 173–200. New York: Columbia University Press.

——. 2006a. "Settlement Patterns and Diversity." In Pyong Gap Min, ed., *Asian Americans: Contemporary Trends and Issues*, 32–53. Thousand Oaks, CA: Pine Forge Press.

——. 2006b. "Asian Immigration: History and Contemporary Trends." In Pyong Gap Min, ed., *Asian Americans: Contemporary Trends and Issues*, 7–31. Thousand Oaks, CA: Pine Forge Press.

——. 2008. *Ethnic Solidarity for Economic Survival: Korean Greengrocers in New York City*. New York: Russell Sage Foundation.

——. 2011. "The Immigration of Koreans to the United States: A Review of 45-Year (1965–2009) Trends." *Development and Society* 40: 195–223.

Min, Pyong Gap, and Chigon Kim. 2012. "The Growth and Settlement Patterns of the Korean Population." In Pyong Gap Min, ed., *Koreans in North America: Their Twenty-First Century Experiences*. Lanham, MD: Lexington Books.

Min, Pyong Gap, and Young Oak Kim. 2009. "Ethnic and Sub-ethnic Attachments among Korean, Chinese, and Indian Immigrants in New York City." *Ethnic and Racial Studies* 32: 225–32.

New York City Department of City Planning. 2009. *American Community Survey (ACS) Demographic and Housing Estimates: 2006–2008*. New York: New York City Department of City Planning.

Oh, Joong-Hwan. 2007. "Economic Incentive, Embeddedness, and Social Support: A Study of Korean-Owned Nail Salon Workers' Rotating Credit Associations." *International Migration Review* 41: 623–55.

Ong, Paul, and John Liu. 1994. "U.S. Immigration Policies and Asian Migration." In Paul Ong, Edna Bonacich, and Lucie Cheng, eds., *The New Asian Immigration in Los Angeles and Global Restructuring*, 45–53. Philadelphia: Temple University Press.

Rinder, Irwin. 1958–59. "Strangers in the Land: Social Relations in the 'Status Gap.'" *Social Problems* 6: 253–60.

Rosenthal, Elizabeth. 1995. "Competition and Cutbacks Hurt Foreign Doctors in the U.S." *New York Times*, November 7.

7. *Jamaicans*

BALANCING RACE AND ETHNICITY

Milton Vickerman

Immigration scholars often speak of gateway cities when referring to urban areas that are disproportionately funneling immigrants into the United States. New York City is particularly important in this respect, and Jamaicans have become a prominent part of the migrant stream there. Over the past four decades they, along with thousands of other West Indians, have given several of the city's neighborhoods a distinct island flavor. In areas such as Crown Heights, East Flatbush, Wakefield, and Laurelton, West Indian-accented English, restaurants advertising patties and roti, and calypso and reggae music blaring from car radios remind visitors of Kingston (Jamaica), Bridgetown (Barbados), and Port of Spain (Trinidad). As the population of West Indians has grown, they have deepened their roots in these neighborhoods and expanded into a number of new ones. In the process, they are complicating the city's racial dynamics by renewing considerations of ethnic identity among blacks but also underlining the continued importance of race.

Although New York City's total West Indian population has increased, in this chapter I focus on Jamaicans because of their disproportionately large numbers—in 2010, there were some 170,000 foreign-born Jamaicans in New York City—and their strong cultural influence. I provide background on their settlement and incorporation patterns and argue that their adaptation to American society is strongly influenced by contradictory pressures—or cross pressures—concerning race, generated by the conflict between attitudes and orientations they bring from Jamaica and new notions of race in the United States. These cross pressures and Jamaicans' economic activities help to determine their position in New York City. In developing this argument, and describing the New York Jamaican community, I draw on census data, data from the Department of Homeland Security, the work of numerous researchers who have studied West Indian New Yorkers, and my own research on these immigrants,[1] as well as personal knowledge as a Jamaican immigrant myself. In using the term *race*, I refer to the belief that socially significant differences between human groups are innate and unchangeable; ethnicity involves groups whose members feel a sense of belonging because of a belief in common ancestry and descent (see Foner and Fredrickson 2004; Weber 1998). By West Indian, I mean people from the Anglophone Caribbean, including the mainland nation of Guyana.[2]

MIGRATION AND SETTLEMENT

Jamaicans and other West Indians have a long history of migrating to other countries in search of a better life (Marshall 1982; Palmer 1990; James 2004). This is not surprising. West Indians come from societies with small, resource-poor economies that are highly dependent on more developed societies. Income, wealth, and land are distributed unequally, and their societies are marked by high levels of unemployment and underemployment. At the same time, because of the proximity of North America, tourism, and the influence of American media throughout the region, as well as the fact that many, perhaps most, West Indians have relatives in the United States and Canada, West Indians are well aware of American affluence and standards of living. Moreover, U.S. and Canadian investment in the region, as well as the American economy's demand for individuals with particular skills, have contributed to the outflow from the West Indies. In fact, migration is a flight response that has become engrained in the culture of West Indian societies (Brodber 1989). This includes not only internal migration from rural to urban areas, but—much more significantly—international migration. Once begun, migration is also network driven, a dynamic that has been reinforced by the family reunification provisions of U.S. immigration law.

Large-scale Jamaican migration to the United States dates from the beginning of the twentieth century, with Jamaicans predominating among the 138,615 West Indians who migrated to this country from 1899 to 1928 (Reid 1939:235).[3] New York City—especially Harlem in the first third of the twentieth century—was the destination of choice. U.S. restrictions, along with the Great Depression, virtually halted emigration from Jamaica after the late 1920s and may actually have reversed the flow. Following World War II, beginning in the late 1940s and taking off in the 1950s, huge numbers of Jamaicans—along with other West

Indians—migrated to Britain (Eisner 1961:147; Smith 1981:151). This movement to the "mother country" was severely curbed when the British government passed the Commonwealth Immigration Act in 1962 (Smith 1981; Dean 1993). Not long after, in 1965, the Hart-Celler Immigration Act in the United States shifted West Indian immigration back to this country, ushering in the present wave, which is still going strong.

A look at statistics collected by the U.S. government shows the dramatic increase in numbers after the passage of the 1965 Immigration Act. In the ten years before 1965, approximately 1,500 Jamaicans per year migrated to the United States; in the decade 1966–1975, Jamaican immigration averaged 12,400 annually. Between 1976 and 1985, the numbers increased further, to about 18,000 per year, in large part a result of the political turmoil, high crime rate,[4] and economic recession that characterized Jamaica through much of the 1970s and into the early 1980s. In 1977, a poll conducted by Jamaican political scientist Carl Stone (1982:63–65) revealed that almost 60 percent of Jamaicans said they would go to live in the United States if given the opportunity. Since the early 1980s, continuing economic difficulties have led to high rates of emigration, including among members of the middle and upper middle class. Especially troubling for Jamaica is the high proportion of skilled Jamaicans who move abroad. International Monetary Fund data show that in the thirty-five-year span from 1965 to 2000, 4 percent of Jamaicans attaining only a primary school education migrated to the United States. This was true of 33 percent of high school graduates—and a remarkable 61 percent of college graduates (Mishra 2006). According to the World Bank, in 2000 the emigration rate among the tertiary-educated population in Jamaica stood at 85 percent, with 42 percent of Jamaican physicians emigrating (World Bank 2011b). Female migrants to the United States have outnumbered males throughout the post-1965 period, a gender difference that is linked, at least in part, to unemployment patterns in Jamaica, which have been consistently higher for women. Between January 2010 and April 2012, for example, the unemployment rate in Jamaica averaged 9.5 percent for men, but 17 percent for women (Statistical Institute of Jamaica 2012). In 2010, 55 percent of Jamaicans obtaining legal permanent residency status in the United States were women (Monger and Yankay 2011), and as chapter 2 shows, the sex ratio for Jamaican immigrants in New York City in 2010 was remarkably low, with 75 males for every 100 females. To a large extent, this disproportionate flow of Jamaican women stems from the nature of American immigration policy and the availability of jobs in the United States. Researchers have noted that in the early years of the recent immigration, Jamaican women found jobs more easily than Jamaican men (see, for example, Foner 1998, 2008).

Within the United States, Jamaicans and other West Indian immigrants are highly concentrated along the east coast, with most living in New York and Florida (and within Florida, in the Miami–Fort Lauderdale metropolitan area).

In 2007–9, New York State and Florida accounted for 36 percent and 28 percent, respectively, of the 627,000 foreign-born Jamaicans residing in the United States.[5] Other notable—but much smaller—concentrations were in New Jersey (6 percent), Connecticut and Georgia (both 5 percent), and Maryland (3 percent). The New York City metropolitan area retains its status as the center of the Jamaican community in the United States. Depending on exactly how this metropolitan area is defined, it accounts for anywhere from one-quarter to one-third of all Jamaican Americans in the nation; in New York City itself, Brooklyn is the most popular borough for Jamaican Americans, followed by the Bronx and Queens.

Particular neighborhoods in central Brooklyn (Crown Heights, East Flatbush, Flatbush, and Flatlands-Canarsie), the Bronx (Wakefield and Williamsbridge-Baychester), and Queens (Cambria Heights, Rosedale, Springfield Gardens–Laurelton, and St. Albans) stand out as Jamaican (and West Indian) neighborhoods (New York City Department of City Planning 1999: 34–40). African Americans are often present in large numbers in West Indian neighborhoods, as well; West Indian and African American neighborhoods are often intertwined and the two groups typically live side by side. Both groups experience extraordinarily high rates of residential segregation from whites in New York City (Crowder and Tedrow 2001; Logan and Deane 2003).

As Jamaicans improve their occupational and income status, they often move to surrounding suburbs or other states that are seen as offering a better quality of life, including better housing and schools. Jamaicans living in suburban Westchester County (and Queens), not surprisingly, have higher household incomes and lower poverty rates than those in the Bronx and Brooklyn. In recent years, there has also been some movement southward, with Washington, DC, and Atlanta, Georgia, being especially popular among highly educated, professional, and well-off Jamaicans. These cities—as well as Miami—have another draw: the warmer climate, reminiscent of the West Indies, as well as closer physical proximity to Jamaica than New York. The Miami-to-Kingston flight takes less than one hour, compared to three hours from New York City.

ADJUSTING TO AMERICAN SOCIETY: CROSS PRESSURES

In grappling with adjusting to life in the United States, issues of race are critical for Jamaicans, who find themselves being pulled in opposite directions by contending, powerful forces or cross pressures—influenced by both homeland and American views of race (Bryce-Laporte 1972).[6]

Race has always been important in Jamaica because of its long history as a slave plantation society. After the end of slavery, and under the long period of

British colonial rule, class correlated strictly with race, and social conflict often manifested itself as class conflict with racial overtones (Curtin 1970; Austin-Broos 1987; Lewis 1968, 1977; Phillips 1977). This occurred because in the pyramidal structure that characterized colonial-era Jamaica, a small but powerful white elite dominated the island's politics and economy. The great mass of the population consisted of African-descended people at the bottom of the pyramid who had the fewest opportunities. In between these two poles lay a mixed-race ("colored") segment that was European in its orientation (Curtin 1970).

The impact of the past lingers on in that many of the largest Jamaican corporations are dominated by white Jamaicans, consciousness of skin shade continues to exist, and class inequality remains high. However, there have also been marked changes. One is that in the decades since Jamaica gained independence in 1962, individual achievement through personal effort—especially through gaining higher educational credentials—has become increasingly important. Although Jamaica's hierarchically ordered education system has been unable to fully accommodate the demands made on it, the belief in the possibility of mobility through education remains influential and, indeed, has become a cultural ideal (Smith 1965). Moreover, as dark-skinned Jamaicans have increasingly achieved upward mobility, the relationship between complexion and social class has started to break down. Many high-achieving—and dark-skinned—Jamaicans feel a high level of self-esteem. Skin color is less important today than it was in earlier decades (Lewis 1968; Richardson 1983; Stone 1988, 1989), and there is a general belief that race is not a barrier to success.

These developments mean that in their day-to-day lives, Jamaicans on the island are not preoccupied with race. Instead, their identity is organized more around the attainment of upward mobility (especially through education). When Jamaicans come to the United States, these attitudes are reinforced by characteristics of the immigrants themselves: Jamaicans possess an immigrant mentality (i.e., as outsiders with a strong desire to succeed), and the most skilled Jamaicans, with qualifications that facilitate successful integration into the American job market, are most likely to migrate (Mishra 2006; Model 2008).

The other side of the cross-pressures equation has to do with American racial realities. Despite significant progress in race relations—witness the election of Barack Obama—American society still discriminates against blacks in a manner to which Jamaicans are not accustomed, and Americans tend to view Jamaicans through a racial frame instead of as ethnics. Furthermore, a widespread expectation is that most blacks will not do well, which runs against the immigrant ethos held by many Jamaicans (and West Indians). The upshot is that while Jamaicans emphasize their ethnic (national) identity, Americans often emphasize Jamaicans' race, as blacks. This conflict between how Jamaicans view themselves and how Americans view them fits with Mary Waters's (1990) argument that identity derives from the interaction between how individuals attempt to define themselves (agency) and society's imposition of labels on individuals and groups.

THE JAMAICAN BACKGROUND

To better understand the nature of the cross pressures Jamaican immigrants experience, it is helpful to briefly elaborate on the factors in Jamaica that have shaped their ideas about race and the kind of identity they bring with them to New York. Jamaicans' focus on individualized achievement through obtaining educational credentials should be seen as a political and cultural response to socioeconomic inequality in Jamaican society.[7] This long-term problem, created and reinforced by 300 years of slavery and colonialism, reached a modern crisis point around the time of Jamaica's independence from Britain in August 1962. Faced with the problem of how to maintain social stability in the midst of social and economic inequality, the mixed-race ("brown") leaders who came into power in Jamaica after independence resorted to the same solutions that had been pioneered by the British rulers under colonialism, an important one having to do with ideology.

Two aspects of postindependence ideology pertaining to inequality and notions of race are significant here. One is the notion that Jamaica is a multiracial society in which various groups live in harmony. The best expression of this is the country's official postindependence motto: "Out of many, one people." Another important aspect of Jamaica's postindependence ideology has been the view that individual Jamaicans, whatever their color or socioeconomic background, can attain upward mobility through hard work and the right educational credentials.

Despite Jamaica's history of inequality, the idea that education is the key to upward mobility has been strongly embraced in Jamaican culture (Norris 1962; Smith 1965; Foner 1973; Kuper 1976; Austin 1987). Jamaicans—especially the underprivileged—hope for a brighter future for their children through education. Their hopes have been nurtured and reinforced by the fact that there are many successful highly educated Jamaicans in the society, as well as famous Jamaicans and other West Indians who rose from humble origins to worldwide fame based on their intellectual achievements. Examples include early twentieth-century novelist Claude McKay, Trinidadian journalist and essayist C. L. R. James, and St. Lucian poet and playwright Derek Walcott.[8] Postindependence upward mobility for dark-skinned Jamaicans has been particularly important in cementing Jamaicans' faith in the uplifting power of higher education. In their minds, these achievements reaffirm the efficacy of schooling.

In reality, many Jamaicans have relied on other means for attaining upward mobility. For ordinary Jamaicans, mass migration to the United States, Canada, and the United Kingdom is particularly noteworthy in this respect. Not only has migration provided Jamaicans with opportunities to achieve upward mobility abroad, but also, and perhaps surprisingly, it created new possibilities in Jamaica as well. In the 1970s, as economic, social, and political turmoil prompted large numbers of white, Chinese, and mixed-race Jamaican business owners to emigrate, substantial opportunities opened up on the island for educated and financially well-off dark-skinned Jamaicans. Ownership of many of the businesses ended up in the hands of the black middle class (Stone 1988). The globalization of Jamaican culture has provided yet another route to upward mobility for some ordinary Jamaicans. For instance, reggae's global popularity has lifted some Jamaicans of humble birth to worldwide fame. Bob Marley and his family are the best example of this. Similarly, in the sport of track and field, Jamaican athletes such as Usain Bolt, Asafa Powell, and Merlene Ottey have risen to global prominence.

The overwhelming demographic predominance of African-descended Jamaicans has buttressed the dynamics I have described. This demographic reality has undermined race's salience by normalizing blackness and daily presenting Jamaicans with many examples of both high achievers and social failures, virtually all of whom have African ancestry. In their minds this effectively severs the link between race and achievement. The average Jamaican is used to seeing people of African ancestry at all levels of society, from homeless people on the street to prime ministers. Importantly, many high achievers are visible in the political system, since most postcolonial Jamaican leaders have been people of color, many of them very dark skinned. This system, itself, plays a key role in undermining the salience of race by organizing politics around a two-party model that draws its strength from a coalition of different classes. The system avoids appeals to race, thereby helping to prevent the subject from becoming a public issue (see, for example, Stone 1972, 1973; Nettleford 1978; Palmer 1989). Instead of race, what does tend to preoccupy Jamaicans are the ongoing machinations of the major political parties, the country's economic problems, and its high crime rate.

One other factor conspires to deemphasize race in Jamaica. Unlike the United States, Jamaica never developed a "one-drop rule," where possession of the merest trace of African ancestry has made an individual categorically black. Instead of a blunt black-white schema, Jamaicans have combined lineage with education, occupation, wealth, and skin shade in assessing race (see, for example, Henriques 1957). Consequently, it might be more accurate to speak of a "shadeocracy" than race when discussing Jamaican society. In present-day Jamaica—and in fact for more than half a century—a person with dark skin who is highly educated, is wealthy, and holds a prestigious occupation is recognized for these characteristics—and is not stigmatized on the basis of skin color. Jamaicans evince a general dislike of viewing the world in racial terms, even while postindependence social change has moved the island's African heritage to the cultural center (Richardson

1983). An unspoken taboo exists about speaking out forcefully on racial issues, and individuals who break this taboo find themselves subject to harsh criticism (see, for example, Nettleford 1978; Post 1978).

JAMAICAN ETHNICITY IN NEW YORK CITY

Although American society tends to impose the label "black" on people of African ancestry, overlooking or ignoring national-origin differences, to Jamaicans themselves, their ethnic identities are important. In New York, Jamaican immigrants view themselves as Jamaicans and West Indians, using the two terms interchangeably—as I often do in this chapter. Although a degree of tension exists between the various Caribbean islanders, several factors offset divisions among West Indians. These include a common history as British colonies, shared cultural elements and language, and regional West Indian institutions such as the University of the West Indies. Migrating to New York City solidifies Jamaican immigrants' "West Indianness" even more as, rubbing shoulders with non–West Indian New Yorkers, they come to recognize their strong similarities with others from the Anglophone Caribbean. That Jamaicans live in neighborhoods with other West Indian immigrants and participate in the annual West Indian Labor Day festival along Eastern Parkway in Brooklyn both reflects and reinforces a shared sense of West Indian ethnicity.

Consistent with their premigration socialization, immigrant sensibilities, and the tendency for the most qualified Jamaicans to migrate, a central defining element of Jamaican (and West Indian) ethnic identity in New York City is a self-perception that Jamaicans are hard-working achievers. Jamaicans tend to express annoyance with the idea that race is more important than educational and occupational qualifications and with assumptions that black people cannot attain success. As one middle-aged manager I interviewed put it:

> I think a man should be qualified for a job. . . . I don't want a job because I'm black. I want a job because I'm qualified. . . . If you make an application here [for a job], they want to know your race. What the hell with my race! I feel right away that you're going to judge me off of that and I am at a disadvantage there. I'm a man! Do I have the qualifications? That [is what] you must find out. (Vickerman 1999:104)

Along the same lines, another respondent, a chemist, stated:

> I think we [West Indians] refuse . . . to really get caught up in the whole racial issue . . . although we are being treated the same way racially. Our thing is . . . to forge ahead just the same. . . . Since . . . we . . . grow up . . . [with] a more

> socio-economic issue in the West Indies—we are not that sensitive to racism; although some, you know, is pretty blatant that you just can't refuse from knowing that it is racism. (Vickerman 1999:95)

Jamaicans measure achievement in New York City in occupational, material, and educational terms, evaluating themselves according to both American and Jamaican standards. Because of Jamaica's much smaller economy, many perceive the United States as presenting huge opportunities and, despite the hard work necessary to get ahead and improve their standard of living in New York, believe that migrating there was the right decision. The data seem to support this assessment. Home ownership is a key measure of success for Jamaicans, and in New York City they are often more likely to own their own homes than the average New Yorker. According to the 2012 American Community Survey, 37 percent of Jamaicans living in the Bronx (compared to 19 percent of non-Jamaicans) own their homes; in Brooklyn, 36 percent of Jamaicans are homeowners, as against 30 percent of non-Jamaicans. Overall, Jamaicans' home ownership rate is lowest in Manhattan (15 percent) and highest in Staten Island (63 percent) and Queens (60 percent).

Another aspect of Jamaicans' cultural orientations and indeed their ethnic identity in New York is a tendency toward conservatism on social issues (Rohter 1997). This social conservatism is ironic in light of the common portrayal of Jamaicans as hedonistic (a useful tourism marketing tool) and troublemakers, but it manifests itself in a variety of ways. For instance, contrary to their portrayal as remorseless killers in movies such as *Predator 2* (1990), *Klash* (1996), and *Marked for Death* (1998), Jamaicans often hold conservative views on law-and-order issues, for example, supporting strong police actions against criminals. In a March 1978 poll, 41 percent of Kingstonians responded that the police use "too little violence" in the apprehension of criminals. Another 27 percent felt that the use of police violence was "just enough."[9] (Kingston, the capital of Jamaica, is the site of much of the violence in the country.) Similarly, in a June 1980 poll, 79 percent of Jamaicans agreed that the army and police were able to protect the country from gunmen (Stone 1982:68–69).

The widespread support for strong police measures stems from the seriousness of the ongoing crime problem in Jamaica (rooted in class inequality, drug trafficking, and political party conflict). As might be expected, poorer Jamaicans on the island, who are often on the receiving end of law-and-order efforts by the government and police, view matters more skeptically and, like many other Jamaicans, are often wary of police (and army) violence in the apprehension of criminals. Nevertheless, even poorer Jamaicans—and the poverty rate declined from 19.1 percent in 2003 to 9.1 percent in 2007 (World Bank 2011a)—have been socialized to respect law and order. Despite Jamaica's high crime rate, this socialization is generally effective, since the society is relatively stable.[10] (Another factor in political stability, it should be mentioned, is that Jamaicans enjoy a great deal of freedom of speech in print and the expanding broadcast media, and enthusiastically criticize politics, politicians, and problems in Jamaican society. Also, as mentioned before, migration acts as a safety valve to relieve social pressures.)

A second example of Jamaicans' social conservatism is that male Jamaican immigrants often hold traditional views on family life. For instance, they regard themselves as heads of their households and domestic chores as women's work. In fact, Jamaican women are very independent and have a long tradition of working outside the home. In the Caribbean, perhaps the best-known example are "higglers," women who dominate the selling of produce in open-air markets. Working women in Jamaica often experience a "double shift," both working outside the home and performing traditional female chores at home. The double shift follows them to New York, but as immigration scholars have shown (e.g., Foner 1998, 2008; Bonnett 1990; Gordon 1990), the process of going abroad increases their sense of autonomy even more—especially since women have often pioneered the serial migration pattern characterizing Jamaicans. It has been common for women to leave by themselves and work for several years in the United States while arranging for partners and children to join them.

Jamaican immigrants' views on child rearing are another area where their conservative social values are in evidence. They dislike permissiveness and believe that children should show respect to their elders. Contrary to American mainstream values, they feel that corporal punishment is an appropriate, in fact desirable, disciplinary tool (see Waters and Sykes 2009). As one second-generation Jamaican high school student put it: "West Indian parents do not tolerate . . . raising your voice [to them]. . . . You must respect your elders and things of that nature—no matter what: always respect them." Not surprisingly, parents' attempts to maintain this kind of traditional authority and to transfer old world values to children can lead to conflict within immigrant families, particularly if the children have an attenuated relationship with Jamaican culture or if the parent in New York is trying to reimpose authority on children who have only recently immigrated from Jamaica.

THE IMPACT OF RACE

Jamaican ethnicity in New York City develops within the context of a society that is highly racialized and is reactive since it increases in intensity as Jamaicans experience more racism (Portes and Rumbaut 1996). The problem is that while Jamaicans may emphasize their ethnicity, their racialization as blacks in the United States—involving a whole range of negative stereotypes—is usually of greater consequence. In other words, Jamaicans may identify as Jamaican or West Indian, but other New Yorkers often just see them as black.

Even Jamaicans who have lived in the United States for many years have trouble coming to terms with the fact that their skin color has such a negative impact on their daily lives and aspirations. Having moved from a society where race is not a publicly debated issue and where blacks are numerically and politically dominant, they find that learning to cope with America's racial order is painful and difficult. American racism, associated with negative notions of blackness, is a major test of adjustment. Here is how a young computer programmer I interviewed put it:

> Race was important [in Jamaica] but not on a day to day basis. The difference I find is that when you get to America, you have to start thinking about race when you walk into the store. . . . In Manhattan you walk into a store; you'll find that people will be following you around: Things like that you have never been accustomed to. To me, what has been a shocker here is to walk on the train and for women to clutch their handbags. . . . That has been, to me, my worst problem to overcome since I have been here. (Vickerman 1999:95)

Most of the Jamaicans I interviewed spoke of subtle racism—such as being followed in stores or, like the computer programmer, women clutching their purses when they approached. A few complained of threats of racial attacks or actual racial attacks. Some of the men reported being stopped and insulted by the police; many feared that such encounters could result in physical abuse, which is why they tended to be wary of the police. Others reported blatant and aggressive discrimination in various public places, like this 51-year-old accountant:

> I go to the track one day a year—the Belmont stakes. . . . There are . . . benches around the place that you can sit on; not reserved, not paid for. Everybody pays $5.00 and you go into the clubhouse. . . . We were feeling a little tired and we went . . . to sit down; have a break before we go have something to eat. And we sat and these people started to tell us that these seats were reserved. So we said, "look, these seats are not reserved. If you want to reserve a seat you have to pay extra because I have one of the tags." . . . And this redneck guy looked around and told us that . . . he used to . . . kill people like us; meaning he used to kill black people! (Vickerman 1999:102)

Discrimination in the workplace is, for Jamaicans, the unkindest cut of all, since it not only directly targets their economic well-being but also the central pillar of their self-image: the notion of hard-working competence built around educational qualifications. Among the men in my study, racial incidents in the workplace varied in detail, but all left a bitter taste. One man, a truck driver, told me of confrontations with his immediate superior over the latter's treatment of black customers. Others spoke of being denied promotions for racial reasons. As one man bitterly put it: "I was doing the work but I would be in charge of all whites. . . . They didn't want me to do that."

The other side of the coin is positive discrimination that works in Jamaicans' (and other West Indians') favor (Kaufman 1995; Kasinitz and Rosenberg 1996; Waters 1999). Some Jamaicans I interviewed believed that employers preferred to hire them over native minorities, especially African Americans. A considerable literature supports this view, indicating that U.S. employers favor immigrants over African Americans because they see immigrants as more reliable and pliable—as more willing than native minorities to work hard and long for low wages and to stay on the job (see, for example, Waldinger and Lichter 2003; Wilson 1997; Vickerman 2007). To the extent that employers do prefer to hire Jamaicans, it is clearly an advantage that West Indians enjoy relative to African Americans.

JAMAICANS' IMPACT ON NEW YORK CITY

POPULATION

The influx of tens of thousands of Jamaican immigrants has obviously had a significant impact on New York City. One impact has to do with sheer numbers. In 2009, in the United States as a whole, only 8 percent of the black population was foreign-born, with 5 percent originating in the West Indies (the other 3 percent is mostly of African origin) (American Community Survey 2007–9). Foreign-born blacks comprise a much larger—and growing—percentage of New York City's black population, accounting for approximately one-third of all non-Hispanic blacks in the city (compared to 10 percent in 1970). Although there is a growing African presence, the overwhelming majority of foreign-born blacks in New York City are West Indian in origin (chapter 2, this volume). The increasing Caribbeanization of the city's black population has a broad range of implications, including the rising influence of West Indians in politics. As of 2011, there were three city councillors of Afro-Caribbean origin and one representative to the U.S. Congress (second-generation Jamaican Yvette Clarke), and New York City's school chancellor was a third-generation West Indian.

ECONOMIC IMPACT

Jamaicans in New York City have remarkably high labor force participation rates, especially among women. In 2010, 79 percent of Jamaican immigrant men in New York City were in the labor force (compared to 76 percent of all men in the city) and 83 percent of Jamaican immigrant women (compared to 67 percent of all New York City women) (chapter 2, this volume). Overwhelmingly, Jamaicans work in private industry, although a sizable proportion are employed in government. Only a small proportion—5 percent in 2009—of foreign-born Jamaicans in the New York City metropolitan area are self-employed. Jamaican immigrant New Yorkers have relatively high household incomes—in 2010, a median household income of $49,374 (chapter 2, this volume)—mainly because many members of Jamaican families are working. These facts indicate that though, in general terms, Jamaican culture influences how Jamaicans adapt to American society—especially where race is concerned—immigrant selectivity accounts for many aspects of their performance in the economy (e.g., labor force participation, household income, and poverty rates) (Model 2008).

One way Jamaicans have affected New York City economically is through concentrating in distinct occupational niches. These niches result from a combination of the structure of opportunities available to Jamaicans in the New York economy (including possible employer preferences); the skills, human capital, and cultural preferences they bring with them; and the operation of ethnic networks through which employment information and referrals flow (see Kasinitz and Vickerman 2001). New Yorkers are likely to encounter Jamaican women working as domestics and in a variety of health care fields. In New York City, 44 percent of Jamaicans (mostly women) in 2009 worked in "educational services, and health care and social assistance" (American Community Survey 2007–9). A path for many Jamaican women is to start out as nursing home or hospital aides (or domestics in private homes), move up to become licensed practical nurses, and then receive additional training to qualify to become registered nurses. College-educated women aspire higher, to become nurse practitioners, health care administrators, or physicians (along with accounting, engineering, law, and university professorships, perhaps the five most prestigious professions in Jamaica).

Private household work, involving care for affluent New Yorkers' young children or the growing number of frail elderly, illustrates how a confluence of factors has created a specific niche for Jamaican women. Indeed, in the post-1965 period, demand from well-off white women for in-home child care has been an important factor drawing many Jamaican women to New York City. Having favorably impressed their employers, these workers created networks that pulled in even more Jamaican women. Alone in a strange country—especially if they worked in distant suburbs—these women tightened their bonds even further through frequent contact. By saving money from their meager wages through rotating credit associations ("partners," in Jamaican terminology), many were able to raise the funds for purchasing household consumer items and sometimes cars, and even for making down payments on houses (see, for example, Bonnett 1981; Kasinitz 1992; Johnson 1997; Louis 2000).[11]

Jamaican men are less occupationally concentrated than women; they are about as likely to work as managers or professionals as security guards. They have, however, created a niche in the jitney van industry. Jamaican (and other West Indian) men responded to gaps in New York's public transportation system by recreating the private response to a public need for better and cheaper transportation that had developed earlier in Jamaica. In Jamaica (and other Caribbean islands), public transportation is often inefficient and unreliable, and some men developed a fiercely competitive network of small vans ("robots") to transport Jamaicans within the big cities (notably Kingston) and throughout the island. In New York City, this transplant was met by a knowing, generally appreciative, nod by West Indians, who found New York City transit buses and subways not frequent or fast enough, especially in outlying areas of Brooklyn and Queens. Although sometimes overcrowded and uncomfortable, the vans come often and are convenient. New York City authorities were initially skeptical about the vans, but ultimately were swayed by the newfound political clout of West Indian politicians to legalize the industry (see, for example, Kasinitz 1992; Tierney 1997; Dao 1999).

RACIAL AND ETHNIC RELATIONS

West Indians' enhanced political clout in the city follows in the New York tradition of new ethnic groups eventually gaining influence on the political scene as their numbers grow. Typically, according to Kasinitz (1992), this rise is facilitated by "ethnicity entrepreneurs" who make it their business to spotlight the ethnic group and push its agenda. In the case of West Indians, this agenda often, but not always, overlaps with that of their African American neighbors, with whom they share common concerns, particularly on the basis of race. West Indians often resemble African Americans in their voting patterns—both groups are overwhelmingly Democratic—and in their support for candidates who they perceive will advance the interests of blacks as a group.

A growing West Indian population is complicating this dynamic, as their greatly increased numbers and residential concentration have enabled West Indians to establish themselves as a distinct ethnic voting bloc and to mobilize on many occasions along ethnic lines. Politically, West Indians have concerns that do not always jibe with those of African Americans—and they have a more intense interest than African Americans in certain issues. West Indians, for instance, championed immigration reform in response to the 1996 immigration act, which penalized immigrants in a variety of ways. Jamaicans are interested in issues of economic development in the Caribbean. At about $2 billion in 2009, remittances constituted 14 percent of Jamaica's gross domestic product (World Bank 2011b), and West Indian American politicians (not to mention ordinary West Indian immigrants) display a keen interest in facilitating this flow.

Jamaicans and other West Indians also, at times, seek to distance themselves from African Americans, asserting their ethnic identity to fend off racism and being lumped together with American blacks. Typically, distancing centers around questions of race and achievement, personal behavior, and family issues—and involves contrasts with poor African Americans who live in or near their neighborhoods. Jamaicans often say they are harder and more consistent workers than African Americans; that they are more law abiding and family oriented; and that they place more value on education.

Yet distancing is only one part of the equation; identification is the other. To a certain extent, this identification is premigration in origin, since Jamaicans, living in Jamaica, have often shared the concerns and rejoiced in the victories of African Americans. For instance, the Black Power movement exerted a strong influence on many young black Jamaicans on the island in the 1960s (Lewis 1977; Palmer 1989), and the leading figures of the civil rights movement—such as Malcolm X and, certainly, Martin Luther King Jr.—were widely admired. Needless to say, Barack Obama's election in 2008 as the first black president was greeted with great joy. Culturally speaking, feelings of commonality with African Americans are especially deep. As one example, in the 1960s and 1970s the boxer Muhammad Ali was hugely popular in Jamaica. But it is in the area of music where we see the most pronounced African American influence, since modern Jamaican music (from the 1960s forward) developed from local Jamaican attempts to emulate African American rhythm and blues and soul music in the 1960s and 1970s (Clarke 1981; Goldman 2000).

In the United States, Jamaicans' intermingling with African Americans in the workplace, neighborhoods, and schools leads to friendships and produces common outlooks on crucial aspects of American society. Living in New York, and having firsthand experiences of racial discrimination there (despite improvements in recent years), gives Jamaicans a better understanding of the African American experience and promotes identification with native-born blacks. In my research, Jamaicans who had lived in New York City for a long time were more strongly identified with African Americans than those who had only recently arrived. Over time, Jamaicans become black in the American sense as their race trumps their ethnicity. This identification as black is illustrated by comments from two men I interviewed in the late 1980s:

> We were doing an audit once where we had to go into a white neighborhood—Marine Park. . . . I was there with my white supervisor and we were driving the state car and he said: "You know, the only blacks around here are maids and gardeners, so when they see a black person driving through they get very fearful." . . . And it was a little scary because, in fact, we were out there for a few hours and I didn't see no black people coming out of those homes. . . . I wouldn't go there in the nights by myself (Leon, accountant). (Vickerman 1999:108)

> The black community, we are stereotyped. Your skin is black and therefore you are supposed to be so and so and so and so. You talk to them, they [the police] really want to talk down to you. You could have ten Ph.D.s. . . . You have some of them who'll tell you who you are and what you are based solely on the color of your skin (Nelson, high level manager). (Vickerman 1999:110)

He summed up the situation this way: "Some of us . . . say we are different . . . but don't fool yourself, you are judged basically on this [skin color]. . . . So I don't . . . get carried away; say, well, I am West Indian, I am treated differently. That's nonsensical!" (Vickerman 1999:152)

THE SECOND GENERATION

The question of incorporation and the impact of race arises with particular force for the U.S.-born children of Jamaican immigrants—the second generation. Their immigrant parents often look back to their homeland for referents when navigating American society. But what of their children who are born in the United States? A central issue is how the second generation will identify themselves—as Jamaicans or West Indians, as blacks, as African Americans, or a combination of all three. Mary Waters (1999) has argued that poor, inner-city, West Indian youth are likely to identify as African American because they experience especially pronounced racial discrimination and social alienation. In contrast, she expects middle-class West Indian youth to identify ethnically as West Indians, in part because they (and their parents) perceive this identity as facilitating upward mobility. Typically these families possess the resources to realize this mobility.

Yet middle-class youth, like many I interviewed in my study, see themselves as partially West Indian but also as American. While some evidence supports Waters's thesis (see, for example, Vickerman 2002), there is also evidence suggesting a gradual blurring of group boundaries between West Indian and African American youth. This process involves a hybridization in which elements from West Indian and African American culture are melding into something new (Kasinitz et al. 2002; Richards 2007).

The cross-fertilization dynamic between second-generation West Indians and African Americans is apparent in the field of popular culture. Just as the development of late twentieth-century Jamaican music was influenced by African American rhythm and blues and soul music, the birth of hip-hop music was influenced by Jamaican immigrants. Specifically, "toasting," a form of reggae in which artists speak words over a soundtrack, helped set the stage, in the Bronx, for the format that became hip-hop. Not surprisingly, a number of early stars in the genre—such as Biggie Smalls, Busta Rhymes, Kool Herc, and Eric B—were of Jamaican ancestry (Goldman 2000). Today, a new generation of West Indian stars—such as Sean Paul and Damian Marley (Jamaican ancestry), Nicki Minaj (Trinidadian ancestry), and Rhianna (Barbadian ancestry)—are normalizing Jamaican and West Indian culture among Americans, including African Americans. But their music is often as American as it is West Indian, if not more so. In the new hybrid culture that is developing among black youth in New York City, it is often difficult to disentangle the Jamaican/West Indian and African American cultural influences.

CONCLUSION

Jamaicans have become an increasingly important part of New York City life because of their growing numbers and cultural influence; at the same time, they are embedded within the larger West Indian community and the even larger African American community. As immigrants, they are primarily focused on the difficult process of adjusting to life in the United States. Sociologist Roy Bryce-Laporte (1972:48) has argued that West Indians operate—as blacks and immigrants—in the United States under "more levels of cross-pressures, multiple affiliations, and inequalities than either native blacks or European immigrants." Among Jamaican Americans, the cross pressures Bryce-Laporte refers to, and that I emphasize in this chapter, relate to conflicts between, on the one hand, views they bring with them based on ideas about race and mobility developed in modern-day Jamaica and, on the other, the realities of racial inequality in the United States. In coming to the United States, Jamaicans enter a society that is more overtly racialized than Jamaican society. Despite marked improvements in the United States in the post–civil rights era, Jamaicans find that in New York they are discriminated against as blacks and often are not expected to do well.

This means that, for Jamaicans, the standard immigrant question of how they will incorporate into American society takes on a distinctly racial edge. The general tendency for their activities to be interpreted within a racial framework in the United States is frustrating, disappointing, and upsetting for Jamaicans, if only because they come from a society that underplays race. Their frustrations may be long lasting. Indeed, as new Jamaican arrivals, steeped in their homeland society's views, continue to come to New York—and as many immigrants go back and forth between New York and the Caribbean—it is even possible that, at least among some first-generation immigrants, the tensions between Jamaican cultural orientations and American racial realities will increase .

There are added complications because Jamaicans are embedded in the African American community not only by American racism but also by choice.

Jamaican immigrants, as I have noted, share many cultural and structural connections with African Americans. Although in some ways the two groups are distinct from each other, overall, Jamaicans come to see themselves as part of the larger black population, something that becomes even more pronounced the longer they have lived in New York.

In considering how Jamaicans will incorporate into American society, the second generation is of great significance. Research shows that second-generation West Indians are merging into the African American population in New York City, but the cultural influence they wield—particularly Jamaicans, the largest national-origin group among them—and their substantial size means that this merger does not equal disappearance. Instead, in New York City, a hybridization process is taking place, in which West Indian and African American youth share and swap cultural elements so that Jamaicans and West Indians are coming, increasingly, to resemble African Americans and, at the same time, African Americans are coming to resemble West Indians. In the end, this hybridization process may be the most momentous legacy of the massive West Indian migration for New York City.

NOTES

1. This research consists of two studies. Between 1988 and 1990, I interviewed, at length, a nonrandom ("snowball") sample of 106 male Jamaican immigrants in New York City. The respondents, who ranged in age from 22 to 72, had lived in the U.S. an average of 11.5 years. Sixty were in white-collar occupations, forty-six in blue-collar work. I also draw on a study I conducted in 1999 with a snowball sample of thirty-seven second-generation West Indians, most of whom originally came from New York City, who were interviewed using a structured questionnaire.

2. Reflecting the history of British colonialism, West Indians from the Anglophone Caribbean typically intermingle in the New York City neighborhoods where they concentrate. These immigrants also include the Guyanese. Although part of the South American mainland, Guyana—the former British Guiana—is historically, culturally, and politically part of the West Indies. In New York City, Guyanese immigrants, especially Afro-Guyanese (as opposed to Indo-Guyanese), generally live and interact easily with immigrants from West Indian islands. Few Spanish-speaking immigrants from the Caribbean live in West Indian neighborhoods.

3. However, it should be noted that large-scale Jamaican emigration to other regions began much earlier; shortly after the end of slavery in 1838, thousands of Jamaicans migrated within the Caribbean and, later, to Central America in search of work (see, for example, Thomas-Hope 1986; Fraser 1990; James 2004).

4. Inequality between haves and have-nots is a basic underlying cause of crime in Jamaica. The situation worsened considerably after the 1960s when the two entrenched political parties—the conservative Jamaica Labour Party and the more left-leaning People's National Party—began using impoverished people in various slums (especially in Kingston) as clients to further their political goals. This led to organized political violence that, typically, has escalated every four years during the country's general elections. This presents the ironic spectacle of an ongoing, entrenched, democratic political process that is accompanied by mass violence. Adding fuel to the fire is that in recent decades, Jamaica has become a transshipment port for hard drugs flowing out of Colombia into the United States. Criminal deportees from Canada, the United Kingdom, and United States have also added to the crime problem (see, for example, Lewis 1968; Levi 1989; Stone 1989; Gunst 1995; Harriott 2007; Millman 2010; Patterson 2010).

5. Approximately 900,000 individuals in the United States claim Jamaican ancestry according to the American Community Survey (2007–9) three-year estimates.

6. The concept of cross pressures is embedded in the literature on West Indian immigrants, even when the term has not been used explicitly. See, for example, Reid (1939) and Basch (1987).

7. In 2004, the bottom 20 percent of the Jamaican population earned only 5 percent of total yearly income in Jamaica, compared to 36 percent earned by the top 10 percent of the population (see World Bank 2011a).

8. The point is not that Jamaicans necessarily consciously model themselves after these individuals. Rather, knowledge about them has been disseminated among the postindependence generations through the educational system. For instance, Trinidadian Eric Williams's classic work, *Capitalism and Slavery*, has long been a staple of many high school curricula.

9. The question posed was: "Do you think the police use too much violence in dealing with suspects?"

10. One key indicator is that since the 1960s Jamaican politics has alternated between the People's National Party and the Jamaica Labour Party. The foundational Westminster model of parliamentary democracy has not faced serious challenge—even during the 1970s when the PNP turned decidedly socialist.

11. In a rotating credit association, each person takes a turn depositing money into a common pot ("throwing a hand"). Each week, a different individual takes the total contribution and this continues until each individual in the group has had the opportunity to make such a withdrawal.

REFERENCES

American Community Survey. 2007–9. American Community Survey Three-Year Estimates. http://factfinder2.census.gov/faces/tableservices/jsf/pages/productview.xhtml?fpt=table.

Austin, Diane J. 1987. *Urban Life in Kingston, Jamaica: The Culture and Class Ideology of Two Neighborhoods*. New York: Gordon and Breach.

Austin-Broos, Diane J. 1987. "Pentecostals and Rastafarians: Cultural, Political, and Gender Relations of Two Religious Movements." *Social and Economic Studies* 36 (4): 1–39.

Basch, Linda. 1987. "The Politics of Caribbeanization: Vincentians and Grenadians in New York." In Constance Sutton and Elsa M. Chaney, eds., *Caribbean Life in New York City: Sociocultural Dimensions*, 160–81. New York: Center for Migration Studies of New York.

Bonnett, Aubrey W. 1981. *Institutional Adaptation of West Indian Immigrants to America: An Analysis of Rotating Credit Associations*. Washington, DC: University Press of America.

—. 1990. "The New Female West Indian Immigrant: Dilemmas of Coping in the Host Society." In Ransford Palmer, ed., *In Search of A Better Life: Perspectives on Migration from the Caribbean*, pp. 139–150. New York: Praeger.

Brodber, Erna. 1989. "Socio-cultural Change in Jamaica." In Rex Nettleford, ed., *Jamaica in Independence*, 55–74. Kingston: Heinemann (Caribbean).

Bryce-Laporte, Roy. 1972. "Black Immigrants: The Experience of Invisibility and Inequality." *Journal of Black Studies* 3 (1): 29–56.

Clarke, Sebastian. 1981. *Jah Music*. London: Heinemann Educational.

Crowder, Kyle D., and Lucky Tedrow. 2001. "West Indians and the Residential Landscape of New York City." In Nancy Foner, ed., *Islands in the City*, 81–114. Berkeley: University of California Press.

Curtin, Philip. 1970. *Two Jamaicas: The Role of Ideas in a Tropical Colony, 1830–1865*. New York: Atheneum.

Dao, James. 1999. "Immigrant Diversity Slows Traditional Political Climb." *New York Times*, December 28, A1.

Dean, Dennis. 1993. "The Conservative Government and the 1961 Commonwealth Immigration Act: The Inside Story." *Race and Class* 35 (2): 57–74.

Eisner, Gisela. 1961. *Jamaica: 1830–1930*. Manchester: Manchester University Press.

Foner, Nancy. 1973. *Status and Power in Rural Jamaica: A Study of Educational and Political Change*. New York: Teachers College Press.

—.1978. *Jamaica Farewell*. Berkeley: University of California Press.

—. 1998. "Towards a Comparative Perspective on Caribbean Migration." In Mary Chamberlain, ed., *Caribbean Migration: Globalised Identities*, 47–60. London: Routledge.

—.2008. "Gender and Migration: West Indians in Comparative Perspective." *International Migration* 41 (1): 3–29.

Foner, Nancy, and George Fredrickson. 2004. "Immigration, Race, and Ethnicity in the United States: Social Constructions and Social Relations in Historical and Comparative Perspective." In Nancy Foner and George Fredrickson, eds., *Not Just Black and White*. New York: Russell Sage Foundation.

Fraser, Peter D. 1990. "Nineteenth Century West Indian Migration to Britain." In Ransford Palmer, ed., *In Search of a Better Life: Perspectives on Migration from the Caribbean*, 19–38. New York: Praeger.

Goldman, Vivien. 2000. "One Drop of Mighty Dread: How Jamaica Changed the World's Music." *CommonQuest* 4 (3): 20–31.

Gordon, Monica. 1990. "Dependents or Independent Workers? The Status of Caribbean Immigrant Women in the United States." In Ransford Palmer, ed., *In Search of a Better Life: Perspectives on Migration from the Caribbean*, 115–38. New York: Praeger.

Gunst, Laurie. 1995. *Born Fi Dead.* New York: Henry Holt.

Harriott, Anthony. 2007. "Yardies and Dons." *Jamaica Journal* 30 (3): 34–39.

Henriques, Fernando. 1957. *Jamaica: Land of Wood and Water.* London: Macgibbon and Kee.

James, Winston. 2004. "Caribbean Immigration." In Howard Dodson and Sylviane A. Diouf, eds., *In Motion: The African-American Migration Experience.* Washington, DC: National Geographic.

Johnson, Kirk. 1997. "Black Workers Bear Big Burden As Jobs in Government Dwindle," *New York Times*, February 2, A1.

Kasinitz, Philip. 1987. "The New Black Immigrants." *New York Affairs* 10 (1): 44–58.

——.1992. *Caribbean New York: Black Immigrants and the Politics of Race.* Ithaca, NY: Cornell University Press.

Kasinitz, Philip, John Mollenkopf, and Mary Waters. 2002. "Becoming American/Becoming New Yorkers: Immigrant Incorporation in a Majority Minority City." *International Migration Review* 36 (4): 1020–36.

Kasinitz, Philip, and Jan Rosenberg. 1996. "Missing the Connection? Social Isolation and Employment on the Brooklyn Waterfront." *Social Problems* 41 (2): 501–19.

Kasinitz, Philip, and Milton Vickerman. 2001. "Ethnic Niches and Racial Traps: Jamaicans in the New York Regional Economy." In Hector R. Cordero-Guzman, Robert C. Smith, and Ramon Grosfoguel, eds., *Migration, Transnationalization, and Race in a Changing New York*, 191–211. Philadelphia: Temple University Press.

Kaufman, Jonathan. 1995. "Help Unwanted: Immigrant Businesses Often Refuse to Hire Blacks in Inner City." *Wall Street Journal*, June 6, A1.

Kuper, Adam. 1976. *Changing Jamaica.* London: Routledge and Kegan Paul.

Levi, Darrell E. 1990. *Michael Manley: The Making of a Leader.* Athens: University of Georgia Press.

Lewis, Gordon. 1968. *The Growth of the Modern West Indies.* New York: Monthly Review Press.

Lewis, Rupert. 1977. "Black Nationalism in Jamaica in Recent Years." In Carl Stone and Aggrey Brown, eds., *Essays on Power and Change in Jamaica*, 65–71. Kingston: Jamaica Publishing House.

Logan, John, and Glenn Deane. 2003. "Black Diversity in Metropolitan America." Albany, NY: University at Albany, Lewis Mumford Center for Comparative Urban and Regional Research.

Louis, Meela. 2000. "Pooled Savings Help Jamaicans Build Business." *Wall Street Journal*, October 17, B1.

Marshall, Dawn. 1982. "The History of Caribbean Migrations." *Caribbean Review* 11 (1): 6–9, 52–53.

Millman, Joel. 2010. "Jamaica's Growing Violence Threatens Retiree Economy." *Wall Street Journal*, August 11. http://online.wsj.com/article/SB10001424052748704532204575397882614635158.html.

Mishra, Prachi. 2006. "Emigration and Brain Drain: Evidence from the Caribbean." IMF Working Paper, Washington, DC: International Monetary Fund.

Model, Suzanne. 2008. *West Indian Immigrants: A Black Success Story?* New York: Russell Sage Foundation.

Monger, Randall and James Yankay. 2011. *U.S. Legal Permanent Residents: 2010.* Washington, DC: Department of Homeland Security.

Nettleford, Rex. 1978. *Caribbean Cultural Identity: The Case of Jamaica.* Kingston: Institute of Jamaica.

New York City Department of City Planning. 1999. *The Newest New Yorkers 1995–1996.* New York: Department of City Planning.

Norris, Kathleen. 1962. *Jamaica: The Search for an Identity.* London: Oxford University Press.

Palmer, Colin. 1989. "Identity, Race, and Power in Independent Jamaica." In Franklin W. Knight and Colin A. Palmer, eds., *The Modern Caribbean*, 111–28. Chapel Hill: University of North Carolina Press.

Palmer, Ransford. 1990. "Caribbean Development and the Migration Imperative." In Ransford Palmer, ed., *In Search of a Better Life: Perspectives on Migration from the Caribbean*, 3–18. New York: Praeger.

Patterson, Orlando. 2010. "Jamaica's Bloody Democracy." *New York Times*, May 29. http://www.nytimes.com/2010/05/30/opinion/30patterson.html?sq=Orlando&st=Search&scp=1&pagewanted=print.

Phillips, Peter. 1977. "Jamaican Elites: 1938 to Present." In Carl Stone and Aggrey Brown, ed., *Essays on Power and Change in Jamaica*, 1–14. Kingston: Jamaica Publishing House.

Portes, Alejandro, and Ruben Rumbaut. 2006. *Immigrant America: A Portrait.* Berkeley: University of California Press.

Post, Ken. 1978. *Arise Ye Starvelings: The Jamaican Labour Rebellion of 1938 and Its Aftermath.* The Hague: Martinus Nijhoff.

Reid, Ira D. A. 1939. *The Negro Immigrant.* New York: Columbia University Press.

Richards, Bedelia. 2007. "West Indian Roots and American Branches: Ethnicity, School Context and Academic Engagement among Afro-Caribbean Students." Ph.D. dissertation, Johns Hopkins University.

Richardson, Bonham. 1983. *Caribbean Migrants*. Knoxville: University of Tennessee Press.

Rohter, Larry. 1997. "The Real Caribbean: Paradise Stops at the Beach's Edge." *New York Times*, February 16, Section 4:1, 1.

Smith, M. G. 1965. *The Plural Society in the British West Indies*. Berkeley: University of California Press.

Smith, T. E. 1981. *Commonwealth Migration*. London: Macmillan.

Statistical Institute of Jamaica. 2012. "Unemployment Rates by Age Group." http://statinja.gov.jm/LabourForce/UnemploymentRatesByAgeGroup.aspx.

Stone, Carl. 1972. *Stratification and Political Change in Trinidad and Jamaica*. Beverly Hills, CA: Sage.

——. 1973. *Class, Race, and Political Behaviour in Urban Jamaica*. Kingston, Jamaica: Institute of Social and Economic Research.

——. 1982. *The Political Opinions of the Jamaican People (1976–81)*. Kingston, Jamaica: Blackett.

——. 1988. "Race and Economic Power in Jamaica." *Caribbean Review* 16 (1): 10–16.

——. 1989. *Carl Stone on Jamaican Politics, Economics, and Society*. Kingston, Jamaica: Gleaner.

Thomas-Hope, Elizabeth. 1986. "Caribbean Diaspora—the Inheritance of Slavery: Migration from the Commonwealth Caribbean." In Colin Brock, ed., *The Caribbean in Europe*. London: Frank Cass.

Tierney, John. 1997. "Man with a Van." *New York Times Magazine*. (August 10), 22.

Vickerman, Milton. 1999. *Crosscurrents: West Indian Immigrants and Race*. New York: Oxford University Press.

——. 2002. "Second Generation West Indian Transnationalism." In Peggy Levitt and Mary C. Waters, eds., *The Changing Face of Home*, 341–66. New York: Russell Sage Foundation.

——. 2007. "Recent Immigration and Race: Continuity and Change." *Du Bois Review* 4 (1): 1–25.

Waldinger, Roger, and Michael I. Lichter. 2003. *How the Other Half Lives*. Berkeley: University of California Press.

Waters, Mary. 1990. *Ethnic Options*. Berkeley: University of California Press.

——. 1996. "Ethnic and Racial Identities of Second-Generation Immigrants in New York City." In Alejandro Portes, ed., *The New Second Generation*, 171–96. New York: Russell Sage Foundation.

——. 1999. *Black Identities: West Indian Immigrant Dreams and American Realities*. New York: Russell Sage Foundation.

Waters, Mary, and Jennifer E. Sykes. 2009. "Spare the Rod, Ruin the Child? First- and Second-Generation West Indian Child-Rearing Practices." In Nancy Foner, ed., *Across Generations: Immigrant Families in America*, 72–97. New York: New York University Press.

Weber, Max. 1998. "Ethnic Groups." In M. Hughey, ed., *New Tribalisms: The Resurgence of Race and Ethnicity*, 17–30. New York: New York University Press.

Wilson, William Julius. 1997. *When Work Disapears*. New York: Vintage Books.

World Bank. 2006. *Global Economic Prospects*. Washington, DC: World Bank.

——. 2011a. "Jamaica." WorldDataBank. http://databank.worldbank.org/ddp/home.do?Step=2&id=4.

——. 2011b. "Jamaica." In *Migration and Remittances Factbook, 2011*. http://econ.worldbank.org/WBSITE/EXTERNAL/EXTDEC/EXTDECPROSPECTS/0,,contentMDK:21352016~pagePK:64165401~piPK:64165026~theSitePK:476883,00.html.

8. Liberians

STRUGGLES FOR REFUGEE FAMILIES

Bernadette Ludwig

Liberians in Staten Island? Most people are surprised to hear that thousands of West Africans live in Staten Island. In fact, Liberians are one of the newest foreign-born groups in New York City, only coming in substantial numbers in the last ten or fifteen years. Many of them have arrived as refugees—unlike most other newcomers to the city from abroad—and many have settled in Staten Island. Whatever their legal status on arrival, Liberians' lives in New York are shaped by the wars, persecution, and sometimes torture they or their family members experienced in their home country.

In this chapter I set out to show how Liberians are adjusting to life in New York, in a part of Staten Island where they have created a vibrant "Little Liberia." I begin by describing the dire situation in Liberia that led many to leave and come to America, and then give an overview of the neighborhood in Staten Island where many live. A major focus of the chapter is on Liberian families and the struggles different family members encounter as they adapt to American society. While a majority of parents hold onto Liberian culture and customs,[1] many of the younger generation, who usually came to New York as (young) children or were born in the United States, do not share these traditions and actively embrace (urban) American culture. The resulting strains between parents and children on different cultural paths are compounded by the lack of intergenerational communication as well as the challenges of living in poor, crime-ridden neighborhoods. In addition, Liberians and their families continue to be deeply affected by the experiences of war in Liberia—including torture, the loss of loved ones, sexual violence, dangerous escapes through war zones, and fear for the lives of their relatives—and the fact that many have not sought or received adequate psychological counseling.

In discussing these topics, I draw on ethnographic fieldwork among Liberians in Staten Island, which I conducted between the spring of 2009 and spring 2012. The field research included semistructured interviews using interview guides, informal conversations, and participant observation. I also make use of other data sources: a qualitative study of health concerns in Staten Island's West African community (Reed and Ludwig 2010); a survey of Liberian American youth and focus groups with Liberian parents, both conducted by the International Rescue Committee (IRC) between 2008 and 2010; and refugee arrival data from the Office of Refugee Resettlement, Refugee Processing Center, and the U.S. State Department.

THE JOURNEY TO STATEN ISLAND

The brutal civil wars that raged in Liberia from the late 1980s to the early 2000s underpinned the recent migration to the United States—and color the lives of all Liberians who arrived. This includes those already living in the United States before the wars but who feared for the lives of relatives, many of whom they later sponsored to come to this country.

The first civil war, sometimes referred to as the Great War in Liberia, started in 1989 and lasted until 1996 (Levitt 2005). The war began with a failed coup attempt to oust Samuel Doe, the first indigenous (Krahn ethnic group) president, who had come into power in a coup d'état in 1980. Prior to 1980 and since its founding in the mid-nineteenth century, Liberia had been ruled by Americo-Liberians, who trace their origins to freeborn and formerly enslaved African Americans and African Caribbeans who immigrated to Liberia in the nineteenth century and to Africans "repatriated" after being intercepted at sea following the abolition of the Atlantic slave trade. In the pre-1980 years, most indigenous Liberians were treated like second-class citizens. Thus when Doe became president, the vast majority of ethnic groups in Liberia saw this as the beginning of equal rights for all Liberians. However, Doe soon exercised preferential treatment for members of his own ethnic group, the Krahns, which was a major factor leading to the first civil war, in which two main factions battled for control; the first civil war came to a close when one of the leaders of the rebels, Charles Taylor, was elected president in 1997. Two years later, in 1999, a second civil war erupted to overthrow Taylor, and only ended in 2003, with Taylor's resignation and the presence of a United Nations peacekeeping mission (for a detailed description and analysis of the foundation of the Liberian state and the Liberian civil wars, see Berkeley 2002; Dolo 2007; Levitt 2005).

The civil wars were long and atrocious. They involved child soldiers, mutilations, torture, and sexual violence—and general violence that pervaded the entire country. Many Liberians are still traumatized as a result of the violence they experienced or witnessed. Liberians described some of the atrocities at meetings held by the Truth and Reconciliation Commission in Liberia and in communities where Liberians had moved abroad:

> My father's body was terribly mutilated. My mother's stomach was ripped open. She was eight months pregnant. I was so frightened I couldn't even touch them. My sister had been shot right in the middle of her head. I was in a terrible state. I couldn't even look at them closer because I was just in shock. I mean even to see my father was hard. I could just recognize him by his watch which was still on his hand. (Advocates for Human Rights 2006:146)

> Without a search warrant, they went from room to room searching for the alleged hidden arms. In the meantime, the entire household which included my father, step-mother, my siblings and myself were tied with nylon twine on chairs and beaten with gun butts and any object they could lay their hands on. I was severely beaten with a gun butt in my abdomen. I sustained serious abdominal injury that led to me undergoing abdominal surgery in Ghana. The same soldier that beat me in my abdomen also pierced my feet with sharp rusty iron. The scars of this barbaric treatment are on my feet to this date. The blows to my abdomen caused me to faint. My first cousin who was also tied tried to reach me and help me stand. Seeing his effort, one of the armed men who referred to himself as Turtle shot my cousin in his forehead killing him instantly. They never found the arms and ammunition that were allegedly hidden in the house. Yet, they took away my father for interrogation. He was detained for a few days and released. When he returned home I observed that he had lost one of his front teeth as a result of being beaten while in detention. (Advocates for Human Rights 2006:189–90)

It is estimated that the wars caused at least 250,000 fatalities and made almost 50 percent (1.5 million) of Liberia's population refugees or internally displaced people (Alao et al. 2000; Ellis 1999; Advocates for Human Rights 2006). Many Liberians fled the country by any means possible, which meant walking for days or months, crossing rivers, all the while hiding and fearing for their lives. The majority of Liberian refugees who escaped the fighting and crossed the border sought refuge in neighboring West African countries such as Sierra Leone, Guinea, and the Ivory Coast. But unstable political conditions in these countries forced Liberian refugees to flee anew, and many ended up in one of the refugee camps such as Danané in the Ivory Coast or Buduburam in Ghana. As one person who fled explained:

> In 1990, we ran to Sierra Leone. We took a bus there and lived in Bo-Waterside among the Sierra Leoneans for one year. When there was an attack on the border, we fled to Guinea. That was in 1991. We lived on a football field in Conakry for one month. We entered Côte d'Ivoire later that year. We went to Toulépleu and lived there with the Ivorians for six years. In 1997 we returned to Liberia. We went back to live in Sinkor right before the presidential election. We spent one year in Monrovia until we had to run again. . . . We came back to Toulépleu in September 1998. In September 2001 I came to Ghana. I came alone, and then my family joined me here. (Advocates for Human Rights 2006:322)

In the refugee camps, some individuals were selected for permanent resettlement in faraway countries like Australia, Canada, and the United States. Resettlement in a third country is one of the three durable solutions for refugees identified by the Office of the United Nations High Commissioner for Refugees (UNHCR), with repatriation and local integration in the first country of refuge the other two. From the mid-1990s to mid-2000s, the United States resettled more than 25,000 Liberian refugees who had been living an average of five years in refugee camps before they finally started their new lives in safety in this country.

Every year the U.S. president sets an annual quota, usually around 80,000, that determines how many refugees from which geographical regions are admitted to the United States (Haines 2010). In U.S. legal parlance, "refugee" is a status for admission to the country; in the scholarly and policy literature, refugees are often defined as those who have fled their native countries because of persecution or fear of persecution, in contrast to immigrants who come to the United States mainly to be reunited with family members and for economic reasons (Tepper 1980). In the case of Liberians in the United States, those with refugee, asylee, or permanent resident status later were able to petition the U.S. government for their relatives to join them—including spouses, unmarried children (under the age of 21), and parents—under the Family Reunification program that is part of U.S. refugee policy. In fact, the vast majority of Liberian refugees in New York City were admitted through this program.

The procedure is complicated. The sponsoring relatives in the United States ("anchors") have to file an AOR (Affidavit of Relationship) with a local refugee agency, showing proof that they are in a position to provide housing and financial resources for the relatives joining them.[2] Once the AOR is filed and processed, the family member seeking to be reunited with her or his family in the United States—and waiting in a refugee camp—hopes to get to the next step, which is being called for an interview with a refugee officer from the U.S. Citizenship and Immigration Service, which is part of the U.S. Department of Homeland Security (DHS). In this interview, DHS staff seek to determine the overseas relative's eligibility for refugee status under U.S. law. It is important to note that only individuals recognized by the UNHCR as refugees under the 1951 Convention are eligible for these interviews and consequently for resettlement.[3] Individuals not only have to show that they have suffered persecution in the past or have a well-founded fear of persecution if they returned to Liberia but also have to provide proof that they are related to the person who filed the AOR. This is sometimes more difficult than one imagines, as refugees usually only flee with what they can carry and do not take birth certificates or other documents.

A Liberian in the refugee camp who is approved for resettlement in the United States has to pass a medical exam before entering this country. Prior to departure, the majority of adult refugees attend a cultural orientation program intended to prepare them for their new lives in America and also to "develop realistic expectations about life in the United States" (Center for Applied Linguistics 2010). In conversations with Liberian refugees in Staten Island, it was clear that this program did not sufficiently prepare them. Most Liberians expected the U.S. to be "like heaven" or "the answer to their dreams." They did not anticipate that they would have so many new financial responsibilities—for example, having to pay (relatively high) rent and utility bills in addition to repaying loans from the U.S. government for the airfare from West Africa to the United States—and they were surprised and disappointed by the realities of what the buildings and neighborhoods looked like. Some Liberian refugees mentioned that they were shocked when they saw potholes when they arrived at John F. Kennedy Airport. One former resettlement case worker told me, "They [Liberian refugees] picture America as very sophisticated. I mean even if America is a good place but the way they picture it in their mind, the mental picture they create, is not what they see. When they get to JFK, and see how JFK looks, and they come outside and see that there are some potholes, it's like a shock."

According to data from the Office of Refugee Resettlement (2010), more refugees from Liberia were resettled in New York than any other state, and, within New York, Staten Island was the major area of resettlement. In fact, Park Hill, located on the North Shore of Staten Island, ranks just behind Philadelphia as the second most common destination for officially resettled Liberian refugees during the last twenty years. Between 1990 and 2010, 1,889 Liberian refugees were resettled in Staten Island, compared to 2,550 in Philadelphia (Refugee Processing Center Data 2010). The Park Hill neighborhood was selected by refugee resettlement agencies not only because many of the Liberians sponsoring relatives from the refugee camps were already living there but also because the area has affordable housing available to individuals without a credit history in the United States. Those originally resettled in Staten Island were frequently joined by other Liberian refugees over the years who had been initially settled in Minnesota, Pennsylvania, or other states and were drawn to Staten Island by family connections, friendships, climate preferences, job opportunities, and the availability of public transportation. The majority who were initially resettled in Staten Island have ended up staying there; only a few, usually those achieving significant economic upward mobility, have moved to other neighborhoods in Staten Island or to New Jersey and Philadelphia. Liberian refugees in Staten Island also have been joined by Liberians who entered the United States by different paths, for example, as students or immigrants. Community organizations and the IRC (Rowbottom 2009) estimate that upward of 6,000 Liberians lived on Staten Island in 2009, suggesting that the American Community Survey figure of 2,120 Liberians for 2007 is too low.

When they first moved to Staten Island, many Liberians were surprised by the quality of housing available to them—typically small, old apartments in poorly maintained low-income housing. Some refugees who had been sponsored by relatives had received photographs of the relatives standing in front of impressive skyscrapers in Manhattan—leading the refugees still in West Africa to think that these would be their new homes in the United States. Most Liberians, moreover, lived in houses before the civil wars. As humble as these houses were, they were not apartments in a huge complex, which newly arriving Liberians saw as a step down. Still, all Liberians were happy to be in the United States after years in refugee situations and to be reunited with their relatives.

Upon arrival, Liberian refugees were not only assisted by their anchors—the relatives who sponsored them to come to the United States—but also by refugee resettlement agencies. These agencies are nonprofit organizations founded to provide services for refugees; they receive federal and private funding to aid refugees in adjusting to life in the United States. The agencies helped Liberians with enrolling in government programs such as Medicaid and food stamps, for which refugees are immediately eligible to apply, as well as employment services such as job training and placement. Being classified as refugees by the U.S. government entitles individuals to these employment (and other) services and access to government benefits, including Supplemental Security Income, Medicare, and Refugee Cash Assistance, thereby putting them in a privileged position compared to immigrants (Singer and Wilson 2006). Liberian youths who were admitted to the United States as refugees were able to attend after-school programs operated by resettlement organizations or community organizations that received funding from the Office of Refugee Resettlement.

A significant number of Liberians on Staten Island did not come to the United States under the official refugee category, and were unable to benefit from the array of programs available to refugees. The lack of access to the programs is a common complaint of Liberians without the legal status of refugee or asylee. As a Liberian immigrant mother of three children said:

> If you came here as an immigrant, you are not entitled to that [summer camp] program. In order for your child to be qualified for the program, he had to come here as a refugee or whatever word you use . . . 1090 something. Yes, you see that's a big difference, I want to say. . . . I tell you, you come here as an immigrant, . . . you supposed to have opportunity. What I have seen, no . . . if you came here with a green card, as an immigrant, this program is not for you, it's for the other people. . . . Because IRC have the program one year, our children attended it. The next following year . . . they found out we came as immigrants and so we're not entitled to it.[4]

The nonrefugees include Liberians who came to the United States in a variety of ways. Some filed for political asylum while already in the United States, which many were eventually granted. Numerous Liberians obtained green cards through the diversity immigrant visa program, which has made 55,000 permanent resident visas available annually by lottery to people from countries with low rates of immigration to the United States (see chapter 2, this volume). Still others came as immigrants, sponsored by relatives who had entered the United States legally but not under the refugee category. The legal status of many other Liberians on Staten Island is temporary or murky. For example, some Liberians who fled the war first received Temporary Protective Status (TPS), which gave them permission to remain and work in the United States for a period of time. Once the U.S. government ceases to issue TPS for nationals of a certain country, the U.S. president can declare nationals eligible for Deferred Enforced Departure (DED). Some Liberians have had this temporary status (first TPS, now DED) for close to twenty years without any hope of making their stay in the United States permanent as neither of these statuses provides a path to legal permanent residency.[5] Those holding DED status must regularly file paperwork with the U.S. Department of Homeland Security, although not all Liberians fulfill this requirement. Sometimes, they are so focused on daily survival issues that they neglect to file the papers or they have difficulty navigating the bureaucratic maze, in a number of cases because they are illiterate or semiliterate. Those who fail to annually renew their DED status or have overstayed student or visitor visas end up as undocumented immigrants. Although Liberians who did not enter the United States as official refugees have limited access to programs designed for refugees, over the years they have been able to take advantage of other recent initiatives open to all low-income residents of Staten Island's North Shore that provide services to Liberian youth and often mediate between them and their parents when serious tensions or conflicts arise.

Whether refugees or immigrants, most Liberian adults have ended up in low-wage jobs because they arrived without adequate formal education (less than secondary education) or possession of their diplomas. Many are home health aides (overwhelmingly in Staten Island) and have security guard positions (in

Staten Island and Manhattan) with irregular hours, including night shifts. Some who started out as home health aides have taken a one- to two-month course to become certified nursing assistants, which improves their wages somewhat but still involves night and weekend shifts. However, the urgency to earn money to pay bills and provide for their families on both sides of the Atlantic has forced most Liberians to work long hours and has prevented many from pursuing additional schooling to secure better-paid jobs with more family-friendly hours.

LIBERIANS ON STATEN ISLAND

To many New Yorkers, Staten Island is known as the "forgotten borough" (Brown 1994) and it represents an anomaly in the city; it is not linked to any other borough by the subway system, and the only public transportation connecting it to the rest of New York City are buses from Brooklyn and the Staten Island Ferry from the Whitehall Ferry Terminal at the tip of lower Manhattan.

A DISTINCT BOROUGH

Staten Island differs from the other boroughs in its demographic makeup. Not only does it have a much smaller population (469,000 in 2010) but, until recently, Staten Island was overwhelmingly white; and whites are still numerically dominant. In 1980, a remarkable 85 percent of Staten Island's residents were non-Hispanic white, and only 7 percent were non-Hispanic black. In 2010, according to the census, 64 percent of Staten Island's population was non-Hispanic white and 10 percent non-Hispanic black—in contrast to New York City as a whole, where 33 percent were non-Hispanic white and 23 percent non-Hispanic black.

The immigrant population has rapidly expanded on Staten Island, adding new diversity to the borough in the last few decades. Parts of Staten Island have the flavor and characteristics of "new destinations" (Massey 2010), a term often used to refer to cities and towns across the country that have only recently experienced a rapid growth of immigration. In 1980, when 24 percent of New York City residents were foreign-born, the figure was only 10 percent in Staten Island; most immigrants on Staten Island then were Europeans who had arrived years earlier compared to newly arrived Asians, Latin Americans, and Caribbeans who had begun to dominate the immigrant population in the city as a whole.

By 2010, a fifth of Staten Island residents were foreign-born, with Mexicans and Chinese the two biggest groups. (Reflecting the large Italian American population in the borough, Italians comprised the third largest group of immigrants.) The immigrant presence is especially pronounced on the North Shore—the northern part of Staten Island (see chapter 2, this volume). This section of

Staten Island has a much larger non-Hispanic black population than elsewhere in the borough—a fifth of the population of North Shore Community District 1 was non-Hispanic black in 2000. It is in this part of Staten Island that Liberians have become a new part of the ethnoracial mix.

LITTLE LIBERIA

The North Shore neighborhood of Park Hill is the place where most Liberians in Staten Island and New York City are concentrated. It is a predominantly black neighborhood, made up of many African Americans who have been joined by West Africans (mainly Liberians) as well as some West Indians and Latinos (primarily Mexicans). Because so many Liberians have come to live in Park Hill, parts of the neighborhood have, in truth, become a Little Liberia.

A walk down Park Hill's main shopping area—Targee Street—gives a sense of the neighborhood. Mom-and-pop supermarkets advertise that they accept WIC (Women, Infants, and Children program) and food stamps; laundromats, phone stores, and beauty parlors are interspersed among many empty storefronts. There are a few African-themed stores that advertise that they offer African food as well as African DVDs.

The heart of Park Hill is the Park Hill Apartments, built in the 1960s. Park Hill residents and other Staten Islanders refer to them as Park Hill, the Park Hill projects, or the projects. The buildings of the apartment complex physically resemble those owned and run by the New York City Housing Authority but in fact, they are not; they are a mix of privately owned and federally subsidized low-income housing. About two-thirds of all residents of the buildings are of Liberian heritage, and the remaining third are a mix of African Americans and other West African, Caribbean, and Hispanic immigrants. A small Liberian community existed in the buildings in the 1980s, and the number mushroomed as a result of later resettlement efforts of the refugee agencies.

The Park Hill apartments continue to be a site of crime, violence, gang activity, and the drug trade. The area is decidedly dangerous, something Liberians become all too aware of when they move there. The frustrations that one Liberian parent expressed in a parent focus group were voiced by many others as well:

> What I do not like about the North Shore? Park Hill, kids hanging out on the street corners, instead of being in school. They are out selling drugs, smoking, taking drugs, and getting involved with gangs and related issues. I strongly agree that there must be a reason for all of this, but is this enough to give up their future, or give up all the hopes and dreams their parents had when they brought them to this country. Raising kids in Park Hill or the North Shore depends on both the parents and the child.

In the 1980s—before the arrival of Liberians—the neighborhood acquired the labels "Crack Hill" and "Kill[a] Hill"—names which have continued to stick (see, for example, the recent documentary by Liberian-born producer Gerald "Gee-Bee" Barclay, *Killa Hill: The Park Hill Documentary* [2009]). The names were made famous by songs by the Wu-Tang Clan, a hip-hop group, many of whose members grew up in the Park Hill apartments. As one of their songs goes, "From Park Hill, the house on haunted hill / Every time you walk by your back get a chill" ("Gravel Pit," Wu-Tang Clan 2000).

In addition to the unsafe conditions inside the six-story buildings in the fifteen-acre complex, and in the nearby surroundings, signs of decay are everywhere—water leaks, broken windows, chipped ceilings, and rodents—although some of the buildings underwent renovation in 2011 and 2012.

Nevertheless, in the face of such dreary conditions Liberians have created a bustling community. Especially on weekends, the building hallways and streets become alive with chatter in Liberian English and women dressed in colorful African garments. People may approach those they do not know, whom they believe to be Liberian, asking, "Are you Liberian?" If they are, they get a smile and a hug. If, as one definition has it, a community consists "of a population carrying on a collective life through a set of institutional arrangements" (in Hallman 1984:33), then Park Hill is not just a place where Liberians live, but a Liberian community. Many community activities take place in common areas in the basement of the apartment buildings, and in community organizations (including the Staten Island Liberian Community Association) whose offices are on Park Hill Avenue, in churches, and on the sidewalks.

One of the most visible centers of the lively Liberian community is the market held daily on the sidewalk outside one of the apartment complex buildings. During the warmer months, as many as twenty African women sell vegetables and food including African peppers, palm oil, cassava leaves, potato greens, and smoked fish, as well as clothing, shoes, and CDs. One could say that the African women are adapting their African lifestyles to Staten Island's landscape. The market women buy many of the vegetables in New Jersey and Brooklyn and bring them to the neighborhood. This sidewalk market provides market women, who are from Liberia, Sierra Leone, and Ghana, with a type of employment in which many were already engaged in West Africa. Selling at the market also allows them to be in close proximity to their homes, where they can keep an eye on their children and grandchildren after school hours. For those who buy products at the market—as well as those involved in selling—the market is crucial in combating the isolation that many older, often semiliterate or illiterate, Liberians experience in the community. The market allows Liberians, especially those in the older generation, to socialize and an opportunity for women to leave their apartments. "We can sell at the small market," one Liberian told me, "get our African food and meet our kind."

The market is not only cherished by local Liberian residents but also appeals to Liberians and other West Africans who live elsewhere in Staten Island. There they can buy fresh vegetables and other food frequently not available at their neighborhood grocery stores and catch up with the latest Liberian gossip. One parent said, "When I miss home I go down to Park Hill to buy African food, meet friends, and visit family members."

RELATIONS BETWEEN PARENTS AND CHILDREN

The family is a critical institution for all immigrants and refugees, and those from Liberia are no exception. As Portes and Rumbaut (1996, 2001) note, many members of immigrant and refugee families—especially those of lower socioeconomic status—acculturate to their new society at a different pace.[6] The differences are particularly pronounced for immigrant and refugee youths, on the one hand, and refugee and immigrant parents, on the other, and often lead to conflict and misunderstandings between the generations (Birman 2006; D'Alisera 2004; Foner 2009; Lewig et al. 2010; Waters 1999; Ying and Han 2008; Zhou and Bankston 1998).

(ENGLISH) LANGUAGE ISSUES

As happens in other immigrant and refugee groups (Birman and Trickett 2001), Liberian youths who arrived as young children or teenagers and U.S.-born second-generation Liberian Americans generally adopt aspects of American culture faster than their parents do. The Liberian community in Staten Island provides an example of what Portes and Rumbaut (2001:53–54) refer to as "dissonant acculturation"—"when children's learning of the English language and American ways and simultaneous loss of the immigrant culture outstrip their parents'." The young people's greater familiarity with and adoption of U.S. norms and culture can empower them and threaten immigrant parents' authority.

Language, it should be said at the start, is not generally a major issue between the generations in Liberian families. Many studies note that children's acquisition of English causes a serious divide with their immigrant or refugee parents (Birman 2006; Huisman et al. 2011; Portes and Rumbaut 2001; Zhou and Bankston 1998). This is not the case for Liberians, mainly because English is the national language in Liberia and is spoken and understood by the majority of Liberians.

Although Liberians speak English, many adult Liberians also speak one or more Liberian languages such as Bassa, Kpelle, and Vai. In New York, children are exposed to these languages only when their parents use them with relatives; none of the parents I met has taught their offspring an indigenous language. Partly, this may have to do with parents' effort to ease their children's transition into American society, but it also has roots in Liberia. There, English is regarded as the language of the educated, and speaking only other languages is often equated with being illiterate and from the rural areas, sometimes referred to as "country people" (see also Cooper 2008), compared to residents of Monrovia, the Liberian capital. Consequently, in New York, members of the younger generation speak English with their parents and grandparents, while the latter sometimes use other languages. Often, parents do so out of habit, but at times they choose to speak, for example, in Bassa to exclude children from their conversations.

Most of the younger generation, moreover, speak American English, while their parents typically speak Liberian English. Sometimes, youth forget to code-switch when they are talking to their parents. "Sometimes I call my mom and I'll be talking like this and she is like, 'Slow down, I can't understand you,'" said one 22-year-old who had come to the United States as a young child. "So then I have to remember, oh, I am talking to my mom, let me switch into my Liberian accent."

Interestingly, some children and young adults said they speak Liberian English not only with their parents but also with their Liberian American friends—perhaps an indication that as the younger generation becomes adults they will (re)embrace aspects of their Liberian heritage. Sometimes Liberian children will choose aspects of being Liberian, such as speaking Liberian English at school, to exclude other students from their conversations. However, many young children and teenagers prefer not to identify as Liberian. This is not surprising, given the mocking that children often experience in school on a daily basis because they are African—including insults such as "Liberians live in trees" or "Liberians have tails" and being called "monkey" and "African booty scratcher." Children are not only ridiculed about their African origins but are also taunted because the wars in their native country made them refugees. An employee of a refugee organization who works with Liberian youths explained that when she visited a high school to invite Liberian students to a conference about refugee youths in Staten Island's North Shore, "[They looked] the other way when I used the word *refugee*. Like, 'Not me,' 'That's not me.' . . . Being called a refugee was a bad thing. They did not want to be seen as refugees."

In addition to speaking English before they arrived, most Liberians had been exposed to and had incorporated other aspects of American culture before they came to the United States given the longtime and very significant American influence in their home country. In Liberia, for example, those in urban areas often used American canned food products. American fashion inspired by hip-hop has been a guide to stylish dressing in major cities, including Monrovia and Buchanan. According to UNHCR staff who worked with Liberians in refugee camps, Liberians, unlike most other Africans, orient their dress style to U.S. fashions. My conversations with Liberians revealed that if people in Liberia spoke about traveling outside the country, it was implied that the destination would be somewhere in the United States, mainly because a significant number of Liberians had relatives living in this country for decades. The perception of the United States as their motherland—even among those without any Americo-Liberian ancestry—meant that the vast majority of Liberian refugees regarded their resettlement in the United States as a logical choice and did not anticipate much need for acculturation. Unfortunately, the adjustment turned out to be more difficult than they anticipated.

VIEWS OF LIBERIAN CULTURE AND THE LIBERIAN WAY OF PARENTING

The move to New York exposes Liberians to new norms and customs—and often leads to strains and tensions within the family. While children at times engage in various strategies to distance themselves from their Liberian background, and sometimes from their Liberian-born parents as well, the parents are distressed that their children have little knowledge of Liberian culture and are becoming "too American." The older generation regards Liberian culture as superior to American culture, especially in terms of its emphasis on respect for elders, and they feel that Liberian culture puts a much greater stress on the need to strive to do well and pursue educational opportunities, especially since these opportunities are not available in Liberia.

Parents and children have different views of Liberian culture. Youths who did not grow up in prewar Liberia have different memories of the country, if any at all, than adult Liberians for whom distinctions in Liberia—"before the war," "during the war," and "after the war"—have great resonance. Moreover, for most of the parent generation, Liberia and Liberian culture represent home and familiarity, a source of pride, and a place to which they eventually seek to return. For the younger generation, Liberian culture and their parents' traditions frequently stand for "cultural backwardness"—views that are learned or reinforced in interactions with their American peers and reports in the media. These views echo those described by JoAnn D'Alisera (2009:121) among young Sierra Leoneans she studied in Washington, DC, who felt bombarded by media images of "the starving/diseased African child." In addition to these one-sided depictions of the African continent and its people, Liberian youths also hear frequent taunts from American and other immigrant youths who hold notions of Africans as "sleeping in trees" or "running in the jungle without clothes."

Among the Liberian youths I have met on Staten Island, the impact of these negative representations of Africa is compounded by the shame some feel because many parents have—by American standards—low (formal) educational levels and continue to work in low-skilled jobs. A woman who works with a local nonprofit association that provides programming to North Shore youths explained, "Some of them [Liberian children and teenagers] are so embarrassed by their parents. Because their parents cannot read and write. When they go to school, they are embarrassed because of their identity [as African/Liberian]. They want to disassociate themselves from being Liberian." To the older generation, being Liberian does not come with the same stigma. Several Liberian adults I spoke with said that in looking for jobs, they felt they received preferential treatment from potential white American employers because they were Liberian or African rather than native-born African Americans.

Reversal of roles between adults and children occurs in many immigrant and refugee families when parents depend on their children to help them navigate American society (Birman 2006; Birman and Trickett 2001; Portes and Rumbaut 2001). In the Liberian case, as I have noted, it is not a matter of the children interpreting or translating for parents, which is a common source of tension in other newcomer families. The issue is that the young people are exposed to more information about U.S. society and institutions and, more important, that they sometimes control the information, for example, about their performance in school, that the parents receive. The result is often diminished parental control, and discomfort among children who have to take on roles—such as intermediaries with schools, health care providers, and government bureaucracies—that they are unprepared to assume (see also Birman 2006).

Especially interesting in the Liberian case is that this role reversal actually started before migration in many families, during the wars. Children who were separated from parents in the midst of fighting and the flight to safety had to take on parental roles for themselves or for younger siblings when they were still in Africa. When the families were reunited in the United States, and lived together again, parents sought to reestablish their authority and rights as parents but were often met with resentment from children who thought that their parents had abandoned them during the wars and subsequent flight. Parents, however, who had been separated from children during the war felt that they had no alternative in Liberia but to flee and that they simply were unable to protect all of their children.

A further subject of disagreement between the generations concerns discipline and child-rearing methods (Foner 2009; Waters and Sykes 2009). Liberian children learn quickly that there are limits to corporal punishment in the United States. They often assume (falsely) that any form of corporal punishment is prohibited, although in fact parents in New York State are legally allowed to hit a child with an object provided no serious injury results (Waters and Sykes 2009). Many Liberian youth have been known to return from school to tell their parents that they can no longer spank them. In some instances children, not always fully aware of the potential consequences, have called 911 after being punished physically by their parents. Rumors are rife in the Liberian community about parents who were jailed after the children called 911 and about children who were taken out of their parents' custody. The rumors are likely to be exaggerated, yet there have been several cases of Liberian parents being charged with assault and endangering the welfare of children (see for example Calzolari 2008).

For many parents, disciplining a child the Liberian way consists of spanking the child if she or he "gets out of line." They feel that this form of discipline is an intrinsic part of Liberian culture and necessary for responsible Liberian parents to employ. That many parents suffered considerable trauma during and after the wars and consequently are not emotionally available to interact with their children may reinforce parents' practice of resorting to the Liberian way of discipline rather than, say, having a conversation or trying to reason with their children. When children challenge parents' right to punish them the way they see fit, parents perceive this as a challenge to their authority. One 60-year-old father of six described how most Liberian parents believe their authority is being undermined in the United States:

> Here [in the United States], the children come first. You don't beat the children here. . . . But that's different in my culture back home. It's different. . . . We've got to have the control, and we've got to take care of our children. We don't allow our children to take care of us. Here, in America I see . . . the kids talking back to their parents any way they want to. That's because of maybe the culture. In our culture, that can't happen. We discipline our kids. We use a rod.

Anxiety about the possibility that the New York City Administration for Children's Services will take away their children because of suspected child abuse or neglect is omnipresent in the community, among parents as well as Liberian service providers. Liberian parents are also worried about the influence of school personnel. Many told me that the schools try to influence Liberian youth to say that their parents are abusing them; they believe that at a school hearing parents will ultimately lose owing to linguistic and cultural barriers and false stereotypes about "negligent and uncaring African parents." One parent said, "People in Staten Island have the notion that African parents are mean to their children. With these low expectations of us, there is not much we can do, so sometimes you just sit there and you watch your children go astray."

Parents are also disappointed that school officials, including teachers, do not discipline their children the way the parents would like; parents believe the teachers are not strict enough and do not use corporal punishment the way teachers did in Liberia. One parent stated: "Back home in school the teacher would discipline the children. When you send the children to school they are in the teacher's charge. The teacher cannot say they will send them home to the parent to discipline. What the child did happen[ed] in the teacher's presence and the teacher will correct it."

Parents who are summoned by a school for their children's (alleged) misbehavior face a host of obstacles in meetings with teachers. Many parents feel intimidated because teachers in Liberia are regarded as important authority figures. Linguistic barriers present another problem. Many Liberian parents in Park Hill have limited literacy skills and difficulty understanding American English; for their part, teachers are unable to understand Liberian English or Liberian accents. Some parents may also prefer to speak Bassa or Krahn, for example, but schools fail to inquire about the need for interpreters. Parents assert that teachers have negative—and erroneous—stereotypes about Liberian children and teenagers, labeling them as aggressive and deviant. In fact, an American who works at a refugee organization told me that teachers in the schools Liberians attend often associate the Liberian community with violence, and this spills over into their attitudes toward Liberian students.

> They [teachers] associate the community with violence. I overheard this conversation in the teacher's lounge. . . . Somebody was [saying,] . . . "Oh, don't you know that the Liberians . . . can come to this country for free . . . because they took people out of the jails in America and sent them back to found this country [Liberia]. Haven't you guys read your history about this?" And another one said, "Maybe that's why they [Liberians youths] are so violent."

Parents' alienation from, and difficulty in dealing with, the schools can translate into disengagement from them, which is interpreted by school officials and teachers as parents' lack of interest in their children and their schooling. Currently, one of the refugee organizations is launching a program to bridge the cultural gap between Liberian parents and school officials.

Apart from discipline, there is the issue of how children should interact with parents more generally. In Liberia, children are only supposed to speak to parents when spoken to, never to talk back, and always to show deference to their elders. "When someone older than you is speaking," explained a 34-year-old mother of three, "you're not even allowed to talk back to them, but in America here, you can do it." Another parent explained: "Back home the relationship between a parent and a child is strict. Parents dictate to their children. They say, 'I am the breadwinner, therefore, you have to do what I say.' In America it is different."

Liberian youth see how their American peers question their own parents' orders or talk back to them and observe the way American families are represented on television. When they try to behave with their parents in a similar way, they are told that this is not the Liberian way.

Data from the IRC youth surveys show that many young people are frustrated by Liberian parenting styles. This was particularly pronounced among the younger survey participants (ages 9–18); nearly half said that the relationship with their parents was a major source of stress. Many Liberian youths complained that their parents yelled at, rather than encouraged and reasoned with, them. Children also said that parents spent too much time working away from home and disapproved when parents tried to replace time spent with them with money and material items (Rowbottom 2009). Younger children especially did not understand why their parents often had more than one job—one full time and another part time. Parents, however, are struggling to earn an income to support their families in the United States and in Liberia. The types of low-income jobs that most Liberians have require them to work nights and weekends, and this puts an additional strain on family life and cohesion.

Some Liberian parents, in a desperate attempt to keep or regain control over children who parents fear will become—or may already be—involved in drugs, gangs, or teenage pregnancy, move their entire family to a different state in the hope of removing children from influences of the "wrong crowd." Occasionally, a Liberian parent will send a child to Liberia, and quite a number threaten to do so. A stay in Liberia, they believe, will prevent exposure to the vices of the Park Hill neighborhood such as crime and drugs; it will also provide the opportunity for the children to learn Liberian culture. The despair felt by some parents is so strong that they would rather their children grow up in a postwar society than in an American inner-city neighborhood.

NEW OPPORTUNITIES FOR PARENTS AND CHILDREN

So far I have painted a rather negative picture of intergenerational relations, but there are several encouraging signs as well. Despite strains with parents, young people usually have strong emotional ties with their parents that include a deep sense of obligation to them. It is not unusual, for example, for older youths to work to contribute to the household income while they attend college or during the summer months when they are not in school—and to feel that this is something they ought to do and want to do.

Parents may be worried about children going astray, but many young people are doing well—and the two generations take great pleasure in the achievements. Several parents proudly showed me certificates and graduation programs that featured their children or grandchildren. Children's high school and college graduation photos decorate Liberian living rooms—given a prominent place in a mélange of photos of relatives in Liberia and President Obama (and his family).

Like other immigrant parents (Foner 2009; Waters and Sykes 2009), a number of Liberian parents are also changing their views of—and actual—child-rearing practices in the context of their new lives in New York. Some told me that they have come to appreciate new, and less authoritarian, forms of discipline in the United States, with more open communication between the generations. One parent explained: "There are some things I did not enjoy with my own father. This is what I have with my children, and it is all because I came to the USA. Coming to this country helped me a lot. I can talk to my children about anything and my children can also talk to me. I enjoy this kind of relationship I have with my children."

Although the children of Liberian refugees are adopting many American ways, at the same time they appreciate certain aspects of the Liberian community in Park Hill. In the youth survey, nearly two-thirds said that having friends in their neighborhood was the number one asset of living in the North Shore, and this was even more important for females. Liberian teenagers share common experiences and feel comfortable spending time with and confiding in their Liberian American peers. Liberian youth also stated they liked living in Park Hill because many Liberians live there. However, young people's connection to Liberian culture tends to be limited, largely confined to eating Liberian dishes. They are unfamiliar with many Liberian traditions and often hear about Liberian culture in a negative way, when parents berate them for not conducting themselves in the Liberian way.

Local organizations oriented to Liberian youths in Park Hill have begun to fill this void, teaching children and teenagers about various aspects of Liberian culture (while at the same time often providing help with homework). Many associations have a major focus that attracts youths to the programs, the most common being soccer. More than half of those in the North Shore youth survey—regardless of their gender—said that soccer was the sport that most interested them. Involvement in soccer in youth programs in Staten Island's North Shore also provides a connection—and shared interest—with parents, since soccer is very popular among the older generations of Liberians as well. A Liberian father recounted how his former teammates—with whom he had played in Liberia when he was a young adult and who now live in New York and other states—participated in a soccer tournament against a group of Liberian youths in Park Hill on Labor Day weekend in 2005. At this gathering, Liberian families came together not only to watch the game but also to celebrate Liberian culture and eat Liberian food for an entire weekend. He said, "We schedule a soccer game. . . . We play on the Stapleton playground. Everybody bring food. We have fun the whole Friday night. Saturday we play. . . . After that we have a party that night. . . . It went on until 7 o'clock in the morning."

An initiative started by a young Liberian woman, who was born in Liberia but came to New York as a child, centers on dance. She became interested in dance when she was in a refugee camp in Ghana, and this interest continued after she moved to the United States. She found solace in dance as she struggled as a teenager to adjust to life in this country and to become reacquainted with her mother, from whom she had been separated for several years. Her goal in starting a dance program was to give Liberian children and other youths in the community the opportunity to learn traditional West African, as well as modern American, dance.[7] By exposing Liberian youths to their parents' culture she has been able to expand their knowledge and understanding of Liberian culture beyond Liberian food and "Liberian discipline" and to provide positive elements of Liberian culture with which children and teenagers can identify. At the same time, her program introduces parents to modern dance through public performances. Initially, parents were skeptical about the value of ballet and other forms of dance not traditional in Liberia, but since then, with their children acting as "cultural ambassadors," the parents have started to appreciate them. In this way, the children, one might say, are serving to acculturate their parents to aspects of the United States.

CONCLUSION

Many Liberians have found refuge in Staten Island after escaping violent and bloody civil wars in their native country. Their adjustment to life in the United States and to Staten Island has not always been smooth, and in the process families have had to overcome many obstacles. Liberians who settled in the Park Hill neighborhood found themselves in an area that has a long history of safety concerns, violence, drug trafficking, and gang activities. In the face of these problems, Liberians have created a Little Liberia that offers comfort and a connection to their heritage culture. Thus, it is not surprising that most Liberians, including those living in other parts of the United States, consider the neighborhood to be like "Africa in the United States." The Africanization of the neighborhood is evident in an outdoor market during the warmer months, numerous Liberian churches, soccer games in the surrounding parks and playgrounds, people wearing African garments on the street, and Liberian parties held in the apartment buildings' basements.

These activities and features of the neighborhood are enjoyed by all generations. At the same time, relations in the family, between parents and their children, are often strained. Parents are struggling to overcome trauma from the wars, subsequent flight, and years of living in crowded refugee camps where they waited in uncertainty about their future. Their priority in New York is to earn a living to support their families in this country and in Liberia, and they bring cultural beliefs with them about family relations that conflict with those in mainstream America. Parents are often not physically and emotionally available for their children, who are dealing with their own problems stemming from the refugee experience, adolescence, and adaptations to life in New York. Liberian children and teenagers, as I have shown, often challenge their parents' authority and culture as they embrace American cultural values, adding to tensions with their parents. Liberian parents tend to cling to Liberian traditions and methods of parenting in the hope of keeping their children from becoming prey to inner-city vices, although there are signs that some are changing in the New York context as they become familiar with and sometimes adopt aspects of accepted American parenting styles.

Liberians have been coming to New York City in large numbers for only a short while—since the 1990s—and the community is therefore a new one. Teenagers as well as adults generally were born in West Africa, and a second generation, born in the United States, is only now coming on the scene and is mostly younger children. It remains for future studies to explore the experiences of this growing second generation, as well as the identities, family relations, and cultural patterns of those born in West Africa as they live longer, and establish deeper roots, in New York City.

ACKNOWLEDGMENTS

I would like to thank Nancy Foner for the opportunity to contribute to this volume and for her helpful edits and suggestions, as well as Sara Rowbottom, Adama Kromah, and Joe Dugbo for their comments. I am also grateful to the Liberians living in Staten Island and those working with them for sharing their experiences with me. Part of this research was supported by the National Science Foundation (NSF/CUNY AGEP SBES # 0753623).

NOTES

1. In this chapter, "parents" refers to biological or adoptive parents, single parents, grandparents, and guardians who are raising Liberian children. While there are many ethnicities and thus cultures in Liberia, all individuals I spoke with talked about Liberian culture and not, e.g., Bassa or Loma culture.

2. This is to meet the standards set by the U.S. Refugee Resettlement Program.

3. The "1951 Convention Relating to the Status of Refugees" is the key legal document in defining who is a refugee, their rights, and the legal obligations of countries.

4. The 1090 is the I-94 U.S. immigration form that denotes an individual as a refugee and grants access to certain programs.

5. As of this writing, the DED is set to expire on March 31, 2013.

6. Acculturation is the process in which newcomers learn new cultural norms and eventually also accept them, although some cultural elements that immigrants bring with them may also become incorporated into the broader American culture (see, e.g., Alba and Nee 2003).

7. About 75–100 young people were participating in the program in 2011.

REFERENCES

Advocates for Human Rights. 2006. *A House with Two Rooms: Final Report of the Truth and Reconciliation Commission of Liberia Diaspora Project*. Saint Paul, MN: DRI Press. http://www.theadvocatesforhumanrights.org/uploads/A+House+with+Two+Rooms.pdf.

Alao, Abiodun, John MacKinlay, and Funmi Olonisakin. 2000. *Peacekeepers, Politicians, and Warlords: The Liberian Peace Process*. New York: United Nations University Press.

Alba, Richard D., and Victor Nee. 2003. *Remaking the American Mainstream: Assimilation and Contemporary Immigration*. Cambridge, MA: Harvard University Press.

Berkeley, Bill. 2002. *The Graves Are Not Yet Full: Race, Tribe, and Power in the Heart of Africa*. New York: Basic Books.

Birman, Dina. 2006. "Acculturation Gap and Family Adjustment." *Journal of Cross-Cultural Psychology* 37 (5): 568–89.

Birman, Dina, and Edison J. Trickett. 2001. "Cultural Transitions in First-Generation Immigrants." *Journal of Cross-Cultural Psychology* 32 (4): 456–77.

Brown, Chip. 1994. "Escape from New York." *New York Times*, January 30.

Calzolari, Anne Marie. 2008. "Spank Your Children and You'll End Up in Jail." *Staten Island Advance*, March 8. http://www.silive.com/news/index.ssf/2008/03/spank_your_children_and_youll.html.

Center for Applied Linguistics. 2010. "Cultural Orientation Programs and Resources." Cultural Orientation Resource Center. http://www.cal.org/co/overseas/overview.html.

Cooper, Helene. 2008. *The House at Sugar Beach: In Search of a Lost African Childhood*. New York: Simon and Schuster.

D'Alisera, JoAnn. 2004. *An Imagined Geography: Sierra Leonean Muslims in America*. Philadelphia: University of Pennsylvania Press.

—. 2009. "Images of a Wounded Homeland: Sierra Leonean Children and the New Heart of Darkness." In Nancy Foner, ed., *Across Generations: Immigrant Families in America*, 114–34. New York: New York University Press.

Dolo, Emmanuel T. 2007. *Ethnic Tensions in Liberia's National Identity Crisis: Problems and Possibilities*. Cherry Hill, NJ: Africana Homestead Legacy.

Ellis, Stephen. 1999. *The Mask of Anarchy: The Destruction of Liberia and the Religious Dimension of an African Civil War*. New York: New York University Press.

Foner, Nancy. 2009. "Introduction: Intergenerational Relations in Immigrant Families." In Nancy Foner, ed., *Across Generations: Immigrant Families in America*. New York: New York University Press.

Haines, David W. 2010. *Safe Haven? A History of Refugees in America*. Sterling, VA: Kumarian Press.

Hallman, Howard W. 1984. *Neighborhoods: Their Place in Urban Life*. New York: Sage.

Huisman, Kimberly A., Mazie Hough, Kristin M. Langellier, and Carol Nordstrom Toner, eds. 2011. *Somalis in Maine: Crossing Cultural Currents*. Berkeley, CA: North Atlantic Books.

Levitt, Jeremy. 2005. *The Evolution of Deadly Conflict in Liberia: From "Paternaltarianism" to State Collapse*. Durham, NC: Carolina Academic Press.

Lewig, Kerry, Fiona Arney, and Mary Salveron. 2010. "Challenges to Parenting in a New Culture: Implications for Child and Family Welfare." *Evaluation and Program Planning* 33 (3): 324–32.

Massey, Douglas S., ed. 2010. *New Faces in New Places: The Changing Geography of American Immigration*. New York: Russell Sage Foundation.

Office of Refugee Resettlement. 2010. "Refugee Arrival Data." http://www.acf.hhs.gov/programs/orr/resource/refugee-arrival-data.

Portes, Alejandro, and Rubén G. Rumbaut. 1996. *Immigrant America: A Portrait*, 2nd ed. Berkeley: University of California Press.

——. 2001. *Legacies: The Story of the Immigrant Second Generation*. Berkeley: University of California Press.

Reed, Holly, and Bernadette Ludwig. 2010. "Urban and Underserved? A Pilot Study Investigates Health Concerns and Health Care Access among Liberian Refugees in Staten Island, New York City." Paper presented at International Conference on Urban Health, New York City, October 27.

Refugee Processing Center. 2010. "Refugee Arrival Data." http://www.wrapsnet.org/.

Rowbottom, Sara. 2009. *The Issues and Assets of African Youth on Staten Island's North Shore: A Community Assessment Report*. New York: International Rescue Committee.

Singer, Audrey, and Jill H. Wilson. 2006. *From "There" to "Here": Refugee Resettlement in Metropolitan America*. Washington, DC: Brookings Institution.

Tepper, Elliot, ed. 1980. *Southeast Asian Exodus: From Tradition to Resettlement: Understanding Refugees from Laos, Kampuchea and Vietnam in Canada*. Ottawa: Canadian Asian Studies Association.

Waters, Mary C. 1999. *Black Identities: West Indian Immigrant Dreams and American Realities*. Cambridge, MA: Harvard University Press.

Waters, Mary C., and Jennifer E. Sykes. 2009. "Spare the Rod, Ruin the Child? First- and Second-Generation West Indian Child Rearing Practices." In Nancy Foner, ed., *Across Generations: Immigrant Families in America*, 72–97. New York: New York University Press.

Wu-Tang Clan. 2000. *The W.* Compact disc. Sony.

Ying, Yu-Wen, and Meekyung Han. 2008. "Parental Acculturation, Parental Involvement, Intergenerational Relationship and Adolescent Outcomes in Immigrant Filipino American Families." *Journal of Immigrant and Refugee Studies* 6 (1): 112–31.

Zhou, Min, and Carl L. Bankston. 1998. *Growing Up American: How Vietnamese Children Adapt to Life in the United States.* New York: Russell Sage Foundation.

9. *Dominicans*

COMMUNITY, CULTURE, AND COLLECTIVE IDENTITY

Silvio Torres-Saillant and Ramona Hernández

DOMINICANS IN THE NEW GREAT WAVE OF IMMIGRATION

At the start of the twenty-first century, Dominicans—along with people from China, Mexico, and Jamaica—headed the list of groups having the largest share of what Nancy Foner has called the "new great wave of immigration" to New York City, an influx that began in the late 1960s and is still going strong (Foner 2000:13). At the end of the twenty-first century's first decade, *Avatar*'s Zoe Saldaña, the Passaic-born daughter of Dominican immigrant Aridio Saldaña, reigned as an up-and-coming Hollywood star; the Puerto Rican composer and performer Lin-Manuel Miranda's award-winning Broadway musical *In the Heights* (2007) was set against the backdrop of the Dominican neighborhood of Washington Heights; the fiction writer Junot Díaz, a native of the Dominican Republic who grew up with his immigrant mother in New Jersey, earned the 2008 Pulitzer Prize in fiction with his novel *The Brief Wondrous Life of Oscar Wao*; and in 2007 third baseman Alex Rodriguez, the New York–born child of Dominican parents, signed a contract with the New York Yankees that made him the highest-paid player in baseball history.

By the end of the decade, one could find Dominicans in high places throughout American society and particularly in New York City. But the less favorable characteristics of their incorporation into the fabric of the city in recent decades also stand out. On the whole, socioeconomic indicators show that Dominicans have done poorly as compared with other groups. They have often found themselves clustered in low-level service and manufacturing jobs, and even professionals with high levels of schooling at the time of immigration have often suffered serious social declines, typically unable to obtain employment in the field of their credentials (Foner 2000:99, 93, 17). Dominican women, who frequently took the lead in the decision to pursue emigration, have outnumbered men in moving to New York; in 2010, among the Dominican foreign-born, there were 71 men for every 100 women in the city (chapter 2, this volume). In terms of gender relations, women generally appear to have enhanced their position in the family as a result of migration to the United States, but given the high proportion of female-headed households (which from an economic viewpoint are a disadvantage), the gender gain does not seem to have translated into much material advancement (Pessar 1982, 1987, 1995).

The story that explains why New York became the principal destination for Dominicans coming to the United States hearkens back to the city's role in the latter half of the nineteenth century as the leading port interacting with the Dominican Republic during periods of intense U.S. involvement in the Caribbean country's affairs. In the past four decades, the presence of a large Dominican community in New York has been an important draw. As for the factors that have pushed so many Dominicans out of their ancestral homeland in the newest great wave of migration to New York City, economic realities in the Dominican Republic have been critical: since the 1960s, the Dominican Republic has failed to provide sufficient economic opportunities for the majority of the employable population or a decent education for the children of the less empowered, leaving the majority of citizens without a sense of hope in a future at home. The observations of Hispanic studies scholar Frank Graziano, who has looked at the conditions of undocumented migrants from the Dominican Republic, may well apply to those who enter or remain in the United States legally. The departure of Dominicans may be "voluntary insofar as one makes a conscious decision to embark, while others in a similar situation opt to stay home; and it is involuntary insofar as the choice is forced by lack of domestic options for the alleviation of poverty" (Graziano 2006:2).

A number of studies have shown the high rates of poverty in the Dominican Republic. A 1994 survey conducted jointly by the Pontificia Universidad Católica Madre y Maestra and Instituto de Estudios de Población y Desarrollo in Santo Domingo (the capital city) found that 65 percent of interviewees 18 years of age or older classified themselves as poor; three years later, when the survey was repeated, as many as 76 percent did so (Hernández 2002:181). In 1993, the government's national planning office (Oficina Nacional de Planificación) identified 60 percent of the country's homes as poor, a number that fell only to 56 percent in a report issued in 1997. As Graziano observes, immigrants from the Dominican Republic come not because they are lured by notions of the American Dream, but because the vast majority are in search of "basic economic stability," which they pursue by obtaining a green card via protracted legal transactions through the U.S. Consulate in Santo Domingo, or, in the worst of scenarios, by defying the gravest of dangers in illegal boat trips to Puerto Rico (Graziano 2006:3).

The search for economic stability has brought Dominicans to the United States in large and increasing numbers since the late 1960s.[1] By 1990, according to census counts, an estimated 520,000 Dominicans were living in the United States, the actual size of this population no doubt appreciably larger since official figures undercount undocumented residents, whose number is estimated to be high. A decade later, a report released by the Lewis Mumford Center, based on the 2000 census, estimated the total number of Dominicans in the country at 1,121,257 (Logan 2001). By 2010, according to American Community Survey estimates, the national figure had risen to 1.5 million (Pew Hispanic Center 2012). Dominicans continue to outnumber all other immigrant groups in New York City and in 2010 ranked ninth among immigrant groups in the entire nation.

In 1960, New York City had a little over 13,000 Dominican residents (Haslip-Viera 1996). By 2008, the number was a remarkable 585,429, most of them foreign-born but a growing proportion (about two-fifths) born in the United States (Caro-López and Limonic 2010). Although nearly half the Dominicans in the country now live in New York State, they have found their way into every state of the union. The most numerous contingents reside in New Jersey, Florida, Massachusetts, Pennsylvania, Rhode Island, Connecticut, California, Maryland, and Texas.

The migration from the Dominican Republic has fluctuated over the years, partly in response to U.S. policy changes, including the 1996 Illegal Immigration Reform and Immigrant Responsibility Act, which required sponsors to have an income 125 percent above the poverty line for a family of four in order to sponsor a relative from abroad. Consequently, the 20,387 Dominicans legally admitted into the United States in 1998 represented less than half the number admitted just seven years before. The same act also led to a dramatic increase in the number of Dominicans sent back from the United States. Whereas U.S. authorities deported 1,082 Dominicans in 1992, by 1998 the number had grown to 2,498, with a Dominican dignitary protesting that 8,000 deportees arrived in the Dominican Republic in August 1999 alone (Hernández 2002:178–79). More recently, the number of deportees has escalated further. A study by David Brotherton and Luis Barrios (2011:12) estimates that between 30,000 and 50,000 deportees arrived in Santo Domingo between 1996 and 2008 and that the rate of forcibly returned individuals at the beginning of the second decade of the twenty-first century was nearly 300 per month.

On the whole, the overall picture of people of Dominican ancestry in New York City displays conflicting signs of rise and decline, progress and stagnation, allowing for alternative projections as to the kind of future the community will forge as Dominicans endeavor to assert their presence in the city in the decades to come. The pages that follow explore some of these trends and developments, beginning with a look at the historical roots of Dominican migration to the United States and basic background on socioeconomic characteristics of the Dominican population in New York City before considering a number of other themes, including the question of transnationalism, building a Dominican American community and culture, in neighborhoods as well as through literature, and issues of ethnoracial identity and belonging.

BETWEEN RECENCY AND LONGEVITY

If the Dominican population in New York has reached an unprecedented level in the twenty-first century, this does not mean that this community is altogether new, or that it does not have deep historical roots. Despite the long contact of Dominicans with New York, a way of speaking about them as newcomers continues to recur. "There was virtually no Dominican migration to the United States till the 1950s, none, none. But once Trujillo [the dictator since 1930] was assassinated in 1961, and then, of course, after the U.S. invasion of 1965, suddenly, then, thousands of Dominicans came to the United States," emphatically says *Democracy Now!* cohost Juan Gonzalez, the principal narrator of the 2010 documentary film *Nueva York* about New York City's relationship with the Hispanic world. Yet, as the exhibition *Nueva York: 1613–1945* at the New York Historical Society (in collaboration with the Museo del Barrio) makes clear, in 1613 "a free mulatto from Santo Domingo" named Juan Rodrigues became the very first non–Native American resident of the territory that would subsequently become New York, predating the settlement of Europeans (Wallace 2010:22).

Perhaps it is not surprising that as Dominicans have become a larger and more important group in New York City, scholars of Dominican descent, in particular, have been affirming the longevity and rootedness of Dominicans in the city (Torres-Saillant 1991, 2000a; Cocco de Filippis and Gutiérrez 2001; Méndez 2011). Indeed, the emphasis in scholarship on Dominicans has implications for the way they are seen—and wish to be seen—in New York and thus for issues of identity as well as political inclusion.

To some extent, the discovery of Juan Rodrigues has offered invaluable reinforcement to Dominican scholars who have long fought a narrative that shortens the temporal length of the Dominican presence in New York and that incorrectly abbreviates a history that goes back to the nineteenth century. A narrative of recency, it has been argued, may reinforce the notion that Dominicans are quintessential newcomers who have not yet paid enough dues to be accorded equality among other ethnic groups that can boast of the credentials that seniority confers.

Many scholars of Dominican ancestry also regard the stress on Dominicans as a transnational people par excellence in a similar way, concerned that a sole focus or overemphasis on Dominicans as a people on the move detracts attention from the story of adversity, endurance, and survival that Dominicans have experienced through many generations of effort to build community and forge a home in New York.

THE PRE-1960s PAST

People who trace their origin to the Dominican Republic have lived in the United States at least since before the proclamation of Dominican independence on February 27, 1844, when Juan Pablo Duarte, the ideological architect of the nation, studied English in New York (Duarte 1994:40). Throughout the nineteenth century, as a result of U.S. involvement in Dominican affairs from as early as the administration of President James Polk in the 1840s, contact between people from the small Caribbean nation and their powerful neighbor to the north remained constant. After the American Civil War, U.S. interest in the Dominican Republic evolved into a fervent desire to annex the country to the territory of the union. President Ulysses S. Grant embraced this cause with passion, though fierce opposition from influential U.S. legislators and popular nationalist leaders in the Dominican Republic thwarted the plan. Even so, the United States eventually dominated the Dominican economy, controlled fiscal life in the country by means of a protectorate from 1905 to 1940, ruled the nation directly through a military government from 1916 to 1924, disarmed the civilian population, and instilled in Dominicans a predilection for American consumer goods, pastimes, and popular culture.

As a result, the United States, with New York as its epicenter, became a natural destination for Dominican migrants, initially involving statesmen, political exiles, entrepreneurs, and intellectuals—on the whole, people with sufficient means to finance a move to more auspicious surroundings. Among these were the children of poet laureate Salomé Ureña and Francisco Henríquez y Carvajal, an intellectual family whose lives Dominican American author Julia Alvarez has captured in her novel *In the Name of Salomé* (2000). Most notable among the entrepreneurs was Francisco Rebajes, who achieved a degree of distinction unmatched by any other Dominican businessperson until the outstanding success of fashion designer Oscar de la Renta, who would become a household name in the United States toward the end of the twentieth century. Rebajes arrived in New York City's Harlem in 1922, took menial jobs of all sorts, roamed the streets with a gang of penniless intellectuals, and eventually discovered his talent for using the hammer and anvil to make beautiful and marketable tin, copper, and metal images of various kinds, ultimately attracting a large clientele. After opening his first store in Greenwich Village in 1934 and single-handedly "centering the craft industry along Fourth Street" by the 1940s, his company opened outlets all over the country until he sold his factory operation and original designs to move to Spain in 1958 (Alig 1953; Greenbaum 1996:70–72).

Among those who came from the Dominican Republic before the 1960s, two others stand out for their remarkable careers. Maria Montez, known affectionately as the Queen of Technicolor in the heyday of her Hollywood stardom during the 1940s, became a famous entertainment personality. Her native city of Barahona, where today the airport carries her name, remembers her with pride. Having played major or leading roles in such Hollywood hits as *Arabian Nights* (1942), *Cobra Woman* (1943), *Bowery to Broadway* (1944), *Gypsy Wildcat* (1944), *Tangier* (1944), *Sudan* (1945), *The Exile* (1947), and *Pirates of Monterey* (1947), Montez remains "the object of an extensive fan cult thirsting for nostalgia and high camp" many decades after her death (Kanellos 1994:552). Another Dominican who achieved celebrity was Porfirio Rubirosa, who became famous as an adventurer and playboy. This modern-day Dominican Casanova numbered among his successive and famous wives Doris Duke, from the family of the tobacco magnates and philanthropists memorialized in the name of Duke University; the show business celebrity Eva Gabor; and the heiress Barbara Hutton, granddaughter of Frank W. Woolworth, founder of the famous store chain. Rubirosa's life of luxury was subsidized by his former father-in-law, Rafael Leónidas Trujillo, who ruled the Dominican Republic as a personal hacienda between 1930 and 1961.

Apart from these personalities, an array of political dissidents and other expatriates came to the United States during the thirty-year rule of the ruthless Trujillo dictatorship as well as an equally substantial number of agents of the regime who served the Dominican tyrant by promoting his interests in American society. Among the former, the most politically committed organized rallies that repudiated the dictatorship and joined the New York chapter of the Dominican Revolutionary Party, which would become a major political institution in their homeland after the fall of Trujillo. Among the latter stands out Ambassador Minerva Bernardino, who ironically went on after the end of the dictatorship to receive periodic honors for humanitarian service and women's rights advocacy. Her less-well-known brother Felix W. Bernardino, a henchman of the dictator, ran a reign of terror against the anti-Trujillo émigré opposition during his years as consul general of the Dominican Republic in New York.

The foregoing background forms part of the overall narrative of the U.S. Dominican experience even if research has yet to establish in precisely what ways this early history enters the cultural memory of the community that evolved following the great exodus that began in the 1960s. One can find a clear link in voluntary associations, a prominent feature of U.S. Dominican neighborhoods (Georges 1984; Sassen-Koob 1987). The available data suggest that several of the social clubs and community organizations that gained visibility in Dominican neighborhoods as soon as the group became numerically significant from the 1970s onward actually had their start in associations that originated to promote or repudiate the Trujillo regime (Torres-Saillant and Hernández 1998:80). As time passed, those associations lost touch with their ideological beginnings and became "expressive," "affective," or even "instrumental" venues serving diverse needs for community members.

CONTOURS OF THE COMMUNITY

Originally, Dominican settlers traveled to the United States in the company of familiar forms of worship. Given their cultural ties through birth or ancestral origins to the island of Santo Domingo, a land conquered and colonized under the banner of Catholic Spain, Dominicans are mostly Catholic though they simultaneously display African-influenced forms of worship. Many Dominican homes in New York, for instance, make provisions for small shrines that pay homage to Catholic saints, especially the Virgin of Altagracia, the patron saint of the Dominican people. However, the accoutrements that normally decorate the small altars (flowers, lighted candles, food, water, rum, and other earthly goods) often recall the trappings of Santería and other African-influenced Caribbean religions, reflecting the fundamentally syncretic nature of Dominican religious life (Duany 1994).

As of 2008, 62 percent of the Dominican community in New York City was foreign-born. In 2005 a sizable 34 percent of the community lived in poverty, the number rising to 43 percent among female-headed families in that year—a rather daunting source of stress considering that a significant proportion of Dominican families are of this type. In 2000, 38 percent of Dominican families in New York City were headed by women, with the figure climbing to 47 percent in 2008 (Hernández and Rivera Batiz 2006; Hernández and Argeros 2010). In terms of education, in 2008, 44 percent of Dominicans 25 years of age or older had not graduated from high school (Caro-López and Limonic 2010). In 2005, the per-capita income of Dominican households amounted to $13,423, almost 50 percent less than the rate for the overall population of the city. The median age of the Dominican population was 29.2 in 2000, lower than that of other major racial and ethnic groups, and did not show much change in the course of the next decade (Ramírez 2002; Hernández and Argeros 2010).

In 2000, the occupational distribution for members of the Dominican labor force 16 years of age or older in New York City remained close to the breakdown from the previous census (in 1990) when 30 percent were operators, fabricators, and laborers; 28 percent, service workers; 26 percent in technical, sales, and administrative support; 12 percent in managerial and professional positions; and 5 percent precision production, craft, and repair workers (Ramírez 2002). But even in its socioeconomic profile, the Dominican population of New York City seems to refuse a linear narrative of misery or prosperity. In terms of postsecondary instruction, in the last decade more students of Dominican descent were enrolled in the City University of New York (CUNY) than any other single national group. In the first five years of the twenty-first century, U.S.-born Dominicans had a higher percentage of college graduates as compared to the overall U.S.-born Latino population in the city (Hernández and Rivera Batiz 2006). In 2008, 24 percent of U.S.-born Dominicans in New York City 25 years of age and older had achieved a bachelor's degree or higher—with the figure at 34 percent for Dominican women adults born in the United States (Caro-López and Limonic 2010:18).

Washington Heights is still a heavily Dominican neighborhood—and remains the symbolic heart of the city's Dominican community—but since 1990, Dominicans have increasingly been moving to the Bronx. By 2008, the Bronx had the largest proportion of Dominicans in the city, and sections of Queens and Brooklyn also continued to have significant numbers (Caro-López and Limonic 2010).

To a large extent, the texture of the group's daily life, its distinguishing characteristics, its sounds, its smells, its rhythm—in short, the sum of sensory elements that many would deem integral to the community's culture—are manifested in the city's many heavily Dominican neighborhoods. Dominican-based ethnic enclaves in New York such as one finds in Manhattan's Washington Heights visibly display the community's tropical colors with numerous bodegas, supermarkets, beauty salons, travel agencies, and restaurants contributing to what could be regarded as a Dominicanization of the physical surroundings. Observers of the community typically highlight the energy and vitality of the group, especially as the number of neighborhood business establishments has tended to grow apace with the continuous arrival of Dominican residents in formerly depressed areas, for example in parts of the south Bronx. However, socioeconomic portraits of the community indicate that Dominican New Yorkers, as a group, are lagging behind blacks and other Hispanics economically; they have the lowest median household incomes ($37,680 in 2008) among the five largest Latino groups in New York City (Caro-López and Limonic 2010:10). Among the reasons for this situation, Dominicans have low levels of English language proficiency and often lack the levels of education and specialized skills that the job market increasingly requires. Exacerbating their precarious economic condition, Dominicans often retain economic commitments to relatives in their native land (Hernández 2002).

TRANSNATIONALISM OF THE DOMINICAN KIND

Understanding the transnational links among Dominicans to their homeland is a complicated endeavor. For one thing, there is the risk of minimizing the extent to which close and continuous cross-border connections have a long history. Given the Dominican Republic's history of colonial and neocolonial rule, people ancestrally connected there, like their counterparts everywhere in the Caribbean, have had their everyday lives determined by circumstances and events occurring both in their land of birth and in countries overseas for more than five centuries (Torres-Saillant forthcoming). What may appear as new dynamics today in the context of the massive Dominican migration to the United States can be seen as representing a stage in the evolution of the relations between the Dominican Republic and its geopolitical overlord. Perhaps even more important, overemphasizing transnational ties can have the effect of shifting attention away from developments among Dominicans in New York.

A particularly dramatic example is Navy Petty Officer Ruben Rodriguez, one of the 225 victims of American Airlines flight 587, which crashed in Queens, New York, as it took off from JFK Airport on November 12, 2001, bound for Santo Domingo. A veteran of the U.S. military mission in Kosovo who had served for seven months on the *USS Enterprise*, Rodriguez had just returned to New York from participating in the U.S. attack on Afghanistan when, before taking on his next military assignment, he decided, as a respite, to go to the Dominican Republic to reconnect with his extended family. This tragic case illustrates the circumstances that have led a number of scholars to think of Dominicans in the United States as a transnational community that spans borders—in which individuals maintain loyalties, remain connected, and engage in a variety of practices linking them to the homeland (Duany 1994; Guarnizo 1994, 1997; Levitt 2001). Yet the fact that Rodriguez was a U.S. Navy officer who had gone to war on behalf of this land also shows the depth of his groundedness in the United States as the country of his citizenship and civic duty, his strong affective ties to the "old country" notwithstanding.

The transnational approach in migration scholarship in the United States that has developed since the 1990s has focused heavily on Dominicans, with many scholars touting Dominicans "as a classic example of transnationalism" (Duany 2011:3, 5). Peggy Levitt, the author of a well-known study of the relationship of people in a Dominican town she calls "Miraflores" and emigrants from the town who have settled in Boston, examined transnational relations between the two branches of this population. Her study suggests that "Mirafloreños" in the Dominican Republic have grown "so dependent on the money, ideas, and values imported from Boston that migration has become an integral part of their everyday lives" (Levitt 2004:250). The tendency to analyze the Dominican experience from the perspective of transnationalism has become widespread on topics ranging from the political interconnections of Dominicans in the ancestral homeland and overseas to the dynamism of middle-class Dominicans in south Florida, Dominican American literature, Dominican music in New York, the position of Dominican women, and changing gender roles among second-generation Dominican youths (Sagás and Molina 2004).

Whether or not Dominican Americans can be regarded as members of a transnational community, scholars have done little to show to what extent this transnationality differs from that of other U.S. ethnic minorities that owe their development to migratory flows in the jet-plane era. It is also important to pay attention to the impact of the interlaced coexistence of U.S.-born and immigrant individuals—with immigrants more likely to maintain close connections with the homeland and the second generation generally having much weaker ties there. A telling detail in this respect is the foreign birth of well-known Dominican American writers (with the exception of Julia Alvarez and Angie Cruz) and their continued engagement with the homeland in their work. The same is true in the realm of visual arts, in which nearly all painters and sculptors who have achieved a measure of visibility belong to a middle-class wave of migration that left the Dominican Republic beginning in the 1980s, many of them trained at the Altos de Chavon School of Design in La Romana, Dominican Republic, and New York City's Parsons The New School for Design.

A notable feature of political leaders in the U.S. Dominican community is their need to remain attentive to the dual sensibilities of their political constituency, which includes many with their hearts set on the affairs of one of the major parties back in the Dominican Republic as well as others who recognize the U.S. arena as the most appropriate setting for their political involvement and commitment. Interestingly, many members of the community who have attained legislative positions in the United States were born in the Dominican Republic, such as New York State Senator Adriano Espaillat, New York City Council member Diana Reyna, Montgomery County (Maryland) Council member Thomas Perez, Providence Municipal Council member Miguel Luna, and Rhode Island State Senator Juan Pichardo, to name only a few Dominicans who have held public office since the beginning of the twenty-first century.

A study by Ana Aparicio (2006) of young Dominican leaders in New York, including second-generation activists, shows a trend away from involvement in homeland politics. The new younger local leaders appear to have retreated from the emphasis on homeland politics that had occupied their predecessors in the 1960s and seem more committed than their elders to forging coalitions with other ethnic groups in New York, chiefly Puerto Ricans and African Americans (Aparicio 2006:3–4).

To the extent that the second generation is engaged with elements from Dominican culture, this has as much, perhaps more, to do with experiences in New York as with regular practices connecting them to their parents' homeland. Second-generation individuals, the majority of whom reside in New York neighborhoods with a substantial representation of Dominicans of various generations, remain attached to their native cuisine even as they inevitably develop a taste for American food, which for many often becomes synonymous with the products of the large fast-food chains. They may call attention to their ethnicity by waving the flag of the Dominican Republic at parades and other festivities or at public events such as baseball games that feature major Dominican stars like Sammy Sosa, Pedro Martinez, or Alex Rodriguez. They generally consume merengue and *bachata* among their favorite rhythms, reproducing their parents' musical taste while, at the same time, enjoying the sound of hip-hop and the other popular music forms that the U.S. entertainment industry offers to audiences of every new generation.

Second-generation individuals often call themselves Dominican though they may not know much about their parents' native land; when travel becomes a possibility many think of the Dominican Republic as their first option. It is rare that they lack close kinship ties to people "back home." Quite often the grandparents that young Dominican Americans look to for affection or permissiveness live across the Caribbean sea in a Dominican city or rural town, a dynamic that is probably more typical of families at the lower ends of the class scale and is sometimes complicated by the considerable volume of intermarriage in New York so that only one parent may be Dominican. What is clear, though, is that the interplay of here (New York) and there (the Dominican Republic) is an element of Dominican American culture, and those in the second generation typically do not regard their loyalty to the United States as requiring a delinking from their parents' homeland.

Among immigrants, as well as the second generation, there is, on one side, a continuous negotiation of traditions, behaviors, and beliefs from the ancestral homeland—that may, though need not, be reinforced by actual ties or ongoing relations with people there—and, on the other, the transformative thoughts, values, and practices derived from the experience of living as an ethnic minority in the United States. Thus, Dominicans in New York are influenced by notions of political identity and national belonging prevalent in the Dominican Republic, which emphasize an all-encompassing "Dominicanness" as a basis of social identity and inclusion. At the same time, in the context of ethnic self-assertion and racial differentiation and exclusion in the United States, Dominicans emerge as a differentiated cultural group with a distinct place—and identity—in the city's ethnic and racial hierarchy. The creative tension produced by the confrontation of the legacies brought or inherited from the ancestral homeland and the sensibilities forged in the United States largely accounts for the texture of cultural life among New York Dominicans. To look at it another way, at times they embrace a worldview that breaks with ideologies from the old country and at times they distance themselves from views that hold sway in American society.

BUILDING COMMUNITY, IMAGINING THE FUTURE

The process of building a Dominican community has involved the creation of new institutions and events that are visible in the public sphere, and a growing involvement in politics in the city.

The Dominican population's sense of collective selfhood as a settled community with an imaginable future has manifested itself in the type of legacies it has seen fit to recognize. Witness the dedication ceremony that took place in the early afternoon of Saturday, August 6, 2011, on the corner of Audubon Avenue and 190th Street in Manhattan's Washington Heights. Under a severe summer sun, without great fanfare, Manhattan Borough President Scott Stringer, a Jewish New Yorker, and city council member Robert Jackson, a longtime African American resident of Washington Heights, had come to join their Dominican American colleagues in the public naming of Miguel Amaro Way, in honor of a community activist who was instrumental in the creation of the annual Dominican Day Parade. Present among their Dominican-descended colleagues in public office were State Senator Adriano Espaillat, Assemblyman Guillermo Linares, and city council member Ydanis Rodriguez, together with old-time district leaders Maria Luna and Maria Molina.

The elected officials, community activists, neighbors, friends, and members of the Amaro family came to memorialize the legacy of a man who had imagined a future for Dominicans in the city. Judith Amaro, head of the Miguel Amaro Foundation, with the support of her brother Mao, worked closely with the office of council member Ydanis Rodriguez and enlisted the support of the other Dominican American legislators who knew Amaro to secure a place for her father in the community's public memory by naming the street. People congregated on the sidewalk immediately outside the building where Miguel Amaro lived with his family in 1982. In that year he convened a group of his peers in his fifth-floor apartment to discuss the idea of creating an organization that would put together an annual Dominican parade to match the existing ethnic parades in the city at the time. He thought that such a parade would provide New York Dominicans, immigrant as well as U.S.-born, with an empowering resource by enhancing their visibility as a social force in the city while also stimulating a sense of their own collective identity. Having come to New York from Santiago, Dominican Republic, in the 1960s, Amaro harbored a deep faith in community advancement and ethnic advocacy, trusting that symbolic politics could have material consequences. A graduate of Brooklyn College, Amaro dedicated his life almost entirely to community activism. When he died in 1987, the Dominican Day Parade had become a force to contend with, a symbol to New York's political establishment about the resolve of Dominicans to enter the conversation about the distribution of power among the various ethnic segments of the city's population.

On the second Sunday of August 1982, the first Dominican Day Parade marched up Audubon Avenue for some twenty blocks with appropriate pomp and circumstance, culminating in a cultural festival that featured music, dance, poetry readings, speeches, and other performances on a stage located against the back wall of the George Washington High School building on Amsterdam Avenue between 190th and 191st streets (Aparicio 2006:73–74). Silvio Torres-Saillant, one of the original committee members, recalls the insistence of the organizers on leaving a positive impression, understanding that the image of the community was at stake. This concern came in part from the difficulty the committee members had encountered while seeking the permit that would legally allow the parade and festival to take place. They had had to appear several times before Community Planning Board No. 12 to address several board members' fears about the possibility of vandalism, rioting, or a buildup of garbage on the streets. The collective desire to safeguard the community's image became apparent at the end of the festivities, when many participants spontaneously joined the organizers as they proceeded to clean the area and dispose of the trash, leaving the streets, sidewalks, and park discernibly cleaner than the marchers had found them when the parade began.

Much has happened since Dominicans in New York decided to appear in public view by themselves rather than as one of the multiple Latin American segments of the annual all-Hispanic Desfile de la Hispanidad in October (Hispanic Celebration Parade). Wishing to display their ethnic identity more widely, they soon secured a permit to march in Midtown Manhattan. For nearly three decades now, tens of thousands of Dominican New Yorkers have congregated there every August to flaunt their ethnicity, their flag, and their resolve to affirm their belonging in the city. Since the members of the original committee withdrew from the project a few years after its founding, the Dominican Day Parade has seen ups and downs, with periodic crises over control of the organization's leadership, vision, and resources. Many, including some members of the founding committee, have charged that Nelson Peña, who seized the helm of the organization some twenty years ago, has used the initiative for advancing his own personal interests in disregard of the ideals that brought it into being in 1982 ("Al rescate" 2011:1–2). But despite internal conflicts, the Dominican Day Parade continues to stand as an institution that Dominicans throughout the city and beyond regard as symbolic of their presence in the United States and as a venue to showcase their political gains and potential for further advancement. Today, New York politicians of all stripes, ethnically and ideologically speaking, judge it wise to show up at the parade and enjoy a photo opportunity fraternizing with Dominicans. That other Dominican parades have subsequently sprouted in several parts of New York State and elsewhere in the country where Dominicans live in meaningful numbers attests to the success of Amaro's initiative, one that, looked at in retrospect, epitomizes the story of Dominicans in New York, with its trials and tribulations, hopes and disappointments, failures and triumphs. One could argue that when Amaro appealed to his coethnics in 1982, he was tapping into a yearning that many Dominicans harbored for making their presence felt in the city going back several decades.

Dominicans have also asserted, and gained, a presence and significant influence in New York City politics. By 2011, the New York City Council had four Dominican members (Julissa Ferreras, Diana Reyna, Ydanis Rodriguez, and Fernando Cabrera) as well as a state assemblyman (Guillermo Linares) and state senator (Adriano Espaillat) from New York City.

Dominicans have a long history of community organizing in New York, going back to the 1960s when Dominican education and cultural activists in Washington Heights advocated for an instructional agenda sensitive to the needs of Dominican students (Hoffnung-Garskof 2008). By the early 1970s activists Socorro Rivera and Victor Espinosa formed part of the leadership that, through Community School Board No. Six , promoted a vision of inclusion and empowerment for Dominicans in Washington Heights (Hoffnung-Garskof 2008:109). To a large extent, the longevity of Dominican organizing in New York may account for the success of community efforts enabling Gregorio Luperon High School in Washington Heights to survive "various policy reforms" that ran counter to the school's mission to educate mostly newcomer Dominican youths in New York (Bartlett and Garcia 2011).

Whether organizing to improve the schools their children attend, to elect candidates to office to represent them, or to create a parade to celebrate their presence in New York, Dominicans have long struggled to build community and to secure a place of belonging in the city as an ethnically distinct group.

EMERGENCE OF A DOMINICAN AMERICAN CULTURE IN ARTS AND LITERATURE

The genesis of what could be called a U.S. Dominican culture in the arts and literature dates back to the late nineteenth and early twentieth centuries with the contributions of writers, musicians, and other public figures (Torres-Saillant 1991, 2000a; Cocco de Filippis and Gutiérrez 2001; Rodríguez de León 1998). Examples come most readily from the field of literature, with writers whose roots in this country preceded the large migratory flow that began in the 1960s.

The award-winning poet Rhina P. Espaillat, born in Santo Domingo in 1932, came to the United States with her family at the age of five. Starting out in Washington, DC, by 1939 the family had settled in New York, where the young Rhina grew up without much contact with Dominican neighbors. Her poetic gift and early command of the magic of the English language brought her to the attention of her teachers, who supported her submission of poems to popular publications such as the *Ladies' Home Journal*. A published poet in early adolescence, by the time she reached 16 Espaillat had become the youngest member ever to have been inducted into the Poetry Society of America. After enjoying modest literary celebrity as an up-and-coming American poet and graduating from Hunter College, Espaillat taught English in New York City public schools, married her Jewish colleague Alfred Moskowitz, and took on the demands of raising a family. On the side, she continued to build her literary dossier by writing and publishing in magazines, literary journals, and poetry anthologies. Retired from teaching and her sons already raised—having been "a joy to edit" and needing "no revisions," as she evocatively puts it in the dedication to one of her books—Espaillat (2004) took to poetry with a vengeance. Her volumes of verse have earned her a string of honors that include the Gustav Davidson Memorial Award, the T. S. Eliot Poetry Prize, the Howard Nemerov Sonnet Award, the 2001 Richard Wilbur Award, and the 2003 Stanzas Prize, apart from her inclusion as one of the eighty writers nationwide invited by the first lady and the Library of Congress to participate in the National Book Festival held in Washington, DC, in October 2003. The reader will note that her poetry volumes—*Lapsing to Grace* (1992), *Where Horizons Go* (1998), *Rehearsing Absence* (2001), *Mundo y palabra/The World and the Word* (2001), *Rhina P. Espaillat's Greatest Hits* (2003), *The Shadow I Dress In* (2004), *Playing at Stillness* (2005), and *Her Place in These Designs* (2008)—often include at least one poem in Spanish. Despite her literary development in isolation from proximity to any Dominican neighborhood—her life since she married taking place in a predominantly Jewish area of Queens—she eventually connected with her coethnics and became involved in the literary activities of Dominicans who wrote primarily in Spanish. Among the tangible outcomes of that relationship, Espaillat collaborated with Dominican poet César Sánchez Beras, contributing the English translation of the poems in his collection *Trovas del mar*, now available in a bilingual edition (*Troves of the Sea*, 2002).

Equally illustrative of a Dominican presence in New York prior to the major influx since the 1960s is Julia Alvarez, the poet and fiction writer who currently enjoys wide recognition on the literary scene. The offspring of a family of professionals and diplomats with several generations of ties to the United States, Alvarez was born in New York City in 1950, over a decade before the great wave of migrants that would lead to the development of large Dominican settlements in the United States. At the time of her birth and early childhood, the still relatively small Dominican population did not display an ethnically distinct location in New York or have the troubling socioeconomic profile that the community does today. Generally light-skinned and boasting a higher education, Dominicans who lived in New York City over five decades ago shared a favorable socioeconomic status although they were divided by political allegiances, some allied with and others opposed to (and victimized by) the Trujillo regime back home. Their class positions often fit the description one gets of Alvarez's extended family in her autobiographical essays "An American Childhood in the Dominican Republic" (1987) and "My English" (1992), which capture key stages of the writer's early education when, having been taken to live in her parents' Caribbean homeland, she attended the private Carol Morgan School where American diplomats sent their children. As a result, when Alvarez's family came back to New York in 1960, their manner of incorporation into U.S. society was strikingly different from the path of most subsequent generations of Dominican immigrants, whose class background placed them in a position of social disadvantage from the moment of arrival (see Hendricks 1974).

A prolific and talented writer, Alvarez has mined Dominican history, the memory of her family's adjustment to life in the United States, and the old country's folklore in book after book. Following her first best-selling novel, *How the Garcia Girls Lost Their Accents* (1991), Alvarez published *In the Time of the Butterflies* (1994), a moving evocation of the lives of the Mirabal sisters, three women assassinated by the Trujillo dictatorship; *¡Yo!* (1997), a clever return to the Garcia girls story in which the other characters offer their perspectives on Yolanda, the narrator of the earlier novel; and *In the Name of Salomé* (2000), which explores the lives of the Henríquez Ureña family, focusing on parallels between poet laureate Salomé Ureña's civic involvement in nineteenth-century Santo Domingo and her daughter Camila's psychologically transformative years in early twentieth-century Poughkeepsie, New York. In her poetry—*Homecoming* (1984, 1996) and *The Other Side/El Otro Lado* (1995)—Alvarez delves into the tensions emanating from her dual Dominican and American cultural background, while her children's books celebrate Dominican history, legend, and the cultural contrast between life in Vermont and the northern Cibao region of the Dominican Republic: *The Secret Footprints* (2000), *How Tia Lola Came to Visit/Stay* (2001), *Before We Were Free* (2002), and *A Cafecito Story* (2002). Given Alvarez's literary prominence, she, more than any other Dominican writer, has been able to bring Dominican characters and situations, imaginary and historical alike, to a wide American readership.

A picture of the Dominican community that more closely resembles the socioeconomic portrait of U.S. Dominicans in the post-1965 migration appears in the works of writers who are themselves offspring of that exodus. The highly acclaimed collection *Drown* (1996) and the Pulitzer Prize–winning novel *The Brief Wondrous Life of Oscar Wao* (2007) by Junot Díaz, the novels *Geographies of Home* (1999) by Loida Maritza Pérez, *Soledad* (2001) by Angie Cruz, *Song of the Water Saints* (2002) by Nelly Rosario, *Erzulie's Skirt* (2006) by Ana-Maurine Lara, and the short fiction collection *My Daughter's Eyes* (2007) by Annecy Baez all depict individual characters and families plagued by the consequences of their unfavorable class location and the marginality of their ethnic environment.

The characters that populate their stories face obstacles that stem from being trapped in settings where they lack basic amenities such as decent-quality schools, clean neighborhoods, adequate health services, and simple physical safety. Their awareness of being racialized, and their cultural otherness with respect to a distant and indifferent mainstream, are thrust upon them by the ordinary drama of the struggle for material and psychological survival. Key among the common features of these works is the memory of the Dominican past as a source of strength, even while the writers indict the less democratic characteristics of the homeland culture. Often by reconnecting with Dominican history and family members in the Dominican Republic, the characters enhance their ability to cope with the ethnic, racial, and cultural difficulties and barriers they face in the United States.

ETHNORACIAL LOCATIONS, IDENTITY, AND BELONGING

And so we confront questions of race, ethnicity, and identity. Scholars have noted that Dominicans find it hard to accept the prevailing racial code in the United States that often reduces social identity to a black-white binary opposition in contrast to the less rigid codes of the ancestral homeland that allow for distinct identity spaces between the extremes of white and black.

Dominicans, as sociologist Jose Itzigsohn (2009:125) has noted, see themselves as a mixed-race people and have tried to establish their position in the American racial classification system as nonwhite and nonblack. In his Providence study, Dominicans often distinguished themselves from African Americans and non-Hispanic black immigrants by emphasizing a Hispanic or Latino identity—an identity, Itzigsohn argues, that reflects the way they are often categorized by mainstream American society and that "emerges from social life and social practices in the United States" (2009:166). At the same time, for both first- and second-generation Dominicans, national origin, as Dominicans, was the "main anchor of their identity" that generated the greatest level of emotional attachment (Itzigsohn 2009:131).

Second-generation youths have been shown to strategically deploy a Dominican-inflected Spanish in order to avoid being taken for African Americans. By the same token, more successful and often light-skinned Dominicans who find it possible to assimilate to mainstream society may embrace an outlook like that of the conservative segment of the European-descended majority that minimizes, ignores, or denies the importance of structural (including racial) disadvantages and barriers. A New York–based middle-class male informant interviewed by linguist Almeida Jacqueline Toribio (2003:7) described the United States as a place "where you can set your goals and accomplish whatever you want," while dismissing the tendency of African Americans to remember unpleasant experiences of the slavery period. The informant felt that the readiness of African Americans to pull out "the race card," which he said Dominicans and other Latinos were imitating, stifles their ability to get ahead (ibid.).

A study from the perspective of language and identity, drawing on interviews with high school students in Providence, Rhode Island, found that second-generation Dominicans emphasized that they were not black, but also, owing to exclusion and discrimination experienced by those with darker skin color, did not see themselves as white, either. They maintained an ethnolinguistic understanding of their identity in terms of speaking Spanish, which fostered a sense of their difference from black Americans (Bailey 2001:703–4). Toribio has also explored the extent to which the Dominicans' racial and cultural identity may be "mediated or ascribed via linguistic attributes" (2003). Second-generation Dominicans assert their loyalty to their heritage by pledging "allegiance" to their "vernacular," even while their speech shows considerable erosion of "their parents' language practices."

At the same time, ongoing contact with African Americans has led many second-generation individuals to transcend, indeed reject, the "essentialized ethnic/racial stereotypes of their parents." Many recognize the need to distance themselves from the Negrophobia and the anti-Haitianism that has typified the discourse on nationality and culture in the Dominican Republic. Indeed, a commemoration of the 155th anniversary of Dominican independence from Haitian rule held on February 27, 1999, at the Centro Cultural Orlando Martinez in northern Manhattan sought the cosponsorship of Haitian community and cultural organizations in New York. The program featured a presentation of gagá, a musical and spiritual performance born of the experience of Haitian migrant sugarcane workers in Dominican plantations, and concluded with a reading of the poetry of Jacques Viau Renaud, a Haitian-born poet who grew up in the Dominican Republic, where he died fighting for social justice in the revolution of 1965. Interestingly, records of the patrons using the research resources of the CUNY Dominican Studies Institute at the City College of New York from 1994 through 2004 indicate that Dominican students care more about the study of African heritage in Dominican society than about any other subject of scholarly investigation in the human sciences (Aponte 2011).

There is also what can be called the collective identity of the Dominican community. The making of a Dominican community is the specific product of the U.S. ethnic minority experience and can be discerned in the expressive forms, ideas, and practices that characterize the members of the group. The task of defining any community, of course, is fraught with conceptual dangers, not the least of which is the temptation to construe whole populations as monolithic, uncomplicated blocs on the mere basis of their sharing a common national or ancestral origin. Arguably, every culture harbors subcultural segments within. But Dominicans, like other ethnic minority groups that politically and economically occupy marginal spaces in relation to the dominant mainstream society, generally experience the need to articulate an identity with compelling urgency. Dominicans' perception of living under siege culturally leads to their articulating a collective identity that is itself the subject of scholarly and public discussion.

The collective identity of Dominican Americans differs from that of people in the homeland as well as African Americans and other Latino groups in the continuous wrestling in popular, scholarly, and intellectual discourse with internal diversity. There is the appreciation of African heritage without skewing the vitality of the Iberian background in the formation of the ancestral Dominican culture, the desire to preserve Spanish while refraining from the temptation to privilege that language as a necessary requirement for entering the identity space of the community, and the incorporation of democratic values written into the American creed of equality—all ingredients in the formulation of the collective identity of the group. The Dominican American propensity to embrace diversity is illustrated in the symposium "Up from the Margins: Diversity as Challenge to the Democratic Nation," a multidisciplinary, international undertaking held in New York and Santo Domingo over two consecutive weeks in the latter half of June 2001. Spearheaded by the CUNY Dominican Studies Institute with the support of the Rockefeller Foundation, the symposium brought together Dominican and non-Dominican voices from Santo Domingo, Madrid, San Juan, and various U.S. cities to interrogate the principle of homogeneity that informs official and nationalist discourses on Dominicanness. Over sixty scholars, artists, community advocates, and cultural activists spoke about the need to recognize ethnic, sexual, social, ideological, religious, and other forms of diversity in the Dominican Republic and among Dominicans in the diaspora in the United States, Spain, Puerto Rico, and the Netherlands (Torres Saillant et al. 2004).

CONCLUSION

After decades of large-scale migration, Dominicans have created a dynamic and vibrant community in New York that has a growing political influence and cultural presence, including major literary figures, artists, and public celebrations and events—with a good many of the events sponsored by the CUNY Dominican Studies Institute, headed by one of the authors of this chapter. Dominicans are making their mark as scholars, often through studies of their own group, and are chronicling the development of the contemporary Dominican community as well as bringing out its historical roots in earlier eras.

Dominicans in New York can be viewed, at one and the same time, as immigrants or descendants of immigrants, ethnic Americans, and members of a

Dominican diaspora. There is a pervasive tension between the desire to belong in the United States and the yearning to preserve the most cherished of the old country's values and ways. The many New York Dominicans who see themselves as firmly rooted in this country, and do not regard themselves as birds of passage, achieve their cultural distinctness by altering some social practices associated with the Dominican Republic and by embracing, at least in part, norms of the U.S. mainstream. They also manage to preserve their uniqueness vis-à-vis other U.S. ethnic minorities, the other subsections of the Latino population included, while inevitably incorporating borrowed traits from all of them.

The dynamic process of culture building and creation in New York is taking place in multigenerational social fields. Ongoing migration from the homeland to the United States continues to replenish New York's Dominican population with recent arrivals at the same time as the growing number of U.S.-born children and grandchildren of earlier immigrants come of age. Second- and third-generation members of the group with little Spanish language proficiency find themselves sharing room in cultural, social, and political arenas with individuals who got off the plane only a few years—or perhaps even months—ago and cannot speak English well or sometimes at all. It is out of these complexities that a Dominican community continues to be transformed and reshaped and continues, in the twenty-first century, to leave its stamp on New York.

NOTE

1. Unless otherwise indicated, "Dominicans" and "Dominican community" refer to those who trace their ancestry to the Dominican Republic as well as immigrants.

REFERENCES

Alig, Wallace B. 1953. "Man with a Hammer." *Américas* 5 (May): 6–8, 43–45.

"Al rescate del desfile dominicano." 2011. Almomento.net. http://www.almomento.net/news/1520/ARTICLE/93296/2011-08-09.html.

Alvarez, Julia. 1987. "An American Childhood in the Dominican Republic." *American Scholar* (Winter): 71–85.

——. 1992. "My English." *Punto 7 Review: A Journal of Marginal Discourse* 2 (2): 24–29.

Aparicio, Ana. 2006. *Dominican Americans and the Politics of Empowerment*. Gainesville: University Press of Florida.

Aponte, Sarah. 2011. "Dominican Related Dissertations in the US: An Analytical Approach (1939–2009)." *Camino Real: Estudios de las Hispanidades Norteamericanas* 3 (4): 21–51.

Bailey, Benjamin. 2001. "Dominican-American Ethnic/Racial Identities and United States Social Categories." *International Migration Review* 35: 677–708.

Bartlett, Lesley, and Ofelia Garcia. 2011. *Additive Schooling in Subtractive Times: Bilingual Education and Dominican Immigrant Youth in the Heights.* Nashville: Vanderbilt University Press.

Brotherton, David C., and Luis Barrios. 2011. *Banished to the Homeland: Dominican Deportees and Their Stories of Exile.* New York: Columbia University Press.

Caro-López, Howard, and Laura Limonic. 2010. "Dominicans in New York City 1990–2008." Latino Data Project, Report 31. New York: Center for Latin American, Caribbean and Latino Studies, City University of New York Graduate Center.

Cocco de Filippis, Daisy, and Franklin Gutiérrez, eds. 2001. *Literatura dominicana en los Estados Unidos: Presencia temprana.* Santo Domingo: Buho.

Duany, Jorge. 1994. *Quisqueya on the Hudson: The Transnational Identity of Dominicans in Washington Heights.* Dominican Research Monographs. New York: CUNY Dominican Studies Institute.

——. 2011. *Blurred Borders: Transnational Migration between the Hispanic Caribbean and the United States.* Chapel Hill: University of North Carolina Press.

Duarte, Rosa. 1994. *Apuntes de Rosa Duarte: Archivo y versos de Juan Pablo Duarte,* 2nd ed. Ed. Emilio Rodríguez Demorizi, Carlos Larrazabal Blanco, and Vetilio Alfau Duran. Santo Domingo: Secretaría de Educacion Bellas Artes y Cultos.

Espaillat, Rhina P. 2004. *The Shadow I Dress In.* Cincinnati, OH: David Roberts Books.

Foner, Nancy. 2000. *From Ellis Island to JFK: New York's Two Great Waves of Immigration.* New Haven, CT: Yale University Press.

Georges, Eugenia. 1984. *Ethnic Associations and the Integration of New Immigrants: Dominicans in New York City.* Occasional Paper no. 41. New York: New York Research Program in Inter-American Affairs.

Graziano, Frank. 2006. "Why Dominicans Migrate: The Complex of Factors Conducive to Undocumented Migration." *Diaspora: A Journal of Transnational Studies* 15 (Spring): 1–33.

Greenbaum, Toni. 1996. "Frank Rebajes." In Martin Eidelberg, ed., *Messengers of Modernism: American Studio Jewelry 1940–1960,* 70–73. Paris: Montreal Museum of Decorative Arts and Flammarion.

Guarnizo, Luis E. 1994. "Los Dominicanyorks: The Making of a Binational Society." *Annals of the American Academy of Political and Social Sciences* 533 (May): 70–86.

——. 1997. "The Emergence of a Transnational Social Formation and the Mirage of Return among Dominican Transmigrants." *Identities* 4 (2): 281–322.

Haslip-Viera, Gabriel. 1996. "The Evolution of the Latino Community in New York City: Early Nineteenth Century to the Present." In Gabriel Haslip-Viera and Sherrie Braver, eds., *Latinos in New York: Communities in Transition.* Notre Dame, IN: University of Notre Dame Press.

Hendricks, Glenn. 1974. *The Dominican Diaspora: From the Dominican Republic to New York City—Villagers in Transition.* New York: Teachers College Press.

Hernández, Ramona. 2002. *The Mobility of Labor under Advanced Capitalism: Dominican Migration to the United States*. New York: Columbia University Press.

Hernández, Ramona, and G. Argeros. 2010. "Dominicans in the United States: A Socioeconomic Profile, 2010." Ongoing research on data from the U.S. Census Bureau, authors' tabulations: on file with authors.

Hernández, Ramona, and Francisco Rivera Batiz. 2006. *Dominicans in the United States: A Socioeconomic Profile, 2003*. Dominican Research Monographs. New York: CUNY Dominican Studies Institute.

Hoffnung-Garskof, Jesse. 2008. *A Tale of Two Cities: Santo Domingo and New York after 1950*. Princeton, NJ: Princeton University Press.

Itzigsohn, Jose. 2009. *Encountering American Faultlines: Race, Class, and the Dominican Experience in Providence*. New York: Russell Sage Foundation.

Kanellos, Nicolas. 1994. *Hispanic Almanac*. Detroit: Invisible Ink.

Levitt, Peggy. 2001. *The Transnational Villagers*. Berkeley: University of California Press.

——. 2004. "Transnational Ties and Incorporation: The Case of Dominicans in the United States." In David G. Gutierrez, ed., *The Columbia History of Latinos in the United States since 1960*, 229–56. New York: Columbia University Press.

Logan, John. 2001. *The New Latinos: Who They Are, Where They Are*. Albany, NY: University at Albany, Lewis Mumford Center for Comparative Regional and Urban Research.

Méndez, Danny. 2011. "Culture and the City: Pedro Henríquez Ureña's New York City." *Camino Real: Estudios de las Hispanidades Norteamericanas* 3 (4): 143–68.

Pessar, Patricia. 1982. "Kinship Relations of Production in the Migration Process: The Case of the Dominican Emigration to the United States." Occasional Papers 32. New York: New York University, Center for Latin American and Caribbean Studies.

——. 1987. "The Dominicans: Women in the Household and the Garment Industry." In Nancy Foner, ed., *New Immigrants in New York*. New York: Columbia University Press.

——. 1995. "On the Homefront and the Workplace: Integrating Immigrant Women into Feminist Discourse." *Anthropological Quarterly* 68: 37–45.

Pew Hispanic Center. 2012. "Hispanics of Dominican Origin in the United States, 2010: Statistical Profile." Washington, DC: Pew Research Center.

Ramírez, Marilyn. 2002. "Selected Socioeconomic Information about Dominicans in the States." New York: CUNY Dominican Studies Research Briefs, September.

Rodríguez de León, Francisco. 1998. *El furioso merengue del norte: una historia de la comunidad dominicana en los Estados Unidos*. New York: Editorial Sitel.

Sagás, Ernesto, and Sintia Molina, eds. 2004. *Dominican Migration: Transnational Perspectives*. Gainesville: University Press of Florida.

Sassen-Koob, Saskia. 1987. "Formal and Informal Associations: Dominicans and Colombians in New York." In Constance R. Sutton and Elsa M. Chaney, eds., *Carib-*

bean Life in New York City: Sociocultural Dimensions, 278–96. New York: Center for Migration Studies.

Toribio, Almeida Jacqueline. 2003. "The Social Significance of Language Loyalty among Black and White Dominicans in New York." *Bilingual Review* 27 (1): 3–11.

Torres-Saillant, Silvio. 1991. "La literatura dominicana en los Estados Unidos y la periferia del margen." *Punto y Coma* 3 (1–2): 139–49.

——. 2000a. "Before the Diaspora: Early Dominican Literature in the United States." In María Herrera-Sobek and Virginia Sánchez-Korrol, eds., *Recovering the U.S. Hispanic Literary Heritage*, vol. 3, 250–67. Houston: Arte Público Press.

——. 2000b. *Diasporic Disquisitions: Dominicanists, Transnationalism, and the Community*. Dominican Studies Working Papers Series 1. New York: CUNY Dominican Studies Institute.

——. Forthcoming. "Peregrinaciones Antillanas: Sobre el Saber Hegemónico y a Identidad Diaspórica." *Revista Iberoamericana*.

Torres-Saillant, Silvio, and Ramona Hernández. 1998. *The Dominican Americans*. Westport, CT: Greenwood.

Torres-Saillant, Silvio, Ramona Hernández, and Blas R. Jiménez, eds. 2004. *Desde la orilla: Hacia una nacionalidad sin desalojos*. Santo Domingo: Editora Manatí and Ediciones Librería La Trinitaria.

Wallace, Mike. 2010. "*Nueva York:* The Back Story." In Edward J. Sullivan, ed., *Nueva York: 1613–1945*, 19–81. New York: New York Historical Society.

10. *Mexicans*

CIVIC ENGAGEMENT, EDUCATION, AND PROGRESS ACHIEVED AND INHIBITED

Robert Courtney Smith

Mexicans in New York City are still and again the new ethnic group on the block. I say "still and again" because the Mexican population in the city—despite its large size and steady growth for the last two decades—continues to be thought of as new, and New Yorkers often continue to be surprised by this remarkable growth. By 2010, Mexicans were the third largest immigrant group in New York City. Together with their American-born children, I estimate that the Mexican-origin population was about 450,000. Mexicans have transformed many neighborhoods in the city: "Little Mexicos" have sprung up in all five boroughs.

Mexican migration to New York City is part of a larger trend of Mexican migration to the eastern and central parts of the United States in the last twenty years, driven in part by the federal government's legalization programs of the late 1980s, which fostered family reunification that increased the population of children and teens in particular, and also enabled legalized immigrants to seek out cities with more opportunities for their children (Massey 2008; Zúñiga and Hernández-León 2006). A very high percentage of Mexican immigrants in New York City are undocumented, including many children as well as adults. Legal status is thus a major issue for Mexicans in the city—and a major concern of this chapter.

The chapter begins with a brief discussion of the history of Mexican migration to the New York area, including the increasing number of undocumented. I then introduce the concept of "natural experiment" as a way to better understand questions pertaining to Mexicans' legal status. I consider civic engagement and mobilization in the Mexican community, especially around issues of education and immigration, and Mexican New Yorkers' current invisibility in mainstream politics as well as political prospects. I draw on recent data available from the U.S. Census and the American Community Survey, as well as my own interviews, ethnographic research, and continued engagement with the Mexican community in and around New York City since the late 1980s.

A BRIEF HISTORY OF MEXICAN IMMIGRATION TO NEW YORK CITY

Mexican immigration to New York City began in earnest in 1943, when a migrant, Don Pedro, and his two companions, from the small municipality of Ticuani, Puebla (a pseudonym), came to New York. "We opened the road," is how Don Pedro put it. The geographic region from which most Mexican immigrants in New York City (about two-thirds) have come is called the Mixteca, a zone that includes the contiguous parts of three states: southern Puebla, northern Oaxaca, and eastern Guerrero. The second most common place of origin is Mexico City and the state of Mexico (about 11 percent), while the remaining migrants come from a variety of other places in Mexico. The Sierra Norte, a poor, indigenous region in northern Puebla, has sent more migrants lately, as have neighboring states of Tlaxcala, Tabasco, and even Chiapas.

Most migration from Mexico to New York is economic in that lack of economic opportunity—low incomes and low standards of living—has driven it. But political factors have also been involved. Don Pedro, for example, lived in Mexico City in the early 1940s to avoid political violence in Ticuani at the time of his initial migration to New York. From then until the late 1960s, there was only a trickle of Mexican migration to New York City, mainly involving a few families from Ticuani and surrounding towns. The next significant bump occurred during the political upheavals in Ticuani and Mexico City in 1968—involving student protests and police repression—when a number of young student leaders came to New York. Subsequent push factors from the Mixteca region were a result of peso devaluation, and then the lost decades of the 1980s and 1990s in Mexico—lost in the sense that the economy did not grow. Puebla was among the hardest-hit and worst-off states in Mexico, and one of the slowest to recover economically from these decades of crisis. The Mixteca region is visibly less developed than the rest of the state of Puebla. The roads markedly deteriorate when one crosses the mountains into the Mixteca. There is less water and vegetation, and the links to New York—including signs advertising transport to New York City—seem to be everywhere.

Mexican migration to New York City grew dramatically during the 1990s, and continued to increase, but at a slower rate, between 2000 and 2010. The inflow fueled the remarkable growth in the Mexican-origin population, which includes those born in the United States identifying themselves as Mexican as well as the Mexican-born. In 1990, according to the Census Bureau, the Mexican-origin population in New York City was estimated to be 56,000 (.8 percent of the total city population), growing to 187,000 (2.3 percent of the citywide total) in 2000. By 2010, the figure had risen to 319,000, or 3.9 percent of the total population. Census figures do not include many of the undocumented, who are often afraid to respond to forms from U.S. government agencies. Factoring in census undercounts of New York City's Mexican-origin population (Smith 1996, 2006:19–20), I estimate that the numbers are about 100,000 for 1990, 300,000 for 2000, and 450,000 for 2010.

The huge growth in New York City's Mexican population between 1990 and 2000 was driven in part by the indirect effects of the 1986 Immigration Reform and Control Act (IRCA), which enabled undocumented immigrants to apply for temporary, then permanent, residency if they had been continuously in the United States since 1982 or had worked in agriculture for ninety days during the past year. Mexicans accounted for the second largest number of applications for the legalization program in New York City; the resulting family reunification spurred a huge outmigration from the Mixteca to New York. This is how it worked. Mexicans who were legalized during the late 1980s through IRCA received permanent residency or U.S. citizenship in the early 1990s. (A permanent legal resident, or green card holder, may apply for citizenship after continuous residence in the United States for five years.) Once they obtained this status, they could apply to sponsor the immigration of family members living in Mexico, which, not surprisingly, led to a big increase in the migration of Mexican children to New York in the 1990s (Smith 2006). Many relatives and friends of those who came to New York legally this way—but who themselves were unable to come legally—also migrated during this period as undocumented immigrants.

While the Mexican-origin population in New York City tripled from 1990 to 2000, it increased by 70 percent between 2000 and 2010. By 2000, the exceptional effects of IRCA, enabling families to reunite after many years of separation, no longer operated. Indeed, the 2000–10 period was a very difficult time for undocumented Mexicans to legalize their status. Survey data suggest that the percentage of the most recently arrived Mexicans in New York City without proper legal documents remained high through 2010.

A variety of public policy changes led to the mushrooming of the undocumented population in the nation in the last two decades. Prior to the 1990s, for every 100 undocumented Mexican immigrants who came into the United States, an estimated 85 went back in any given year (Massey et al. 2002, 2008).

This ratio fell as the border became harder, more dangerous, and more expensive to cross—changes that occurred, it should be noted, at a time when many Mexicans had little faith in their country's future owing to the failures of the Mexican economy. At the same time, laws governing the adjustment of status were rewritten during the 1990s, making it harder for the undocumented to legalize. In New York, as elsewhere in the country, undocumented Mexicans who in the past would have been able to adjust their status now had no foreseeable hope to do so. Congressional reforms passed in the late 1990s, for example, instituted a ten-year bar on admission for any person who had spent more than a year in the United States in undocumented status. Hence, if someone married a U.S. citizen, he or she could be made to return to the home country for a full decade before being legally admitted to the United States. The standard for suspending deportation—that is, stopping deportation if a person was picked up by the authorities—increased from hardship to "exceptional and extremely unusual hardship." Having a child who depended on a father's income, for instance, did not meet the higher standard, because, it was felt, the child could go back to Mexico with the parent. (If the child had a serious educational or medical problem, e.g., leukemia, then the hardship could be deemed unusual and exceptional.) The end result was to increase the number of undocumented and to keep them in that undocumented status longer, or indefinitely. To put it another way, being undocumented went from being a transitional to a de facto permanent status for millions in American society. While there were an estimated 3 million undocumented people in the United States in 1990, there were about 12 million in 2006 at the peak right before the financial crisis. In 2011, the number had fallen to about 11 million in the nation as a whole—with a slight fall-off in New York City at the end of the first decade of the twenty-first century (chapter 2, this volume), due in part to declining economic conditions in this country and the New York region.

Mexicans are a much larger proportion of the undocumented population in the United States than they are in New York City. However, Mexicans in New York City have tended to have a higher percentage of undocumented immigrants than other groups, including Dominicans, Chinese, and South Americans, who have been more likely than Mexicans to enter with a temporary (usually tourist) visa and become undocumented ("overstayers") when the visa expires. While some Mexicans are overstayers, many others enter the United States by crossing the border without a visa. Estimates of the percentage of undocumented in New York City's Mexican community are difficult to make. According to the census and the American Community Survey, the proportion of citizens relative to noncitizens (including many undocumented) in the Mexican-origin population has increased slightly over the last two decades. In 1990, 36 percent of Mexicans in New York were citizens and 53 percent noncitizens; in 2009, 44 percent were citizens and 50 percent noncitizens (Bergad 2010). Given census undercounts of the undocumented, however, I would estimate that the proportion of citizens is somewhat lower.

I conducted two surveys of Mexicans at the Mexican Consulate and other public places in New York City, one in 2003 (591 respondents) and the other in 2011 (849 respondents; Smith et al. 2012). The surveys show nearly identical percentages of Mexicans with undocumented status. To be sure, the questionnaires given in the consulate were, I suspect, more likely to sample an undocumented population because a key reason to go there is to obtain an identification card, such as the Matricula Consular, which is issued by the Mexican government and includes a photograph and address in the United States. In both 2003 and 2011, slightly under 90 percent of those surveyed indicated directly or indirectly that they were undocumented; 6 percent were permanent residents, about 4 percent were U.S. citizens, and 2 percent had some other kind of visa.[1] In both surveys, even those who had lived in the United States ten or more years—a little over a half of the 2011 sample—were likely to be undocumented. While it is hard to draw firm conclusions about the percentage of undocumented persons in the Mexican population from these two surveys, they do suggest that it is large—I would estimate at least 50 percent and probably higher—and that, if there continues to be little chance to legalize, the undocumented will remain without legal status for long periods of time.

NATURAL EXPERIMENTS IN IMMIGRATION AND BIFURCATED EDUCATIONAL FUTURES

In social science, a natural experiment occurs when a particular variable or policy factor can reasonably be said to cause a significant difference in some outcome, usually because it affects parts of the same group differently, or affects different but equivalent groups in dissimilar ways. A classic natural experiment occurred through the Gautreaux Assisted Housing Program in inner-city Chicago in 1966, when some of the residents in a housing project that was destroyed were relocated to the suburbs, while the rest were relocated to other housing, including other public housing projects in the inner city. Those who moved to the suburbs did better, because their children attended higher-quality schools and were not in dangerous environments and their parents had access to better jobs. I argue that the United States has set up a not dissimilar natural experiment through its immigration policy over the last generation—providing legalization for some while denying it to others. Mexicans in New York City are one case that shows the different results.

The inclusionary aspect of what can be called the experiment in American policy was IRCA's legalization program. Most of the parents in my research who were legalized were able to do so through this program. The end result was that they were able to work legally, advance in their jobs after long tenure, and earn more money. Critically, working legally enabled many parents to jump from unregulated, low-paid, off-the-books jobs in such places as small restaurants, stores, and factories to the mainstream service economy, where jobs not only came with higher pay and benefits but long tenure also tended to be rewarded. This enabled many of the parents to help their children in ways that their undocumented, lower-earning counterparts were not able to do. If the children were U.S.-born (and thus U.S. citizens at birth), or were legalized before about age 13, they could benefit from opportunities that legal status gave them, including the knowledge that they could go to college and get student loans (see Gonzales 2011; Smith 2012).

The exclusionary aspect of the experiment in immigration policy has been the "moratorium period" making legalization effectively impossible for many undocumented immigrants, which has persisted since the passage of IRCA in 1986, and the many negative consequences for those who continue to be in the legal shadows. In the context of growing numbers of undocumented and their spread to nontraditional destinations, the last quarter century has seen an increasing tendency to demonize undocumented immigrants in the United States and to make life harder for them and their children (Newton 2008). Perhaps the apotheosis of this movement was Alabama's 2011 immigration law, which criminalized a host of normal everyday activities involving undocumented immigrants, including making it a felony to conduct a "business transaction," like renewing a driver's license, with any state governmental body and requiring schools to maintain a registry of their students' immigration status. New York City and State have, by and large, remained much more immigrant friendly, and have supported inclusionary rights such as the benefit of in-state tuition at public colleges for many undocumented immigrant students, and the City University of New York (CUNY) has made special outreach efforts to Mexicans. Nonetheless, when it comes to the question of legalizing immigration status, federal policy is supreme—and restrictive rules, and, as of this writing, lack of a program for legalization, have been severe barriers for the undocumented.

The inability to legalize their status has led to enormous problems and inequalities. Among other things, the undocumented face the threat of deportation—a record number of nearly 400,000 immigrants in the United States were deported in fiscal year 2011—and have great difficulty in getting jobs in the regulated portion of the economy (including government positions). Undocumented parents are more likely to be socially isolated and less likely to take advantage of institutional resources than their documented counterparts. A study of the U.S.-born, citizen children of undocumented immigrants in New York City found that parents' fears of deportation led to lower levels of enrollment of their children in public programs for which the children were legally eligible, including child care subsidies, public preschool, and food stamps (Yoshikawa

2011). While New York State law allows qualified undocumented young people to attend public college at in-state tuition rates—they must have graduated from a high school in the state, for example—they are still unable to work legally once they graduate.

My own research shows that undocumented Mexican youths have lower educational attainment and more negative outcomes as compared to their age peers who have legal status. My project has followed about 100 Mexican-origin youths in New York City over a ten- to fifteen-year period, tracing their academic, employment, and social trajectories. Those who were U.S.-born or legalized before high school (typically gaining legal status through their parents who had managed to legalize their own status) were able to negotiate school better than the undocumented (Smith 2012). Although higher education was one of the few paths of upward mobility open to the undocumented youths, it rarely could be converted into the middle-class lifestyle that college attendance usually brings. Indeed, most of my informants who remained undocumented over ten or even twenty years, and who obtained undergraduate or even graduate degrees, remained in lower-status jobs in the unregulated "immigrant economy" because they were unable to work in the legal mainstream economy. For them, more time on the job did not convert to increased earnings; it only meant that they got older in the immigrant economy, making low wages that rarely or never went up.

The relatively high proportion of undocumented Mexican youths in New York City is one factor explaining why Mexican foreign-born 16–19-year-olds had the highest rate of any immigrant group in the city not enrolled in or graduating from high school—an astounding 41 percent in 2005–9.[2] (This is not, strictly speaking, a dropout rate because a significant number of Mexican foreign-born youths never "dropped in," arriving as teenagers and going straight to work without ever entering the school system.) To give an idea of how the Mexican foreign-born compare to other groups, consider that the next highest rates for major groups were found among island-born Puerto Ricans, at 19 percent, and foreign-born Ecuadorans, 17 percent. The Chinese and Jamaican foreign-born were both at 6 percent. It should be noted that U.S.-born Mexican 16–19-year-olds were far less likely not to be enrolled in or to have graduated from high school than those born in Mexico—the rate for the U.S.-born Mexicans was only 8 percent. Although this is higher than the rate for virtually all other native-born groups, it is still a small percentage and indicates that native-born Mexican teenagers are on a much brighter path to integration than their foreign-born counterparts.[3] The huge difference between U.S.- and foreign-born Mexicans no doubt partly reflects the fact that the native-born are more likely to be fluent in English, although lack of legal status among foreign-born Mexican youth—and, as I have emphasized, inability to change this situation—is also critical.

Figures on college attendance for 2005–9 show a similar picture. Only 6 percent of foreign-born Mexicans in New York City aged 19 to 23 were enrolled in or had graduated from college—far lower than for other foreign-born groups. Indeed, they were the only group with a rate in the single digits.[4] These figures point to an enduring crisis among Mexican-born youth. Fortunately, the Mexican native-born are doing far better. More than half (51 percent) of U.S.-born Mexican 19–23-year-olds were in college or had a college degree, which not only represents a remarkable improvement from 2000, when the percentage was 32 percent, but also puts them squarely in the midst of many other groups such as U.S.-born Dominicans (50 percent), Jamaicans (50 percent), and Ecuadorians (55 percent).

The dramatic increase in college attendance among native-born Mexicans in New York City can be seen as part of a positive integration story taking place among the children of those who have been able to legalize. It is especially noteworthy given that so many Mexican immigrant parents have extremely low levels of education themselves, hardly any with a college degree and in 2010 only about four out of ten even graduating from high school (see table 2.2, this volume). A growing number of U.S.-born Mexicans in New York have come of age with the expectation that they can attend college and hence keep what I have called the immigrant bargain, redeeming their parents' sacrifices by succeeding in school and at work (Smith 2006). These youths are also pursuing many of the same strategies that have been reported for other immigrant groups whose integration trajectories have been more positive, including living with parents into early adulthood to save money for education and pooling resources to buy a house (Kasinitz et al. 2008). As I discuss below, recent CUNY outreach programs to the Mexican community have also played a role in drawing Mexican youth to institutions of higher education—and at a relatively affordable cost.

One sign of changing attitudes to education among Mexican youth comes from my qualitative research in the community. When I began this research in the late 1990s, the answer to the question "Are you going to college?" was too often, "Mexicans don't go to college." Usually, the young people said that they did not know any Mexicans who went to college, that undocumented status would prevent them from going, or that they could not afford college. Since the 1990s, the answers to the question have become more positive. Indeed, a number of young people have asked me for information about CUNY. The change partly reflects the fact that the Mexican youth community has a larger proportion of native-born; the number of school-aged, native-born Mexicans in New York City nearly tripled between 2000 and 2010, while the number of school-aged, foreign-born youth remained largely the same. It is also the case that, in good part owing to efforts by CUNY, Mexican young people have increased knowledge that they can go to college, that it is affordable, and that legal status is not an obstacle to going.

INCREASING CIVIC ENGAGEMENT ON EDUCATION ISSUES

Education has arguably become the issue on which Mexicans in New York City have best mobilized, with the strongest response from mainstream civic institutions, including CUNY and the New York City Department of Education (DOE). Another impetus for mobilization has been the drive to get federal legislation passed that will provide legal status for undocumented young people, allowing them to further their educational and employment careers. The central role of education in community organizing has been a relatively recent development. The focus of community organizing, civic engagement, and political action within the Mexican community has evolved over the last forty years as the community itself has changed, from a largely first-generation immigrant population to one with a growing U.S.-born second generation.

The earliest community organizations were focused on hometown associations, which mainly sought to improve conditions in the communities from which Mexicans migrated by sending back money for such things as better roads, school buildings, and, as I have described elsewhere for Ticuani, a potable water system (Smith 2006). Another early focus was on sports groups in New York City. The earliest Mexican *futbol* (soccer) league in the city was formed in the late 1960s by Julio Sierra from Puebla, and is still in operation. Later, other soccer leagues and baseball leagues formed. The late 1980s and the 1990s saw the emergence of groups oriented to labor rights, which tried to fight the abuses undocumented immigrants experienced and worked with labor unions and immigrants' rights groups. Other nonprofit organizations, such as Casa Puebla and Casa Mexico, both in Manhattan, have focused on immigrants' rights and services, providing assistance with labor problems, for example, and referrals to health care facilities and social service agencies. Mixteca Organization in Sunset Park, Brooklyn, was established in 2000 to provide social services, with an emphasis on health education and prevention. A significant amount of immigrant leaders' political energy was also oriented toward politics in Mexico, especially at the state and local levels. There was a very active mobilization for the 2000 Mexican presidential elections, and many leaders worked to support the National Action Party candidate and eventual winner Vicente Fox, in a historic election that ended the Institutional Revolutionary Party's seventy-one-year monopoly on the presidency. Fox's first visit abroad as president-elect was to thank his supporters in New York in an East Harlem restaurant. This focus by community organizations and leaders on "first-generation issues" of abuses of undocumented immigrants and defense of their rights was understandable given urgent needs, but also tended to overshadow "second-generation issues" of education and college.

The evolution of Mexican community organizations in recent decades—and growing focus on second-generation and education concerns—can be seen in a particularly active and prominent group, Asociación Tepeyac. The founding of the Asociación Tepeyac in New York in 1997 represented an important step because it had an extremely able and dedicated full-time organizer, Jesuit Brother Joel Magallan, who had an organizing background in Mexico. Working on his own at first, Magallan was able to develop Tepeyac into a large nonprofit organization offering a variety of services. He emphasized undocumented immigrant rights and alleged racist enforcement of immigration laws, and organized actions and activities in support of an amnesty and the Antorcha (Torch Run) from Mexico City to Washington in 2011 in support of another legalization program. In the wake of the World Trade Center attacks of September 11, Magallan became the most public advocate for undocumented immigrants affected by the tragedy, and Tepeyac's budget and organization grew manyfold in 2001–2. In the last several years, Tepeyac has turned its attention to mentoring services and the education of youth, an area that had previously been overshadowed by its first-generation immigrant rights work and for which it has received funding from the city council and several foundations. It has formed a youth development arm called Walk, which involves college-age and young adult immigrants or children of immigrants in projects that seek to help the Mexican community, such as lobbying Congress in favor of the Dream Act (an acronym for Development, Relief, and Education for Alien Minors Act; Walk 2010–2011 2011). Tepeyac has positioned itself as a Mexican organization fighting for the rights of all Mexicans in New York and for other undocumented Latino immigrants as well.

Another community organization, La Unión, founded in 2006 and based in Brooklyn's Sunset Park, is concerned with "social, cultural, and economic rights" affecting the second as well as first generation. It has taken on general community development and empowerment issues, including education, and has issued a report about the problems facing Mexican immigrants. On its website, La Unión describes itself as an organization of "people from the global south . . . [whose] 600 members . . . are predominantly from the Mixteca region of Mexico . . . and across Latin America."[5] The group has a social justice agenda, focusing on food justice, youth justice, comprehensive immigration reform, and educational justice. Its Parents Committee and youth organization, Youth Action Changes Things, have worked on educational and immigration issues jointly. A key contribution is La Unión's (2009) publication, "Nowhere to Turn: A Report on the Reality of Mexican Americans in the New York City Public Schools," based on eighty surveys conducted by La Unión's organizers, a focus group, key informant interviews, and a review of DOE policies. Among its findings, the report documents that some staff in the public schools have low expectations of Mexicans. One student reported, "My high school guidance counselor told me to drop out, that I wasn't going to succeed." Another student said, "There is no respect for our culture. When one teacher saw my rosary she took it away. She said it was gang paraphernalia. She didn't understand what my mother's rosary meant to me." Some teachers were reported to tell Mexican students that they will end up pregnant or working—and not going to college—because they are all undocumented. The report also indicates that guidance counseling and high school choice systems have not been working for Mexicans. Guidance counselors in New York City schools are overloaded with work and do not have a chance to meet with all their students; linguistic barriers often prevent parents, who usually speak only Spanish, from becoming more involved in their children's education. Parents who already have the problem of being unfamiliar with school practices in the United States, especially the perplexing school choice system in New York City, often face English-only presentations that leave them bewildered. One mother said that she sought help with her child's math homework, but could not find Spanish-language materials available, so she taught her daughter to do the math as she had been taught in Mexico. The daughter was subsequently accused of cheating because she did not do the work the way it was done in class.

The La Unión report offers concrete suggestions for policy changes, including the recommendation that "a language access audit be done for schools with large numbers of parents with limited English skills, to ensure that schools are complying with [the DOE] Regulation A-663 [requiring schools to provide services in a second language]." It also recommends that guidance counselor–student ratios be reviewed to ensure that individual counselors are not serving too many students. In many New York City public schools, guidance counselors are responsible for several hundred students, making it impossible to meet with all of them to offer college counseling and even to provide adequate services to students who specifically request advice and assistance.

The Mexican American Students' Alliance (MASA), as the name implies, has been particularly important in mobilizing around education issues. It was founded in 2001 in response to what turned out to be a relatively brief cessation of CUNY's policy of in-state tuition for undocumented students after September 11 (the policy had been in effect since 1998). Then-Governor Pataki remedied the situation in 2002, when he signed the New York State In-State Tuition Law, granting in-state tuition rights at public postsecondary institutions to undocumented students who graduated from New York State high schools, or obtained general equivalency diplomas (GEDs) in New York. MASA founder Angelo Cabrera participated in a hunger strike in February 2002 in front of CUNY's Manhattan headquarters on the Upper East Side in support of the law, and was invited to the signing ceremony by Governor Pataki that summer.

Since then, MASA has worked closely with CUNY, as well as the Mexican Educational Foundation of New York (MexEd), which it joined in 2010 to promote educational achievement among Mexicans in New York.[6] MASA runs an after-school program in the South Bronx that mentors more than fifty students a year, offering them homework help and college advice. MASA usually involves parents in the tutoring process, an arrangement that has inspired some of the parents to pursue their GEDs or learn more English.[7] Involving the parents in tutoring brings them into the learning process in a way that many had not previously experienced and helps to familiarize them with aspects of the New York educational system. In other contexts, the inversion of parental authority—with children speaking better English and often having more years of education than their parents—is a common problem; MASA's model, by bringing parents into tutoring, fosters a relationship among the student, parent, and tutor that makes more learning possible. Students in MASA's tutoring program have improved their homework completion rates and raised their scores on standardized tests given in New York City's elementary schools. While MASA focuses on elementary and middle school children, MexEd concentrates on promoting college attendance. In 2010, MexEd provided one-on-one college mentoring for fifty high school students and ran an after-school program one day a week focused on, among other things, building bridges to college from high school. MASA and MexEd have also been closely involved in promoting educational outreach to the Mexican community through close collaboration with CUNY, and more recently with the city's DOE.

PUBLIC INSTITUTIONAL RESPONSE TO MEXICANS IN NEW YORK: CUNY AND THE DOE

CUNY has been an important institution in promoting education among Mexicans, and the DOE has also begun to reach out to the Mexican community. With increasing intensity over the last ten years, CUNY has worked with Mexican immigrants and Mexican Americans in New York. Its outreach to the Mexican community has had several main components, involving both the CUNY central administration and various campuses.

First, and perhaps most dramatic, was the signing of a memorandum of understanding (MOU) in 2005 between CUNY and the Mexican Consulate that obligated both parties to undertake certain actions to promote education in New York City's Mexican community. Then-Consul General Arturo Sarukahn told me that the idea behind the MOU was to institutionalize the agreement so that the programs would continue whatever the change in administrations in Mexico or at CUNY. CUNY Senior Vice Chancellor Jay Hershenson was key in the implementation of the MOU—chairing the CUNY Working Task Force on Strengthening Educational Opportunities for Mexicans and Mexican Americans, headed by Jesus Perez of Brooklyn College's Academic Advisement Center, and ensuring the continuation of the programs, which include outreach to the Mexican community in all five of New York City's boroughs each year. A training program in hospitality management has sought to help more Mexicans, many of whom work in restaurants and hotels, to advance to become managers or entrepreneurs. The Si Se Puede Web site (http://www.cuny.edu/about/resources/sisepuede.html) gives information about CUNY in English and Spanish. The Citizenship and Immigration Project, headed by Alan Wernick, offers free or low-cost legal advice on immigration issues to CUNY students, including assistance to those seeking permanent residence status or citizenship. At Baruch College, a leadership training program in which I serve as the lead faculty member has taught more than 120 emerging Mexican leaders skills in tasks related to nonprofit management and advocacy, and has introduced them to officials in various New York City agencies and institutions to facilitate their work. Baruch College's School of Public Affairs has attracted and indeed actively sought out college graduates who are themselves children of immigrants, including Mexican immigrants, or who work with immigrant communities for its Master's in Public Affairs program. In 2012, CUNY opened a Mexican studies institute headed by Alyshia Galvez, at Lehman College, which has many Mexican students.

These efforts by CUNY have had noticeable results. The number of Mexicans applying to CUNY has increased in recent years. Indeed, the proportion of foreign- as well as native-born Mexican students aged 19–23 in New York City at college who went to a public, as opposed to private, institution increased between 2000 and 2009.[8] This period included the years when CUNY's program of outreach to the Mexican community began to be active. CUNY also supported my own research to learn more about the state of knowledge and beliefs about higher education in the Mexican community. Drawing on several hundred surveys as well as interviews conducted in 2007, the research found that most Mexicans in New York City then believed that it was impossible for the undocumented to go to college, that those who were able to attend had to go full time, and that it cost a great deal of money. Many respondents thought that tuition at CUNY was $20,000 per year, at a time when it was less than $5,000 for a full-time student. CUNY's outreach programs have sought to dispel these myths through institutional contacts and Web sites providing accurate information. These efforts have helped change perceptions in the Mexican community; many who previously thought college was not possible for them now believe that it is and that CUNY offers the best route and best value.

New York City's DOE has also responded positively to Mexican community organizations. Perhaps most important, the DOE has begun to train guidance counselors more systematically in how to deal with undocumented students. Based on my research, I have reported to the DOE numerous cases where undocumented students in New York City high schools not only were not told by their guidance counselors that they could get in-state tuition at public colleges—as New York State law provides—but also were told they could not go to college at all because of their legal status, again, contrary to New York State law. Several years ago, I spoke at a daylong training program for guidance counselors from one city public school district, and asked who among them thought an undocumented immigrant could go to college. Only a few raised their hands. When I told them about the in-state tuition law, many gasped, putting their hands to their mouths. Some came up afterward and thanked me for telling them, upset that they were giving students the wrong information. There have been many other instances in which I have intervened as part of my ethnographic work—for example, when a principal told students they could not go to college because of their status and when a guidance counselor would not help a U.S.-born student fill out a financial aid form for fear it would expose her undocumented parents to deportation. It is encouraging that the DOE has begun larger-scale training to avoid misinforming and misdirecting students. The DOE has also been involved in other projects to assist Mexican students. In 2011, to name one, MASA president Angelo Cabrera was involved in planning a series of community forums sponsored by the DOE and Mexican community groups, with the twin goals of increasing knowledge of educational rights and opportunities among Mexicans and creating bridges between the DOE and the Mexican community.

LOOKING AHEAD: POLITICAL INVISIBILITY AND CIVIC AND POLITICAL MOBILIZATION IN NEW YORK CITY

Although civic engagement over educational issues important to Mexicans has increased a great deal in New York City, Mexicans are still largely political invisible. Despite possessing significant resources and energy, Mexicans in the city confront serious challenges to their political mobilization. In many ways, the Mexican population is almost uniquely situated for political invisibility, even in an immigrant-friendly city such as New York. First, the majority of Mexican immigrants to New York City are not citizens, and many are not even legal residents, and hence cannot become citizens and vote. Estimates of the percentage of immigrants who lack legal status vary, but plausible estimates are that upward of 60–70 percent of recent immigrants who arrived in the last few years lack legal status. In political life, those who do not vote—even citizens who have the right to vote—are politically invisible and discounted.

Second, Mexicans in New York are geographically dispersed throughout the city. To be sure, several substantial concentrations or Little Mexicos have emerged in East Harlem, Jackson Heights, Sunset Park, Brighton Beach, the

South Bronx, Port Richmond, and Washington Heights. However, the absence of one or two main residential concentrations makes political mobilization more difficult than for groups like Dominicans or West Indians, for whom densely settled immigrant neighborhoods in upper Manhattan and Brooklyn have provided the basis for electing representatives, including coethnics, who take that group's needs and issues into account (see chapters 7 and 9, this volume). Because Mexicans are so dispersed, they do not have a heavily populated Mexican neighborhood to serve as an anchor for emerging political leadership. Nonetheless, dispersion does not mean that a group's interest cannot be represented; a non-coethnic politician may take up the cause of a new immigrant group in his or her district to become its proxy advocate, in part because the politician sees the demographic writing on the wall and wants support from the community when its second generation comes of age. Up to now, dispersion has acted against this form of representation for Mexicans, but as the Mexican second generation grows in the coming years this will change.

The crowded field of ethnic politics and high barriers to entry also have contributed to Mexican political invisibility in New York City. At the beginning of the second decade of the twentieth century, other ethnic groups already have an established position in New York City politics, including two well-organized Latino groups, Puerto Ricans and Dominicans, who are larger in number and more residentially concentrated than Mexicans. Rather than pursuing a Mexican candidate strategy—that is, seeking elected office by mainly attracting Mexican American votes by emphasizing ethnicity—Mexican politicians in the future are likely to try and run campaigns that have broader appeal and highlight other substantive issues. The same sort of trajectory is also likely for other growing Latino ethnic groups, such as Ecuadorans, whose populations are not yet large or concentrated enough to offer a solid geographic base for a successful political campaign.

Another difficulty for Mexicans in the quest for elected office in New York City is the costs involved. The spending limit for a New York City Council seat in 2008 was $161,000 each for the primary and general election. While the publicly funded Campaign Finance Board gives every candidate up to $6 for each $1 raised, this still requires candidates to raise nearly $27,000 for each race, that is, a total of $54,000 for the primary and general elections. A city council run is not a small-scale affair, since a city council district has about 150,000 people and thus requires strong organization as well as good financing. The need for organizational capacity and financial resources means that political parties, unions, and civic institutions play a relatively strong role in New York City elections.

Despite the many obstacles to elected political office, a number of emerging, younger-generation Mexican leaders are looking ahead to try to win city council seats and other positions. Outside of formal politics, others are taking civic action to address problems confronting the community. This broad orientation toward civic action is inspiring, especially in a population where so many have been excluded from legal status.

DAMIAN VARGAS—ASPIRING POLITICAL LEADER

Damian Vargas, a second-generation Mexican American, is one such aspiring leader. Born and raised in Brooklyn in Community Board 12 district (Borough Park and Kensington), Vargas lived in that neighborhood for most of his life, moving to Community Board 4 district in Jackson Heights, Queens, partly for his work and partly to open up prospects for his political career. Vargas attended New York City public schools, graduated from a CUNY college, received a law degree from Rutgers Law School, and became a practicing lawyer. He spoke with me about his views of how, as a Mexican, he should negotiate his political future.

His first foray into electoral politics was in 2010, when he sought a seat on Brooklyn's Community Board 12 with the encouragement of city councilman Brad Lander, although he was not picked. (Borough presidents appoint the voting community board members, and half of those appointed are nominated by city council members representing the district. Community board seats are often sought by those with aspirations in politics.) Latinos are a minority in Community Board 12 (only 13 percent in 2000). The largest politically organized voting group is Hasidic Jews, with growing South Asian (Bangladeshi and Pakistani), East Asian, eastern European immigrant, and Hispanic populations. Had Vargas been appointed, he would have been the first Mexican member of that community board. Looking ahead, the increasing number of Latinos in Community Board 12 district could help his chances in the future. By 2011, however, he was living in Queens, in Community Board 4 district, which has a profile that could be more amenable to his being appointed—50 percent Hispanic in 2000, a figure that now is likely to be even higher. Vargas was optimistic that the growing Hispanic population in Community Board 4 district would help his chances. He has become active in the Latino Lawyers Association of Queens County, and reported its interest in his political aspirations. He noted that he was "the only Mexican American attorney in the association," but also felt it was essential to develop a broader base of support in the Latino community.

While sensitive to and concerned about the problems facing the Mexican community—with a large proportion lacking legal status and citizenship, earning low wages, experiencing violations of their human and civil rights, and confronting a "general perception that every Mexican is illegal and simply consuming public resources without contribution"—he did not think he could win an election running on a platform based on these issues, which are, in the main, problems of noncitizens and, hence, nonvoters. He was aware that he lacks a large coethnic base to support him in a run for political office. It is not only that most Mexicans in the city "cannot vote . . . and those that can, are not educated enough about the process." Also, he said that the Mexican community leadership at the time we spoke in 2011 was "fractured" and unable to focus on one candidate. Hence, he planned a strategy emphasizing issues of importance to the larger community, and to put himself forward as a Latino candidate, stressing his pan-ethnic as well as Mexican identity. He said:

> Therefore, I think the most important thing for me, if I run in the near future, is not to position myself as the Mexican candidate, but the candidate who happens to be Mexican. I'm not suggesting that I would distance myself from the Mexican community or not represent their interests, but simply that the best chance for me to make a successful run is to align myself with other groups in addition to the Mexican community. Even in neighborhoods with a large concentration of Mexicans, such as Sunset Park, Corona/Jackson Heights, and East Harlem, Mexican voters are not a large enough group to carry the district. Ultimately, I have to be more Mexican than the Mexicans, so as to not alienate the Mexican community and leadership, and more American than the Americans, so as to not alienate everyone else.

Vargas's analysis points to an interesting dynamic in New York ethnic politics, and ethnic politics more generally. In Vargas's view, he must be seen to be authentically Mexican, representing the Mexican community's interests, but not as "too Mexican" by other groups. In this regard, it has been noted that coalitions between blacks and Latinos are more likely when they perceive that they are in the same boat in society (Meier et al. 2004). Vargas sees that he is in the Latino boat, so to speak; to be successful politically he must be viewed as representing all Latinos, not just Mexicans, as well as representing all his constituents.

When I asked Vargas what issues he would emphasize in a political campaign, he said the most important would be "the creation of jobs, efficient government, improving the educational level of at-risk communities, preserving housing for low-income people, and quality-of-life issues, such as harsher penalties for drunk drivers." These are local concerns—and not overtly focused on one ethnic group. With a platform emphasizing such issues, it is unlikely he would be attacked for being too focused on his ethnicity, and he might be helped by the novelty of Mexicans being a large and growing group in New York City but without much political representation.

MOBILIZATION AROUND THE DREAM ACT

Mexicans in New York City have also mobilized around the Dream Act, which as of this writing is the most visible and viable of the versions of national immigration reform in serious discussion. At the beginning of the twenty-first century, the goal of comprehensive immigration reform, providing a pathway to legal status and ultimately citizenship, had largely fallen off the national political stage. In 2010, the Dream Act was pushed, mainly by undocumented students and their allies, in the waning days before the national midterm elections and had widespread support across the entire U.S. ethnic spectrum. The act would have made qualified undocumented youth eligible for conditional permanent residency, with a six-year-long path to citizenship, requiring completion of a college degree or two years of military service. The Dream Act passed the House of Representatives in 2010, and had fifty-five votes in the Senate—a majority, but five votes shy of the supermajority of sixty votes needed to get legislation passed in the new political climate. President Obama said he would have signed the bill had it come to his desk—but it never did.

The youths mobilizing on behalf of the Dream Act were able to garner so much support because their claims resonated with American mythology (Abrego 2008; Galvez 2009) of rugged individualists succeeding by their own merits—pulling themselves up by their bootstraps, without the aid of the government or other outside assistance. Since undocumented students are ineligible for federal student loans, and usually come from low-income families, they embody the rugged individualist myth more than most groups. That they would legalize their status through higher education or military service emphasized their contributions to American society. While some Americans claimed that those who would benefit from the Dream Act were criminals because of their undocumented status, this claim was neutralized (at least for large segments of the U.S. population) by the fact that many of the students had been brought to the United States by their parents as very young children. Americans think of themselves as fair minded, and it seemed unfair and downright un-American to many to hold children responsible for their parents' acts. That the act failed to pass in 2010 was, I believe, an American tragedy, denying equal opportunity to many hard-working youths whose energy and contributions the United States needs and solidifying the exclusionary barriers facing the millions of undocumented in this country.

Mexicans in New York were part of the mobilization to try to get the Dream Act passed. Mexican leaders in the city eagerly participated in and helped to plan the immigrants' rights marches in spring 2006, as well as the rally in spring 2010 in Washington, DC. Tepeyac, MASA, La Unión, and many other organizations brought students onto the streets in New York City in 2006, and on the mall in Washington, DC, in 2010, in demonstrations demanding comprehensive immigration reform. These protests were lessons in American civic engagement, and an exercise of constitutionally held rights to freedom of assembly and freedom of speech. As such, they show Mexican immigrants embracing two of the strongest traditions in American civic life.

CONCLUSION

The story of Mexicans in New York City in the early twenty-first century is one of progress achieved—but also, less happily, progress impeded. The major problem, as I have emphasized, is the large number of undocumented Mexican immigrants living in legal limbo and, as I write this chapter in early 2012, with little chance to legalize their status. As a result, they are unable to participate in the mainstream economy and political processes, cannot convert their hard work into greater opportunities for their children via a middle-class income, and live in fear of being deported, even though they have worked and, in a good many cases, gone to school in New York for many years. Although U.S.-born Mexicans are U.S. citizens at birth, many live in mixed-status families with parents and often siblings who are undocumented. Beyond their own households, virtually all Mexicans in New York have friends or relatives who lack legal status so that the impact of immigration issues on legal status ripples throughout the Mexican community. Without federal legislation to provide paths to legalization, the difficulties and inequalities facing undocumented immigrants will persist. Major New York City elected officials are vocal in their support of such legislation, but it is largely out of their control. The future of New York's Mexican community is bound up with political events and machinations at the national level in the U.S. Congress.

If this sounds bleak, there are also encouraging signs in the city's Mexican community. As many Mexicans establish roots in New York after two decades of large-scale immigration—and, even more significant, as a growing number of children of immigrants, born in the United States, come of age—they are becoming more involved in New York life, including in civic organizations and political mobilizations. Outreach programs by Mexican organizations and, importantly, CUNY, have begun to pay dividends, and more Mexicans, especially the native-born, are attending college and are poised to move into white-collar and often professional jobs. Mexican American leaders have emerged, some of them planning strategies to seek elected office. The future of the Mexican community, to a significant extent, has to do with the second generation who have grown up in and around New York City. How they are—and are not—becoming part of the fabric of American society is still in play, and a critical subject for further study.

NOTES

1. In the 2003 survey, 88 percent reported being undocumented. In the 2011 survey, 39 percent of the respondents reported being undocumented directly, said that they

had an expired visa (2 percent), or did not want to answer the question (9 percent); 39 percent did not answer the question (surveyors were instructed not to push the issue), which I interpret to mean they were undocumented. If this interpretation is correct, then 89 percent of the 2011 sample is undocumented.

2. I wish to thank Andrew Beveridge, of the Queens College Sociology Department, for these figures. The 2005–9 figures are from the American Community Survey in those years.

3. An exception is mainland-born Puerto Ricans, among whom 10 percent were not attending or had not graduated from high school; the figures for the Chinese, Jamaican, and Ecuadorian native-born were, respectively, 1 percent, 2 percent, and 4 percent.

4. The rate for foreign-born Ecuadorian 19–23-year-olds, the next lowest group, was 26 percent; for Jamaicans, 46 percent; Dominicans, 37 percent; and Chinese, 64 percent.

5. "About Us." La Unión website. http://la-union.org/.

6. The author cofounded MexEd and serves on the board of the merged organization, MASA-MexEd.

7. I am grateful to Steven Alvarez , who has been conducting doctoral dissertation research on MASA at the CUNY Graduate Center, for information on the tutorial program.

8. In 2000, according to American Community Survey data, 64 percent of foreign-born Mexican students aged 19–23 in New York City who were attending college went to a public college; in 2005–9, the figure was 88 percent. Among native-born Mexican students at college in the same age group, 40 percent attended public college in 2000, increasing to 58 percent in 2005–9.

REFERENCES

Abrego, Leisy. 2008. "Legitimacy, Social Identity, and the Mobilization of Law: The Effects of Assembly Bill 540 on Undocumented Students in California." *Law and Social Inquiry* 33 (3): 709–34.

Bergad, Laird. 2010. "Mexicans in New York City, 1990–2009: A Visual Data Base." New York: Center for Latin American, Caribbean and Latino Studies, City University of New York Graduate Center.

Galvez, Alyshia. 2009. *Guadalupe in New York: Devotion and the Struggle for Citizenship Rights among Mexican Immigrants*. New York: New York University Press.

Gonzales, Roberto G. 2011. "Learning to be Illegal: Undocumented Youth and Shifting Legal Contexts in the Transition to Adulthood." *American Sociological Review* 76: 602–19.

Kasinitz, Philip, John Mollenkopf, Mary Waters, and Jennifer Holdaway. 2008. *Inheriting the City: The Second Generation Comes of Age*. Cambridge: Harvard University Press and Russell Sage Foundation.

La Unión. 2009. "Nowhere to Turn: A Report on the Reality of Mexican Americans in the New York City Public Schools." http://la-union.org/wp-content/uploads/2010/10/NowhereToTurnReport_v2.pdf.

Massey, Douglas, ed. 2008. *New Faces in New Places: The Changing Geography of American Immigration*. New York: Russell Sage Foundation.

Massey, Douglas, Jorge Durand, and Nolan Malone. 2002. *Beyond Smoke and Mirrors: Mexican Immigration in an Era of Economic Integration*. New York: Russell Sage Foundation.

McNees, Molly, Robert Smith, Nina Suilc, and Olivia Flores. 2004. "Mexican Immigrants and Health in New York City." New York: United Hospital Fund.

Meier, Kenneth, Paula McClain, J. L. Polinard, and Robert Wrinkle. 2004. "Divided or Together? Conflict and Cooperation between African Americans and Latinos." *Political Research Quarterly* 57 (3): 399–409.

Newton, Lina. 2008. *Illegal, Alien, or Immigrant: The Politics of Immigration Reform*. New York: New York University Press.

Smith, Robert Courtney. 1996. "Counting Migrant Farmworkers: Causes of the Undercount of Farmworkers in the Northeastern United States in the 1990 Census, and Strategies to Increase Coverage for Census 2000." Final Report to Center for Survey Methods Research. Washington, DC: Statistical Research Division, Bureau of the Census.

——. 2006. *Mexican New York: Transnational Worlds of New Immigrants*. Berkeley: University of California Press.

——. 2012. *Horatio Alger Lives in Brooklyn, But Check His Papers*. Unpublished manuscript.

Smith, Robert Courtney et al. 2012. "Survey on Migrant Knowledge of Segura Popular." Final Report to Centro Investigacion y Docenia Economica, Mexico City.

Yoshikawa, Hirokazu. 2011. *Immigrants Raising Citizens*. New York: Russell Sage Foundation.

Walk 2010–2011. 2011. "DREAM ACTing Walk Goes to Washington, DC." October 25. http://walk10.wordpress.com/2011/10/25/dream-acting-walk-goes-to-washington-dc/.

Zúñiga, Víctor, and Rubén Hernández-León, eds. 2006. *New Destinations: Mexican Immigration in the United States*. New York: Russell Sage Foundation.

11. *The Next Generation Emerges*

Philip Kasinitz, John H. Mollenkopf, and Mary C. Waters

New York has long been known as a city of immigrants. With more than a third of its population and almost half of its adult population foreign-born, scarcely an area of contemporary New York life has not been reshaped by the resumption of mass immigration since the mid-1960s. And yet, when we think of how immigration is transforming the city's economic, cultural, and political life, we are reminded that we can see the importance of immigration not only in the lives of the immigrants themselves but also in those of their American-born children, the "second generation." When we ask what sort of New Yorkers the newcomers will be—and what sort of New York they are creating—we must look to this second generation for answers.

By 2009, this American-born second generation constituted approximately 22 percent of the city's population. They were, however, 24 percent of the young adult (aged 18–32) population of the city. Another 11 percent of this age group are members of what Ruben Rumbaut (1999) has termed the "1.5 generation"—born abroad but arriving as children and coming of age in the United States. (Another 23 percent migrated as young adults.) Together, these groups make up more than half of all young adult New Yorkers. They outnumber the children of natives and far outnumber the children of white natives, the group many Americans still think of as the mainstream. Indeed, the norm among young adult New Yorkers today is to have immigrant parents, thus setting the tone for what it means to be a young adult New Yorker. As the oldest members of the second generation now enter their early 40s and the average age is in the early 20s, members of the second generation are beginning to make their impact felt on many arenas of New York life. The growth of this population is made all the more important by the aging of the native population and the impending retirement of the large baby boom cohort. Thus, for better or for worse, the children of immigrants will almost certainly play an expanding role in the city's life in the coming decades (Alba 2009; Myers 2007).

New York is also unusual in that immigration affects all of the city's racial groups. In most of the United States, we think of Asians and Latinos as newcomers and whites and blacks as the native population. Not so in New York, where, particularly in the younger age groups, nearly half of the black population and indeed a third of the white population are immigrants or have immigrant parents. This means that the immigrant versus native cleavage does not map onto racial difference in the ways that it does in most of the United States.

These demographic facts make some observers uneasy. Many worry how the city and nation will be able to adjust to a future without a white majority—indeed, a city in which no racial or ethnic group forms a majority. Others express concern as to whether the economy, particularly in the wake of the recent "great recession," will be able to provide enough job opportunities to absorb the young people now coming of age. In the nineteenth and early twentieth centuries, a strong manufacturing base allowed the integration of many newcomers into an expanding working and lower-middle class. Clearly this route is no longer available and employment must be found in the various service sectors, many of which are nonunionized and have a predominance of low-wage jobs. Can New York City's schools and higher educational system meet the challenge of preparing the newcomers and their children for the managerial and professional jobs of the twenty-first century? What will the more complicated racial and ethnic landscape mean for the city's always contentious politics? Finally, will the children of immigrants coming of age in a time of semiofficially recognized multiculturalism be willing, or able, to be fully incorporated into the city's social and cultural mainstream?

In an effort to understand the second generation and the challenges it faces, we undertook the largest study of this group in the New York metropolitan area to date, the Immigrant Second Generation in Metropolitan New York (ISGMNY) project. Between 1999 and 2001, we surveyed about 2,000 young adult New Yorkers of Chinese, Dominican, Russian Jewish, South American (Colombian, Ecuadoran, and Peruvian), and West Indian immigrant parentage. For comparative purposes, we also surveyed young adult New Yorkers of native black and native white parentage as well as mainland-born Puerto Ricans. The survey was supplemented with in-depth life history interviews with about 10 percent of the respondents and a series of linked ethnographic projects (for details, see Kasinitz et al. 2004 and Kasinitz et al. 2008).

In general, our research suggests that many of the concerns about the incorporation of the new second generation are misplaced. By most measures, the second generation is assimilating into American society very rapidly. Language assimilation is particularly dramatic—a finding that is consistent with research in the rest of the country (Portes and Rumbaut 2001; Tran 2010). Nor is there much reason to worry about "divided loyalties." Few children of immigrants stay deeply connected to their parents' homelands or follow national politics in their parents' countries, which, despite the relative ease of modern transportation, a third have never visited even once. Even fewer second-generation New Yorkers have ever seriously considered moving to their parents' homelands permanently. What is more, the second generation tends to see themselves as Americans and New Yorkers, albeit ethnic ones. They are more likely than other New York residents their age to have grown up in the city (many "native" young adult New Yorkers are, in fact, newcomers from other parts of the United States), and they often identify strongly with the city, its culture, and its institutions.

Yet there are reasons to be concerned about the second generation's future. Racial differences among the groups we studied are marked, if somewhat less so than among the children of natives. By most measures of economic and educational achievement, the black and Latino children of immigrants, while generally better off than black and Latino natives, still lag well behind Asians and whites. Many report experiencing discrimination in daily life. For dark-skinned children of immigrants, negative encounters with the police are common and a source of considerable frustration and alienation (Waters and Kasinitz 2010). Perhaps because of their youth, the second generation also has yet to enter the city's political leadership proportionate to their numbers, although the recent emergence of several high-visibility second-generation politicians suggests that this may be changing.

GETTING AN EDUCATION

Second-generation groups vary in terms of educational attainment. In the ISGMNY sample, the Russian Jews and the Chinese were significantly more likely to have graduated from high school, completed a four-year college degree, or acquired postgraduate education than the other groups and significantly less likely to have dropped out of high school. Of those over 24, the percentage with a bachelor's degree ranged from 64 percent among the Chinese (10 percent higher than for native whites) down to only 26 percent among the Dominicans and South Americans—yet that is still 10 percent higher than the rate for native blacks and Puerto Ricans, as well as much higher than the numbers for their own immigrant parents (Kasinitz et al. 2002).

It is noteworthy that the second-generation group with the highest level of educational achievement in the ISGMNY sample, the Chinese, are also the most likely to have attended New York City public schools. Indeed, while the most educationally ambitious white and African American parents often send their children to private or parochial schools (a pattern also seen, albeit to a lesser extent, among South Americans and Russian Jews), the Chinese seem to have found the islands of excellence within the highly uneven public school system. They are heavily overrepresented in the city's well-regarded selective and magnet schools (as are the Russian, Ukrainian, Korean, and other European- and Asian-origin second-generation groups) as well as in selective programs within neighborhood schools. Until recently, this often required that Chinese parents move to neighborhoods with better public schools. However, changes in New York's public school system in the last decade involving increased school choice and a reduction in the number of neighborhood-based schools, particularly at the high school level, has made it easier to access good schools and programs without moving. Thus in the ISGMNY study, among those who attended high school in the city, the Chinese second generation reported the longest commutes to school (Tran 2011), and this is probably even more true today since commuting long distances to attend high school has generally become more common. At the same time, Latino immigrant parents are often reluctant to have their children commute long distances to "better" schools, particularly when this means hours of travel on public transportation through sometimes dangerous neighborhoods. Thus, choice-based New York City school reforms have probably not served Latino groups as well.

For those who go on to college, there are also marked differences in the quality of schools attended. *U.S. News and World Report* ranks four-year institutions of higher learning on how selective they are, with Tier I as the most selective and Tier IV the least. Of those who went to college in the ISGMNY sample, 23 percent of the Chinese, 16 percent of Russian Jews, and 38 percent of native whites attended Tier I colleges—compared to only 6 percent of native African Americans, 8 percent of the Puerto Ricans, 7 percent of Dominicans, and 7 percent of West Indians. By contrast, 22 percent of college-educated Dominicans, 38 percent of native African Americans, 35 percent of Puerto Ricans, and 39 percent of West Indians had gone to Regional Tier IV schools—as opposed to only 4 percent of the Chinese and 9 percent of the Russian Jewish respondents (Kasinitz et al. 2008).

AVOIDING THE BOTTOM, NOT ALWAYS REACHING THE TOP: THE SECOND GENERATION IN THE WORKFORCE

In New York, as elsewhere, finding a foothold in the labor force is a crucial test for the successful incorporation of the second generation. As large numbers of the children of immigrants have come of age and embarked on independent careers, we can begin to see the roles they will play in the city's future. Nationally, many observers have expressed concern about how this entry into the labor force is being managed, and some scholars have noted the potential for "downward assimilation" of the children of immigrants into a multiethnic "underclass" of inner-city poverty (see Portes and Zhou 1993; Haller et al. 2011; Alba et al. 2011). Herbert Gans's notion of "second-generation decline" and the "segmented assimilation" theory developed by Alejandro Portes and his collaborators both suggest that while some immigrant groups will integrate into the mainstream labor force with relatively little trouble, others, particularly the children of poor and racially stigmatized labor migrants, will find themselves increasingly isolated from opportunities in the mainstream economy. Yet at the same time, the cultural assimilation of many members of these groups may lead to a situation where young people are unwilling or unable to take the generally low-status and low-wage jobs held by their immigrant parents (Gans 1992; Portes et al. 2005; Portes and Rumbaut 2001; Portes and Zhou 1993). Others suggest that a significant portion of the second generation is experiencing "racialization" (see Telles and Ortiz 2008) into an urban underclass that stands outside of the mainstream economy.

Our data generally suggest that this is not what is happening in New York. While groups clearly differ in how—and how well—they are being incorporated into the labor force, most of the second generation seems both more likely to be strongly attached to the labor force than the members of native minority groups and far less likely to work in distinctive ethnic niches than their immigrant parents.

Given the youth of most of the current second generation, however, standard measures of labor force participation are not always the best way to examine the question of labor market incorporation. After all, many young people in the United States today combine part-time work and part-time education and career training well into their late 20s and even later (see Waters et al. 2011). This is particularly true in New York, where the huge City University of New York (CUNY, with more than 270,000 students) encourages people to continue to slowly amass credentials often well past what we traditionally think of as college age (Attewell and Lavin 2008). Furthermore, those young adults who are pursuing educational credentials at older ages and who will eventually obtain relatively high-status jobs may, in their 20s, still have low incomes and appear to have weak labor attachment.

One way to deal with this problem is to look at the proportion in various groups in the most danger of falling into an underclass outside of the mainstream labor force. We can do this by identifying those adults who are not currently employed, enrolled in higher education, or in training programs with a statistic known as the NEET (not in education, employment, or training) rate (Quintini and Martin 2006). First introduced in the United Kingdom, the NEET rate has been used in educational research to examine employability, labor market marginalization, and social exclusion among young people. This measure provides a more expansive, and we feel more useful, indicator of labor market marginality than official unemployment rates, given the age of the second-generation respondents.

Of course, not everyone counted in the NEET rate should be thought of as a potential member of a socially isolated underclass. There could be several reasons for being NEET. Some have chosen to stay home as homemakers or caretakers of young children while others might be trying to succeed in a field (such as the arts) without yet earning a living from it. Yet the existence of much higher NEET rates in certain groups clearly suggests the possibility of long-term social exclusion and is a serious reason for concern.

Looking at the ISGMNY data, we see dramatic differences in the NEET rate among the various second-generation and native groups. Native African Americans showed a NEET rate of nearly 30 percent and for mainland-born Puerto Ricans it was above 25 percent. Both groups were significantly above the rate for native whites (13.3 percent). Among the second-generation groups, however, only Dominicans, the worst off of the second-generation populations on most measures, were significantly more likely to be NEET than native whites, and even they, with a rate of 20.6 percent, were more likely to be in school or the labor force than were native blacks and Puerto Ricans. The Russian Jewish and the Chinese second generation were more likely to be working or in school than were the native whites. South Americans and West Indians showed NEET rates that were about the same as those of children of white natives.

If the second generation does seem to be entering the labor force, what sort of jobs are they taking? We found that the children of immigrants do not generally work in "immigrant jobs," nor, for that matter, do they live in isolated ethnic enclaves. Rather, they are moving quickly into the city's increasingly multiethnic mainstream. While their immigrant parents may run convenience stores, drive taxis, or work as nannies, the second generation is moving into financial services, civil service jobs, and mainstream retail work. The children of garment factory workers, for example, are increasingly making their mark among the city's younger fashion designers. In each of the five immigrant second-generation groups we studied, the most common jobs were retail work, white-collar managers, and clerical positions—exactly the same jobs most commonly held by the children of natives their age.

We compared the occupation and industry profile of the second-generation respondents in our study with those of their immigrant parents and with the city's labor force as a whole. As one might suspect, the immigrant parents were highly concentrated in ethnic niche occupations and were also very segregated by gender. Two out of every five fathers of Chinese respondents worked in restaurants, while more than a third of the mothers of West Indian respondents were nurses or nurse's aides. New York's beleaguered manufacturing sector has continued to play an important role for immigrants, particularly for those immigrant women who (unlike West Indians) do not speak English on arrival. Forty-six percent of the mothers of Dominican second-generation respondents, 43 percent of the South American mothers, and a staggering 57 percent of the Chinese mothers worked in manufacturing, primarily in the garment industry.

The second-generation respondents present a different picture. They are markedly less concentrated in certain occupations than their parents. For example, only 3 percent of the second-generation male Chinese respondents worked in restaurants, and only 9 percent of West Indian female respondents were nurses or nurse's aides. While greater economic opportunity has pushed the second generation away from their parents' jobs, they also report a distaste for stereotypical ethnic occupations. When asked what job he would never take, one Chinese respondent replied, "Delivering Chinese food." When the daughter of a Chinatown jewelry shop owner was asked if her father would like her to take over the business, she laughingly replied, "No, he doesn't hate me that much!"

Even the least successful groups have largely exited from parental niches. There is a striking drop-off in manufacturing employment between the generations. While manufacturing is an important employer of fathers, and particularly mothers, for all second-generation groups in our study except West Indians, second-generation employment in manufacturing is negligible—in fact, even less common than in the general population in the New York metropolitan area. As one Colombian respondent put it when asked if he would consider taking his father's job, "Hey, I don't do that factory thing." To be sure, the second generation has good reason for rejecting their parents' jobs, which they often see—rightly—as hard, low status, and unrewarding. The minority of the second generation that ended up employed in workplaces dominated by coethnics generally earned less and had fewer benefits than those who worked in ethnically mixed workplaces (Kasinitz et al. 2011). But beyond the material advantages of joining the mainstream, many of the young people we spoke to found immigrant jobs distasteful precisely because they were seen as immigrant jobs. As one young Chinese man put it:

> RESPONDENT: My father, he is always working [in a restaurant]. Never home. My mom works like six days a week and my dad works six. . . . I don't think he likes it. It is just to make money, pay my tuition, my brother's tuition, pay the bills.

> INTERVIEWER: Would you ever work that job?
> RESPONDENT: No! Too much running around. My parents work long, long hours. I want to work nine to five! I guess it's all right for someone with his level of education. For them it's good, but not for me. I would not want to do it.

Even among second-generation respondents with few other employment options, ethnicity plays a role in defining a job as appropriate, as the comments of a young Dominican woman, an unemployed high school dropout with an arrest record, indicate:

> RESPONDENT: My mom, she didn't have papers. So she was working under the table . . . cleaning, ironing for people—that's like a Hispanic thing. [It] was a way of getting through rough times.
> INTERVIEWER: Would you ever see yourself working that kind of job?
> RESPONDENT: I never say never, but I wouldn't want to. Because I was raised here! I speak very good English. So, I don't know.

Not surprisingly, many of the second generation have been attracted to New York's large finance, insurance, and real estate (FIRE) sector. Indeed, Chinese and Russian respondents are more likely to work in this sector than native whites or New York City residents as a whole. The sector also employs many South American respondents. Interestingly, FIRE employment is higher among the second generation than among their immigrant parents in every group except West Indians, among whom many immigrant parents already in FIRE employment no doubt have lower status and relatively low-paying jobs within this high-paying sector.

For the most part, however, second-generation respondents report working in the same kinds of jobs most young people in New York City have. Given their age and the era in which they entered the labor market, retailing and clerical work are the first or second most common occupations for every group except native whites, for whom they are the second and third most common. A number of interesting ethnic particularities in the occupational distribution do suggest that some new ethnic niches may be forming: many Chinese work in finance as computer and design specialists; the Russians seem to specialize in work with computers; Dominicans, South Americans, and Puerto Ricans are often financial clerks; and many second-generation West Indians work in health care. The overwhelming story is nevertheless one of similarity with each other rather than recapitulating the group differences evident among their parents. Our education and occupation data show some evidence of downward mobility for mainland-born Puerto Ricans—which might suggest "third-generation decline." But for the most part the second generation are going to school and working with each other, and most do not show any signs of the second-generation decline that distressed some analysts.

How are they doing in terms of income? Generally the move out of the parents' ethnic niches and into the economic mainstream seems to be paying off, at least modestly. Chinese and Russian second-generation respondents have almost exactly the same hourly earnings as native white New Yorkers the same age. The West Indian and Latino second generation earns less, although they actually earn about the same as those native whites who were raised in New York City. They still make considerably more than native blacks and Puerto Ricans.

However, if few of the second generation seem to be clustered at the bottom of the New York City labor force, it is not as clear that they are making significant inroads at the very top. Of course, we can see a smattering of the children of immigrants in almost all of New York's most prestigious firms. This is true for all groups, but particularly so for Asians. For example, Goldman Sachs, the financial giant, now has a sufficient number of young Chinese executives to field a large team to compete in the Hong Kong–style dragon boat races now annually held in Queens. However, as Richard Alba's recent analysis of Wall Street employment shows, other groups are not doing as well in the top occupations. The children of black and Latino immigrants are far underrepresented in these firms relative to their proportion of the population and tend to be concentrated in lower-wage and lower-status positions within the generally high-wage financial sector (Alba and Pereira 2011).

FINDING THEIR VOICE: THE SECOND GENERATION IN NEW YORK POLITICS AND MULTIETHNIC URBAN CULTURE

Like other young people, members of the second generation, on the whole, are not particularly interested in politics, take a jaundiced view of politicians, and are not actively engaged in electoral politics. As immigrant communities have grown over the last decade, however, and as the next generation has come of age, young people from immigrant backgrounds are emerging as leaders of student groups, nonprofit organizations, and even as political candidates.

Perhaps the most dramatic political development in recent years in terms of the second generation's emergence as a political force was the election to Congress of Yvette Clarke, the New York–born child of Jamaican immigrants, in 2008 and Grace Meng, a second-generation Taiwanese American in 2012, as well as the election of John Liu, a 1.5-generation Taiwanese immigrant, as the city's comptroller in 2009. In all three cases, these relatively young politicians got their starts representing largely immigrant districts in the city council or the state legislature. Yet as they sought higher office, they managed to combine a strong appeal to coethnics with an ability to reach beyond their "natural" ethnic base and win the votes of New Yorkers from a wide range of groups. Liu, in particular, was elected with significant African American support as well as the endorsement of many of the city's various ethnic newspapers and other media outlets, and has made little secret of his desire to move up even further in the city's political structure. Their success has been echoed in the election of second-generation members of the city council from Dominican, West Indian, and Korean backgrounds.

Finally, it is worth noting that as New York's second generation sets the tone for New York's urban culture, they may be changing the way that they and other New Yorkers view the city, in some cases in very positive ways. Many of the second-generation young people we spoke to demonstrated a fluid and nuanced approach to the oldest and most vexing of American social divides: race. Much of today's second generation does not fit easily into American racial boxes and categories. Race continues to be a central fact in American life, and racism continues to tragically circumscribe many people's life chances. But racial boundaries are blurring as the categories become more complicated. And young people—both the second generation and those who grow up with them—seem more comfortable with that fact than their elders.

Growing up in multiethnic neighborhoods, like Jackson Heights, Queens (where Indians, South Americans, Irish, and Pakistani immigrants live side by side), or Sunset Park, Brooklyn (where Puerto Ricans, Mexicans, Chinese, Vietnamese, and Arabic-speaking immigrants mix with old-timers with roots in Scandinavia), the young New Yorkers we spoke to were generally comfortable with racial and ethnic diversity. In a world where almost everyone's family is from somewhere else, ethnicity is a source of everyday banter. One 18-year-old told us about how often people tried to guess her identity: "I have been asked if I am Egyptian, Cuban, Greek, Pakistani. I say no, I am Peruvian, Spanish. I like my culture and I am proud to be Peruvian, the Incas and all that." This is not a world of balkanized groups huddled within their own enclaves, but rather of hybrids and fluid exchanges across group boundaries. Most of our respondents took it for granted that having friendships with people of a variety of backgrounds was a good thing, that it made one a better, more fully developed person.

Ironically, in this hyperdiverse world, assimilation—if that is the right word—seems to happen faster and with less angst than in the past. The children of European immigrants who arrived at the beginning of the twentieth century often felt forced to choose between their parents' ways and those of American society. Many were embarrassed when their parents could not speak English and even changed their names to fit in. As the Italian American educator Leonard Covello recalled, "We were becoming American by learning how to be ashamed of our parents" (cited in Foner 2000:207).

By contrast, today's second generation is far more at ease with both their American and ethnic identities. One woman told us that learning Russian from her parents has been beneficial for her because "there's a certain richness that comes along with having another culture to fall back on. People are always intrigued. They ask what does it mean to be Russian and you feel a little special to explain and it adds color to you." Far from being "torn between two worlds," the children of immigrants increasingly make use of the second generation's natural advantage: the ability to combine the best of their parents' culture with the best that America has to offer. Maria, age 23, said that being both American and Colombian was "the best of two worlds. Like being able to keep and appreciate those things in my culture that I enjoy and that I think are beautiful, and, at the same time, being able to change those things which I think are bad."

Unfortunately, the intergenerational progress and rapid assimilation of these young people is often missed in immigration debates that are focused only on recent arrivals. A more long-term view, one that takes into account the progress of the second generation, would do much to inform our local and national conversations over immigration. Our research suggests that such a view would lead to a far more optimistic assessment of the role of immigration in American life.

DARK CLOUDS ON THE HORIZON?

Lest we draw too optimistic a portrait about the incorporation of the new second-generation New Yorkers, a few notes of caution are in order. The first is economic. The data for the ISGMNY study were collected during very good economic times—indeed, toward the end of what was, for the city, a remarkable period of economic growth. We still do not know how the ISGMNY respondents fared in the great recession and the long period of stagnation that has followed. It is worth noting, however, that many of the most successful respondents were concentrated in industries that were particularly hard hit—high tech, construction, and finance (although, of course, New York's finance industry recovered remarkably quickly from a crisis that it had a significant role in creating, to the consternation of its many critics). Since the best-off of the second generation have come the furthest from the lives of their immigrant parents, they usually have had far fewer parental and familial resources to fall back on than their native white contemporaries and colleagues. And what of their younger siblings and cousins—the very large cohort of second-generation New Yorkers who had the historical misfortune to enter the labor force just when the recession hit? Will the second-generation resilience of these relative newcomers help them reinvent themselves in a changing economy? Will the ethnic enclaves they previously avoided suddenly seem more attractive? Or will they find themselves locked out of opportunities by better-established groups, now anxious to safeguard their own position in leaner and meaner times? As of this writing it is too early to say, but there are certainly reasons for concern. Yet it is worth remembering that many members of the previous comparable second generation—the children of the great wave of early twentieth-century immigrants—entered the labor force during the Great Depression. In the long run, that seemingly tragic historical timing eventually turned out to be fortuitous, as this group experienced massive upward mobility and economic assimilation in the great economic expansion of the postwar years.

Even after the present downturn passes, the need to integrate such a large number of young people from immigrant backgrounds into a twenty-first-century labor force presents profound challenges for the city's public educational system and CUNY at a moment when fiscal shortfalls are leading to cutbacks at both institutions. As Alba (2009) has argued, nothing could be more in the interest of the city's elites than the successful incorporation of the next generation of the city's leaders, and as such investment in education at this moment would seem crucial. Yet how to fund this investment during a time of austerity and increased popular reluctance to pay for public goods represents a serious challenge.

There is also the question of emerging differences among various second-generation groups, and between second-generation and native minority groups, in the degree to which they have been able to successfully make use of the educational system. Moves toward greater diversity and increased choice in public education at all levels in the city have, on the one hand, guaranteed that some students from extremely modest backgrounds have access to an excellent education. Yet they have also deepened inequalities within the system (Corcoran 2011). The children of Asian and, to a lesser extent, former Soviet immigrants seem to have done extremely well under this system—better by most measures than the children of native whites. At one of the city's most elite public high schools, the children of East and South Asians and Russians are now the majority. Yet, while their achievements are to be celebrated, it is distressing that that the number of native black and Latino students at such elite high schools—and the highest-regarded CUNY campuses—has fallen in recent years. Even among blacks and Latinos, real cleavages are emerging—although the use of racial terms like "black" and "Latino" tends to obscure this fact. By most measures, the children of some Latino immigrant groups (notably South Americans) are doing better than others, and the children of all immigrant groups, including those from South America and the West Indies, seem to be doing better than native African Americans and Puerto Ricans. It should also be noted that women are doing better in school than men in most of these groups (Lopez 2003). We urgently need new research to understand the different rates of educational success. But we also may need new politics and policies to address these new inequities. In general, we should not let the success of large parts of New York's second generation obscure the problems of the less successful or mask the continuing failure of New York City's institutions to address poverty and social isolation among large parts of native minority communities.

Finally, we should note the effects of legal status. While New York City has never had as large a concentration of undocumented immigrants as have those parts of the country closer to the southern border, many parents of the ISGMNY respondents came to the United States without papers or lived here as undocumented immigrants for some years while their children were growing up. Indeed, it was not at all uncommon for these second- and 1.5-generation New Yorkers to grow up in mixed-status households that included undocumented immigrants, people holding legal temporary visas (such as tourist or student visas), legal permanent residents, naturalized citizens, and birthright citizens. Up until the mid-1990s, this diversity of legal statuses seems to have had fairly little impact on the children raised in such households. Deportation was rare and largely restricted to those with serious criminal records. And while regularizing legal status was never easy for undocumented immigrants, opportunities to do so did exist. Eventually most of those who wanted to become legal were able to do so.

Since the mid-1990s (and at least until this writing in late 2012), this has no longer been the case. The United States has been engaged in what Robert C. Smith has termed a cruel "natural experiment" (chapter 10, this volume). By restricting the opportunities of technically illegal immigrants to obtain legal status, the United States has created an unprecedentedly large population of long-standing semipermanent undocumented workers who are part of the city economically, socially, and culturally but not legally or politically. This is a profoundly troubling situation for a democratic society—one that seems far more likely than downward assimilation to produce an underclass.

For the U.S.-born second generation, despite birthright citizenship, having an undocumented parent often means growing up with economic insecurity and the threat of deportation and, whatever their own parents' legal status, coming of age in communities in which many of the adults are undocumented and lack a political voice (Yoshikawa 2011). As for those members of the 1.5 generation who themselves are undocumented, they confront and must cope with their own lack of basic rights and opportunities in the only country they have ever really known (Gonzales 2011). Having siblings who enjoy many advantages because they were born in the United States or were able to regularize their status by virtue of having arrived earlier underlines the harsh realities and barriers that come with their own undocumented status.

New York City, it must be said, is probably facing the challenges we have mentioned more successfully than most of the United States. New York politicians have not generally stooped to anti-immigrant demagoguery and most of the population seems convinced that the successful incorporation of the children of immigrants is in the city's best interest. The presence of CUNY, with its overwhelmingly immigrant and second-generation students and its tradition of celebrating immigrant achievement, has undoubtedly played an important role in the relative success of the second generation up until now. How it will continue to serve this population in more constrained fiscal circumstances is a key question to be faced in the years to come. More generally, New York City governments have tended to take pro-immigrant stands, even under the Republican administration of Rudolph Giuliani and the Republican/independent administration of Michael Bloomberg. Both mayors criticized their party's national leadership on the immigration issue and both sought to promote the image of the city as a place friendly to immigrants, a stance that was frequently at odds with that taken by local government leaders in other parts of the country. Still, as the current situation regarding legal status makes clear, the incorporation of immigrants—and of the second generation—remains a national problem, one the city cannot solve on its own.

REFERENCES

Alba, Richard. 2009. *Blurring the Color Line: The New Chance for a More Integrated America*. Cambridge, MA: Harvard University Press.

Alba, Richard, Philip Kasinitz, and Mary C. Waters. 2011. "The Kids Are (Mostly) Alright: Second Generation Assimilation." *Social Forces* 89 (March): 762–73.

Alba, Richard, and Joseph Pereira. 2011. "The Progress and Pitfalls of Diversity on Wall Street." Report of the Center for Urban Research, City University of New York, December. http://www.urbanresearch.org/news/new-report-progress-and-pitfalls-of-diversity-on-wall-street.

Attewell, Paul, and David Lavin. 2007. *Passing the Torch: Does Higher Education for the Disadvantaged Pay Off across the Generations?* New York: Russell Sage Foundation.

Corcoran, Sean P. 2011. "How New York Students Have Fared under High School Choice: A Bird's Eye View." Unpublished manuscript, New York University.

Foner, Nancy. 2000. *From Ellis Island to JFK: New York's Two Great Waves of Immigration*. New Haven, CT: Yale University Press.

Gans, Herbert J. 1992. "Second Generation Decline: Scenarios for the Economic and Ethnic Futures of the Post-1965 American Immigrants." *Ethnic and Racial Studies* 15: 173–92.

Gonzales, Roberto G. 2011. "Learning to be Illegal: Undocumented Youth and Shifting Legal Contexts in the Transition to Adulthood." *American Sociological Review* 76: 602–19.

Haller, William, Alejandro Portes, and Scott Lynch. 2011. "Dreams Fulfilled, Dreams Shattered: The Determinants of Segmented Assimilation in the Second Generation." *Social Forces* 89 (March): 733–62.

Kasinitz, Philip, Noriko Matsumoto, and Aviva Zeltzer-Zubida. 2011. "'I Will Never Deliver Chinese Food': The Children of Immigrants in the New York Metropolitan Labor Force." In Richard Alba and Mary C. Waters, eds., *The Next Generation*. New York: New York University Press.

Kasinitz, Philip, John Mollenkopf, and Mary C. Waters. 2002. "Becoming American/ Becoming New Yorkers: Immigrant Incorporation in a Majority Minority City." *International Migration Review* 36 (4): 1020–36.

——, eds. 2004. *Becoming New Yorkers: Ethnographies of the New Second Generation.* New York: Russell Sage Foundation.

Kasinitz, Philip, John Mollenkopf, Mary C. Waters, and Jennifer Holdaway. 2008. *Inheriting the City: The Children of Immigrants Come of Age.* Cambridge: Harvard University Press and the Russell Sage Foundation.

Lopez, Nancy. 2003. *Hopeful Girls, Troubled Boys: Race and Gender Disparity in Urban Education.* New York: Routledge.

Myers, Dowell. 2007. *Immigrants and Boomers: Forging a New Social Contract for the Future of America.* New York: Russell Sage Foundation.

Portes, Alejandro, Patricia Fernandez-Kelly, and William Haller. 2005. "Segmented Assimilation on the Ground: The New Second Generation in Early Adulthood." *Ethnic and Racial Studies* 28 (6): 1000–40.

Portes, Alejandro, and Ruben G. Rumbaut. 2001. *Legacies: The Story of the Immigrant Second Generation.* Berkeley: University of California Press.

Portes, Alejandro, and Min Zhou. 1993. "The New Second Generation: Segmented Assimilation and Its Variants." *Annals of the American Academy of Political and Social Science* 530 (1): 74–96.

Quintini, Glenda, and Sébastien Martin. 2006. "Starting Well or Losing Their Way? The Position of Youth in the Labour Market in OECD Countries." OECD Social Employment and Migration Working Paper No. 39. Paris: OECD.

Rumbaut, Ruben G. 1999. "Assimilation and Its Discontents: Ironies and Paradoxes." In Charles Hirschman, Philip Kasinitz, and Josh DeWind, eds., *The Handbook of International Migration: The American Experience.* New York: Russell Sage Foundation.

Telles, Edward, and Vilma Ortiz. 2008. *Generations of Exclusion: Mexican Americans, Assimilation, and Race.* New York: Russell Sage Foundation.

Tran, Van C. 2010. "English Gain vs. Spanish Loss? Language Assimilation among Second-Generation Latinos in Young Adulthood." *Social Forces* 98 (September): 257–84.

——. 2011. "How Neighborhoods Matter, and for Whom? Disadvantaged Context, Ethnic Cultural Repertoires and Second-Generation Social Mobility in Young Adulthood." Unpublished PhD dissertation, Harvard University.

Waters, Mary C., Patrick Carr, Maria Keflas, and Jennifer Holdaway, eds. 2011. *Coming of Age in America: The Transition to Adulthood in the Twenty-first Century.* Berkeley: University of California Press.

Waters, Mary C., and Philip Kasinitz. 2010. "Discrimination, Race and the Second Generation." *Social Research* 77 (Spring): 101–32.

Yoshikawa, Hirokazu. 2011. *Immigrants Raising Citizens: Undocumented Parents and Their Young Children.* New York: Russell Sage Foundation.

CONTRIBUTORS

NANCY FONER is distinguished professor of sociology at Hunter College and the Graduate Center of the City University of New York. She is the author or editor of more than a dozen books, including *In a New Land: A Comparative View of Immigration* (New York University Press, 2005); *Across Generations: Immigrant Families in America* (New York University Press, 2009); *New Immigrants in New York* (Columbia University Press, 1987, rev. ed. 2001); and *From Ellis Island to JFK: New York's Two Great Waves of Immigration* (Yale University Press, 2000), winner of the 2000 Theodore Saloutos Award of the Immigration and Ethnic History Society.

RAMONA HERNÁNDEZ is professor of sociology at the City College of New York, City University of New York, where she is also director of the CUNY Dominican Studies Institute. She is the author of *The Mobility of Workers under Advanced Capitalism: Dominican Migration to the United States* (Columbia University Press, 2002), named Outstanding Academic Title by Choice 2002; and coauthor, with Sully Saneaux, of *De Mayo a Septiembre: La República Dominicana y la Prensa Extranjera 1961–1963* (Biblioteca Nacional Pedro Henriquez Ureña, 2012). She is the recipient of the Meritorious Order of Duarte, Sanchez y Mella, the Dominican Republic's highest civilian honor.

DAVID DYSSEGAARD KALLICK is senior fellow of the Fiscal Policy Institute and director of the institute's Immigration Research Initiative. He is the principal author of numerous reports for the institute, including *Working for a Better Life: A Profile of Immigrants in the New York State Economy* (2007), *Immigrants and the Economy: Contribution of Immigrant Workers to the Country's 25 Largest Metropolitan Areas* (2009), and *Immigrant Small Business Owners: A Significant and Growing Part of the Economy* (2012).

PHILIP KASINITZ is professor of sociology at the Graduate Center of the City University of New York. He is the author of *Caribbean New York: Black Immigrants and the Politics of Race*; editor of *Metropolis: Center and Symbol of Our Time*; coeditor (with Mary C. Waters and John Mollenkopf) of *Becoming New Yorkers: Ethnographies of the New Second Generation*; and coauthor (with Waters, Mollenkopf, and Jennifer Holdaway) of *Inheriting the City: The Children of Immigrants Come of Age*, which received the 2009 Mirra Komarovksy Book Award from the Eastern Sociological Society and the 2010 Distinguished Book Award from the American Sociological Association.

ARUN PETER LOBO is deputy director of the Population Division at the New York City Department of City Planning. He is the lead author of *The Newest New Yorker* series, which examines immigration to the city, and has published widely on the demographic effects of immigration and methodological issues pertaining to the use of survey data. His most recent work has appeared in the *Journal of Immigrant and Refugee Services* and the *Annals of the American Academy of Political and Social Science*; a forthcoming article on changing racial patterns of coresidence will appear in the *Journal of Urban Affairs*.

BERNADETTE LUDWIG is a doctoral candidate in the Sociology Program at the Graduate Center of the City University of New York. She is currently completing a dissertation, "America Is Not the Heaven We Dream Of: Liberian Refugees in Staten Island, NY," based on three years of ethnographic research among Liberians in Staten Island. She is the cofounder and a board member of Culture Connect, a nonprofit organization in Atlanta, Georgia, that assists immigrants and refugees.

PYONG GAP MIN is distinguished professor of sociology at Queens College and the Graduate Center of the City University of New York and also serves as director of the Research Center for Korean Community at Queens College. The areas of his specializations are immigration, ethnicity, immigrant businesses, immigrants' religious practices, and family/gender, with a special focus on Korean and Asian Americans. He is the author or editor of thirteen books, including *Caught in the Middle: Korean Communities in New York and Los Angeles* (1996) and *Preserving Ethnicity through Religion in America: Korean Protestants and Indian Hindus across Generations* (2010).

John H. Mollenkopf is distinguished professor of political science and sociology at the Graduate Center of the City University of New York and director of its Center for Urban Research. He is the editor, with Maurice Crul, of *The Changing Face of World Cities: The Second Generation in Western Europe and the United States* (Russell Sage Foundation, 2012); and author, with Philip Kasinitz, Mary Waters, and Jennifer Holdaway, of *Inheriting the City: The Children of Immigrants Come of Age* (Harvard University Press and Russell Sage Foundation, 2008), winner of the 2010 Distinguished Book Award of the American Sociological Association.

Annelise Orleck is professor of history, women's and gender studies, and Jewish studies at Dartmouth College. She is the author of three books: *Common Sense and a Little Fire: Women and Working Class Politics in the U.S.* (1995); *Soviet Jewish Americans* (1999); and *Storming Caesars Palace: How Black Mothers Fought Their Own War on Poverty* (2005). She is the coeditor of two books: *The Politics of Motherhood* (1997) and *The War on Poverty: A New Grassroots History* (2011).

Joseph J. Salvo is director of the Population Division at the New York City Department of City Planning. He has broad expertise in the application of small-area data for policies and programs, and on the uses of census data to address the concerns of local government. As a frequent member of various advisory committees to the Census Bureau, he regularly provides input on census issues. He currently serves on the Panel on Priority Technical Issues for the Next Decade of the American Community Survey at the National Academy of Sciences. Most recently, he coedited the *Encyclopedia of the U.S. Census.*

Robert Courtney Smith is professor in the School of Public Affairs, Baruch College, and Sociology Department, Graduate Center, City University of New York. He is the author of *Mexican New York: Transnational Worlds of New Immigrants* (University of California Press, 2006), which won awards from the American Sociological Association's International Migration, Urban/Community Sociology, and Latino/a sections and the 2008 ASA Distinguished Book Award. In 2009–10 he was a Guggenheim Fellow. He is cofounder of the Mexican American Students Alliance and Mexican Educational Fund. In 2008, Asociación Tepeyac named him Youth Advocate of the Year.

Silvio Torres-Saillant is professor of English and has served as William P. Tolley Distinguished Professor in the Humanities at Syracuse University, where he also completed two terms as director of the Latino-Latin American Studies Program. He founded the Dominican Studies Institute at City College, CUNY, which he headed until 2000. Publications include *An Intellectual History of the Caribbean* (2006); *Caribbean Poetics: Toward an Aesthetic of West Indian Literature* (1997); *El Tigueraje Intelectual* (2011); *An Introduction to Dominican Blackness* (1999); and *El Retorno de las Yolas: Ensayos Sobre Diaspora, Democracia y Dominicanidad* (1999). He serves as associate editor of *Latino Studies.*

MILTON VICKERMAN is associate professor of sociology at the University of Virginia. He studies immigration and race and has analyzed patterns of assimilation among West Indian immigrants in *Crosscurrents: West Indian Immigrants and Race* (Oxford University Press, 1999). His current research examines the problematic concept of postracialism. He is also studying the social and political impact of the South's growing Hispanic population.

MARY C. WATERS is the M. E. Zukerman Professor of Sociology at Harvard University, where she has taught since 1986. She is the author or editor of numerous books and articles on immigration, ethnicity and identity, race relations, and young adulthood, including *The Next Generation: Immigrant Youth in a Comparative Perspective* (with Richard Alba, 2011); *Inheriting the City: The Children of Immigrants Come of Age* (with Philip Kasinitz, John Mollenkopf, and Jennifer Holdaway, 2008); and *Black Identities: West Indian Immigrant Dreams and American Realities* (1999).

MIN ZHOU is Professor of Sociology and Asian American Studies and Walter and Shirley Wang Endowed Chair in US-China Relations and Communications, University of California, Los Angeles. Her main areas of research include international migration; ethnic and racial relations; ethnic entrepreneurship, education and the new second generation; Asia and Asian America; and urban sociology. Her most recent book is *Contemporary Chinese America: Immigration, Ethnicity and Community Transformation* (2009).

INDEX